HISTORIC PHOTOS OF
MOBILE

TEXT AND CAPTIONS BY
CAROL ELLIS AND SCOTTY E. KIRKLAND

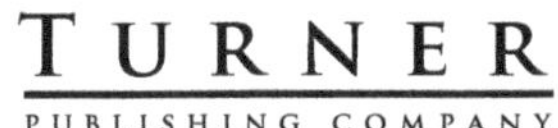

TURNER
PUBLISHING COMPANY

A panoramic view of Mobile taken from the roof of the Cawthon Hotel around 1909. Among other things, the Van Antwerp Building and the tops of trees in Bienville Square are visible.

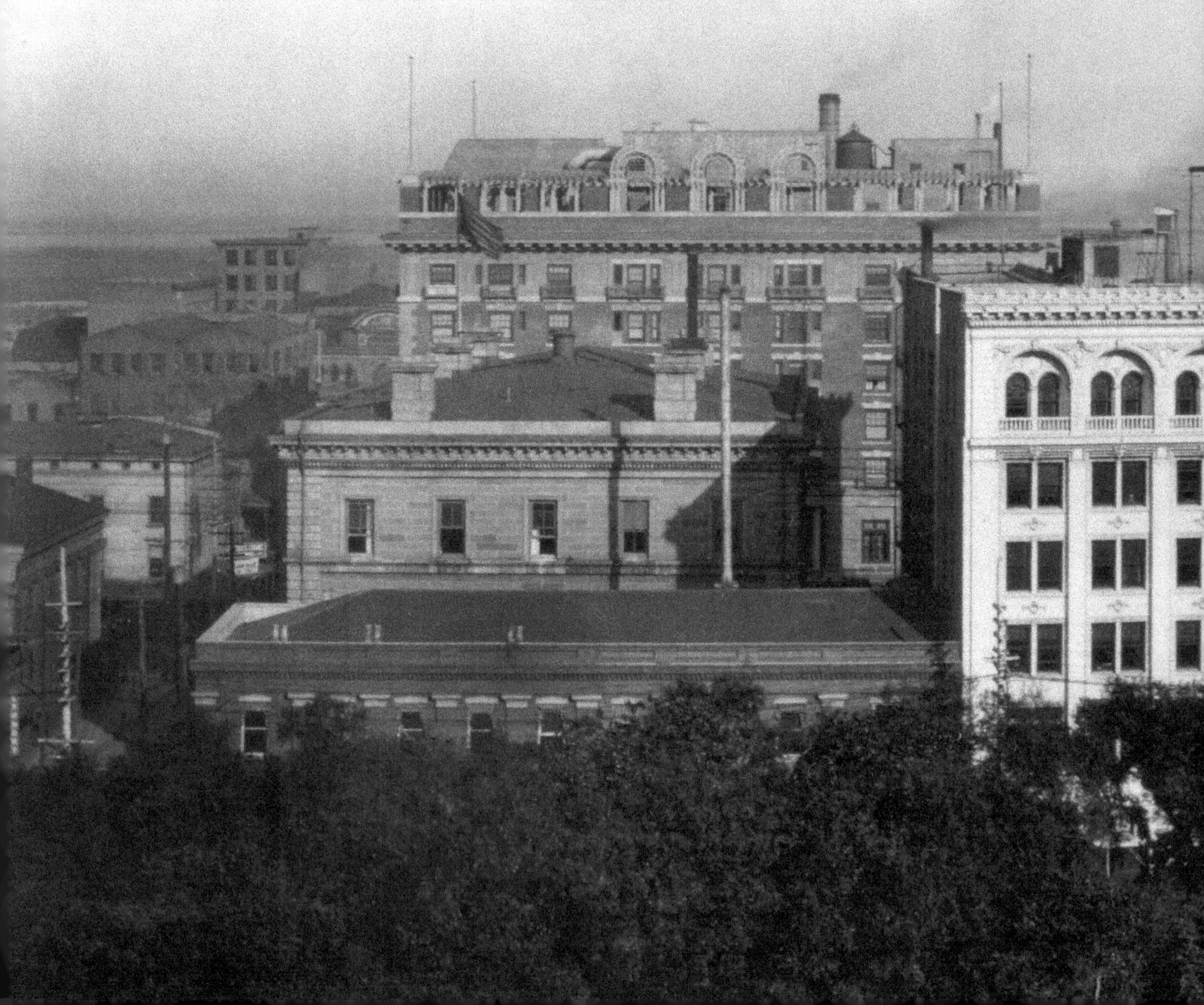

HISTORIC PHOTOS OF
MOBILE

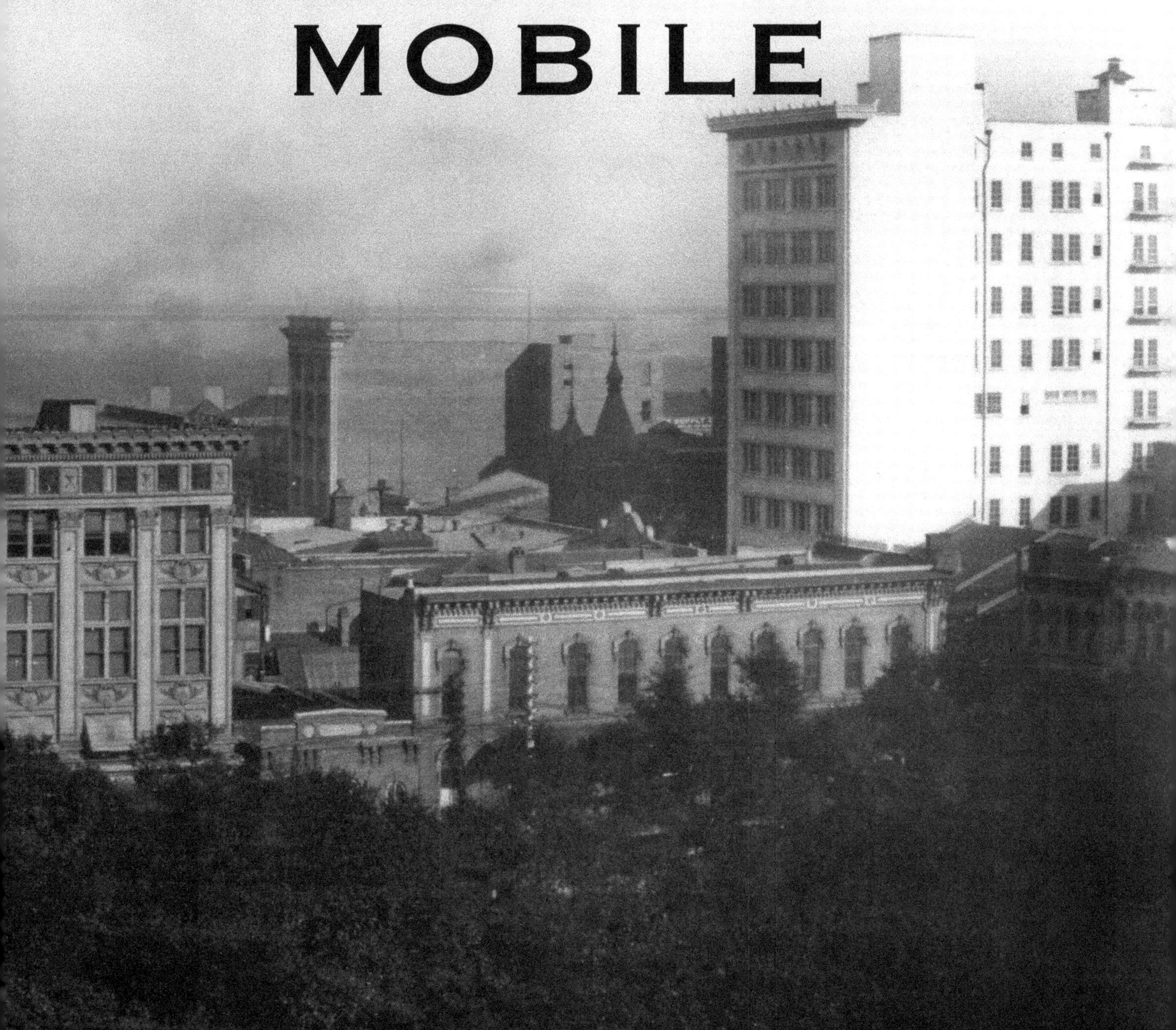

Turner Publishing Company
www.turnerpublishing.com

Historic Photos of Mobile

Library of Congress Control Number: 2007942094

ISBN-13: 978-1-59652-434-7

Printed in the United States of America

ISBN 978-1-68442-010-0 (hc)

Contents

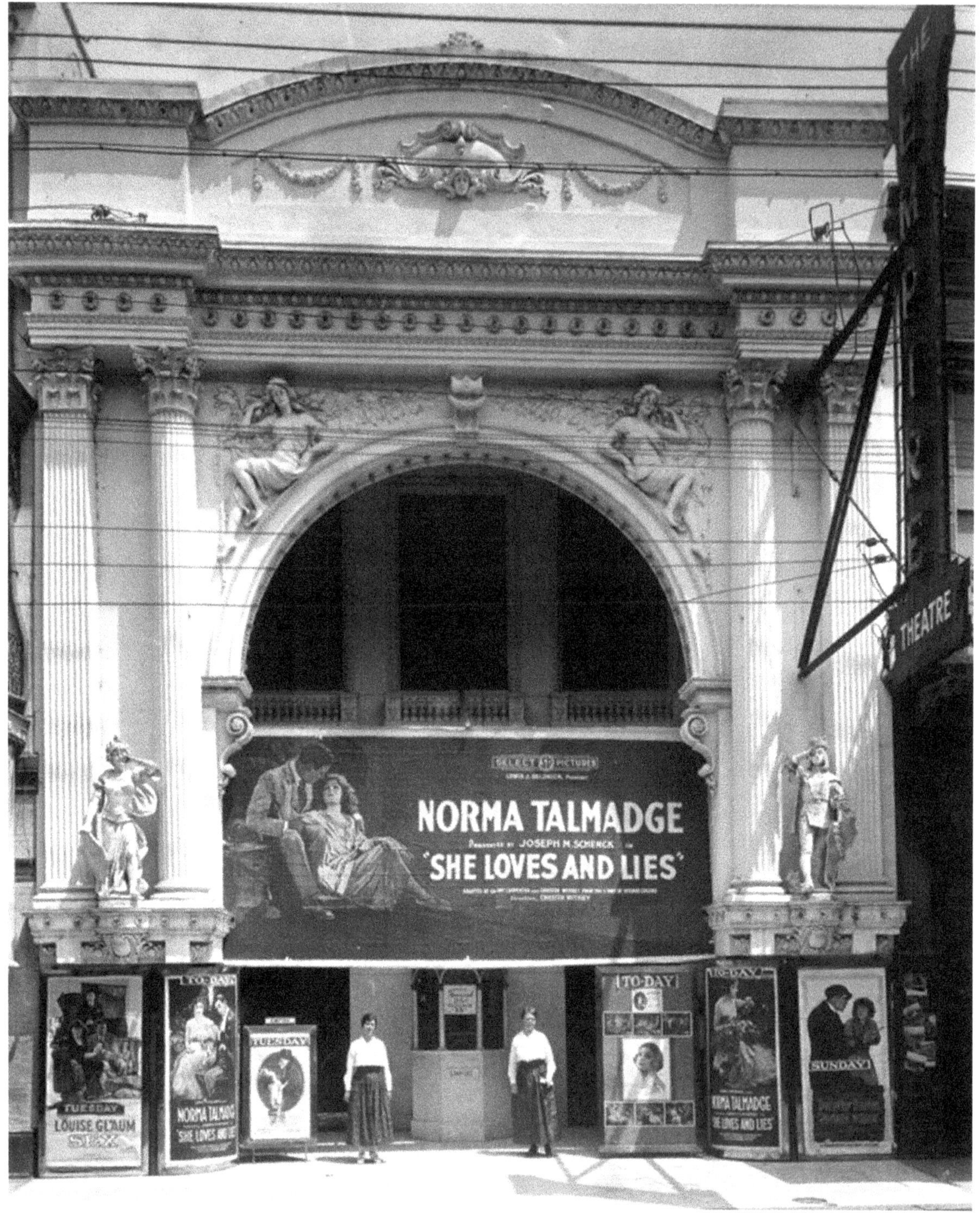

Mobilians came to the Empire Theater on Dauphin Street in 1920 to see Norma Talmadge's *She Loves and Lies,* a comedy about a heiress with multiple personalities. Patrons paid 25 cents for adult tickets. This photograph was taken some years before the Hays Code censored movies like *Sex,* starring Louise Glaum, advertised to the left.

Acknowledgments

This volume, *Historic Photos of Mobile,* is the result of the cooperation and efforts of many individuals, organizations, and corporations. It is with great thanks that we acknowledge the valuable contribution of the following for their generous support:

Clarke County Historical Society
Harris Photo Company
Library of Congress
Mobile Public Library
Museum of Mobile
University of South Alabama Archives

The authors would also like to thank the following individuals for valuable contributions and assistance in making this work possible:

Michael Thomason and Lisa Baldwin, their predecessors at the archives, and Barbara Asmus

Preface

A photograph is a powerful medium. It evokes memories, emotions, and questions. There are thousands of photographs of Mobile residing in archives, both locally and nationally. The goal in publishing this work is to disseminate more widely the extraordinary photographic history of the city of Mobile. We seek to preserve the past with respect and reverence, and hope the images in this book offer an original, untainted perspective that will allow the reader to interpret and observe them.

This project represents the collaboration between Turner Publishing and the University of South Alabama Archives. The researchers and writers reviewed the thousands of photographs contained in the university's archives, selecting those we thought the reader would most like to see. We supplemented those images with photographs from several other local sources as well as the Library of Congress. We greatly appreciate the generous assistance of the individuals and organizations listed in the acknowledgments section of this work, without whom this project could not have been completed.

With the exception of cropping where necessary and touching up imperfections that have accrued with the passage of time, no other changes have been made to the images. The focus and clarity of many of them are limited by the technology and ability of the photographer at the time they were taken.

The work is divided into eras. Beginning with some of the earliest known photographs of Mobile, the first section records the city through the end of the nineteenth century. The second section spans the beginning of the twentieth century through World War I. The following three sections cover the 1920s, 1930s, and 1940s respectively. The concluding section documents the changes that occurred between 1950 and 1979.

We have made an effort to capture various aspects of life in Mobile through our selection of the images herein. To provide a broad outlook, we have included photographs of people, commerce, transportation, infrastructure, religious institutions, and educational institutions.

We encourage readers to reflect as they go walking in Old Mobile. Stroll through the city, its parks, and its streets. It is the publisher's hope that in utilizing this work, longtime residents will learn something new and that new residents will see where Mobile has been, so that each can contribute to its future.

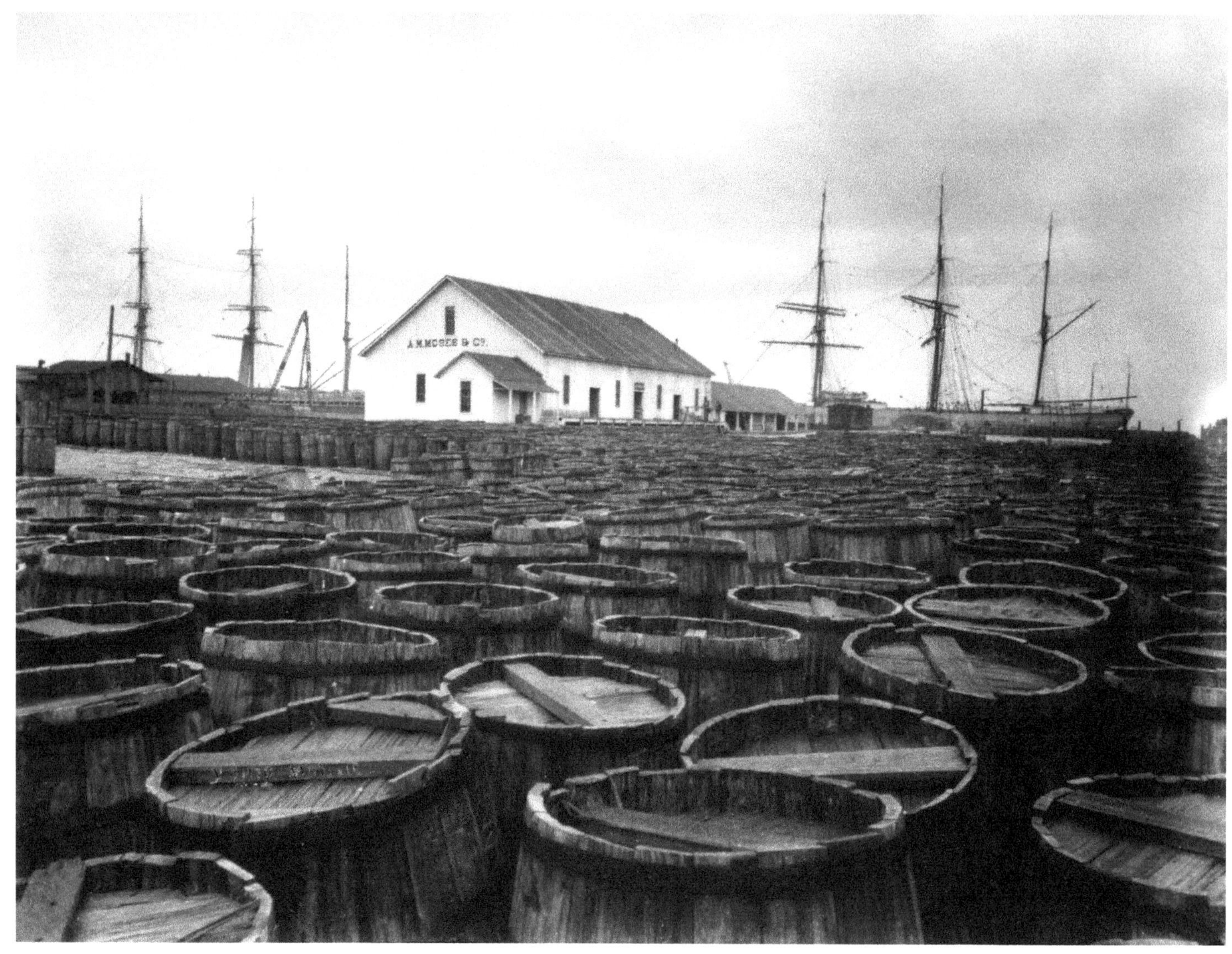

After the Civil War, timber and naval stores from distributors like the Moses Company became an important part of Mobile's economy.

New South City

(1870–1899)

Mobile experienced unprecedented change in the nineteenth century. After the War of 1812, Mobile became an American city but remained an isolated trading center during the early 1800s. The potential of the Port City, however, was unmistakable, and by the 1820s, many entrepreneurs made their way into Mobile, establishing shipping companies and warehouses along the waterfront.

In the decades that followed, Mobile's economic advances were dependent on cotton exportation. Cotton arrived in the city by wagons and trains from Alabama's fertile Black Belt and other regions in the American interior to be shipped to Europe or New England. Merchants and cotton interests in Mobile profited substantially from these exports. These wealthy businessmen formed the earliest social organizations and quickly came to dominate local politics.

Mobile's fortunes came to an abrupt end during the Civil War as a Federal blockade decimated foreign trade. Conditions in wartime Mobile were very poor, particularly when compared against the heady optimism of just a few years before. The city escaped the wartime destruction experienced by other Southern cities, but in May 1865, a waterfront armory with 200 tons of ordnance and munitions exploded, leveling eight blocks of the city and killing 300 workers. The city faced two seemingly insurmountable problems in 1865: rebuilding a major portion of its port facility, and reestablishing its status as a commercial center for a region in economic ruin.

The early years of the New South were unkind to the Port City. Its population decreased as its cotton-dependent economy languished. Industrial growth in other areas of Alabama and the growing prominence of railroad commerce endangered the Port City's future. In 1879, with the city virtually bankrupt, the Alabama legislature repealed Mobile's charter and established the Port of Mobile. The repeal lasted until 1886, by which time Mobile's fortunes had improved. In the 1880s, timber replaced cotton as Mobile's largest export, and municipal improvements like streetcars and telephone lines provided evidence that the city was recovering. Bananas from Central America became a crucial import and helped to revive the port. Prospects of deepening Mobile's ship channel and securing better rail connections to the north also helped usher in a sense of optimism as Mobilians prepared to enter the twentieth century.

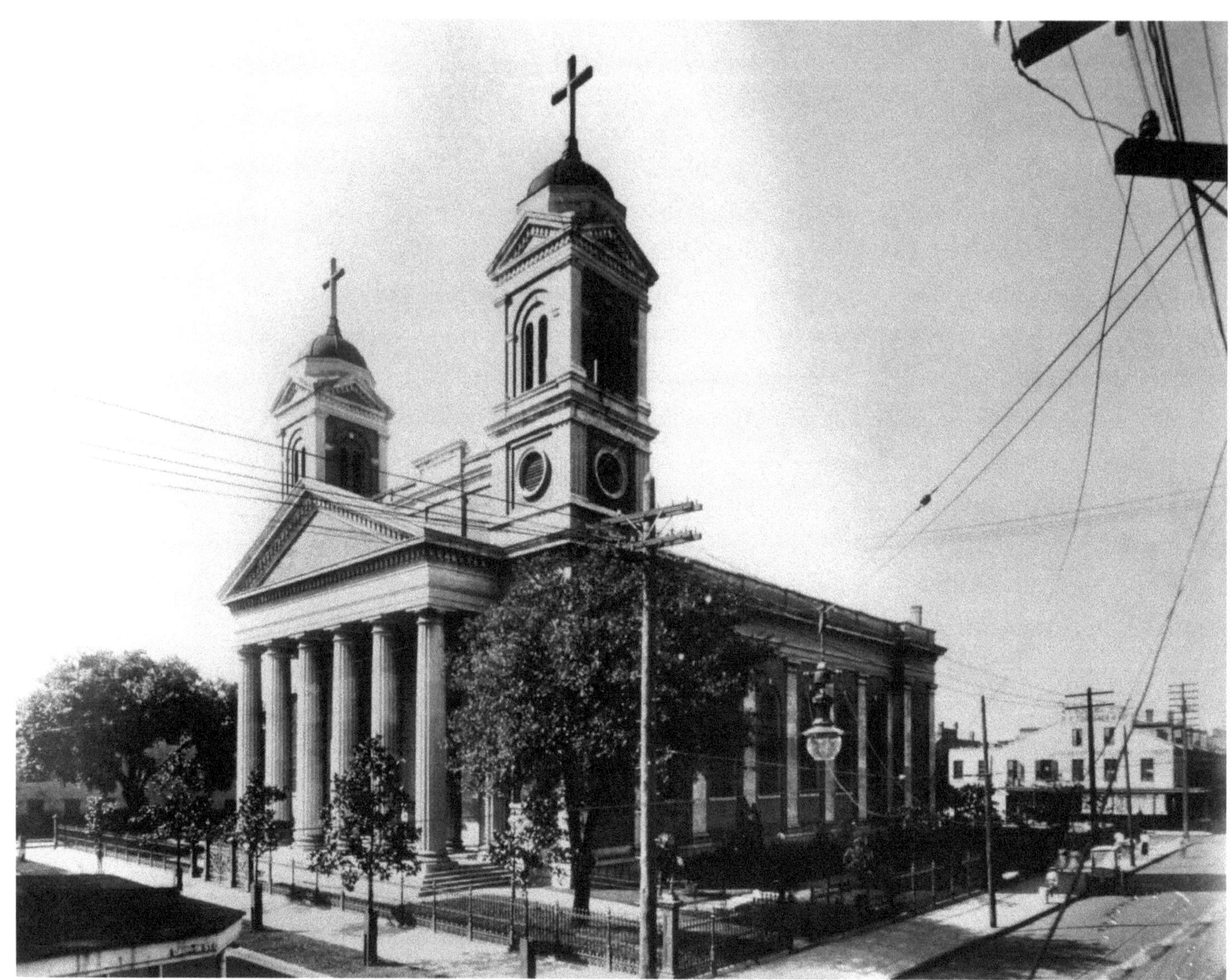

Northeast view of the Cathedral of the Immaculate Conception. The cornerstone of the building was laid in 1835, and it was built between 1834 and 1849 by the architect Claude Beroujon.

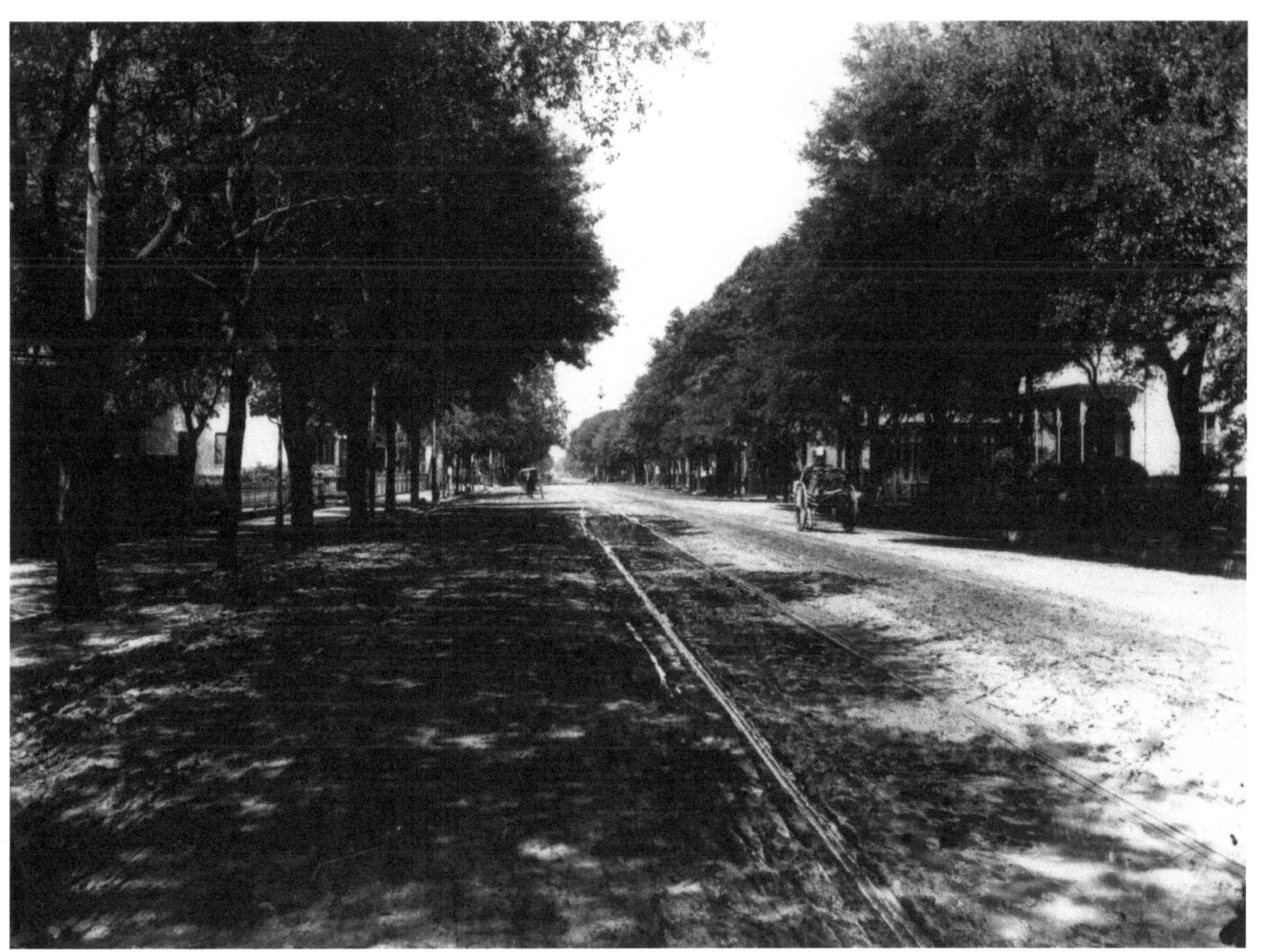

A view of an unpaved Government Street in the 1890s, when carriages were still the preferred mode of travel.

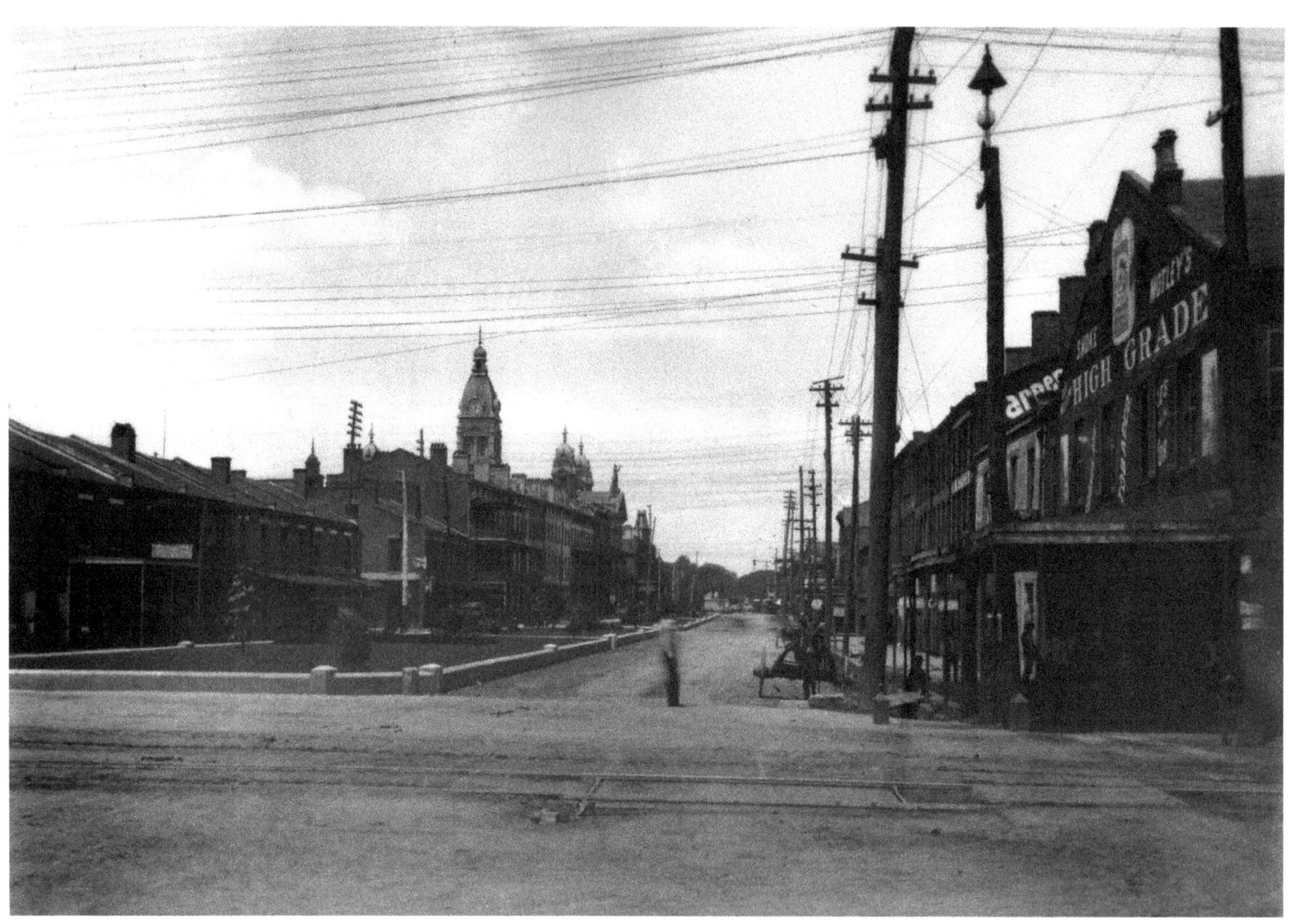

Government Street, looking west from Duncan Place, 1895. The courthouse spires can be seen.

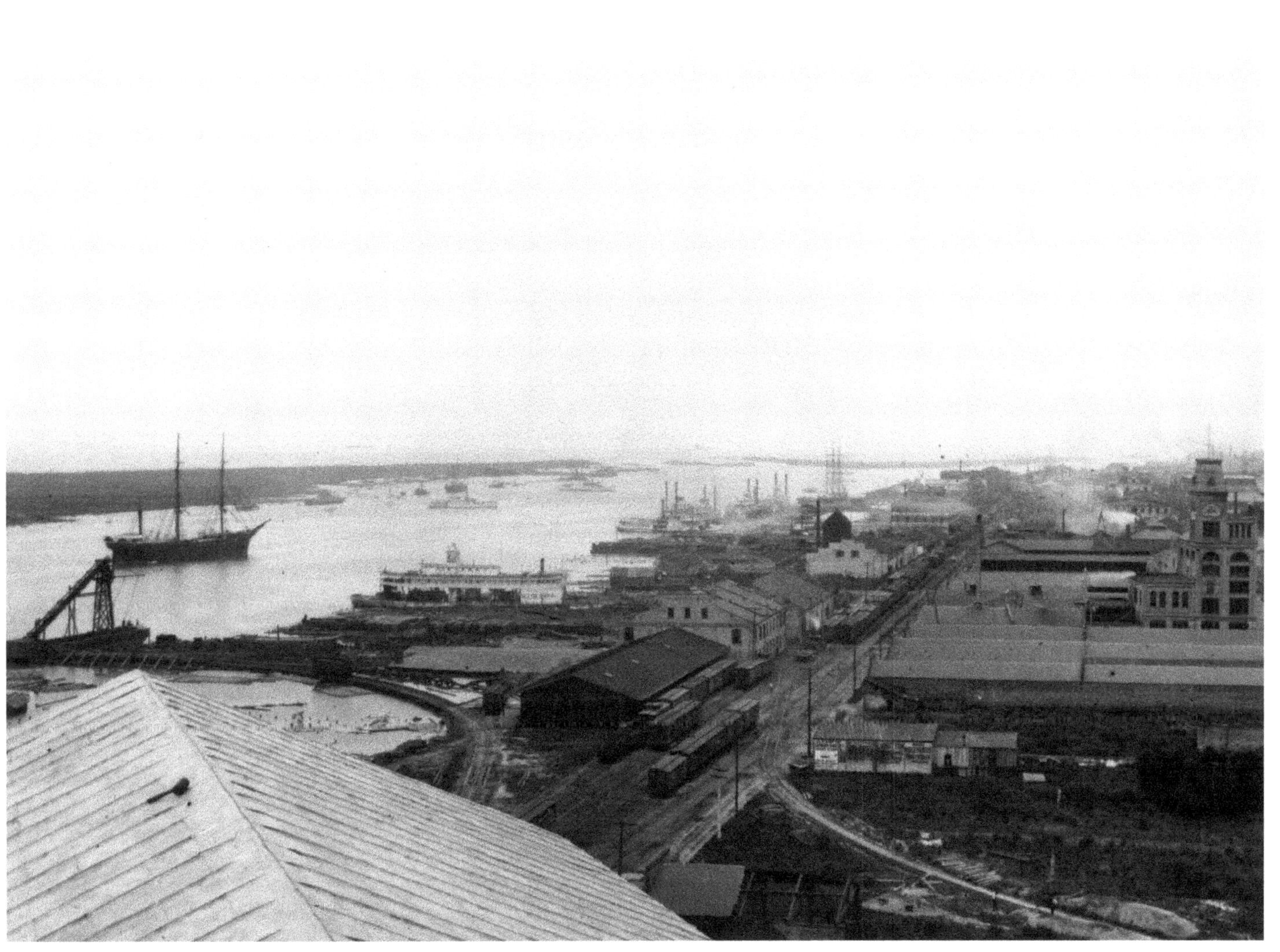

Chartered in 1848 to enhance Mobile's appeal as a commercial center, the Mobile & Ohio Railroad dominated the waterfront by 1895.

The fourth Mobile County Courthouse (1889–1957), designed by Rudolph Benz. This 1895 image shows how ornate the structure was. Erected at a cost of $50,000, it included pilasters, towers, and statuary, as well as a portico, a gable, and an 86-foot clock tower. The statue of the woman holding the flame can now be seen in the atrium of the Museum of Mobile.

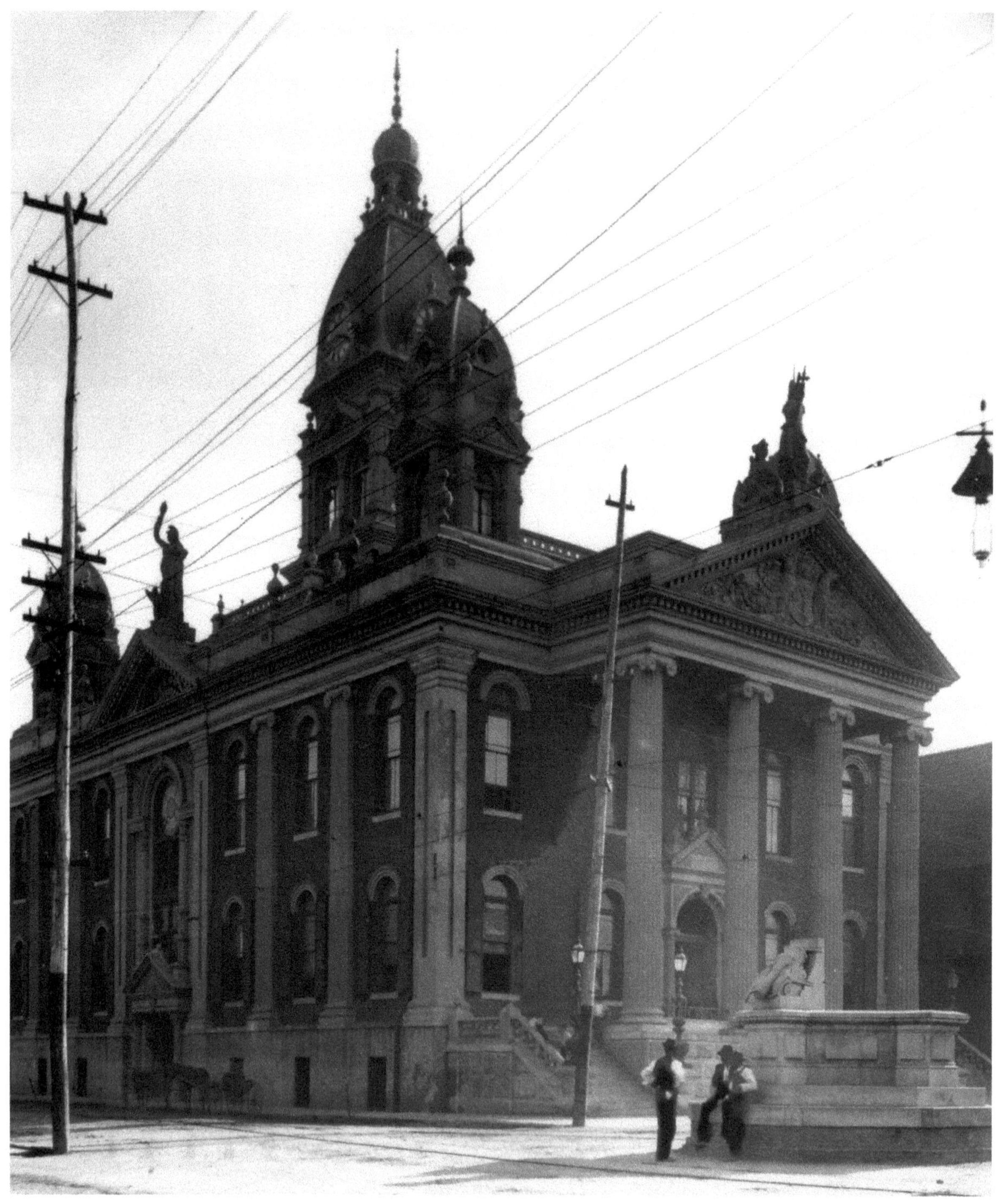

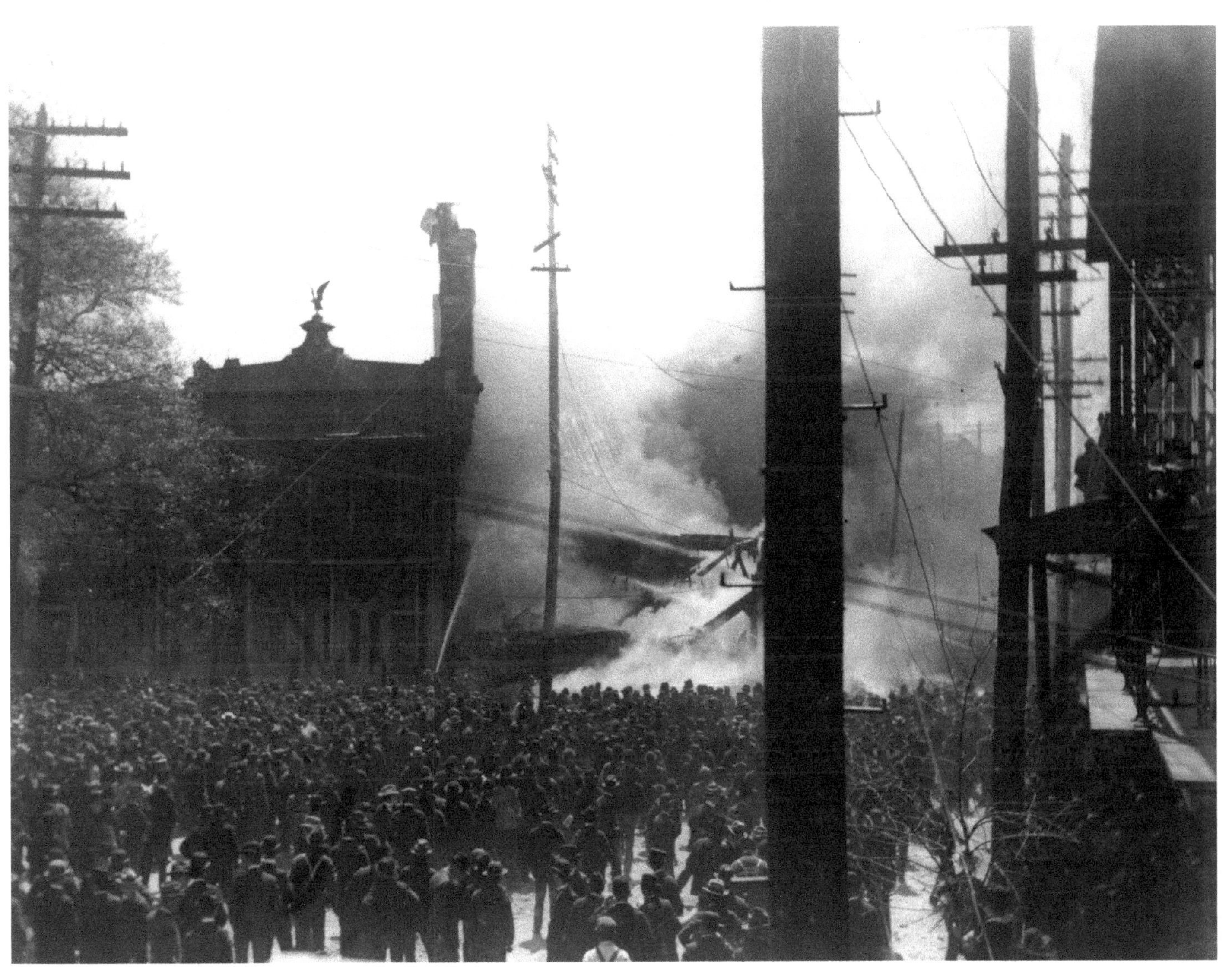

Mobilians watch as the Gayfer's building on Dauphin Street burns in 1899. Fires devastated many antebellum structures in the late nineteenth and early twentieth centuries.

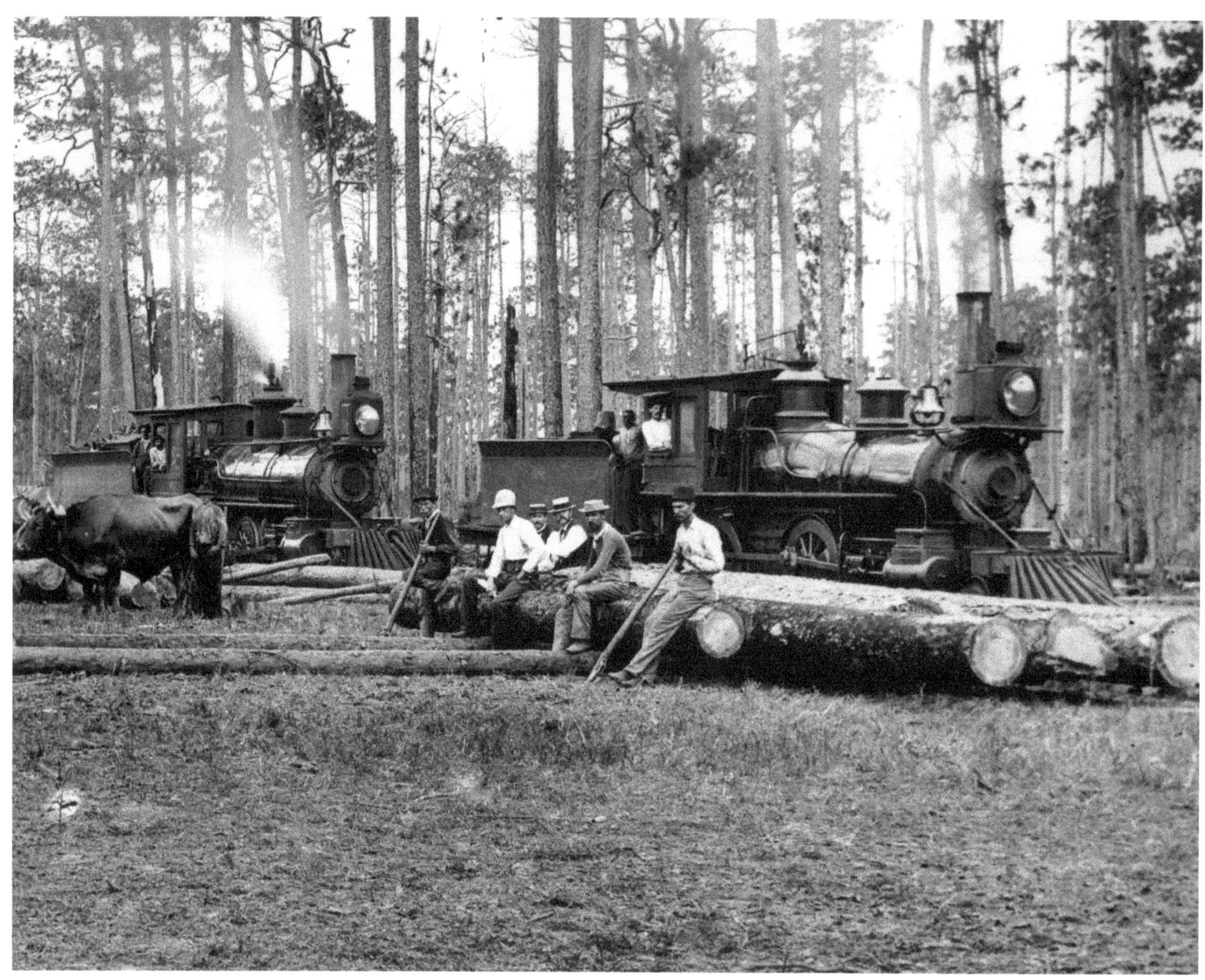

This image depicts some of the forces that drove the area's economy before the twentieth century—cattle, timber, and railroads.

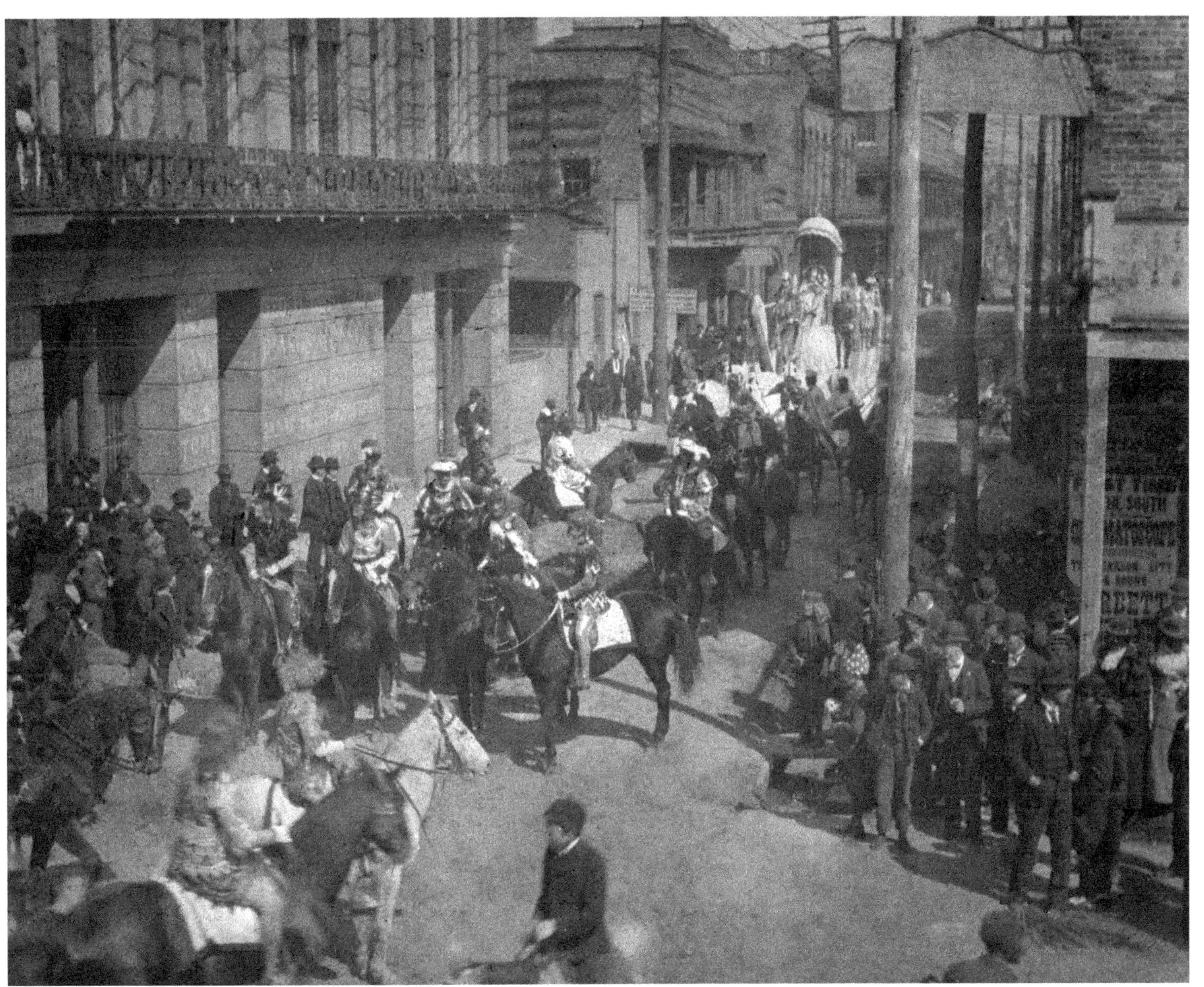

Mobile's Mardi Gras activities date back decades and remain a central part of the city's annual pre-Lenten celebrations. In this photo, taken in 1898, Mardi Gras' King Felix II and his court parade down St. Joseph Street.

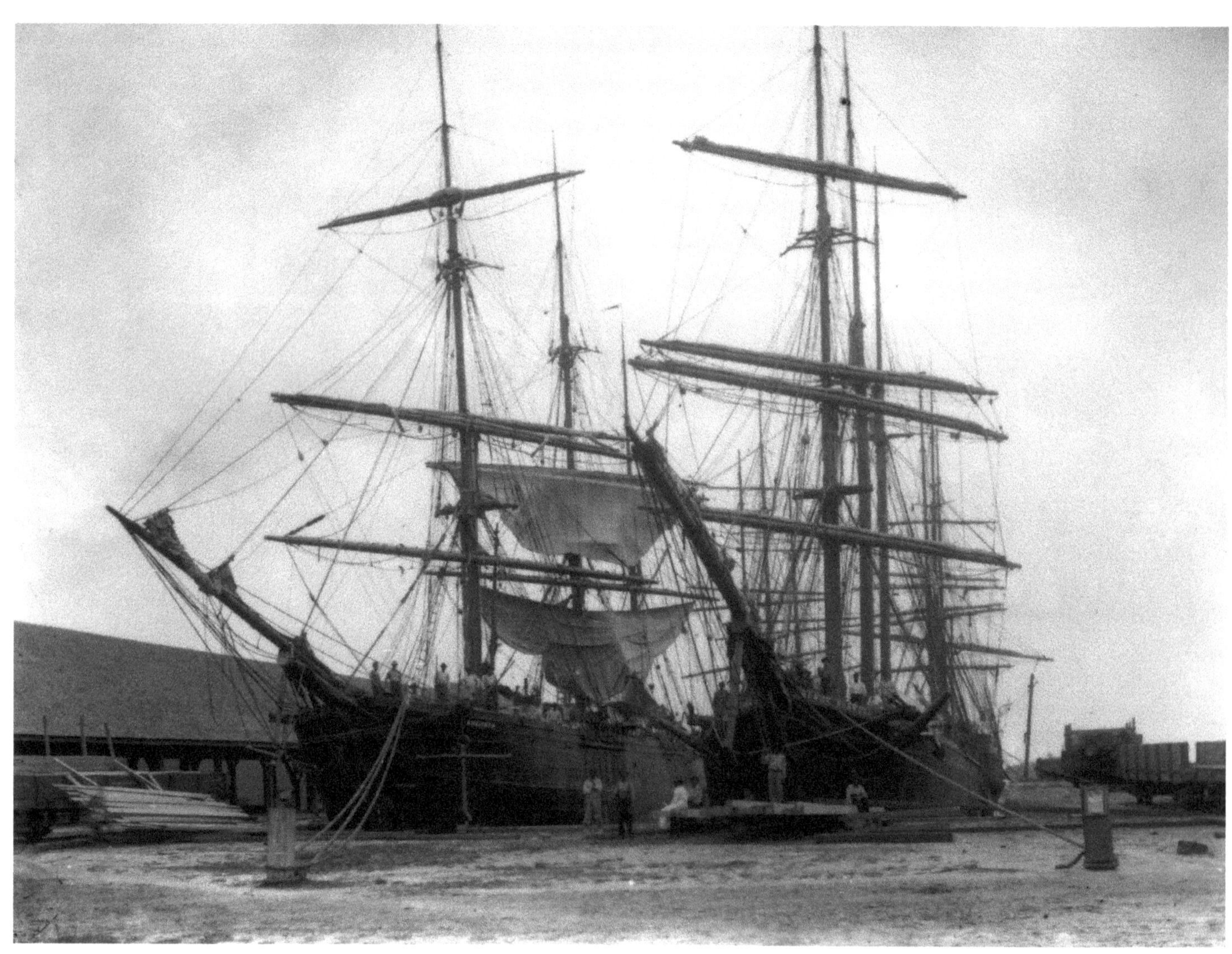

In the 1890s, when this picture was made on Mobile's waterfront, most of the world's cargo still moved under sail. These ships, the *Aucusta* and *Henry Norwell,* are probably carrying timber. The name *Aucusta* may have been an alternate form of *Augusta.*

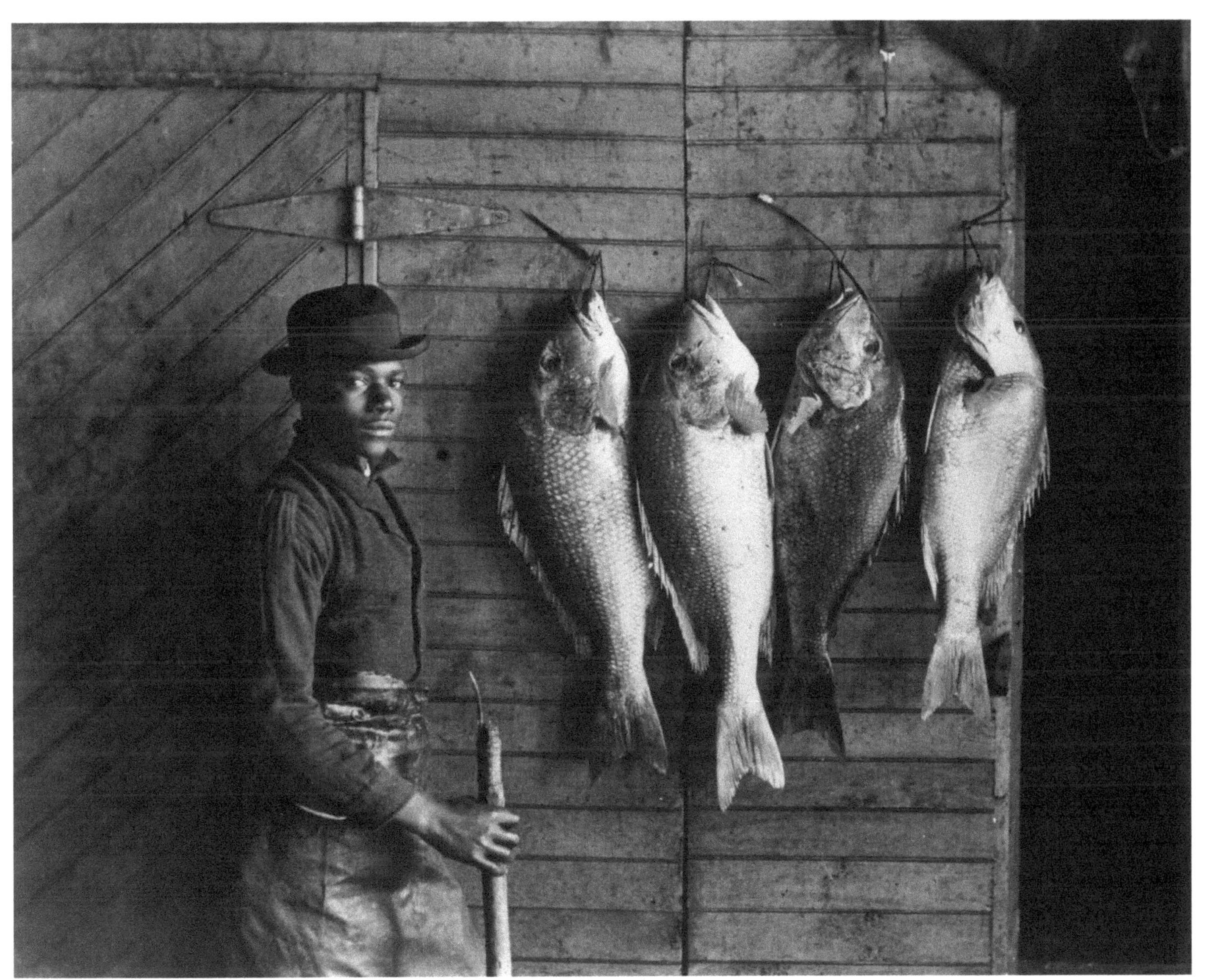

This young man proudly poses with his catch of red snapper (ca. 1895).

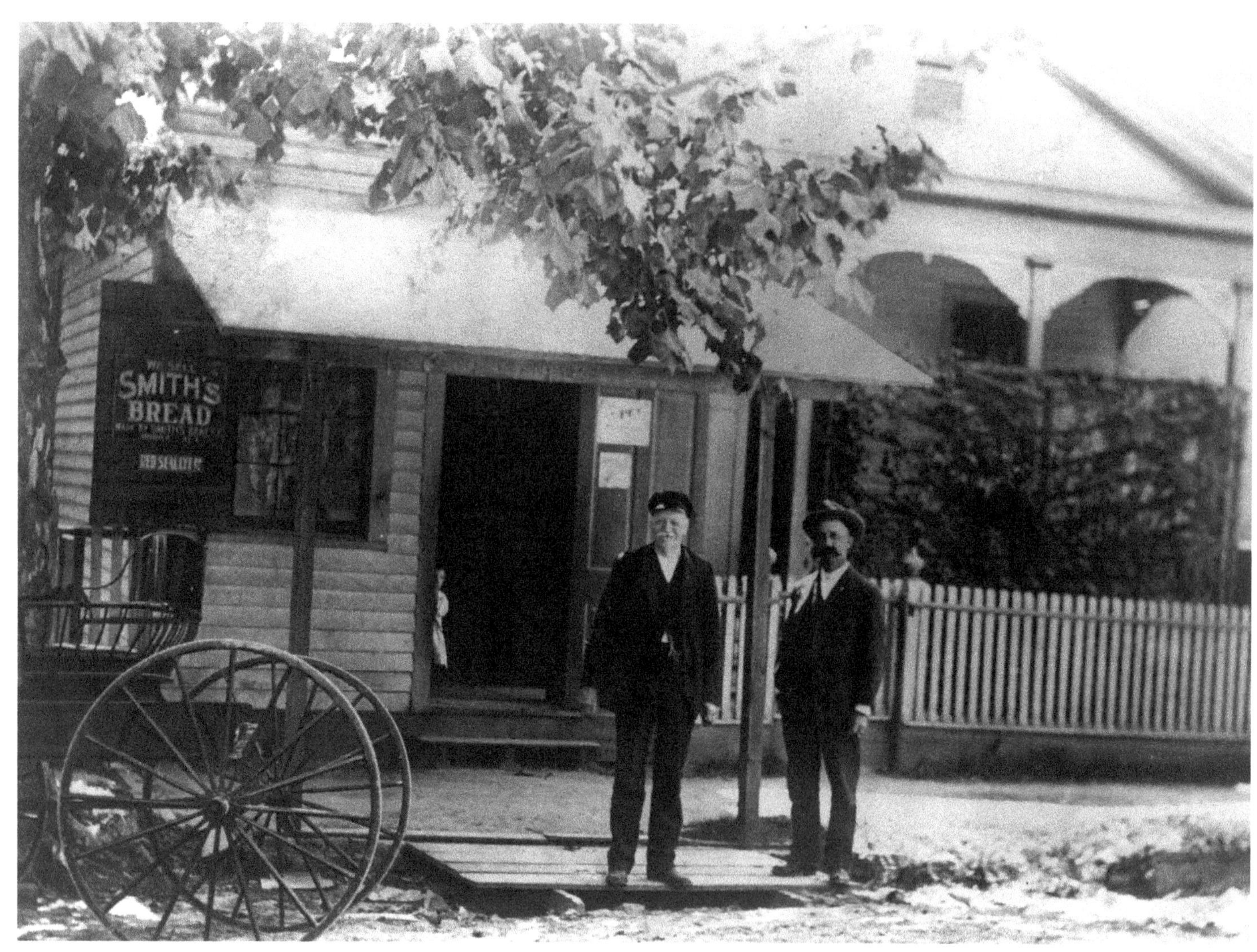

Smith's Bread has been available in Mobile stores for more than a century. This Conception Street store proudly announced they offered it for sale (ca. 1895).

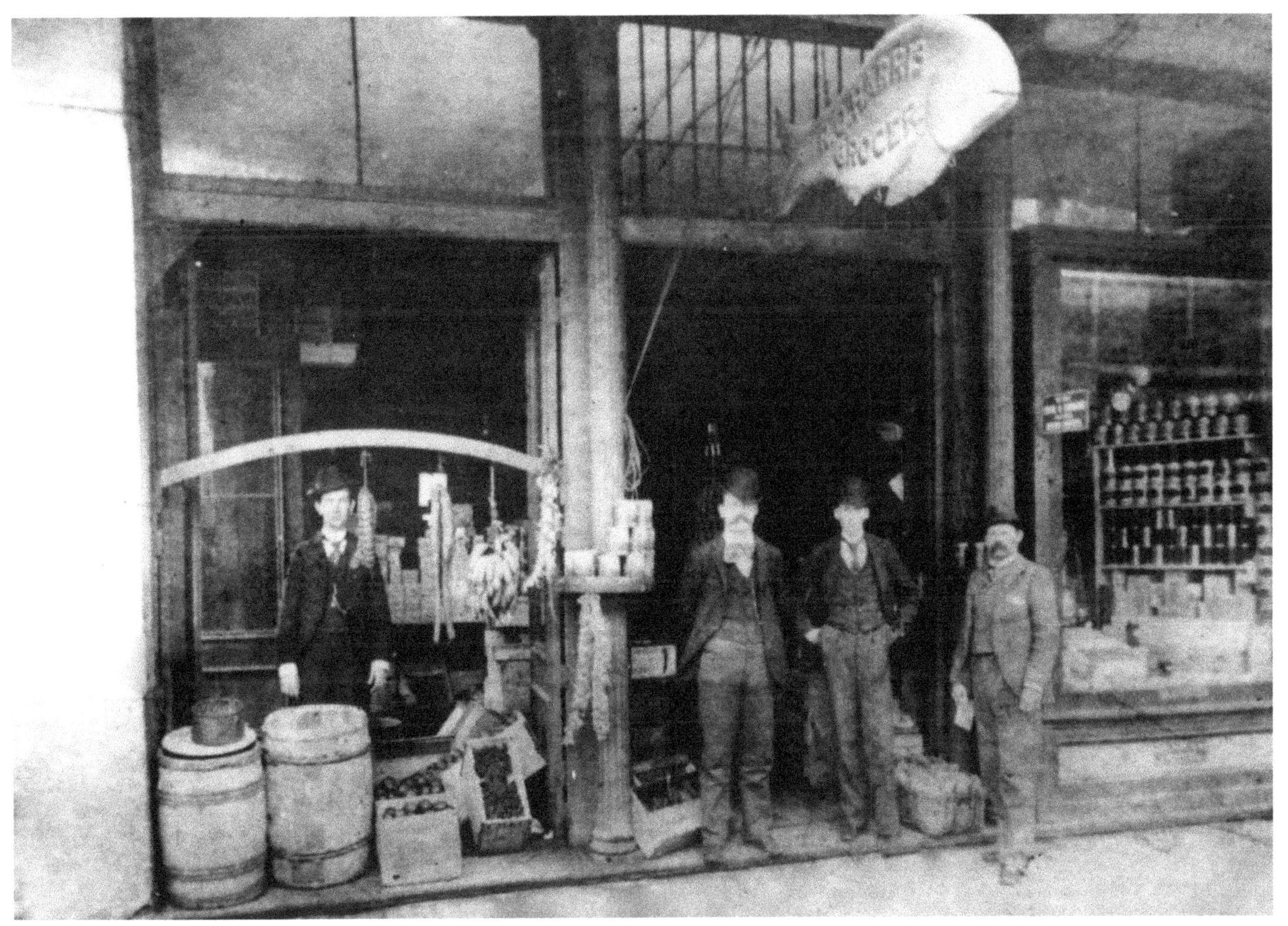

Clerks display fresh produce and dry goods outside the R. O. Harris Grocery at the corner of Dauphin and Joachim streets.

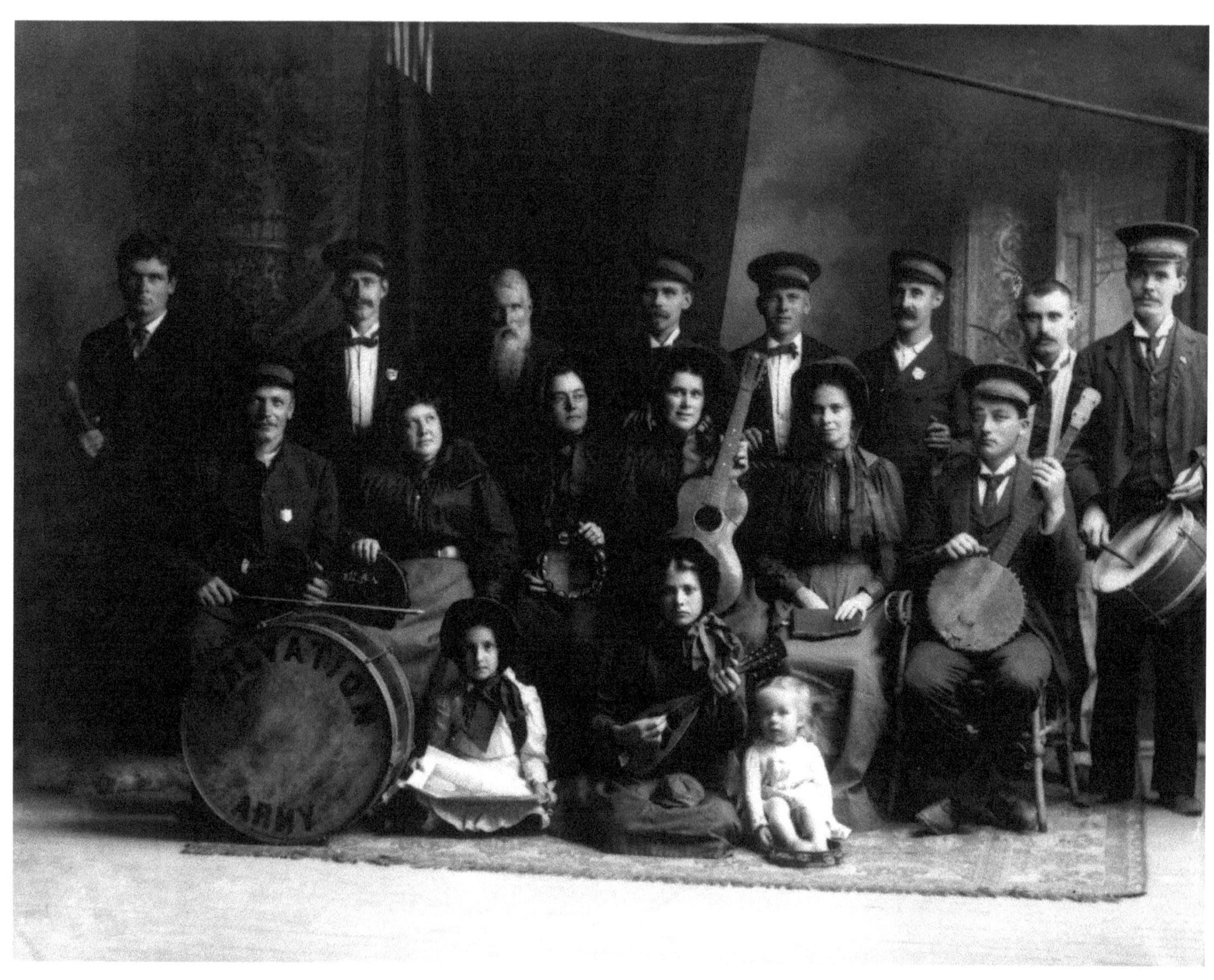

Mobile's chapter of the Salvation Army was established in October 1899 under the direction of Captain James T. Cumbie. Here, its band poses for a portrait in the studio of photographer Erik Overbey.

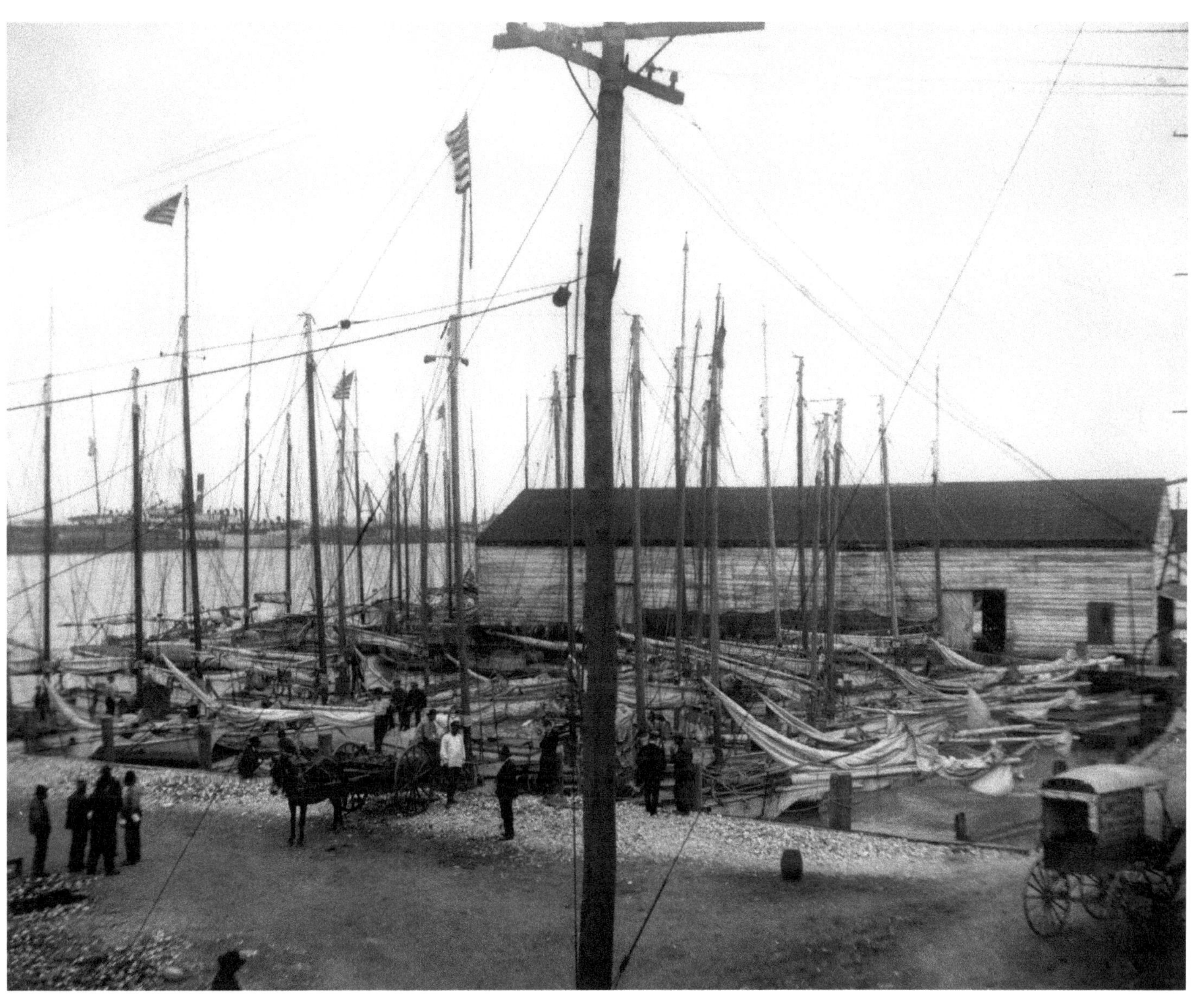

Commercial fishing has always been important to Mobile's economy, as this photograph of a fleet of oyster boats demonstrates (ca. 1895).

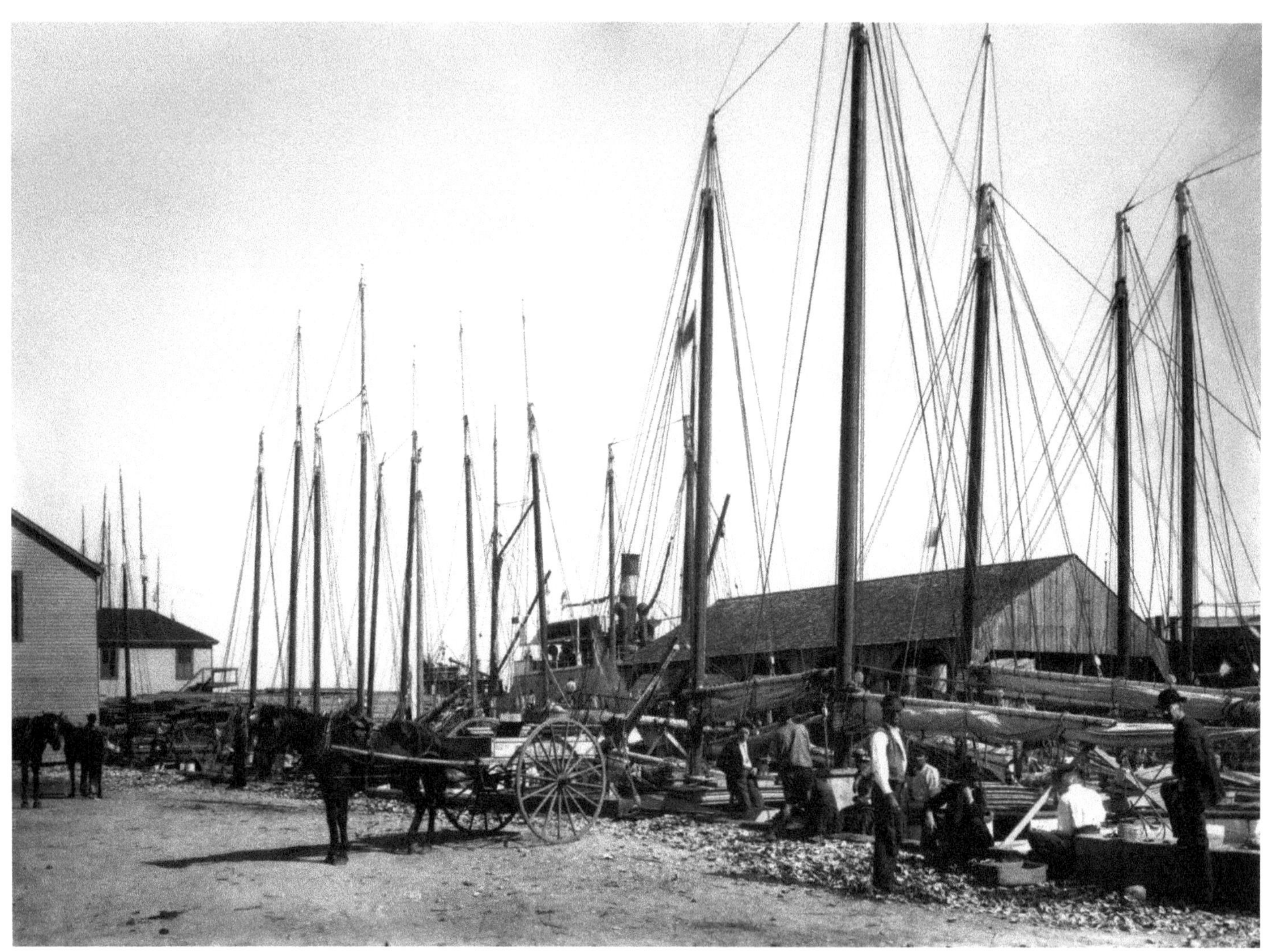

Mobile's oyster docks, 1895.

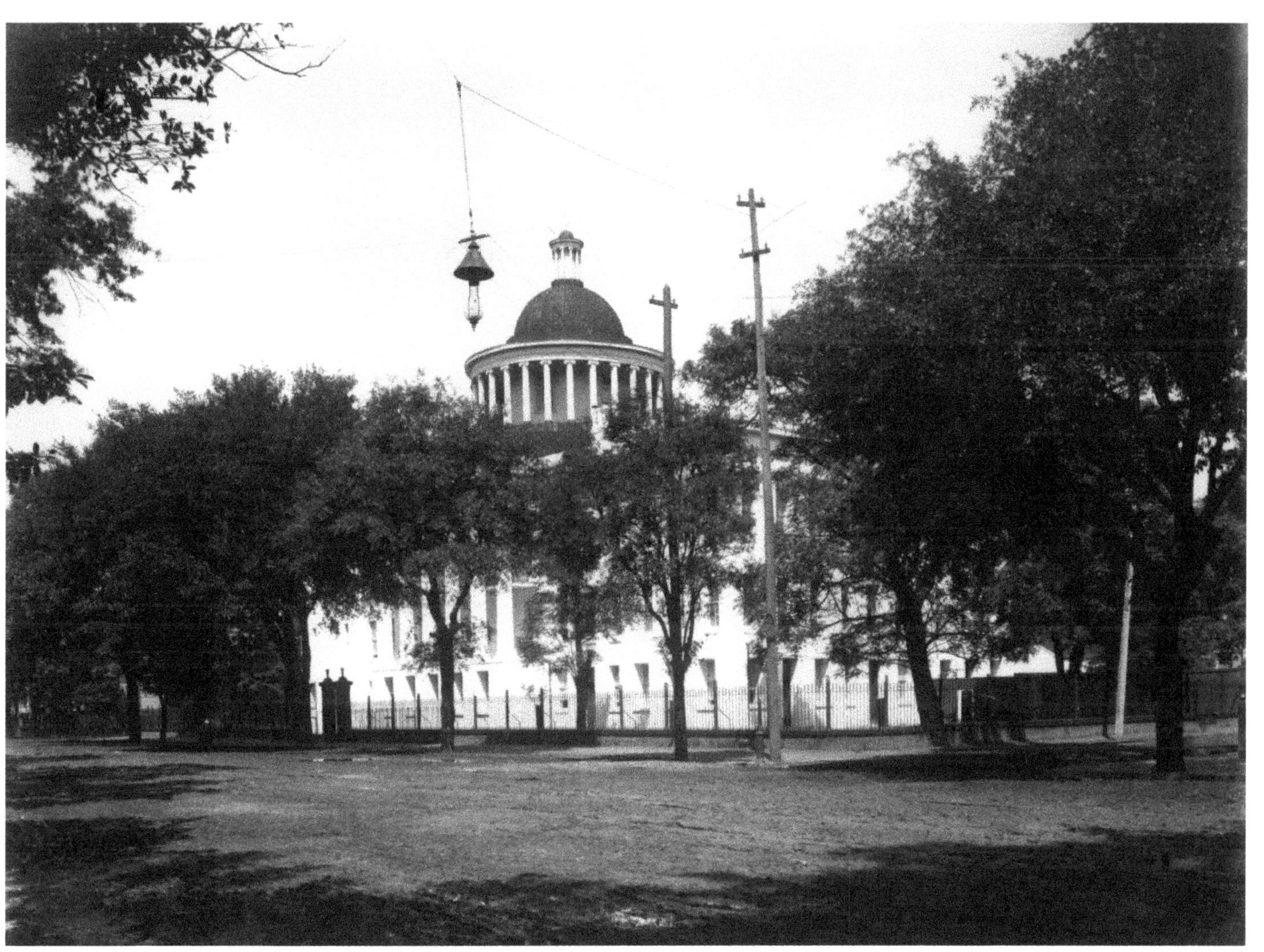

Barton Academy was Alabama's first public school. Built in 1835, it was named for state representative Willoughby Barton, the author of the bill creating Mobile's public school system. The building was used as a hospital for Union soldiers in 1864.

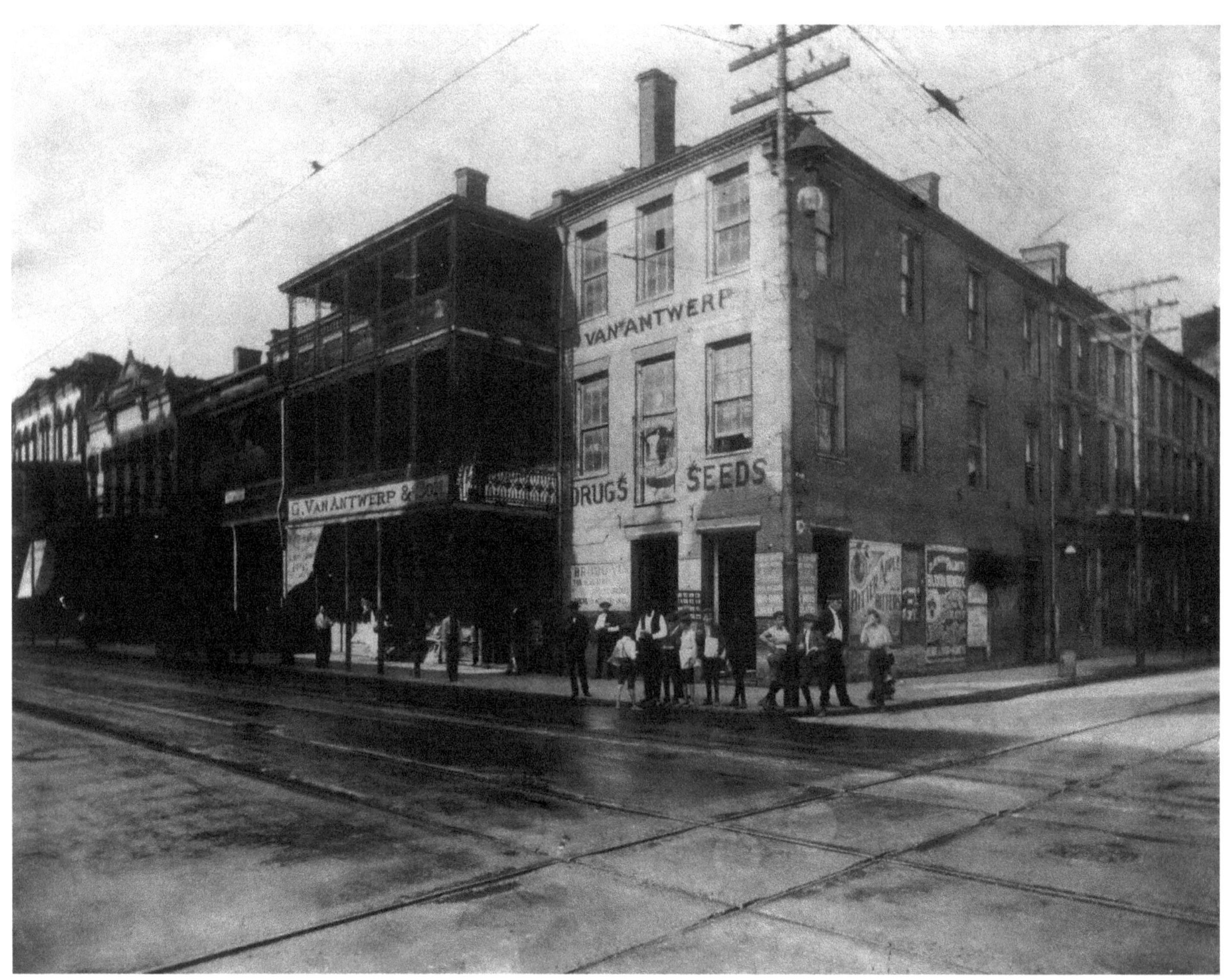

Van Antwerp and Son, located at 2 South Royal Street, sold medicines, soda, mineral water, and seeds.

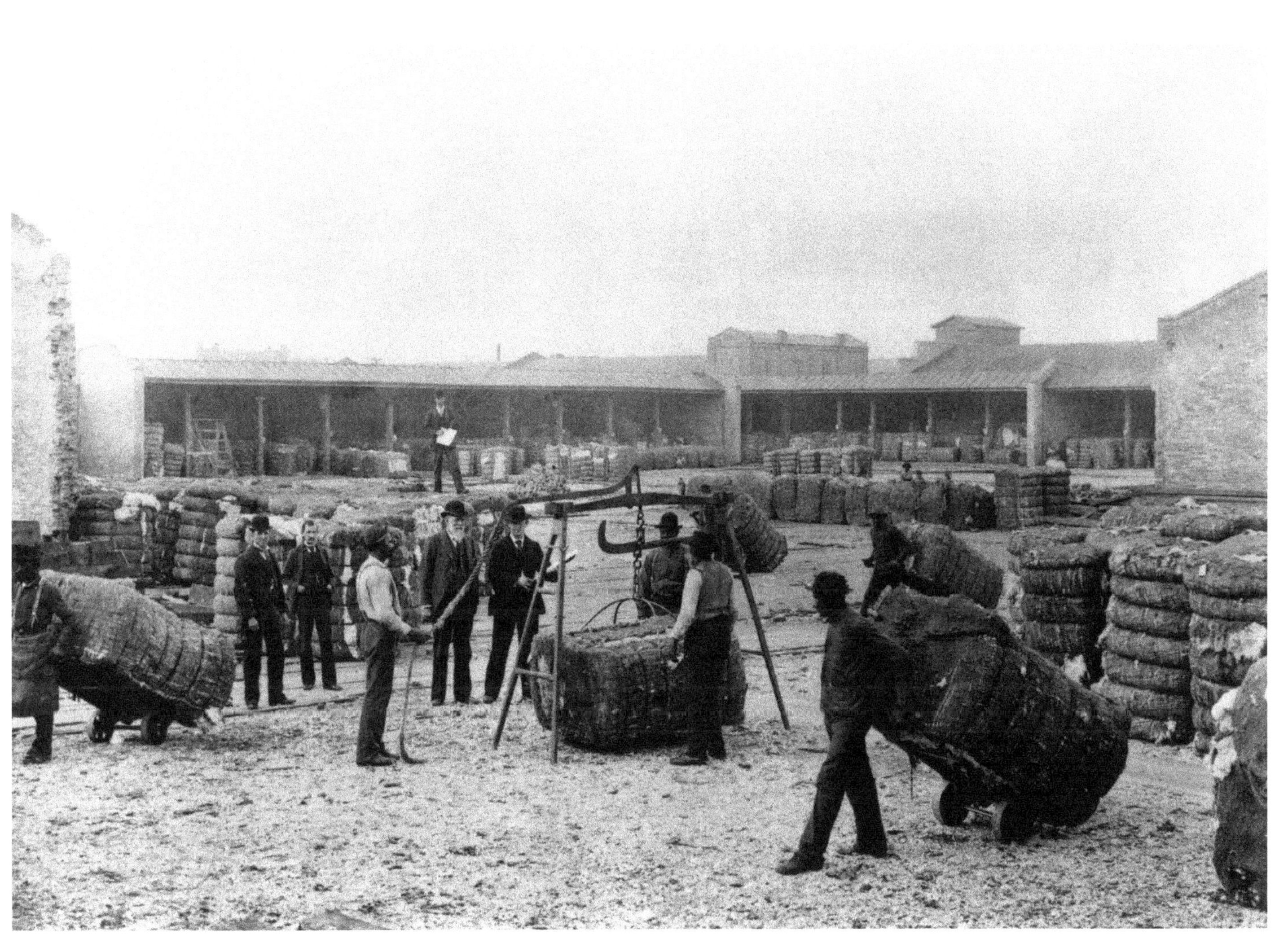

Dockworkers prepare cotton bales for transport from Mobile in 1894.

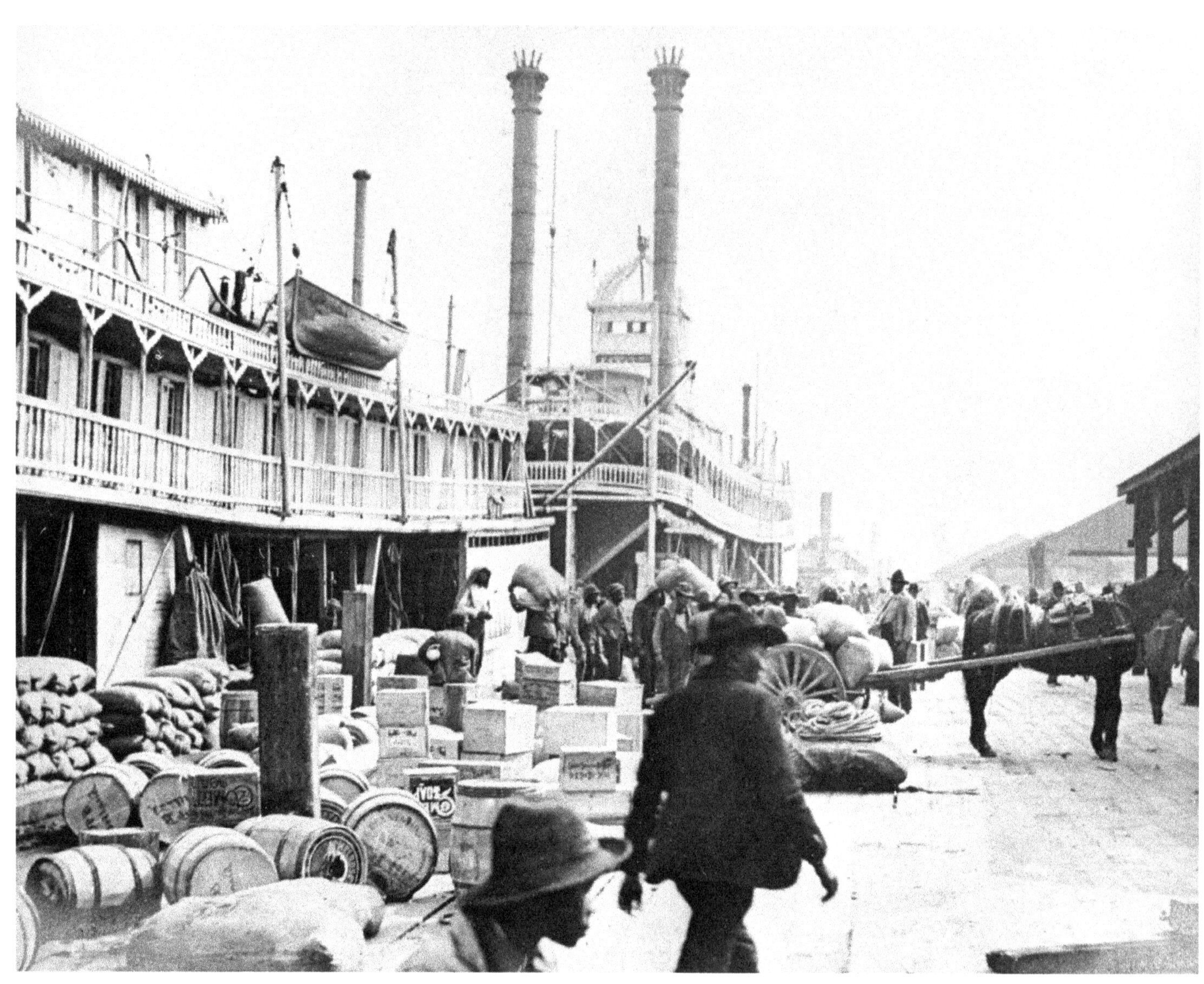

Commerce in Mobile along the river front about 1880. Workers are unloading goods from the riverboats *Hard Cash* and *Mary S. Blees.*

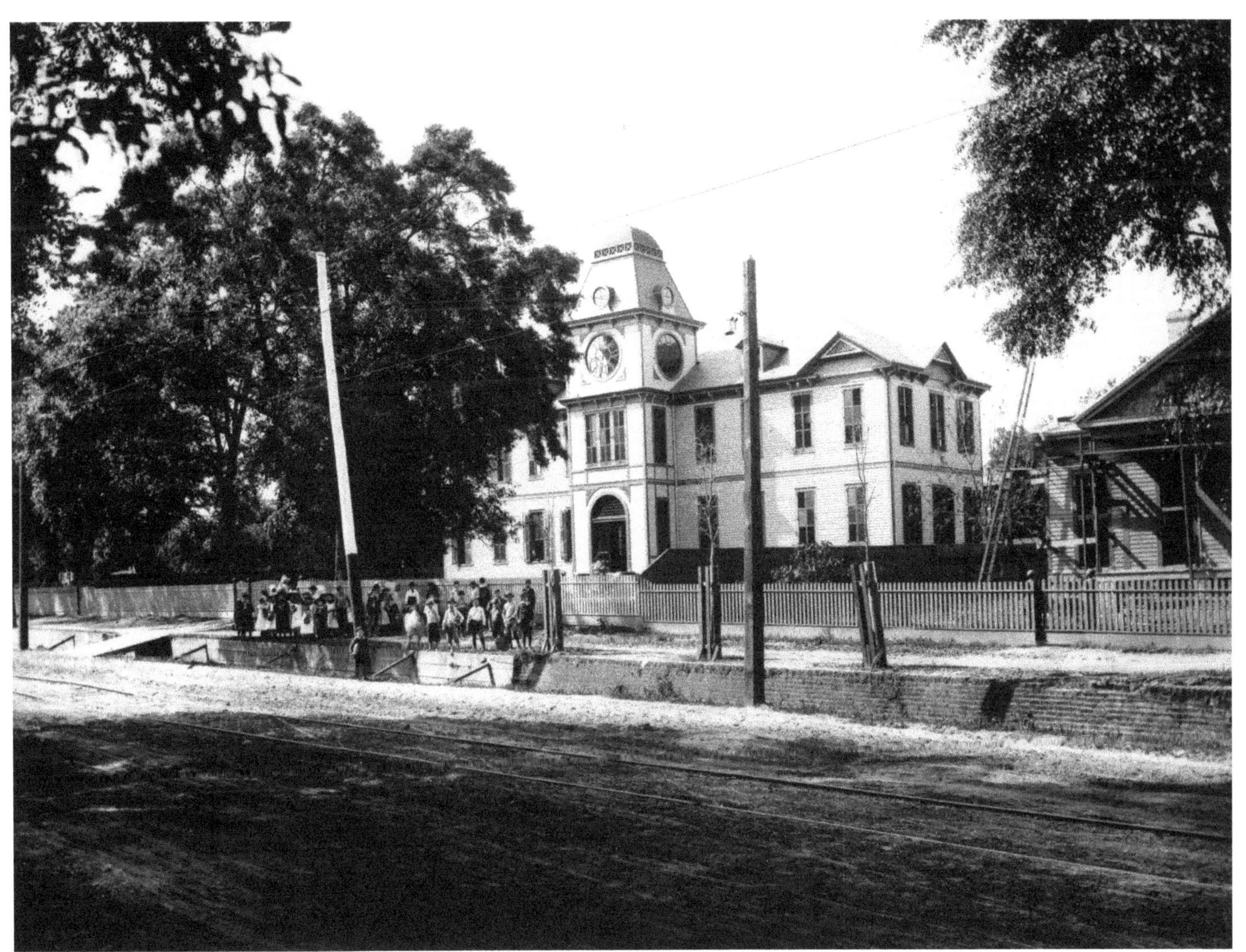

A photograph from around 1899 of the West Ward School, later known as the Admiral Semmes School. It stood on Springhill Avenue, just east of Ann Street, and was built in the Italianate style. It was torn down shortly after the First World War.

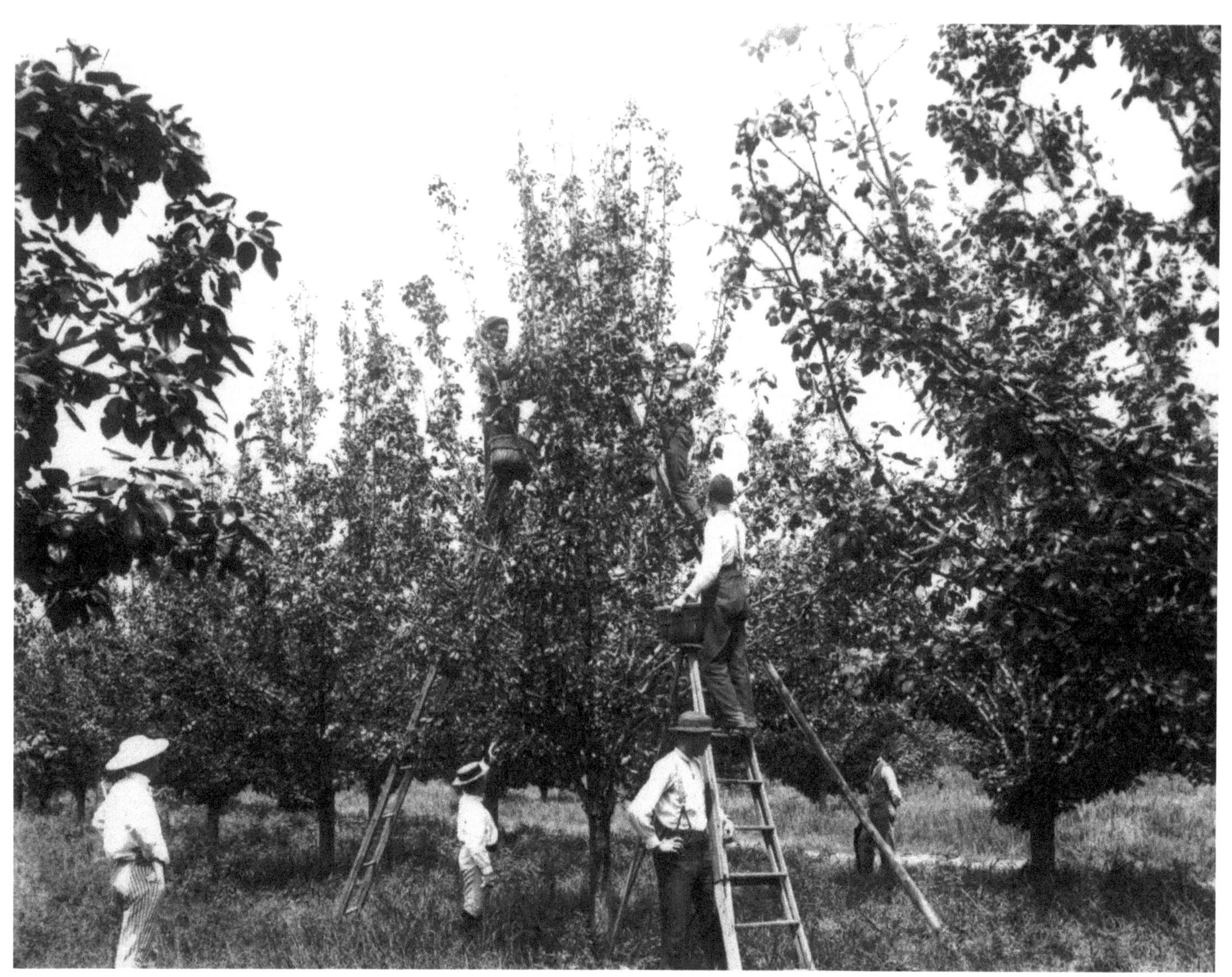

Gathering pears in E. M. Hudson's orchard around 1895.

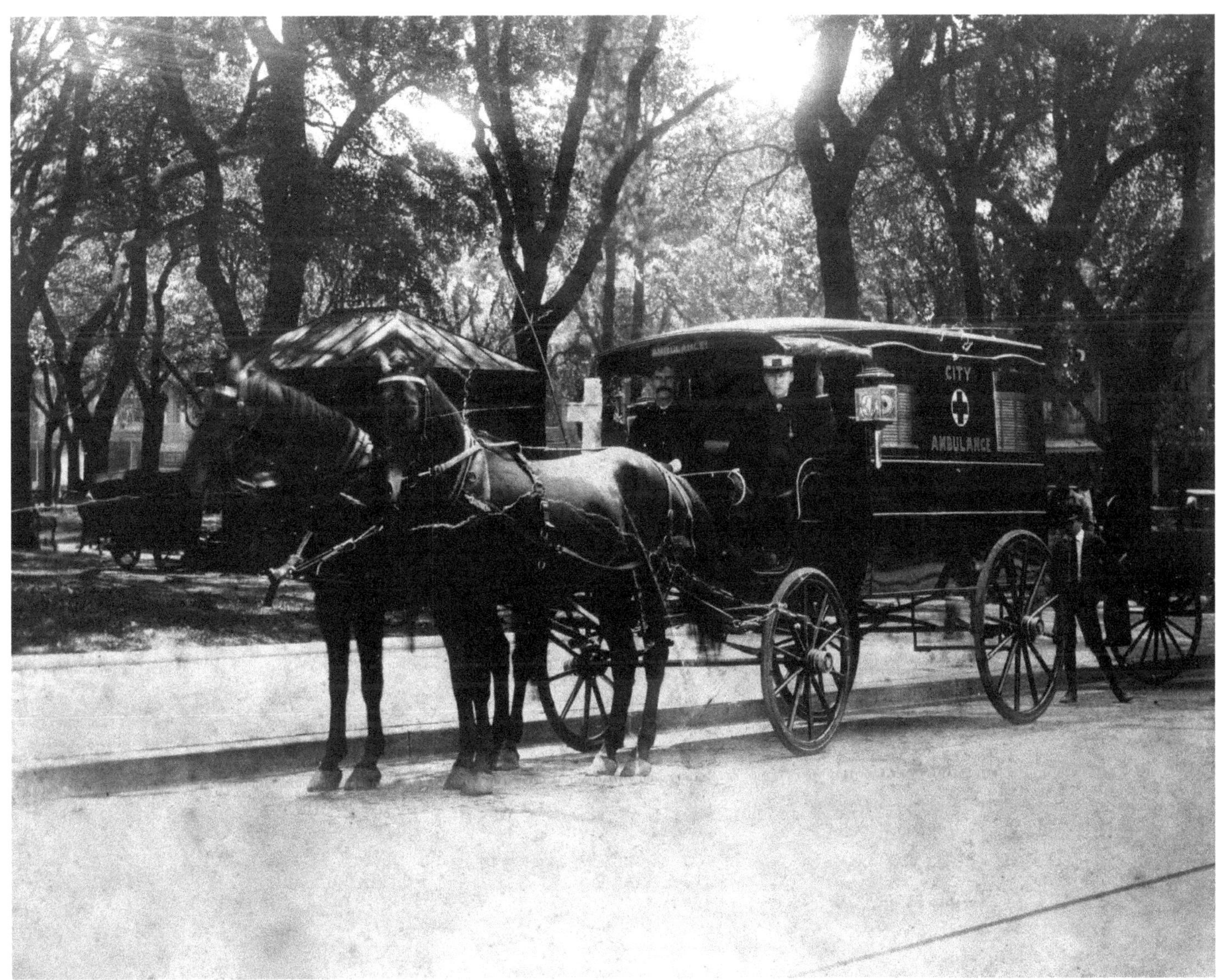

A city ambulance parked in front of Bienville Square about 1899. The square is located on the site of the Spanish Colonial hospital and has been an integral part of Mobile history since the 1850s. It has been the site of celebrations and the place to promenade, relax, and, as this image shows, prepare for an emergency.

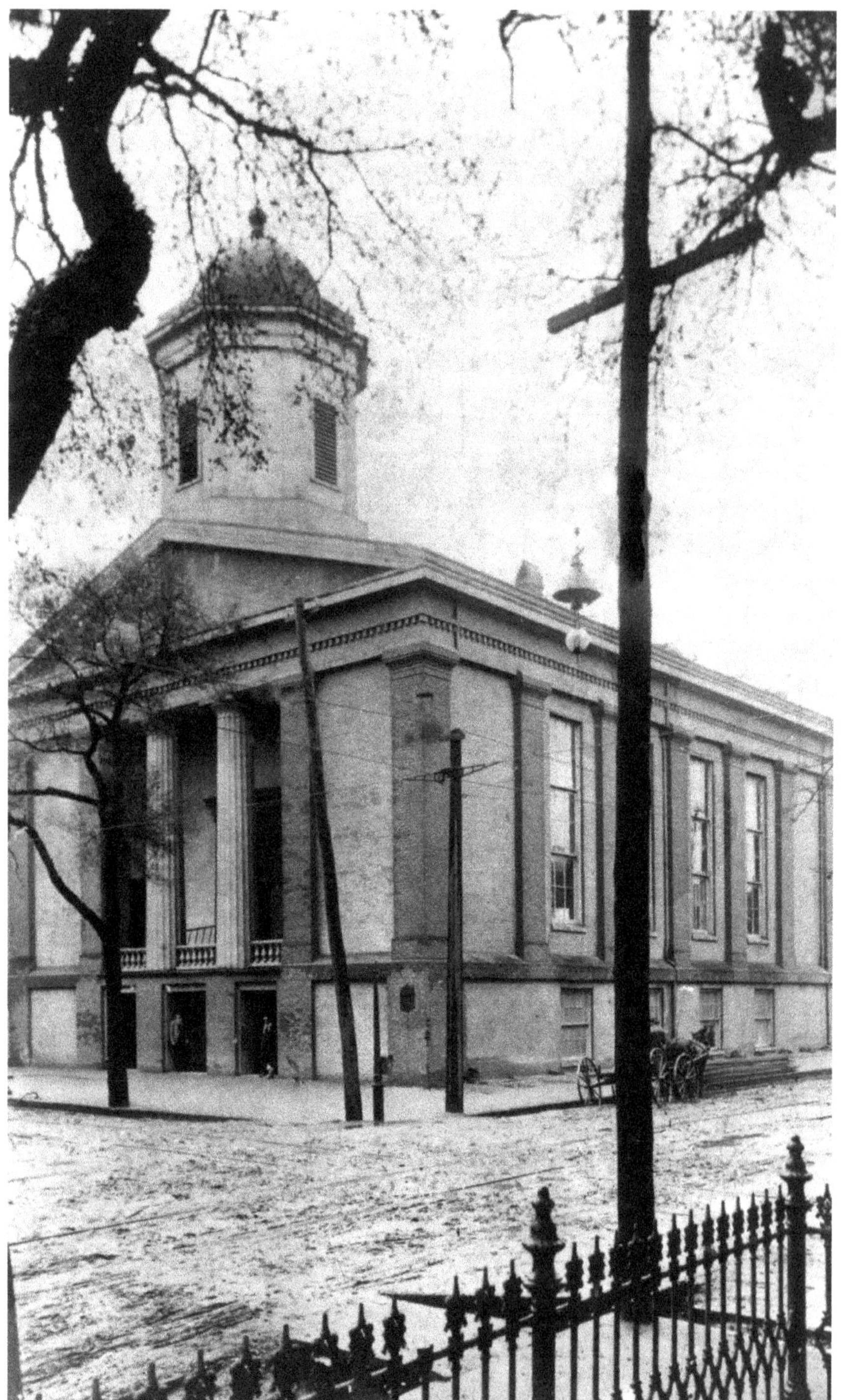

The St. Francis Street Methodist Church was built in 1895. After the 1916 hurricane, the church replaced the steeple with a 150-foot spire that is still visible today.

Near the end of the nineteenth century, the corner of Dauphin and Water streets had an active retail market that included Rhodes & Sons Furniture and the Pollack & Bernheimer Dry Goods Store.

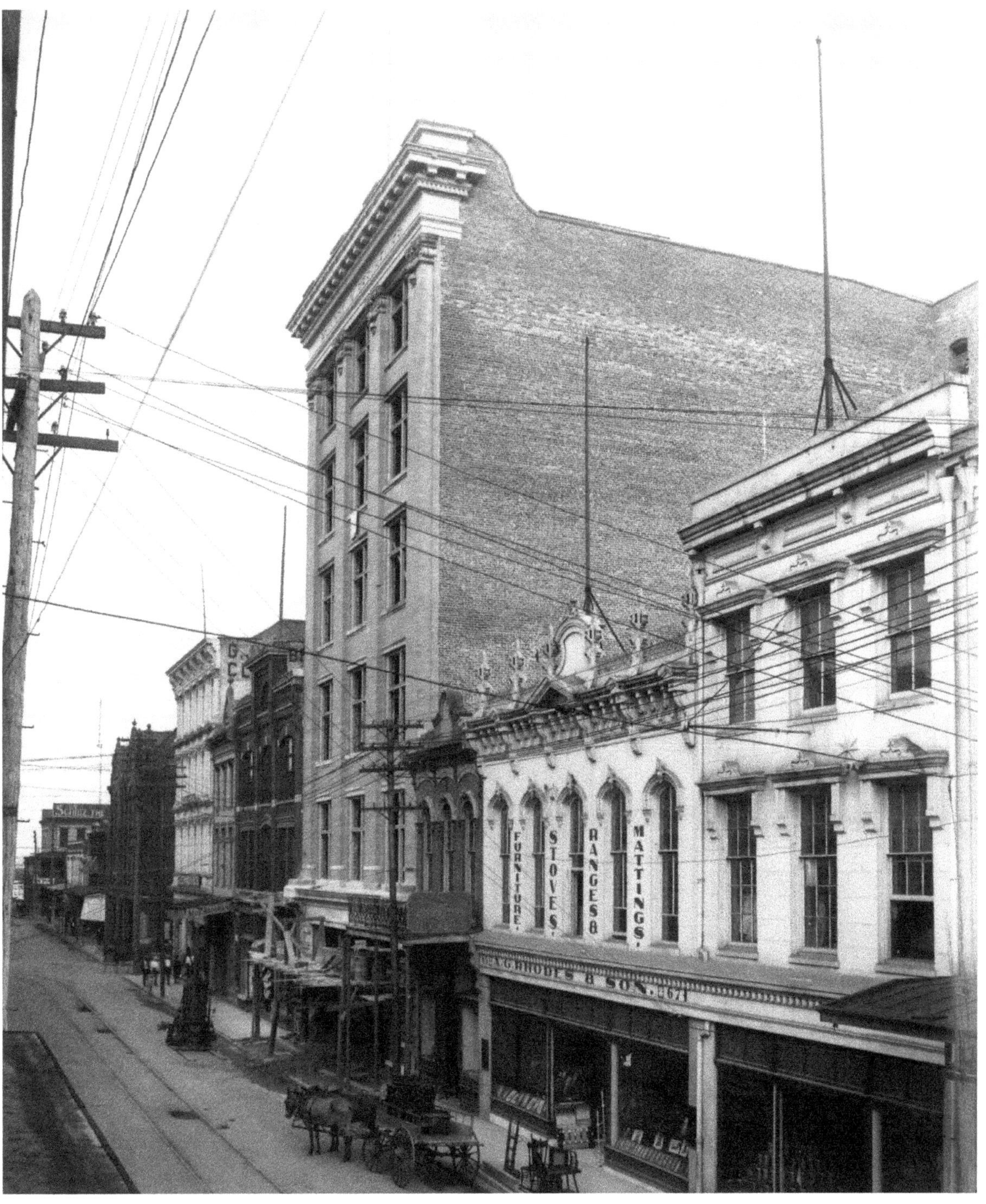

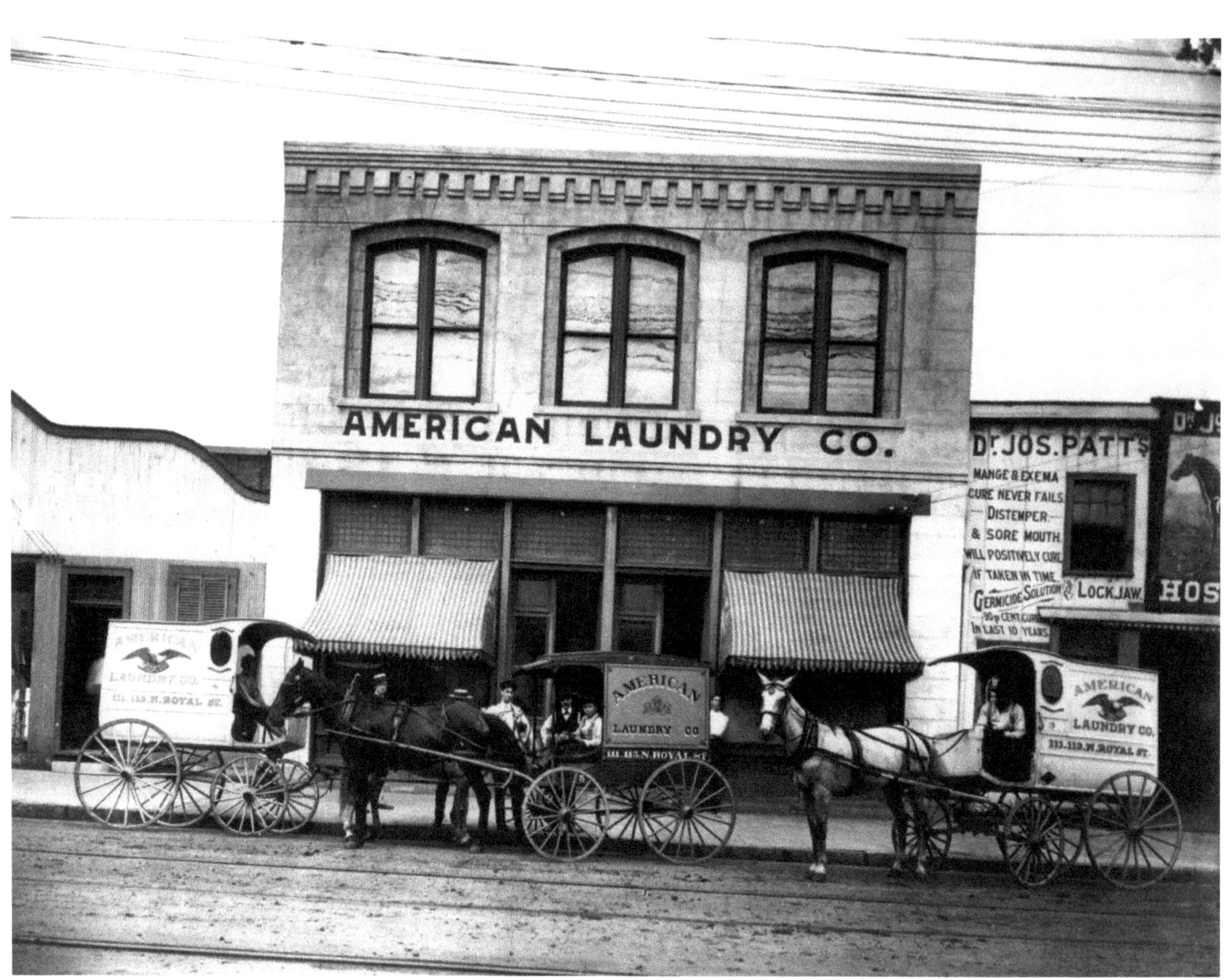

By the late nineteenth century, the American Laundry Company on Royal Street offered a delivery service. Doctor Joseph Patt, whose veterinary office was next door, would move his clinic to St. Michael and Joachim streets in 1908.

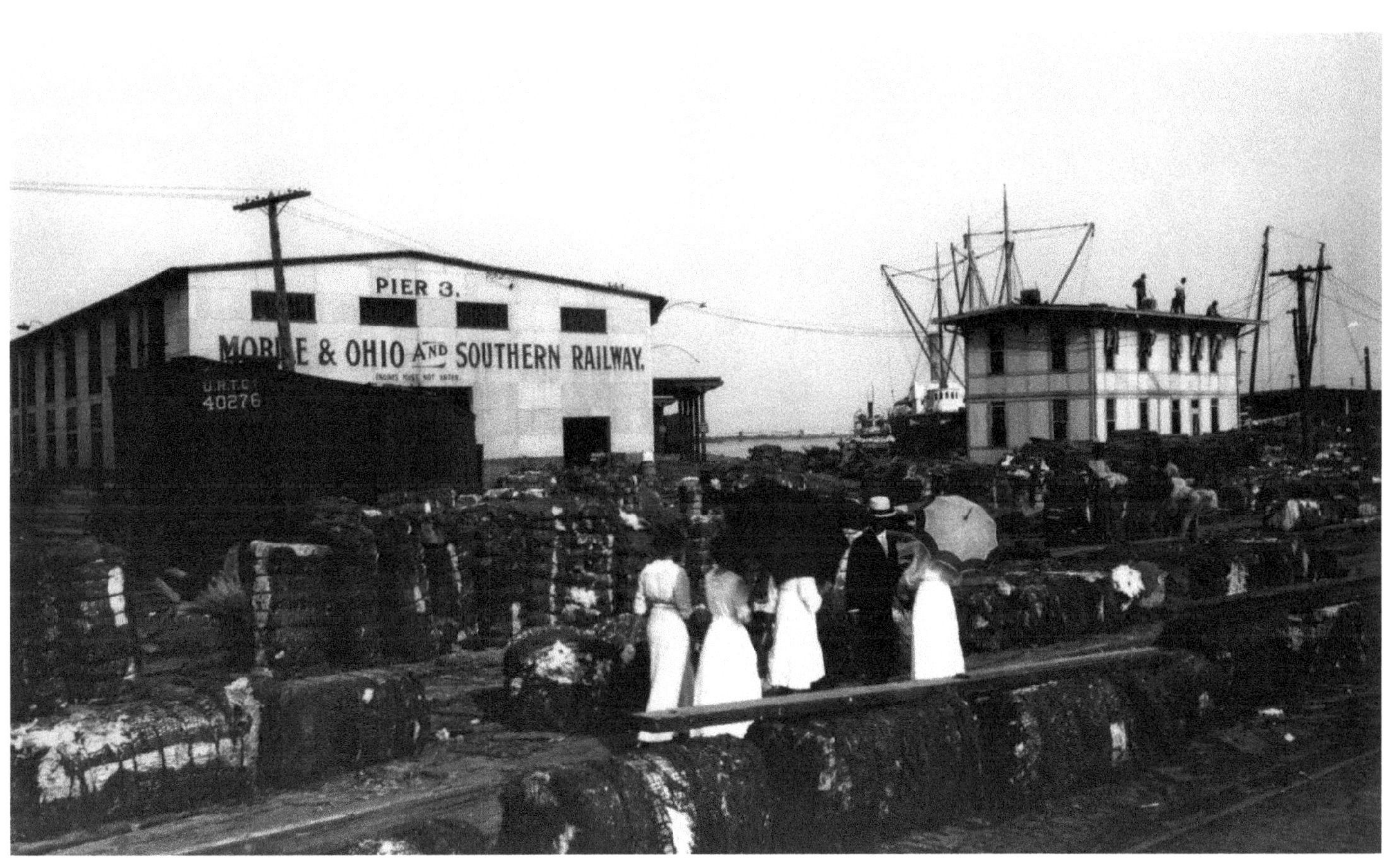

A man escorts four women on a tour of the Mobile & Ohio Docks.

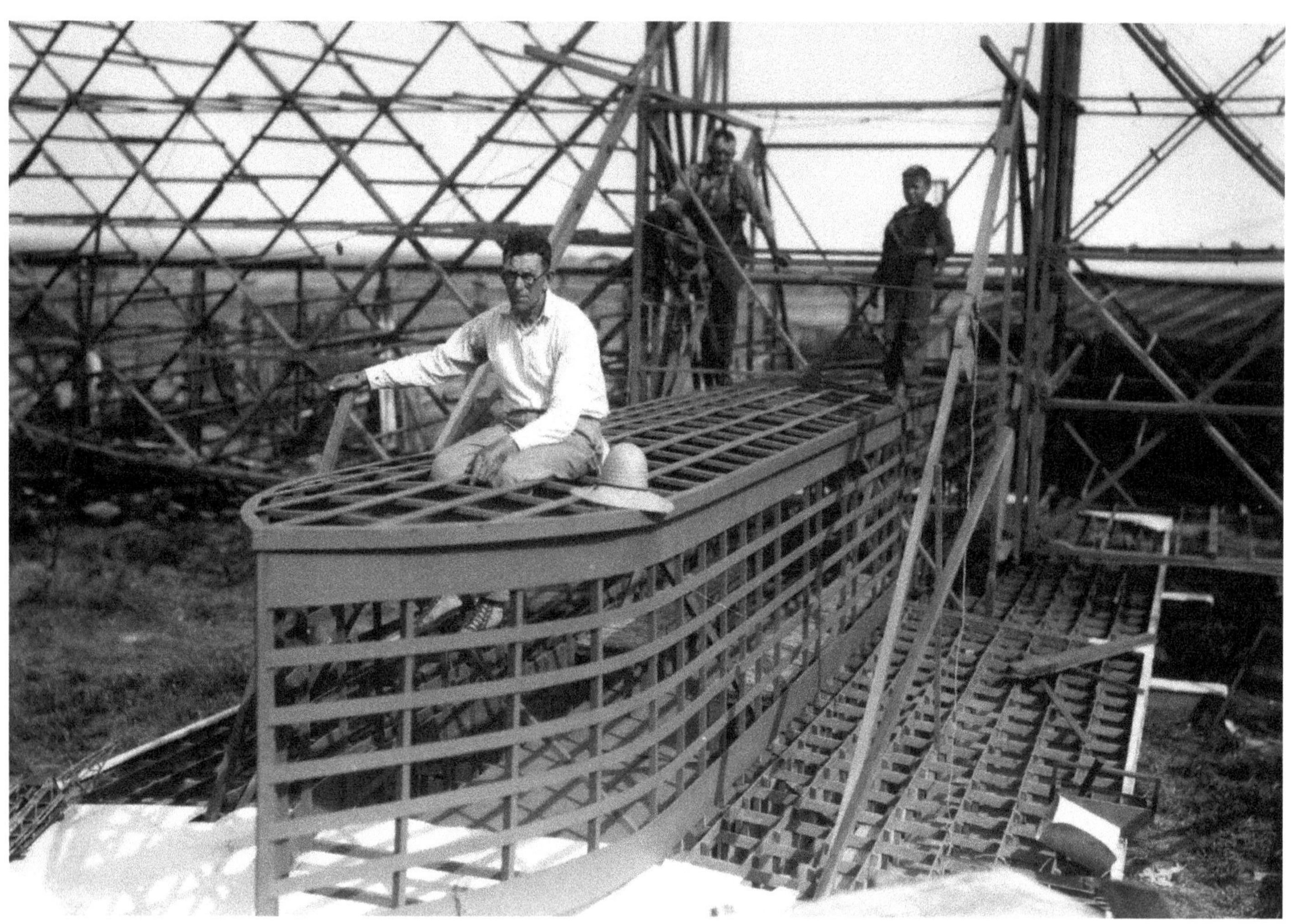

John Fowler, local inventor, sits at the front of one of the planes he constructed and flew. Many people believe that he perfected air flight before the Wright brothers.

Turn-of-the-Century Mobile

(1900–1919)

During the early years of the twentieth century, Mobile continued its slow recovery from a postwar malaise. In 1904, Ollinger and Bruce Company opened the first modern dry dock in the city, absorbing several smaller facilities and bolstering Mobile's ship repair industry. Those early years of the twentieth century ushered in other political and technological changes. In 1901, Alabama ratified a new constitution that disfranchised African-Americans and poor whites and established rigid laws for racial separation. White Mobilians endorsed the state's new constitution, which inaugurated a half-century of oppression and legal segregation. Local politics shifted in 1902 when Mobile established an ordinance segregating streetcars. At the same time, the city began paving streets and strengthening its commercial markets.

A combination of Victorian morality and Progressive politics also contributed to Mobile's changing society. Numerous saloons and gambling houses closed as religious Mobilians applied the Social Gospel to their city. Mobile's fraternal and mystic organizations led the way in resisting prohibition efforts by the Alabama legislature in 1907. The measure passed, but Alabama's Port City refused to acknowledge the law, ensuring a protracted battle between municipal and state governments. By 1910, Progressive-minded businessmen in Mobile, weary of the inaction and corruption of local politicians, established the Mobile Progressive Association and eventually succeeded in changing the city's form of government to an at-large election of three commissioners. The reforming trend continued under the new commission.

Events in Europe interrupted Mobile's Progressive advancements. When the British government recalled all its vessels for wartime service, Mobile's port was once again severely hampered. The Emergency Fleet Corporation, established by the United States in 1916 to accelerate the construction of an American merchant marine, provided an economic boost to Mobile's shipbuilding industry and offset a potential employment crisis. Rapid industrialization of the waterfront during World War I created jobs. Bond rallies combined patriotic fervor with monetary assistance to further the war effort. Although the ships built in Mobile were completed too late to contribute to victory, the economic boost provided by government shipbuilding softened the impact of the postwar depression.

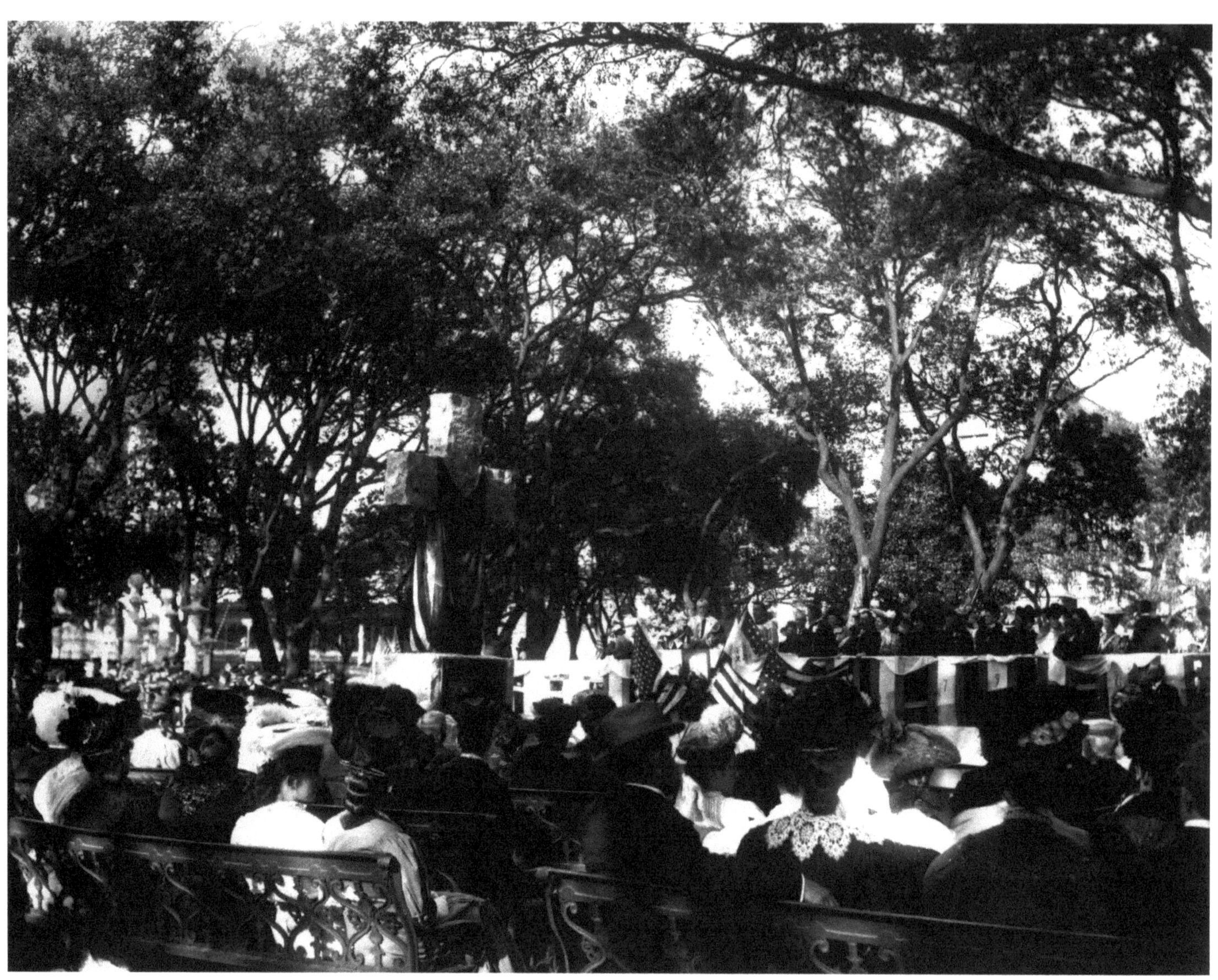

In 1906, Mobilians honored the founder of their city, French explorer Jean Baptiste Le Moyne de Bienville, by unveiling a monument to him in Bienville Square.

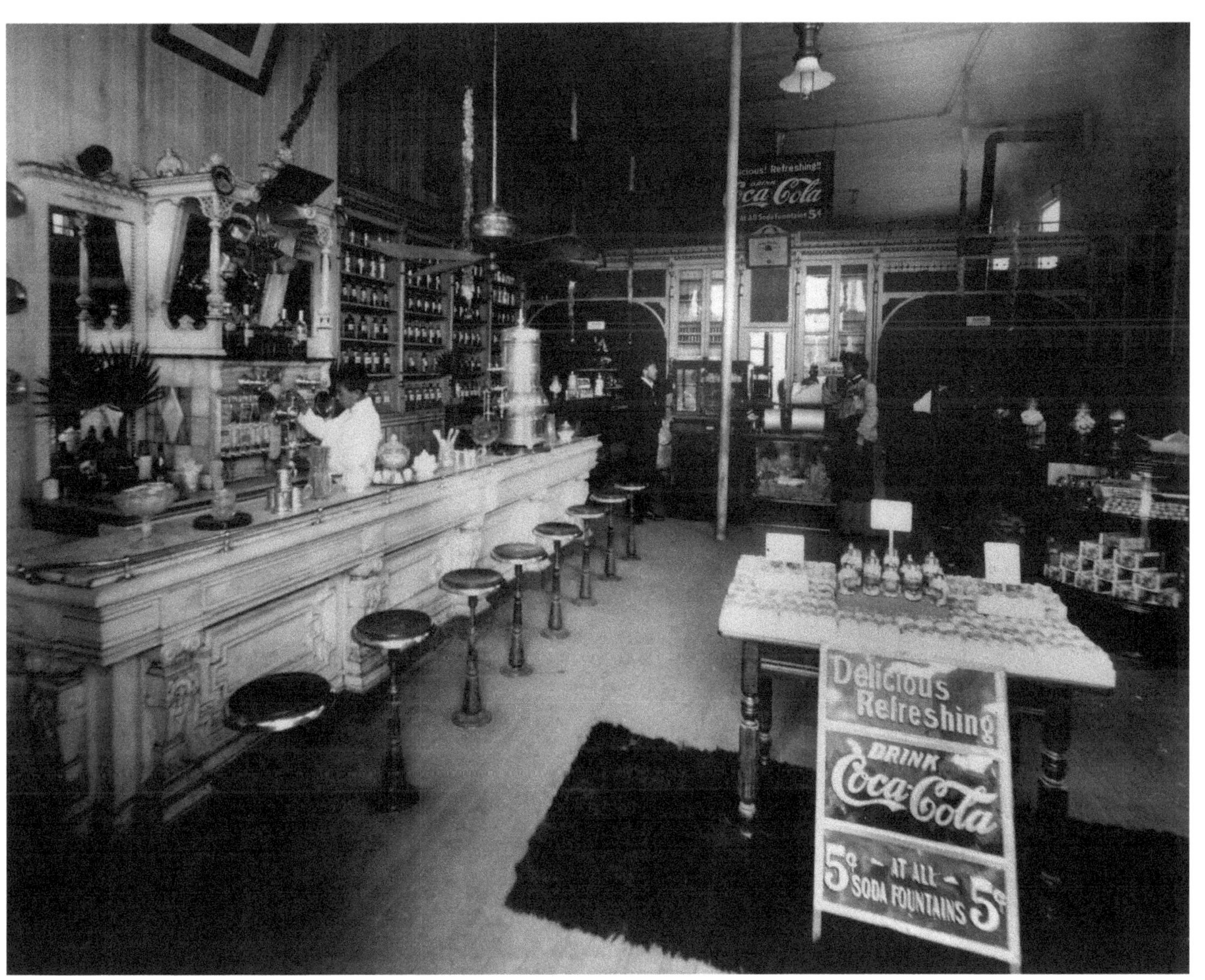

Owned and operated by African-Americans, People's Drugs, located at 522 Dauphin Street, offered a fine example of an early twentieth century drugstore and soda fountain.

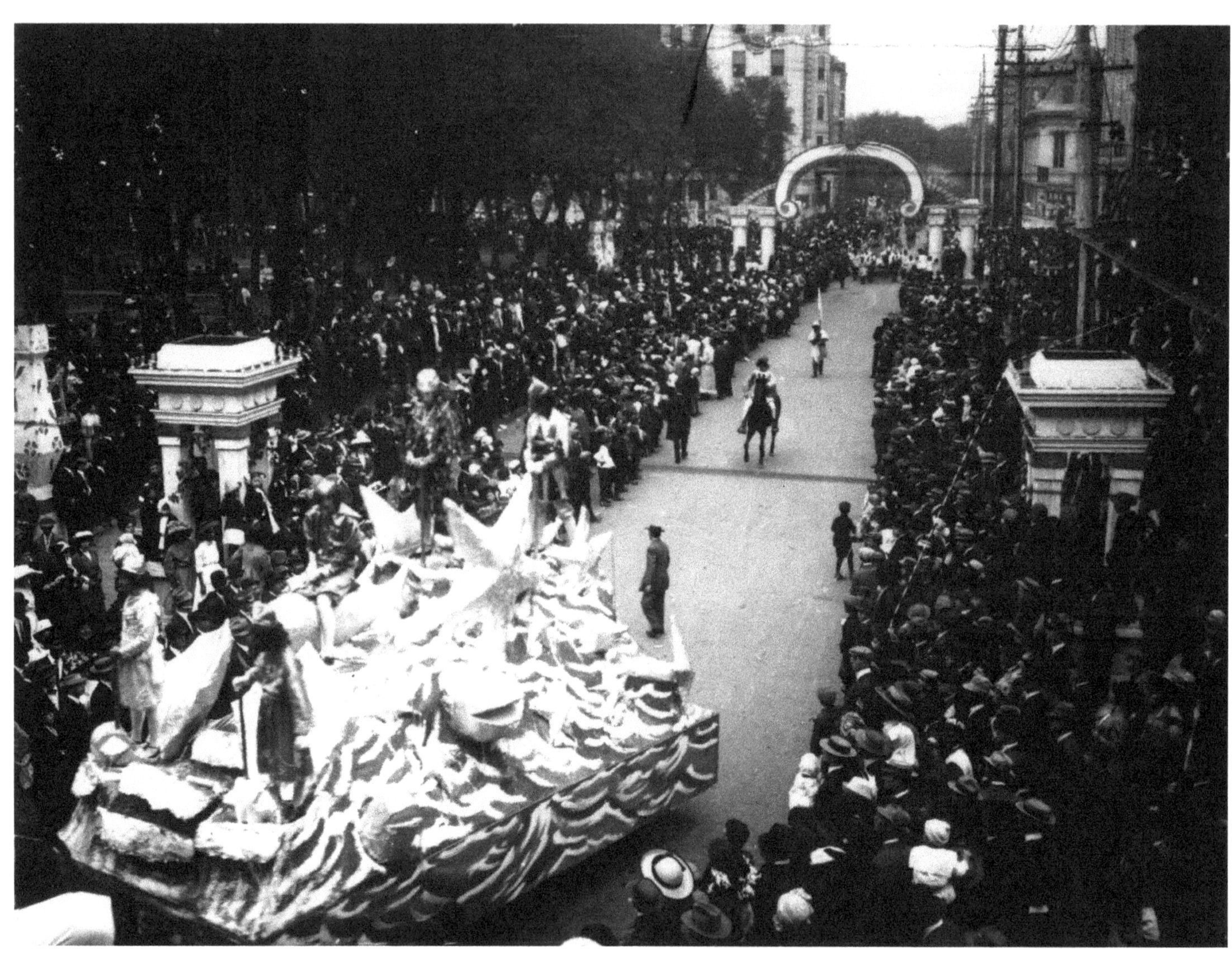

A Mardi Gras float moves down St. Joseph Street about 1900. The stately Bienville Hotel can be seen in the background.

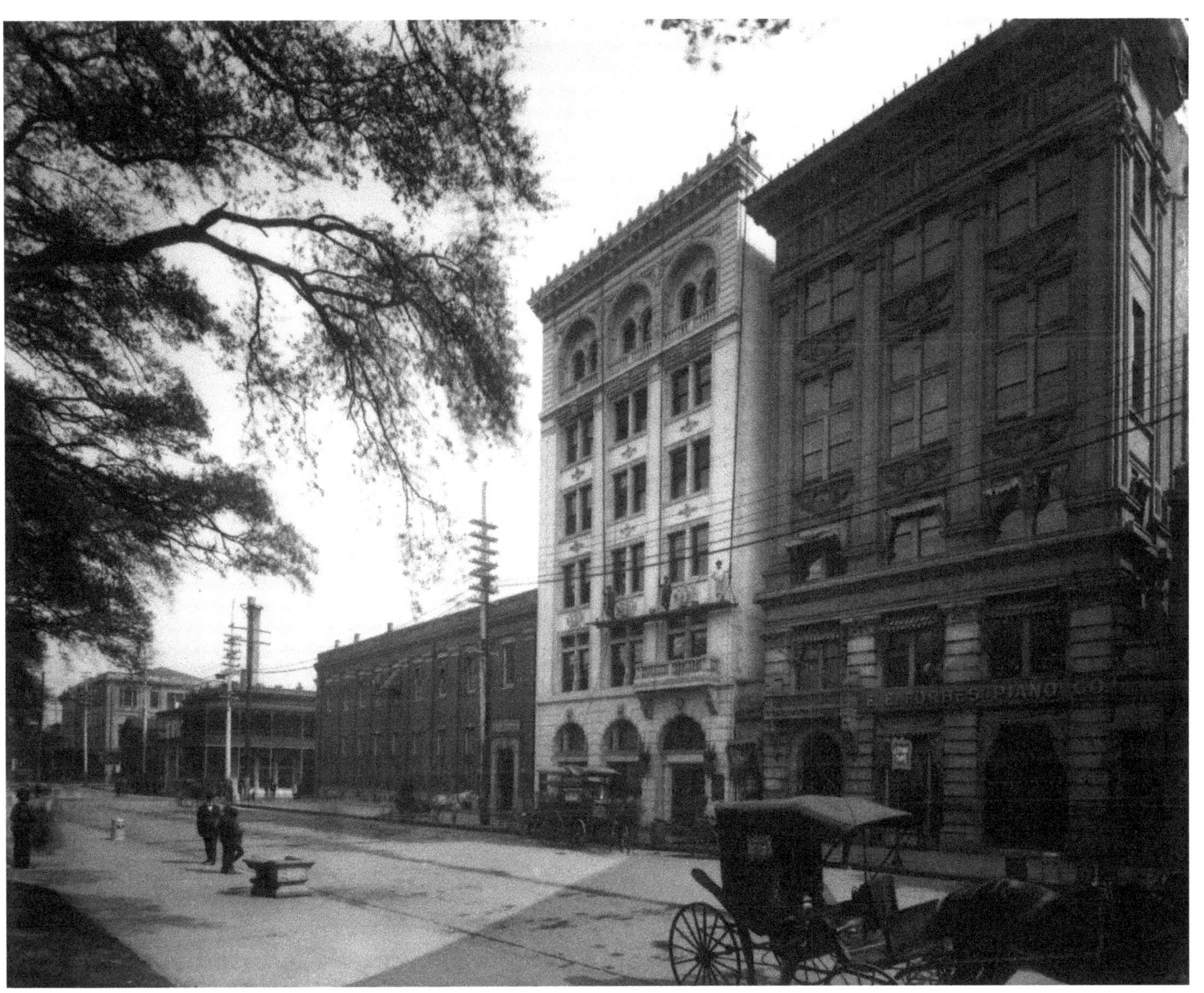

This early twentieth-century photograph shows St. Joseph Street at Bienville Square, looking north. The building on the right was one of Mobile's first steel structures and housed the Forbes Piano Company. Attorneys William B. Inge and William H. Armbrecht, as well as various Masonic lodges, also occupied the building. Quartered in the two adjacent structures were, respectively, the City Bank and Trust and People's Bank.

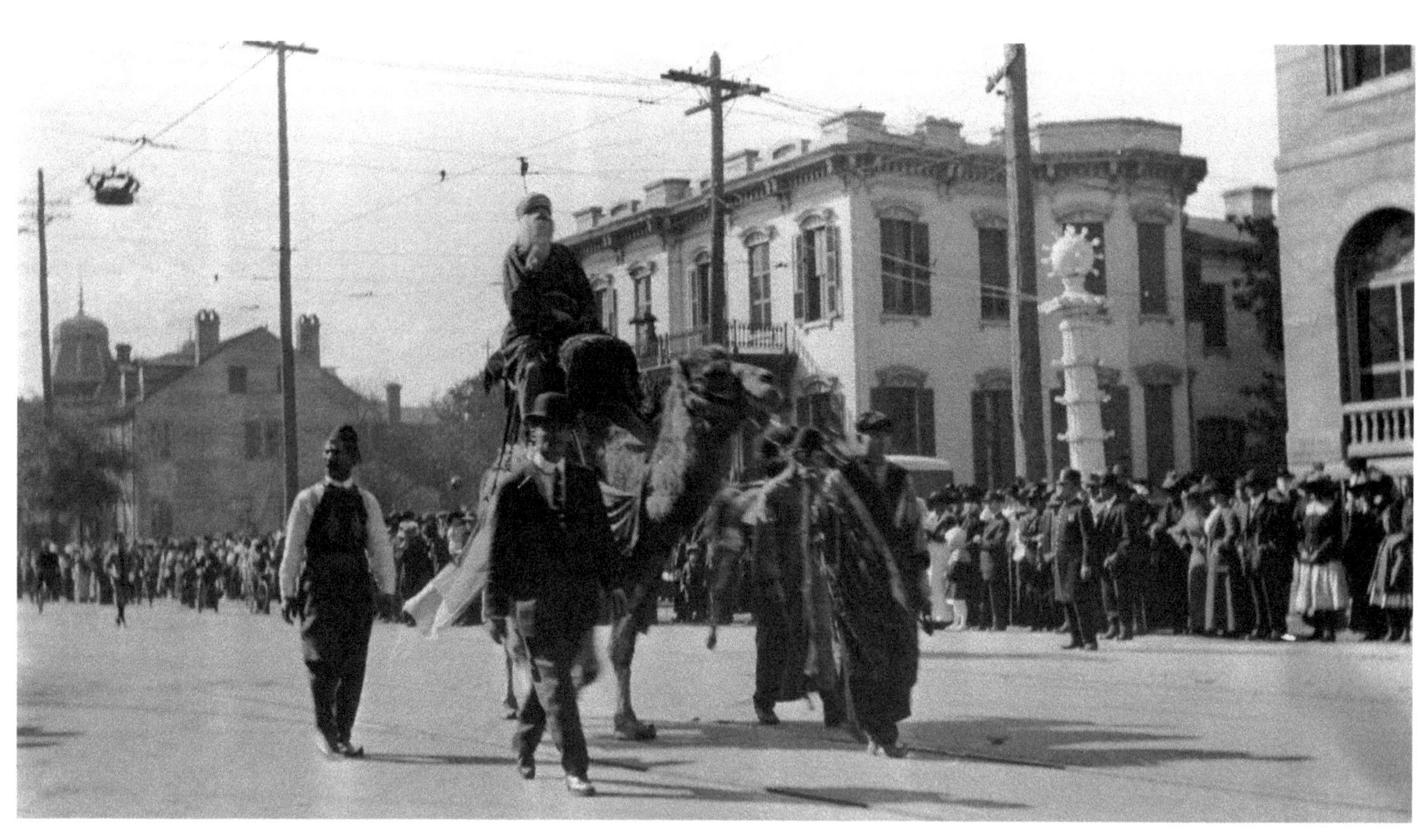

Circus performers, along with their camel, participated in the 1905 Mardi Gras festivities. It is unknown whether that was a regular occurrence.

In this image from around 1907, the Van Antwerp building towers above downtown. Built by George B. Rogers, it was Mobile's first skyscraper and would remain the city's tallest building for a number of years.

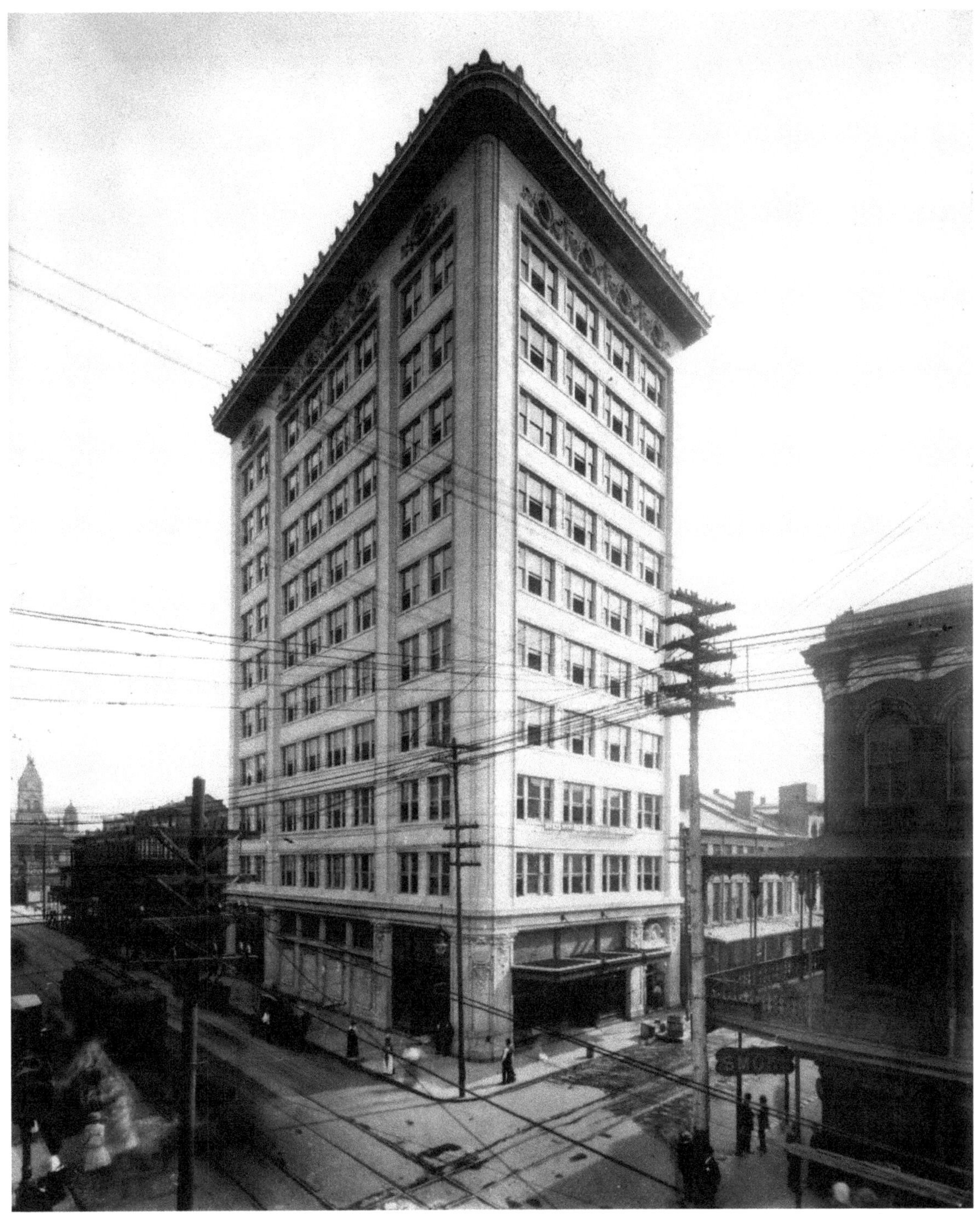

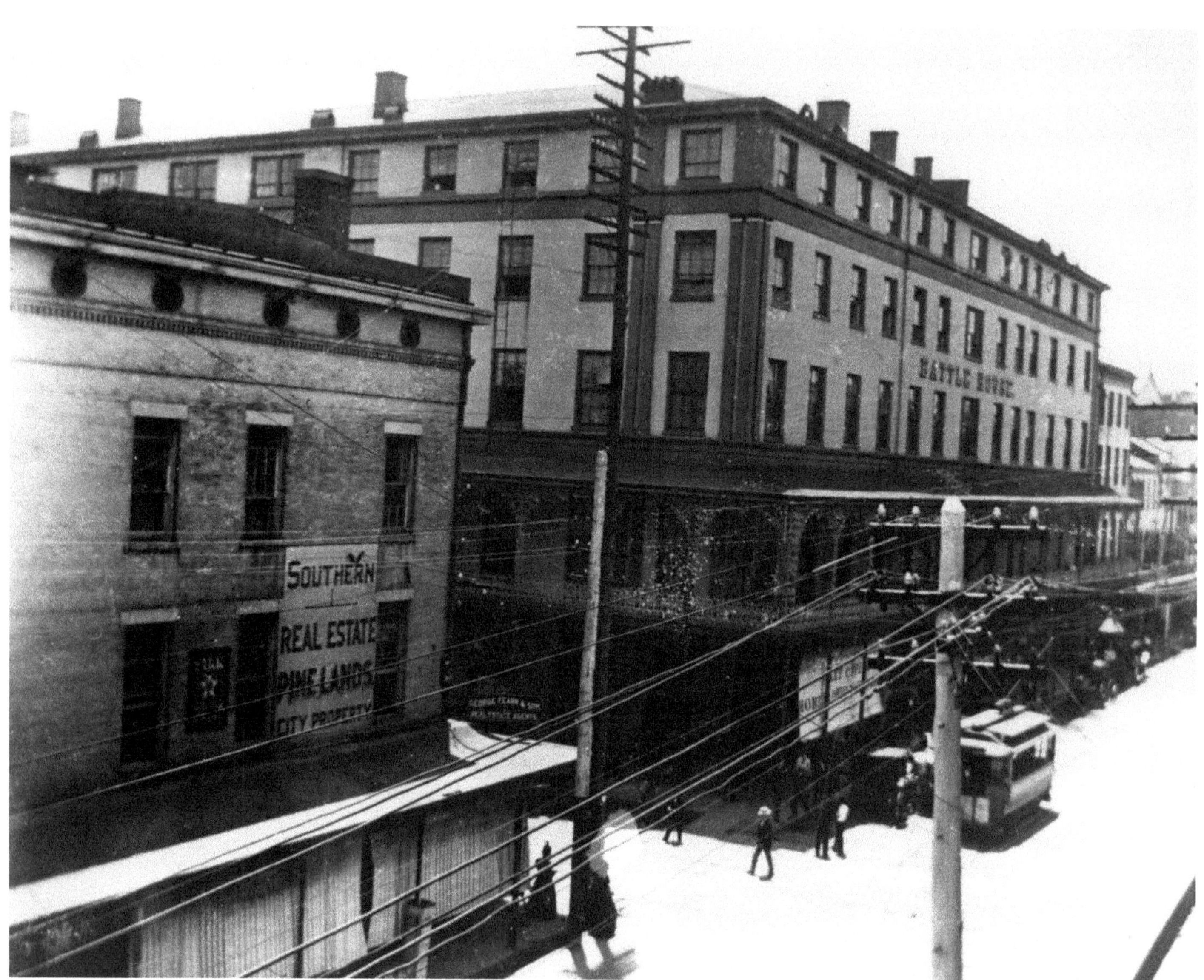

Built in 1852, the Battle House Hotel was a true five-star luxury inn. It featured 240 guest rooms, which were usually occupied by rich planters from Alabama's interior, in town to buy or sell cotton or slaves. The original building burned to the ground in 1905 but was rebuilt in 1908. It then fell into increasing disrepair and was vacant some 30 years before reopening with much fanfare in May 2007. Among the notables who stayed at the hotel were Henry Clay, Amelia Earhart, Jefferson Davis, Woodrow Wilson, and Edwin Booth.

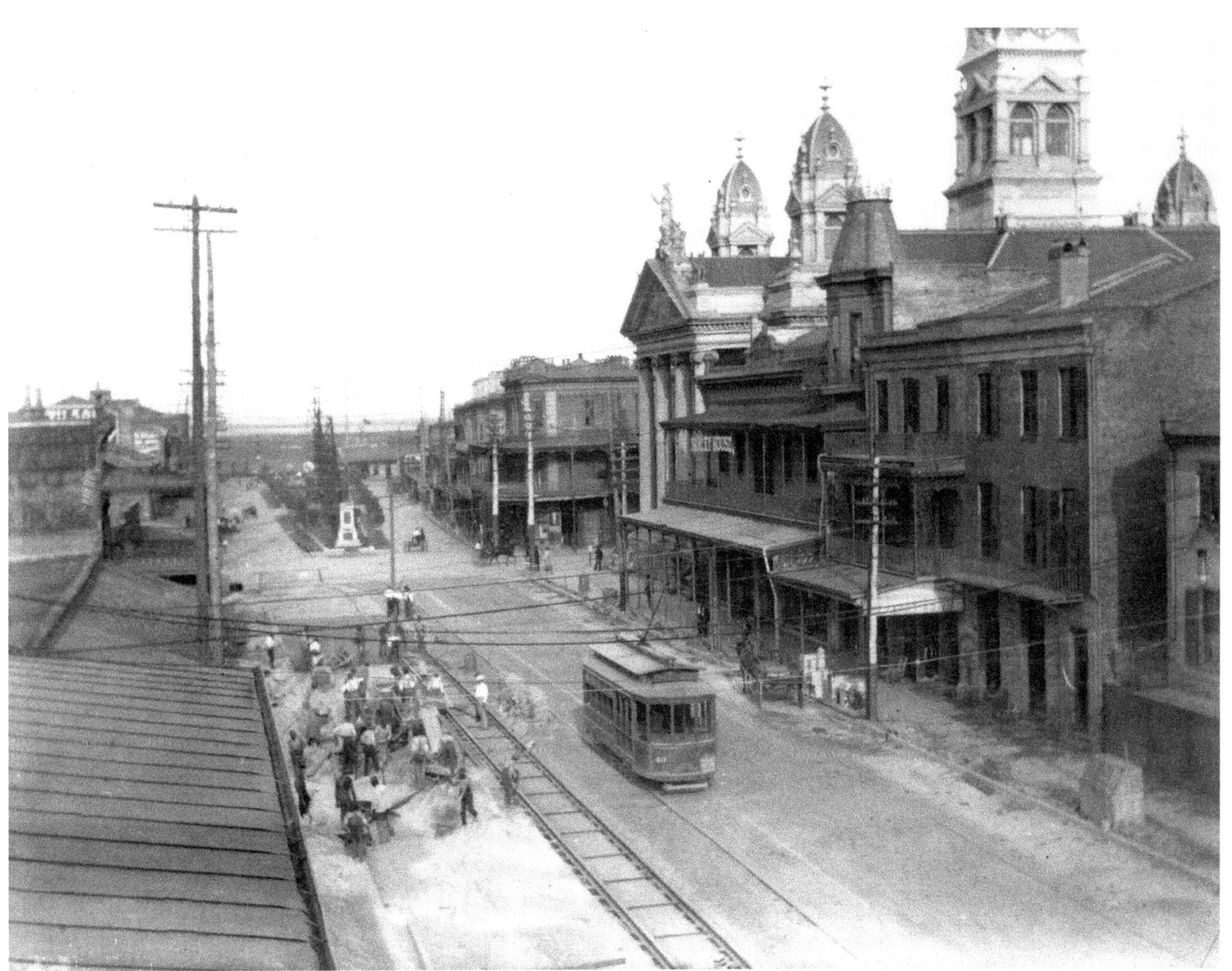

This September 16, 1904, photograph shows Government Street, looking east toward the river. The Benz courthouse is on the right. Two years after this image was taken, the 1906 hurricane struck and much of the building's statuary toppled. Next to the courthouse is Farley Brothers grocery store.

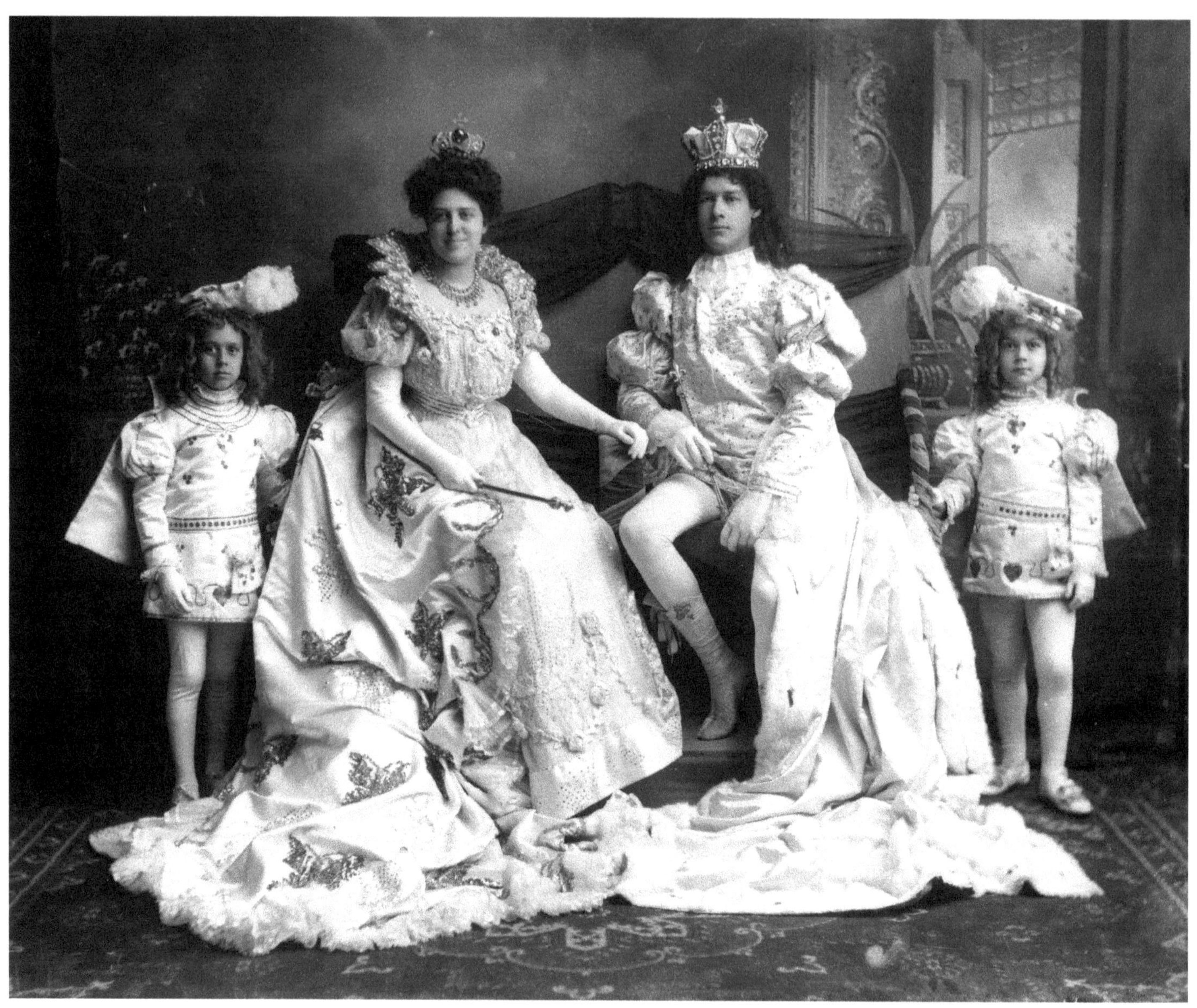

The 1907 Mardi Gras court, Thomas Wilkins Sims as King Felix, with his consort, Virginia A. Lyons (Mrs. Charles Blakeley), accompanied by their pages, LeBaron and Marion Lyons. Although the Mardi Gras season was still brief and parades were rather simple affairs, the trappings of the royal "family" were quite lavish.

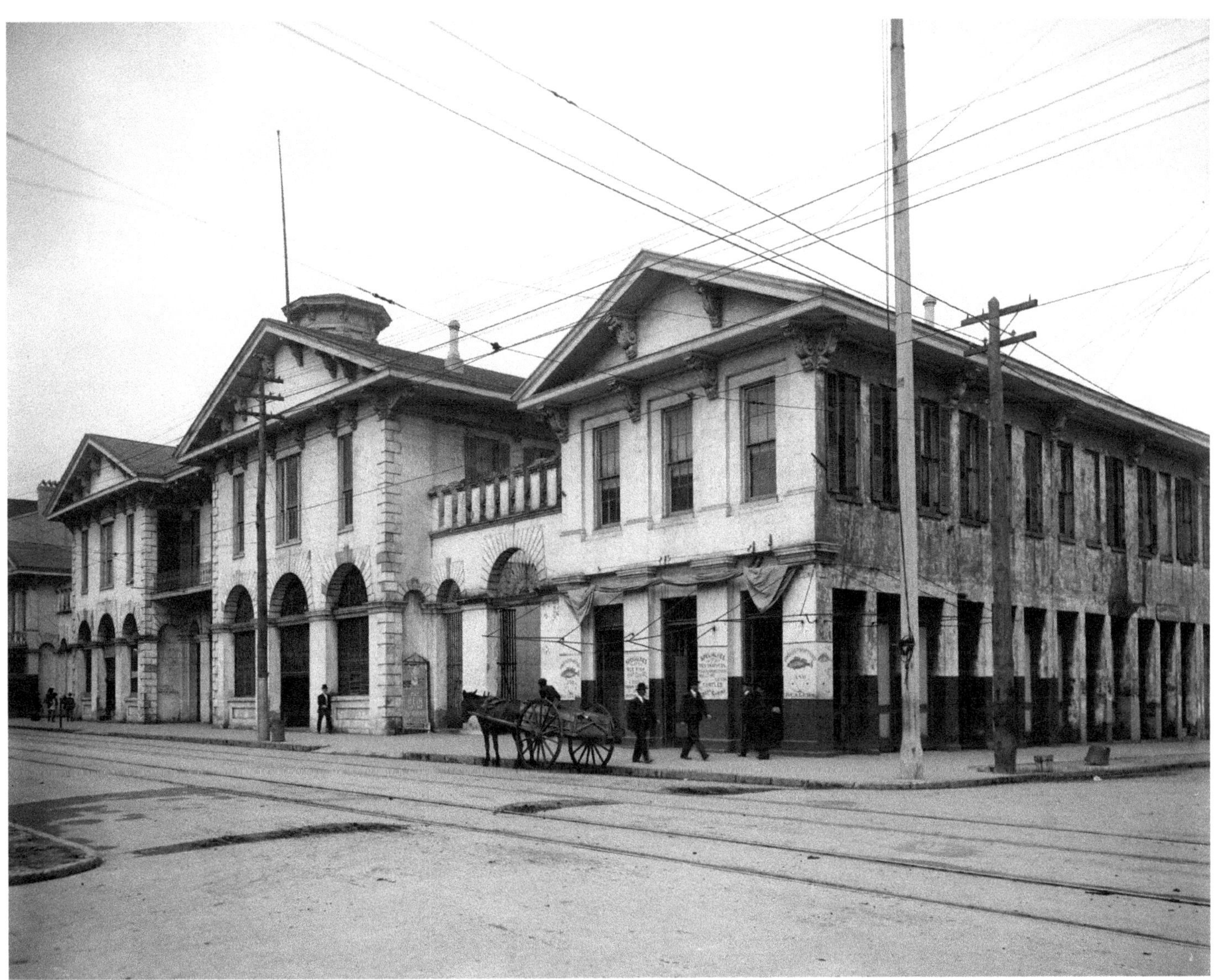

Built during the height of antebellum prosperity, the Mobile City Hall and Southern Market was a natural meeting place. City offices were on the top floor, and the bottom floor had large entryways with open rooms where vendors sold fresh fish, meats, produce, and a variety of other goods. Signs listed such specialties as red snapper, turtle, and catfish. The Museum of Mobile now occupies the building.

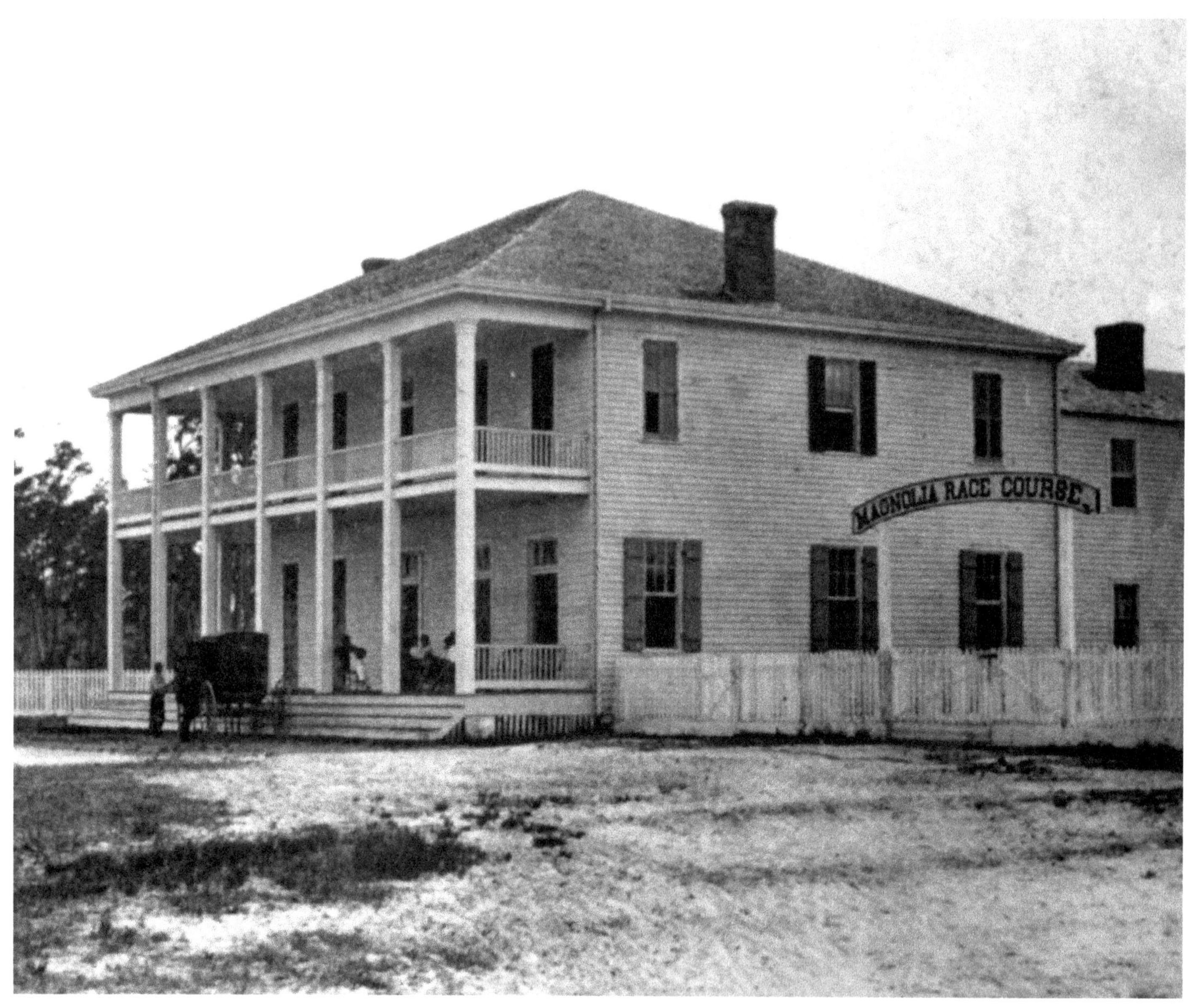

The Magnolia House at Arlington Fairgrounds, about 1900. Located just south of the city, the fairgrounds was the site for an annual agricultural show, held since 1873, that grew to include horse races, automobile displays, and art exhibits. The fair is still held today, but now it is known as the Greater Gulf States Fair, and the venue has moved to West Mobile.

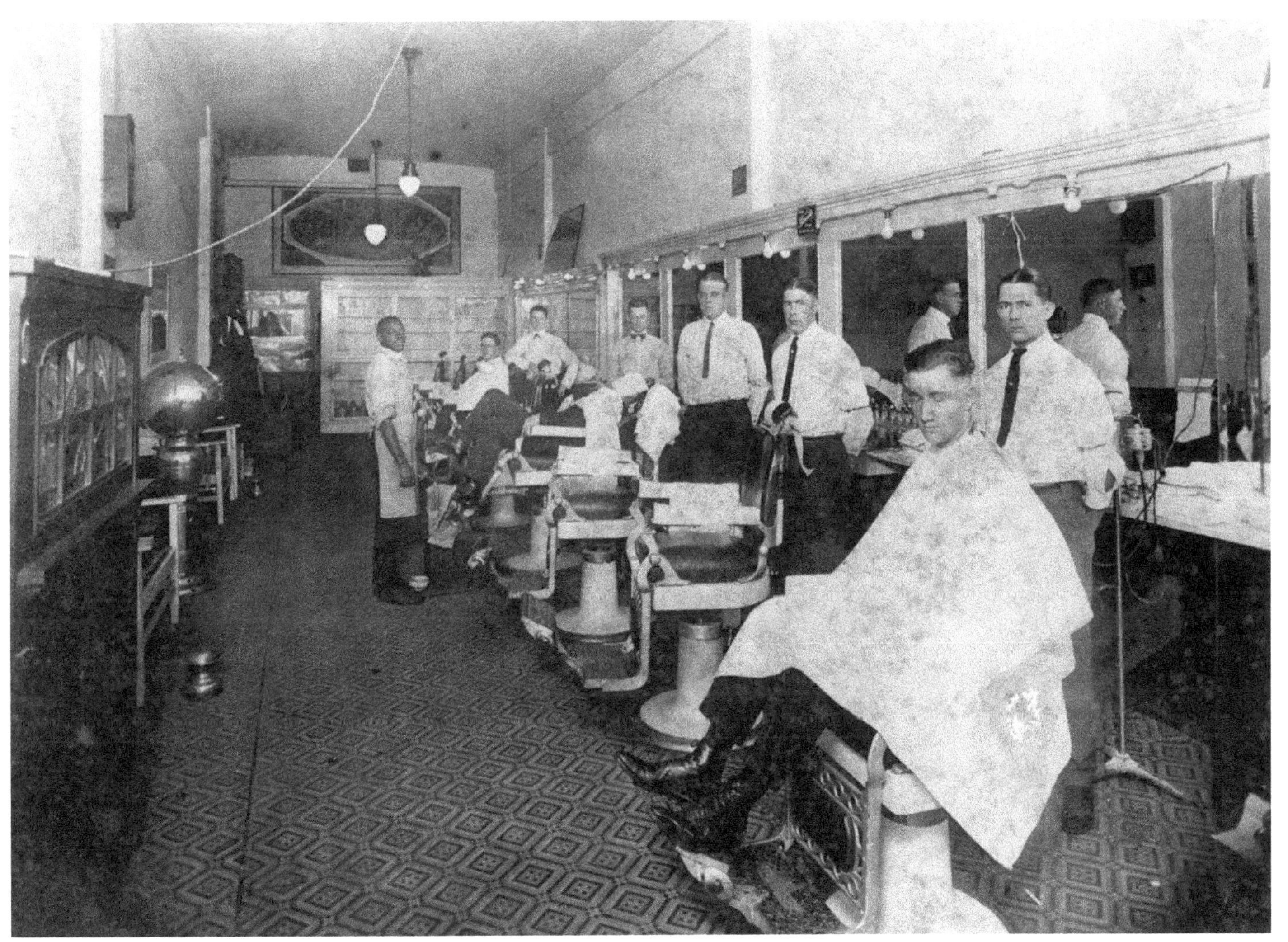

Foster's Barbershop on Royal Street. The barber on the far right is John Stacey Vereen.

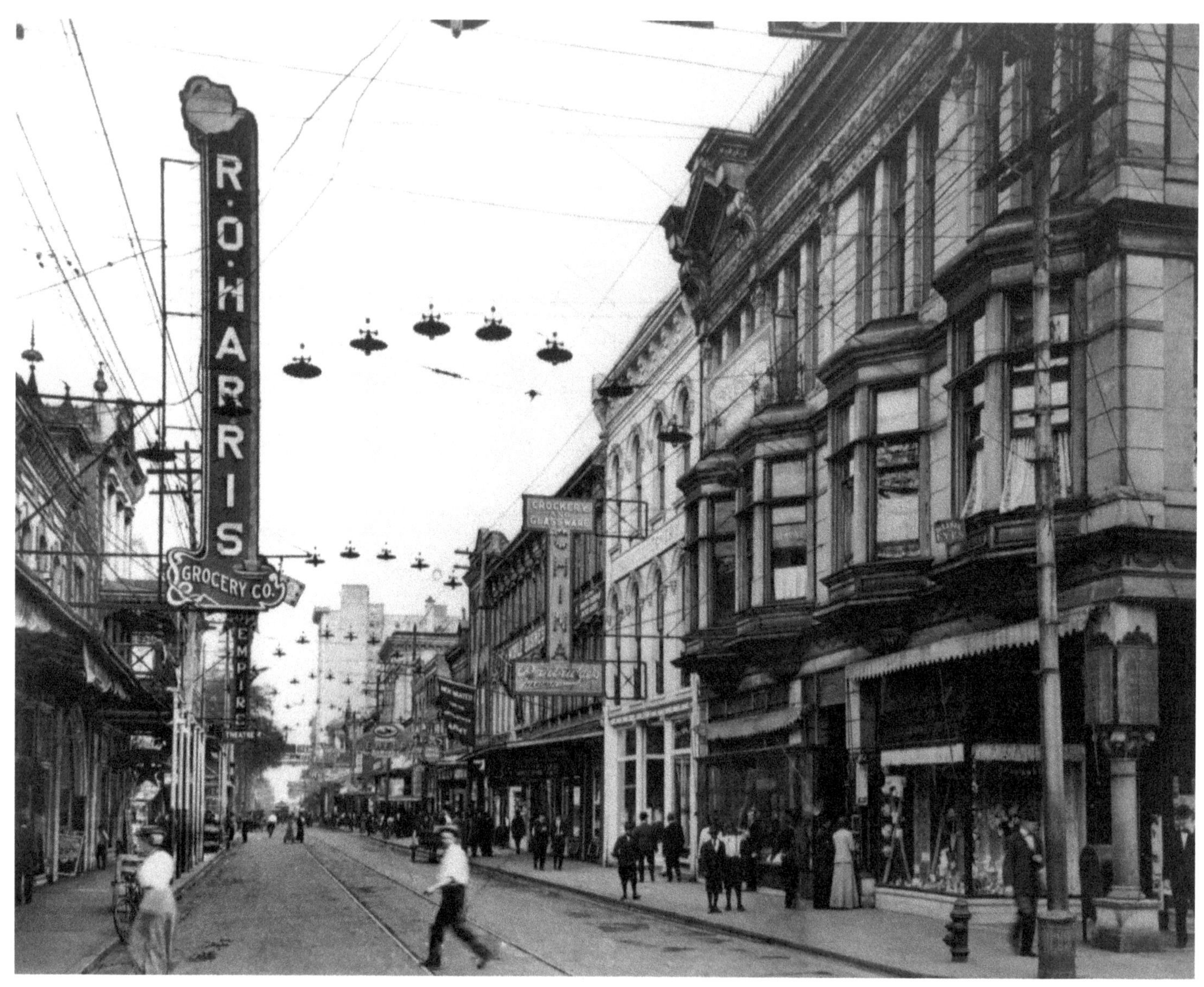

Dauphin Street, looking east from Joachim Street (ca. 1900). To the left are Harris Grocery and the Empire Theatre. A sign in the background reads, "Men Wanted for the United States Army."

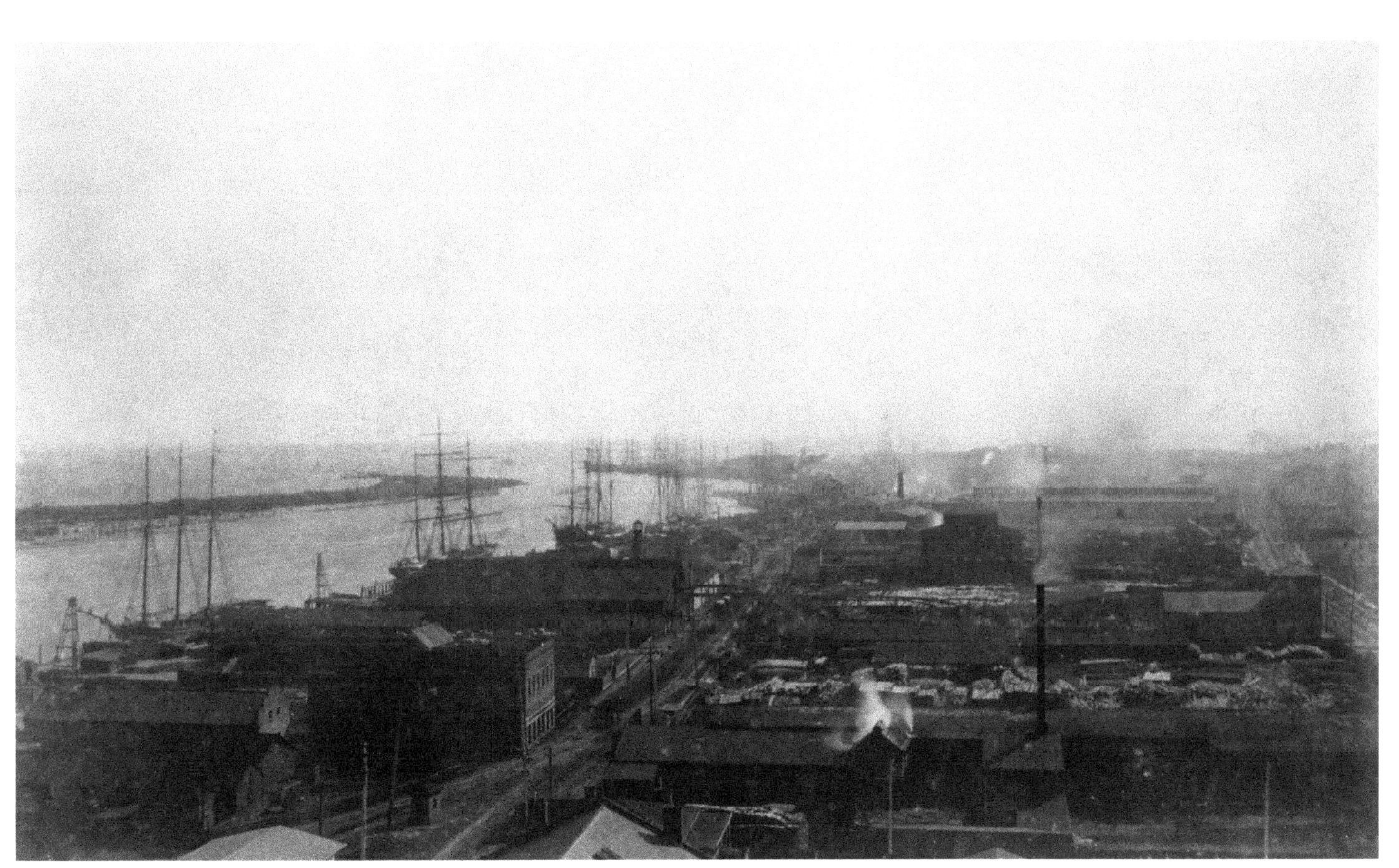

Large cargo ships carrying timber, cotton, and other commercial goods line the docks of Mobile in the early twentieth century.

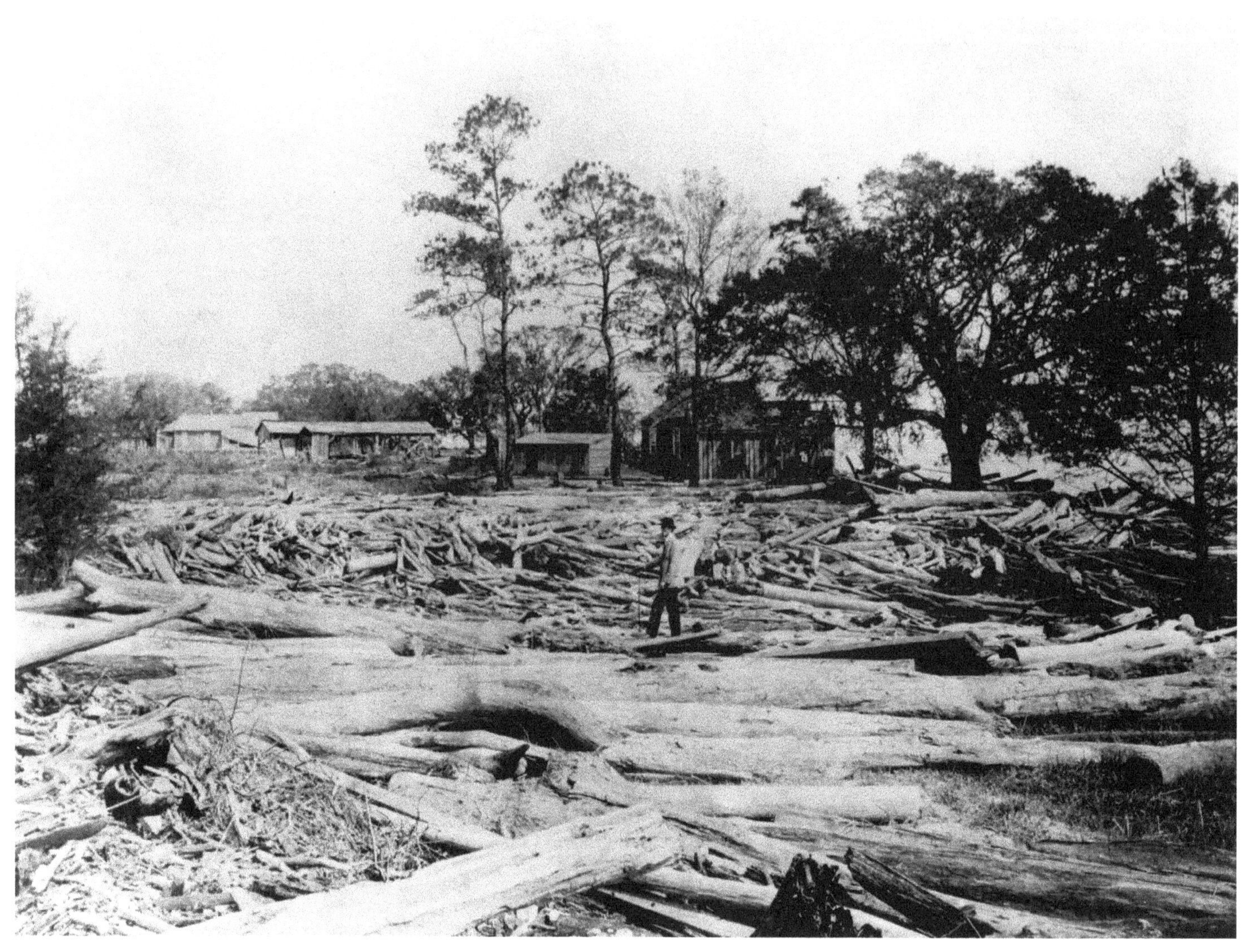

Damage from the hurricane of 1906. This structure used to sit on Bay Shell Road, along the waterfront just outside Mobile's city limits. The occupants had to flee for their lives in the midst of the storm.

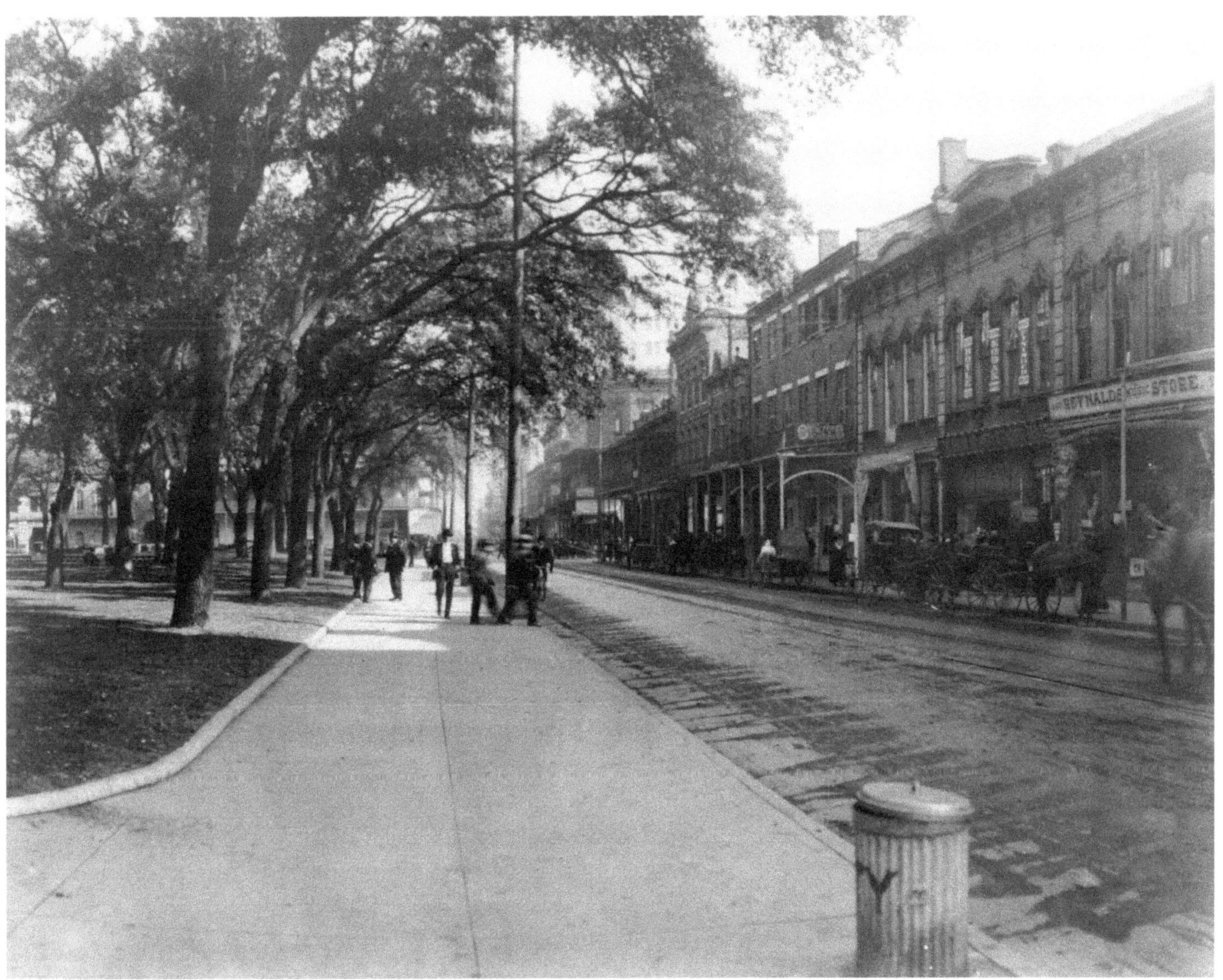

Bienville Square provided a venue for businessmen to gather and discuss the events of the day, as in this image from 1909.

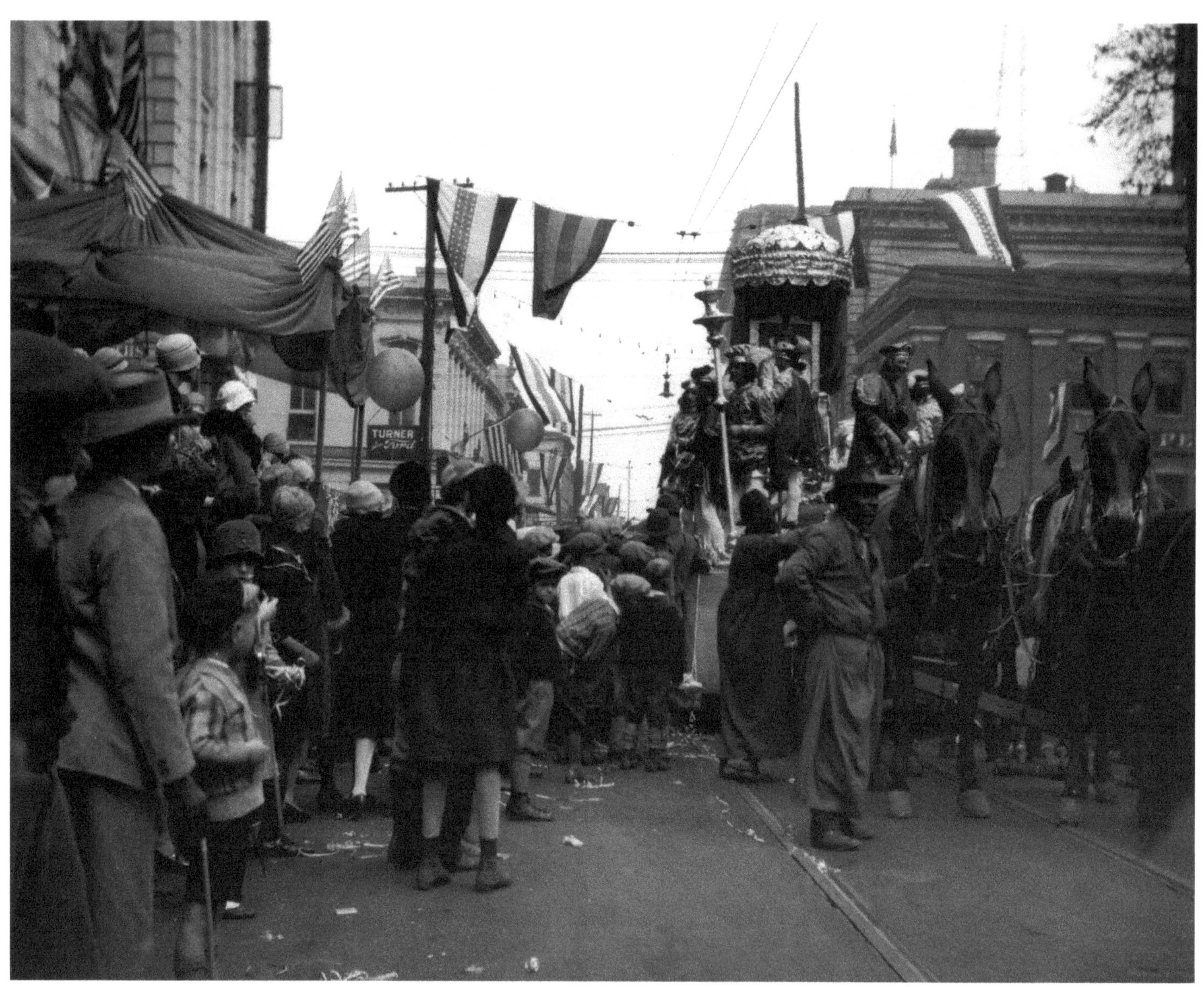

Riding on the King's float, members of one of Mobile's mystic societies throw candy and serpentine to eager children during this Mardi Gras parade on St. Louis Street.

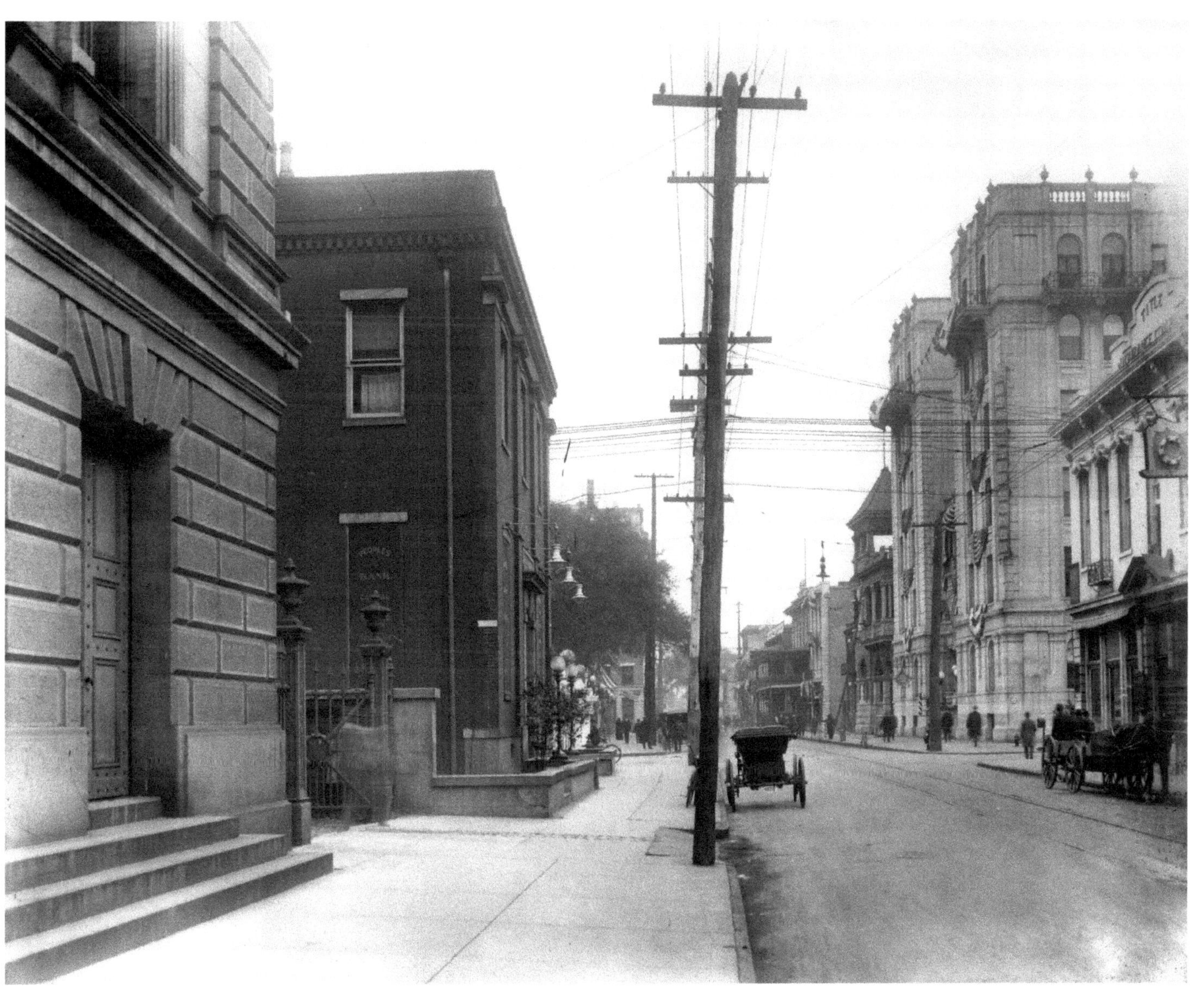

Saint Francis Street, looking west near St. Joseph. On the left is People's Bank. Beyond the intersection Bienville Square is on the left and the Bienville Hotel is on the right.

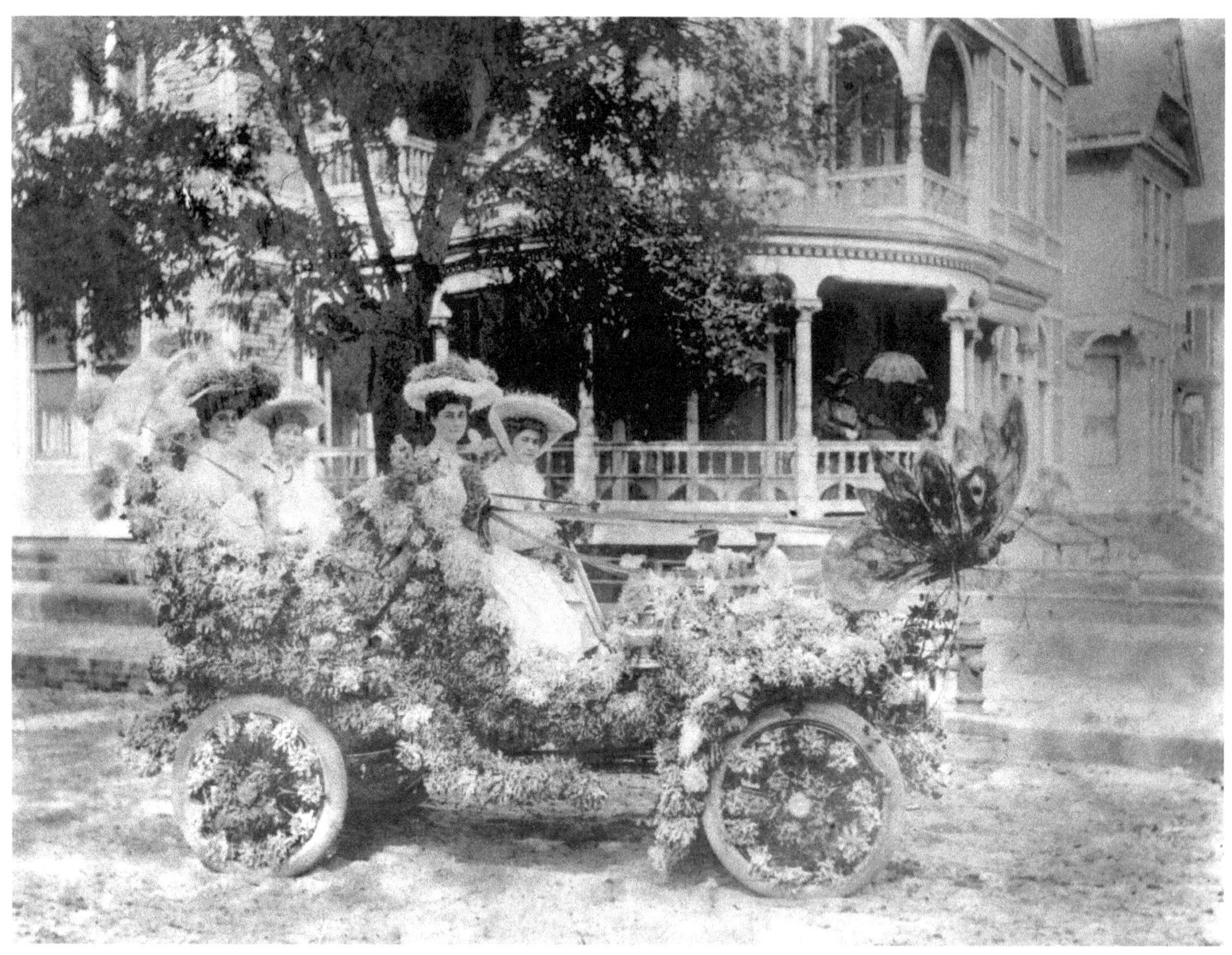

The Floral Parade became a regular part of the Mardi Gras celebration in 1929. Before that time, decorating a car with flowers was a popular way for Mobilians to take part in the festivities. This image was taken around 1910.

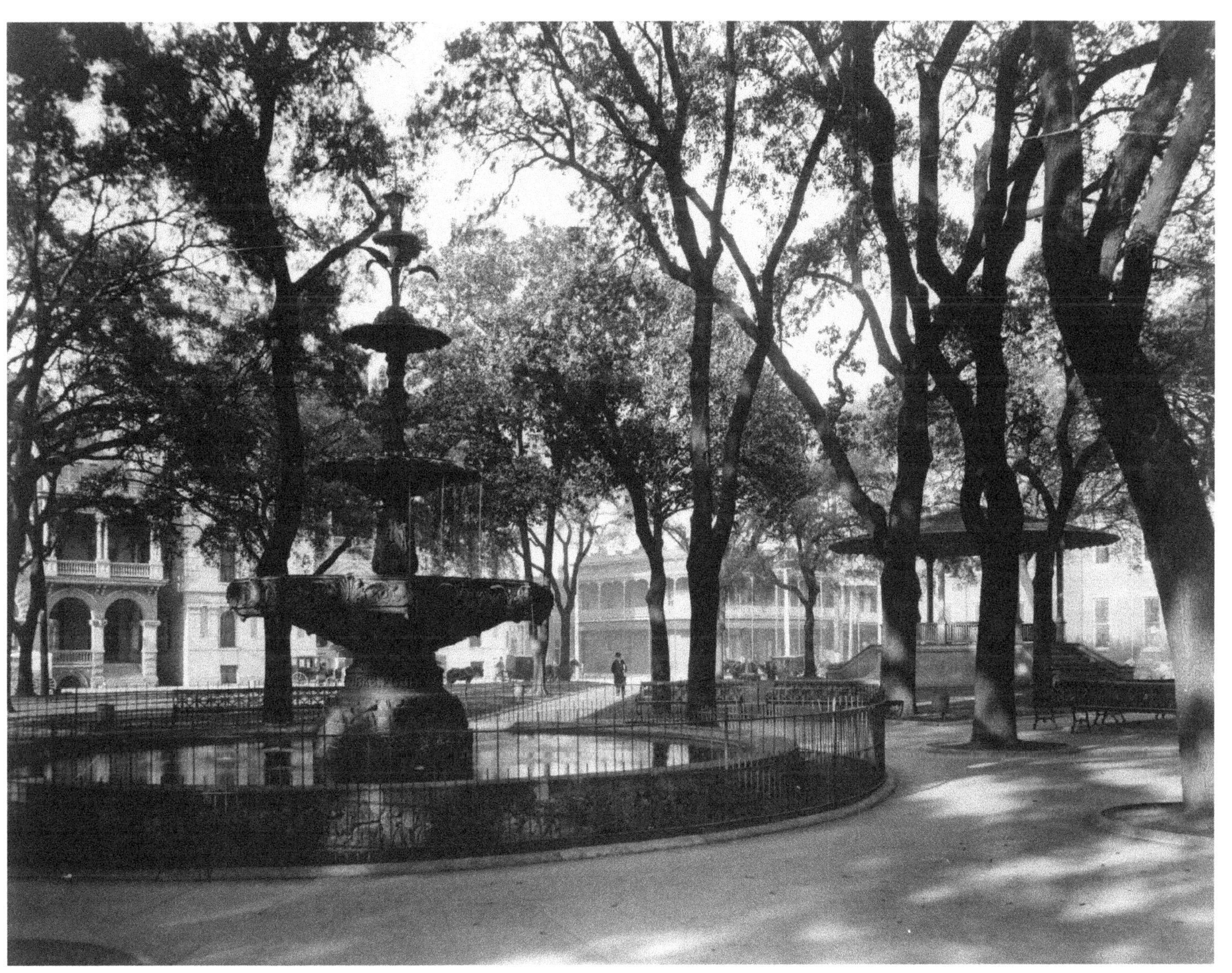

The fountain in Bienville Square shown in this 1906 photograph was installed in 1890 in honor of Bienville Water Works president Dr. George. A. Ketchum.

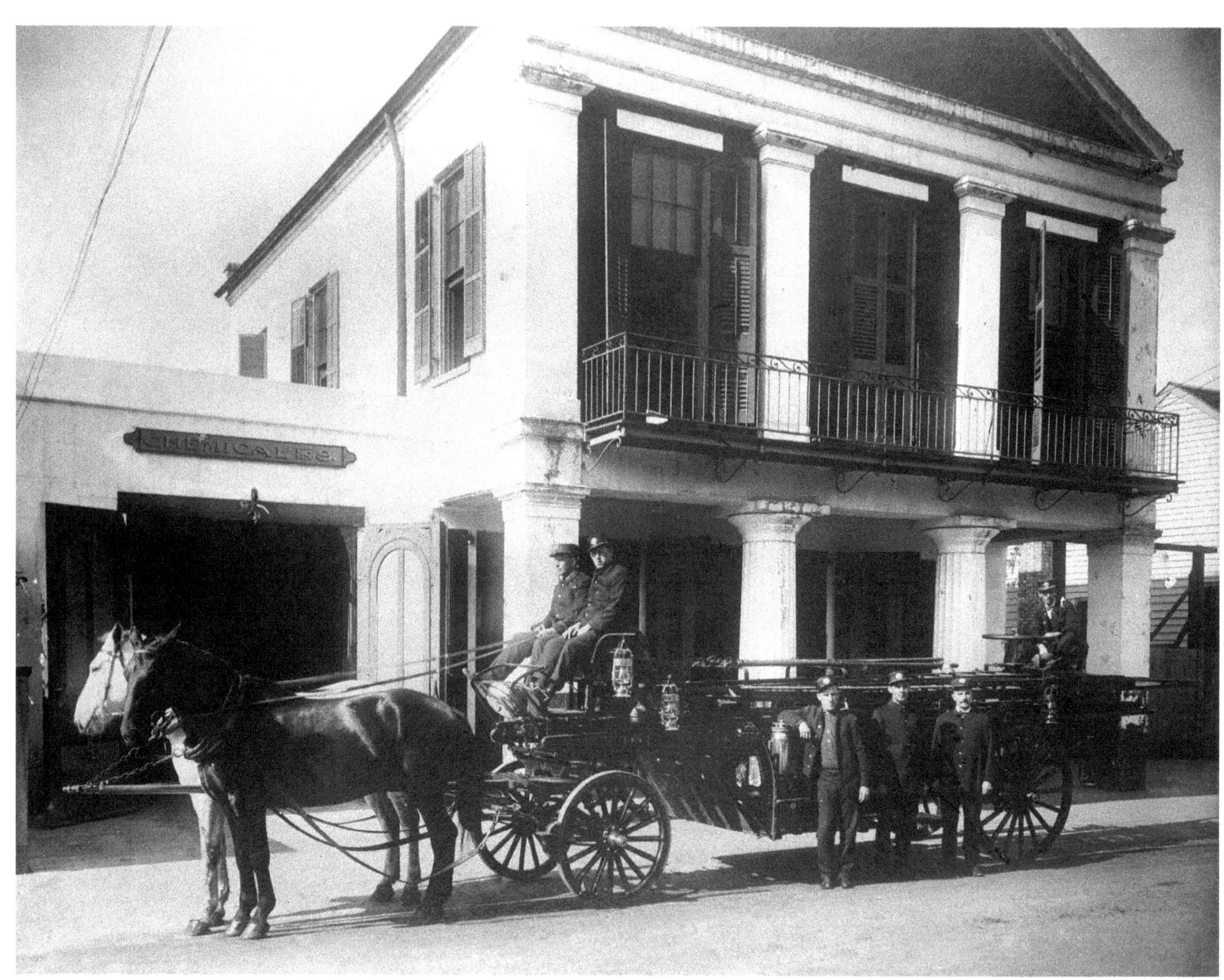

In response to criticism about the effectiveness of the all-volunteer fire companies that had spontaneously developed over Mobile's history, the city established a municipal fire department in September 1888. Here is the Washington Fire Engine Company, which was originally started in 1843. Their headquarters on North Lawrence Street was built in 1851.

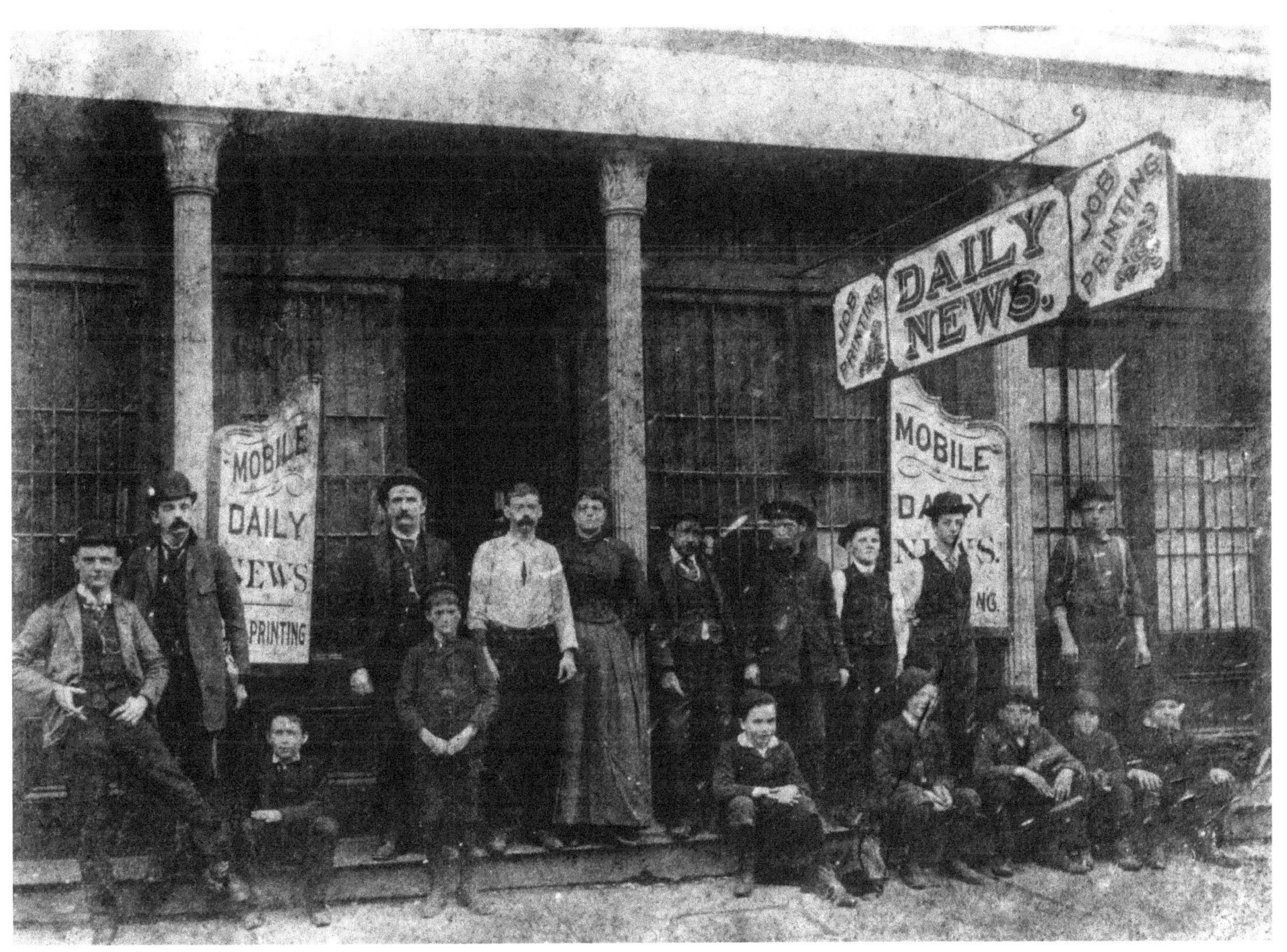

A group of *Mobile Daily News* employees gather outside their offices at 59 St. Michael Street about 1900. Unlike today, when Mobile has only one daily newspaper, in the early twentieth century, there were three dailies, two weeklies, a monthly, and several branch offices for other cities' newspapers.

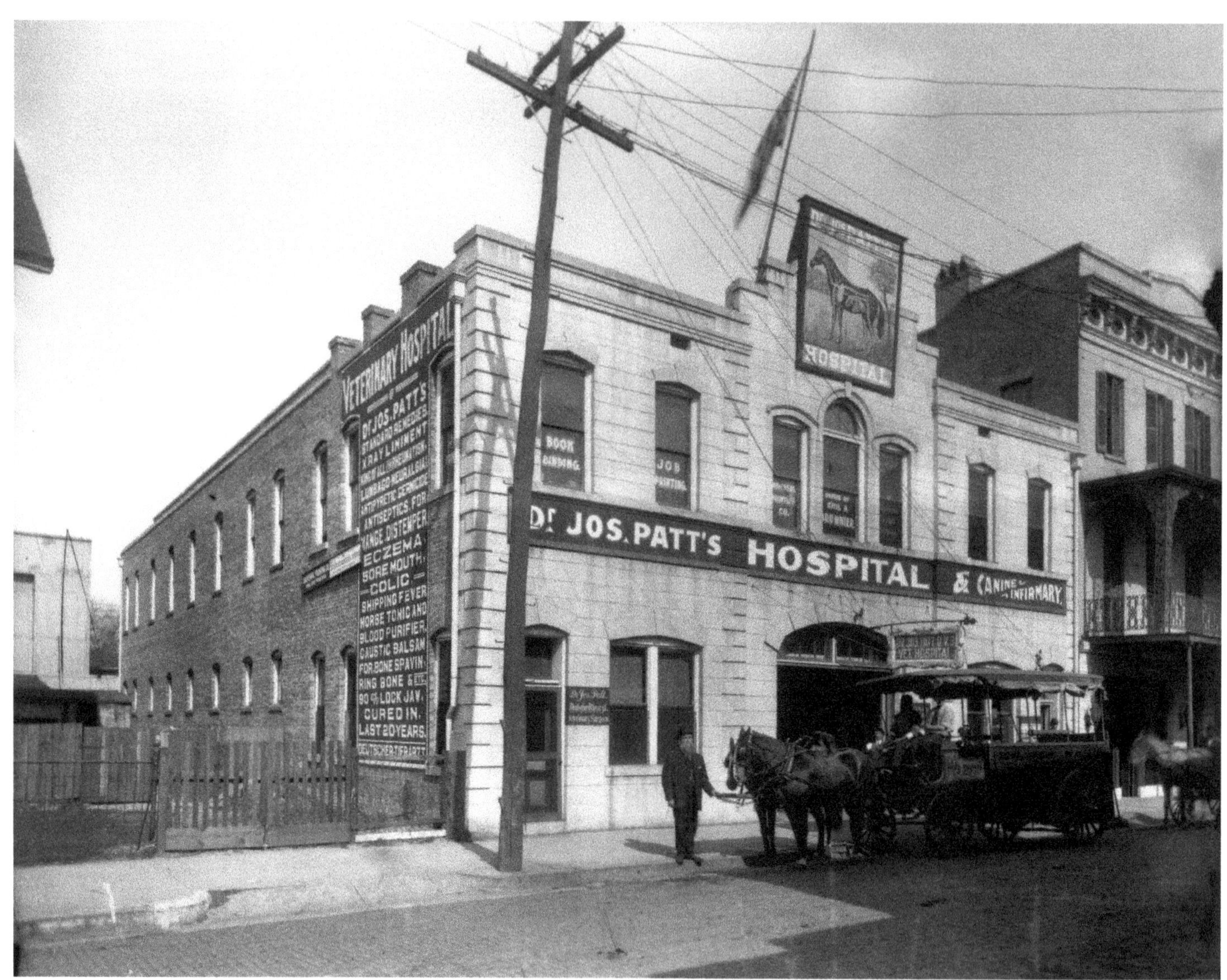

Doctor Joseph Patt's Veterinary Hospital, after relocating to the corner of St. Michael and Joachim streets. Doctor Patt's horse-drawn ambulance waits outside in case of an emergency. He claimed to be able to cure "rheumatism, lumbago, neuralgia . . . distemper, eczema . . . colic," and fevers of all sorts. E. A. Brunnier, a publisher, rented the second floor. By 1920, Patt's business succumbed to the advances of technology, and he went from treating horses to repairing automobiles. Ten years later, McKeen Motor Company purchased the building and undoubtedly removed the portrait of the horse.

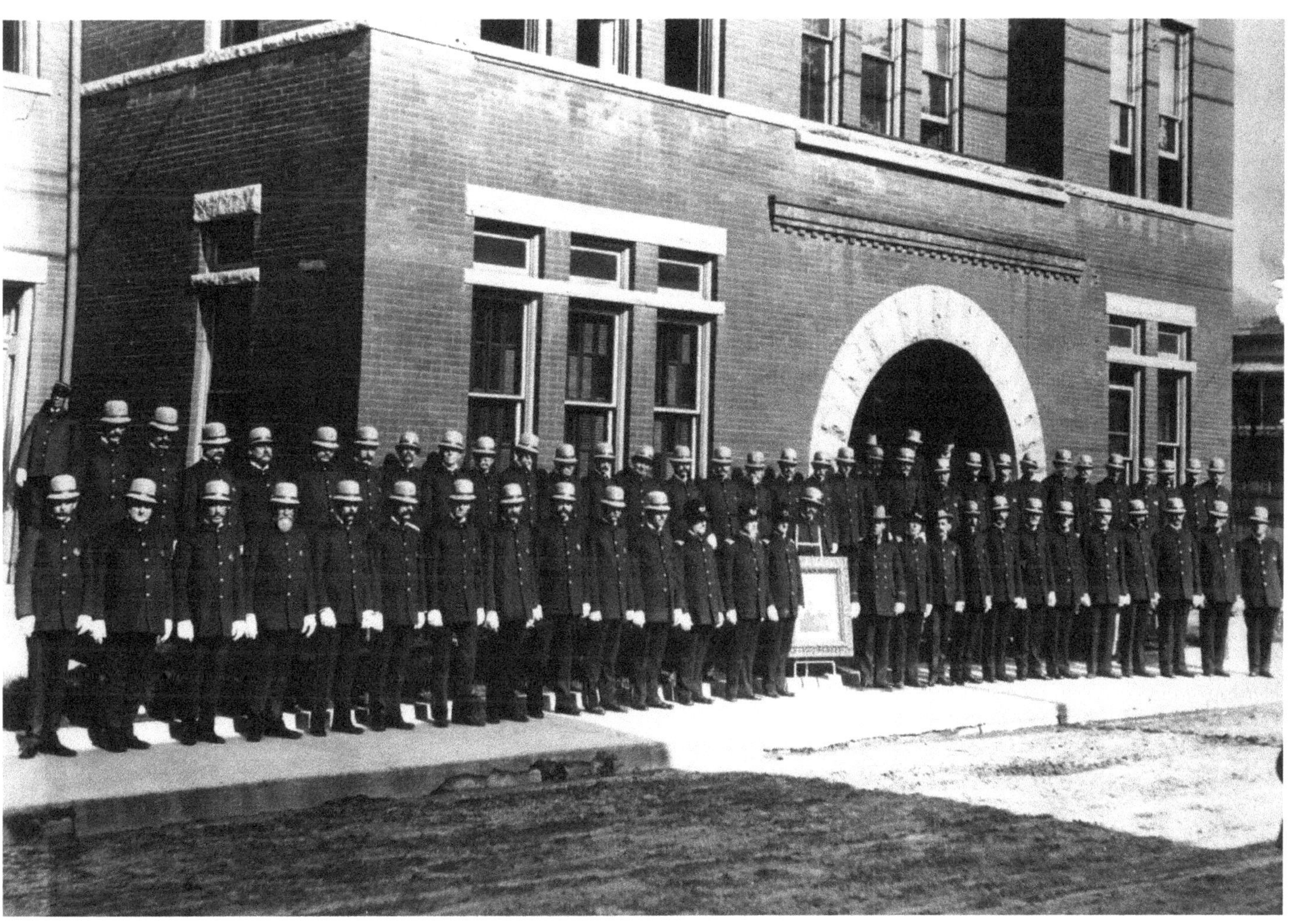

This photograph from 1901 shows Mobile police officers lined up in front of the police building on St. Emmanuel to honor Officer Edward McGrath Morris, pictured in the center. The 25-year veteran was mortally wounded March 31 while attempting to arrest two escaped convicts in a rail yard. He died the next day.

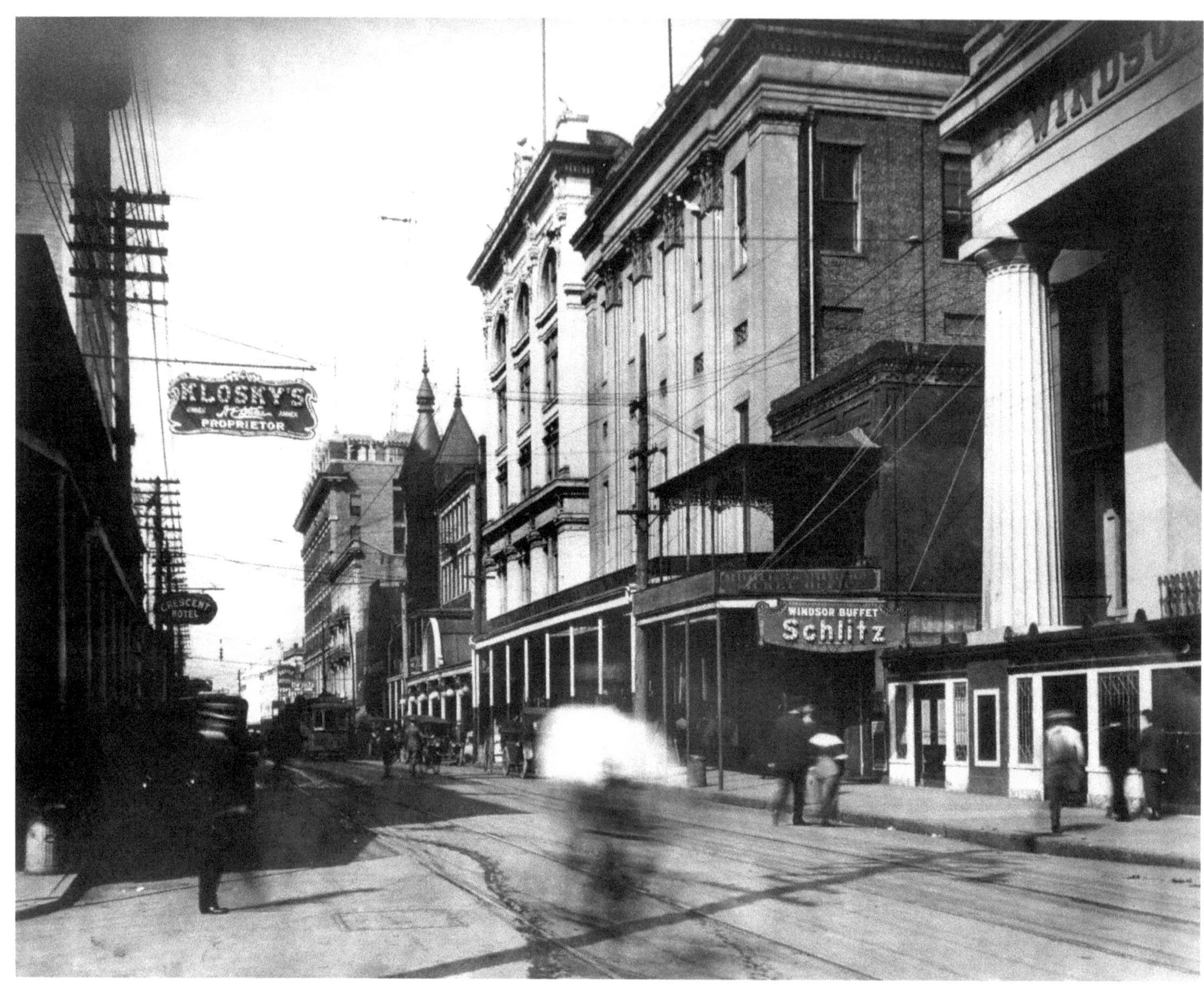

A view of North Royal Street, taken from Conti, 1912. In the background is a streetcar in front of the Crescent Hotel.

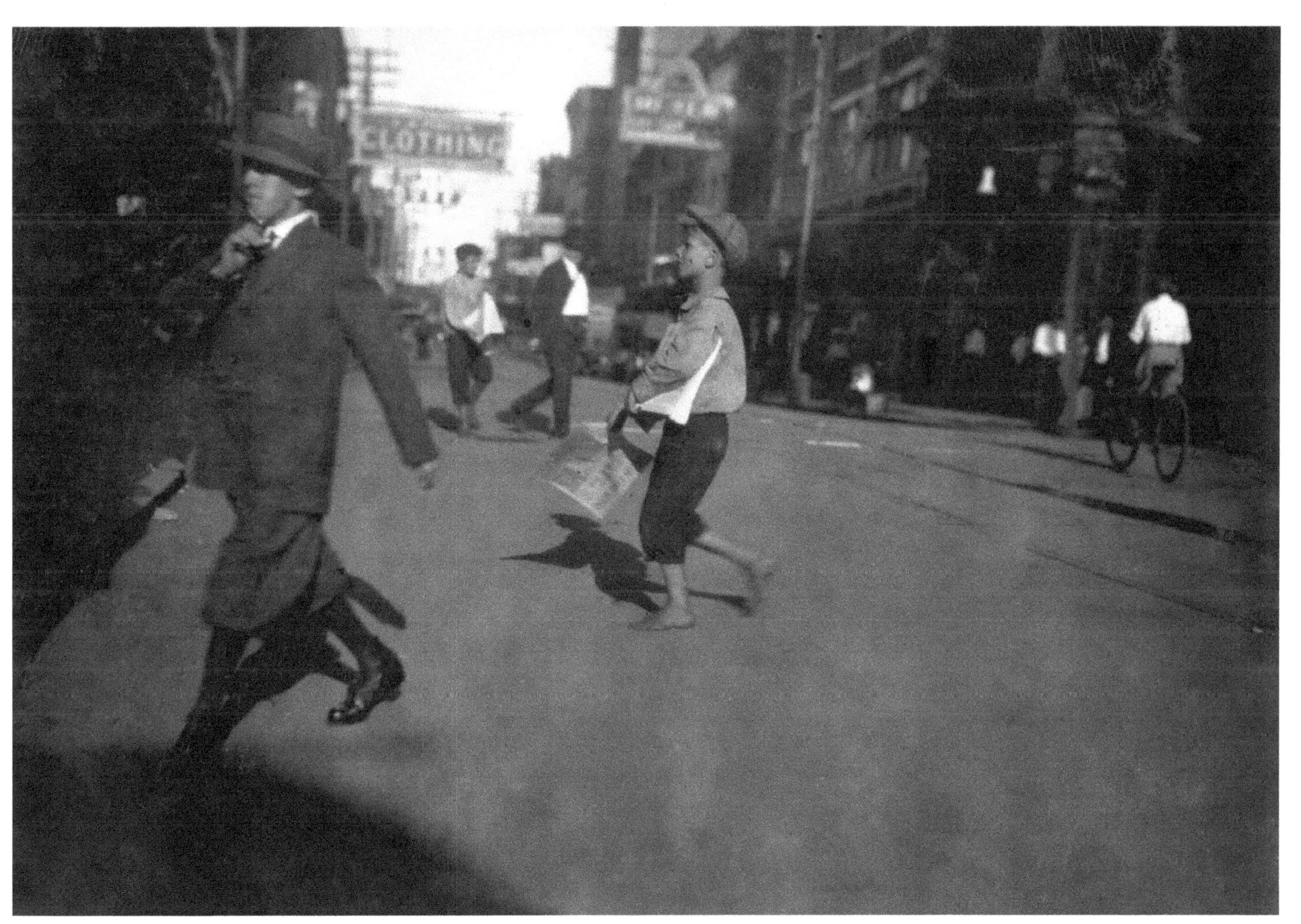

A barefoot newsboy peddles papers on a Mobile street in October 1914.

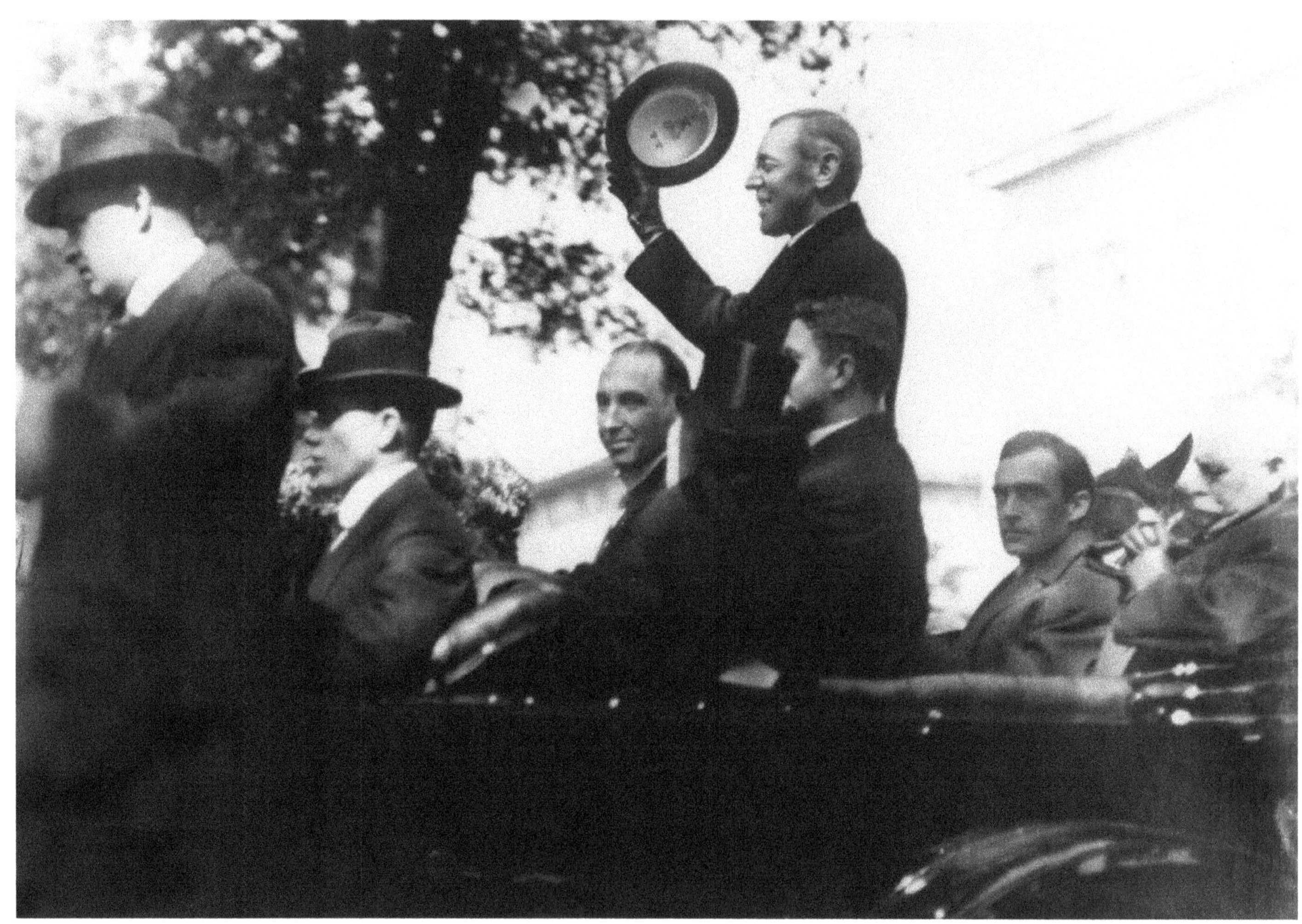

President Woodrow Wilson came to Mobile in October 1913. His visit was the first by a major Democratic politician since William Jennings Bryan in 1898. The president came to Mobile to address the Southern Commercial Congress at the Battle House Hotel. In his remarks, he spoke of good relations with Latin America and chastised European countries for squeezing economic concessions from the region.

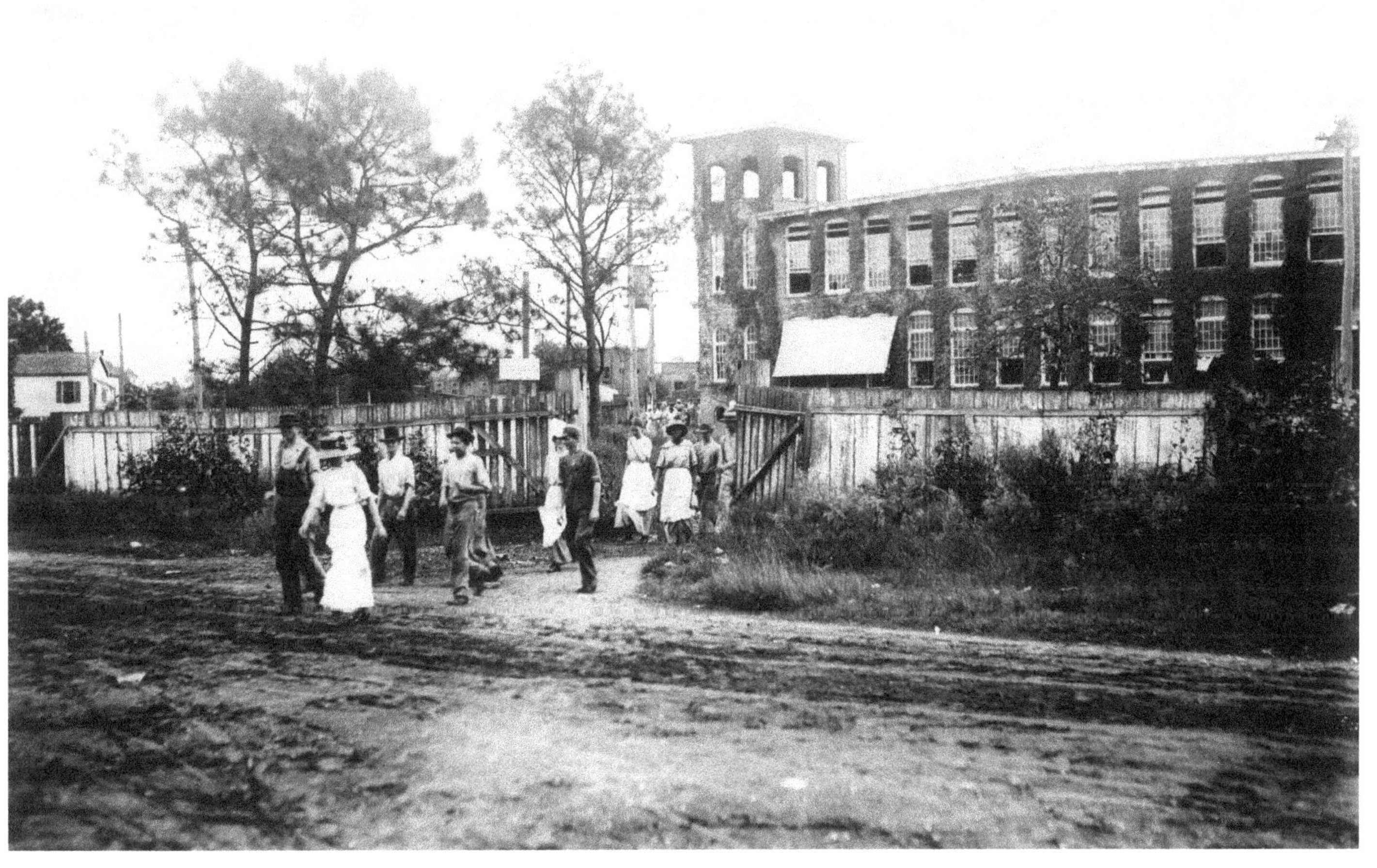

Like other cotton mills throughout the South, the Barker Mill near Mobile relied on women and children for much of its labor force. It was insular, having its own commissary and school. In October 1914, photographer Lewis Hine, a national crusader against child labor, visited the mill and concluded that the workers there were treated better than most in the South.

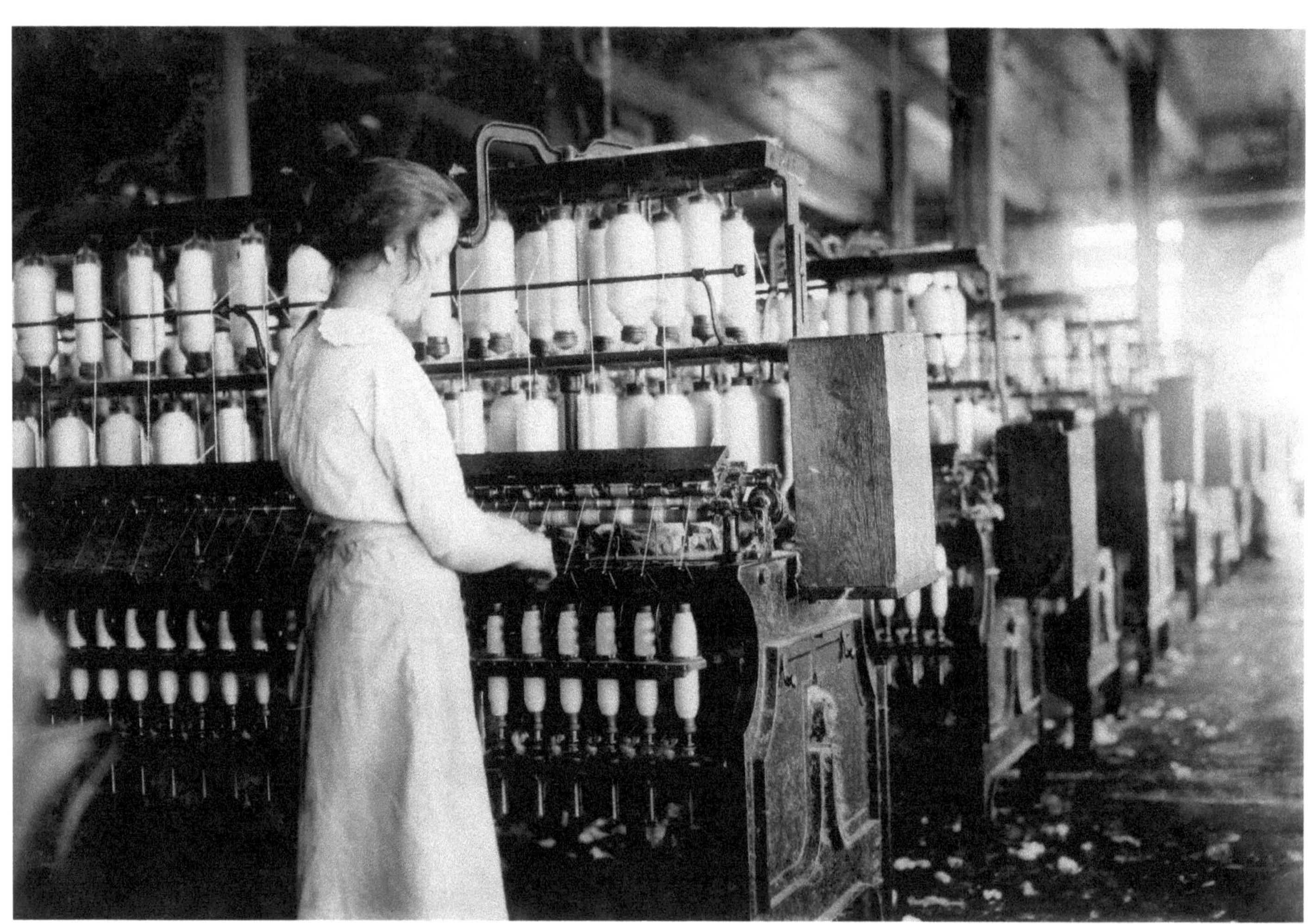

A young woman works the line inside the Barker Cotton Mill. Hine took this photograph to demonstrate working conditions inside the plant.

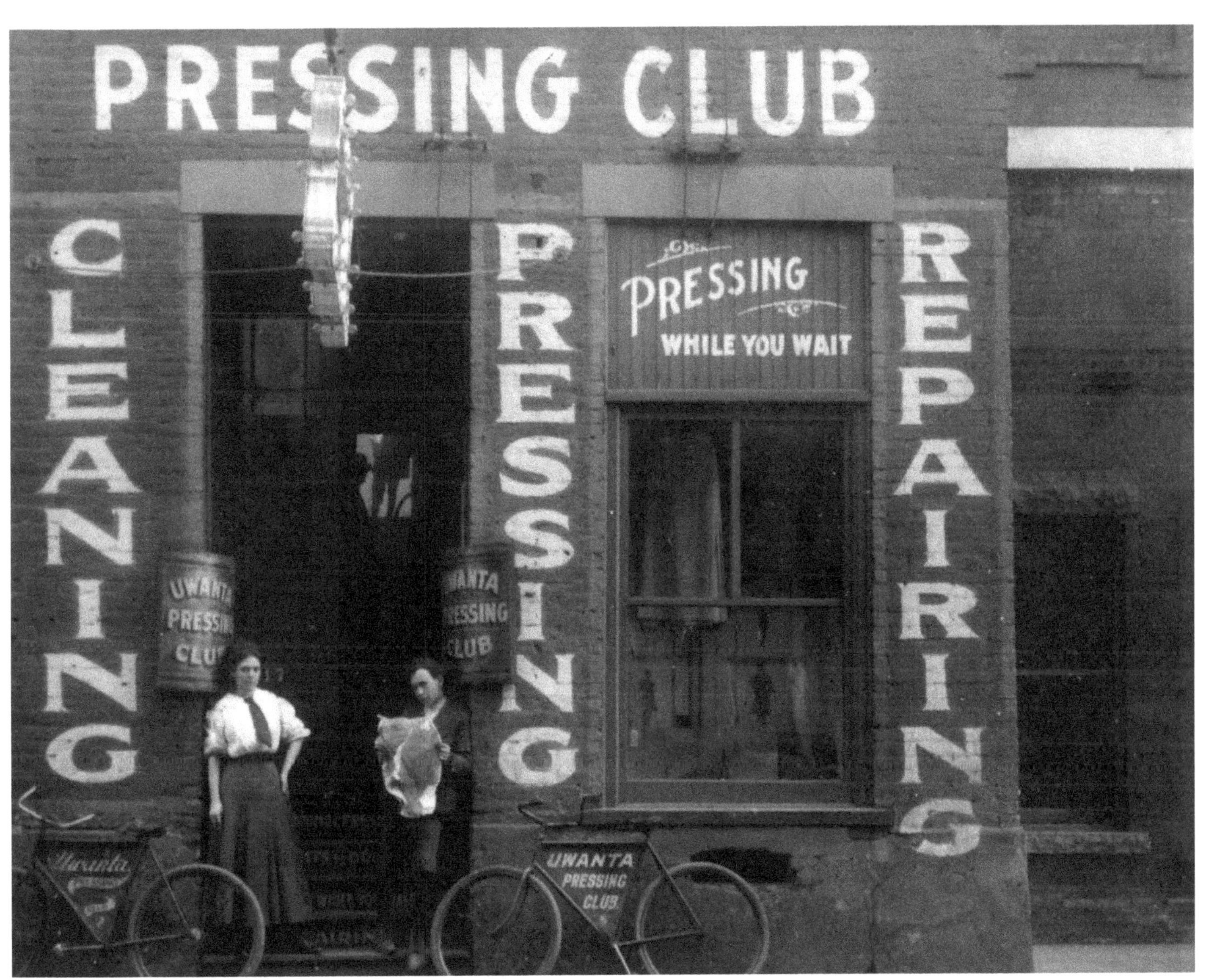

The Uwanta Pressing Club on North Royal Street specialized in cleaning, pressing, dyeing, and repairing clothing.

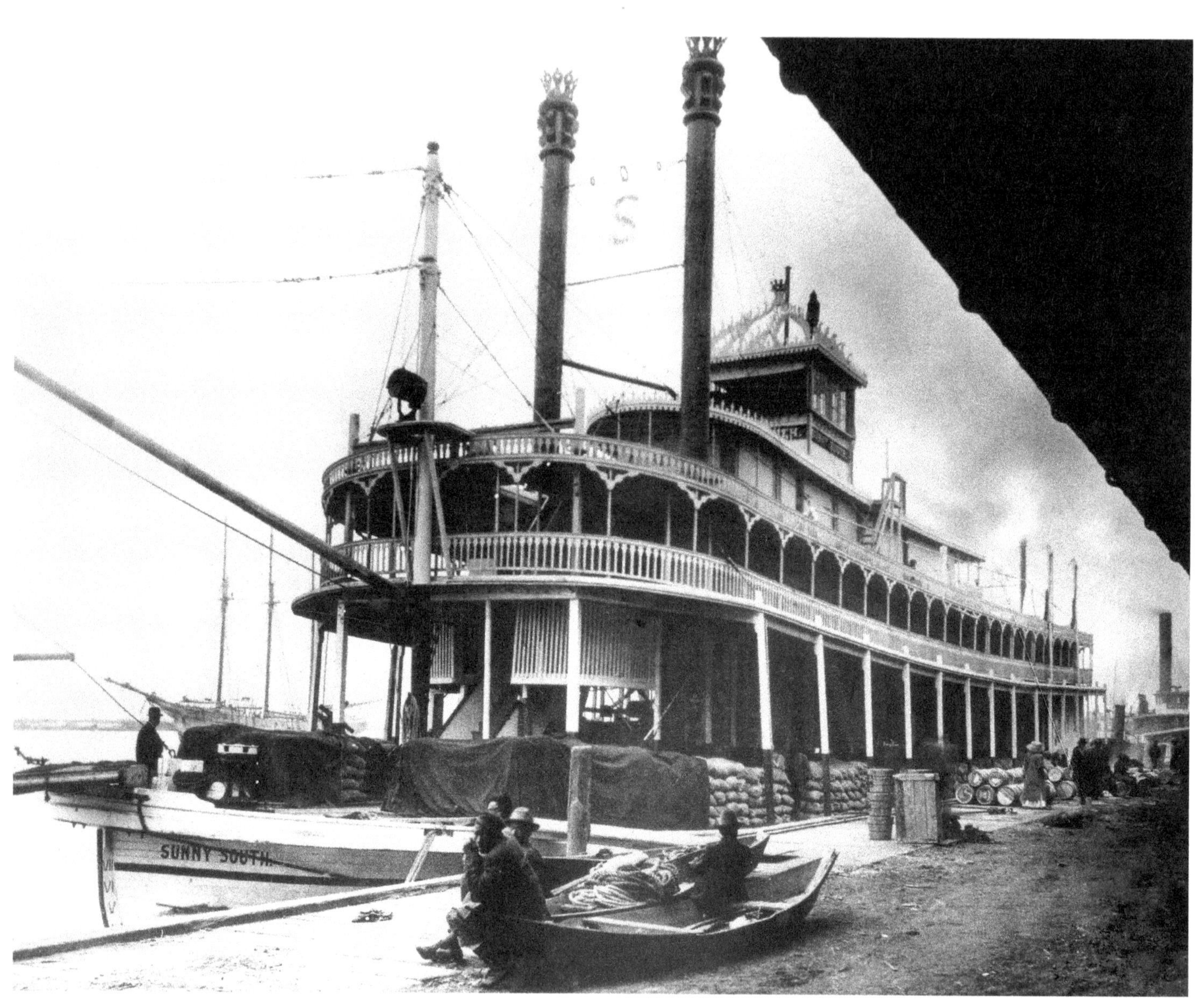

In the early twentieth century, the *Sunny South* riverboat ran from Mobile up the Tombigbee River. Two years after this 1914 photo was taken, she capsized in Mobile Bay.

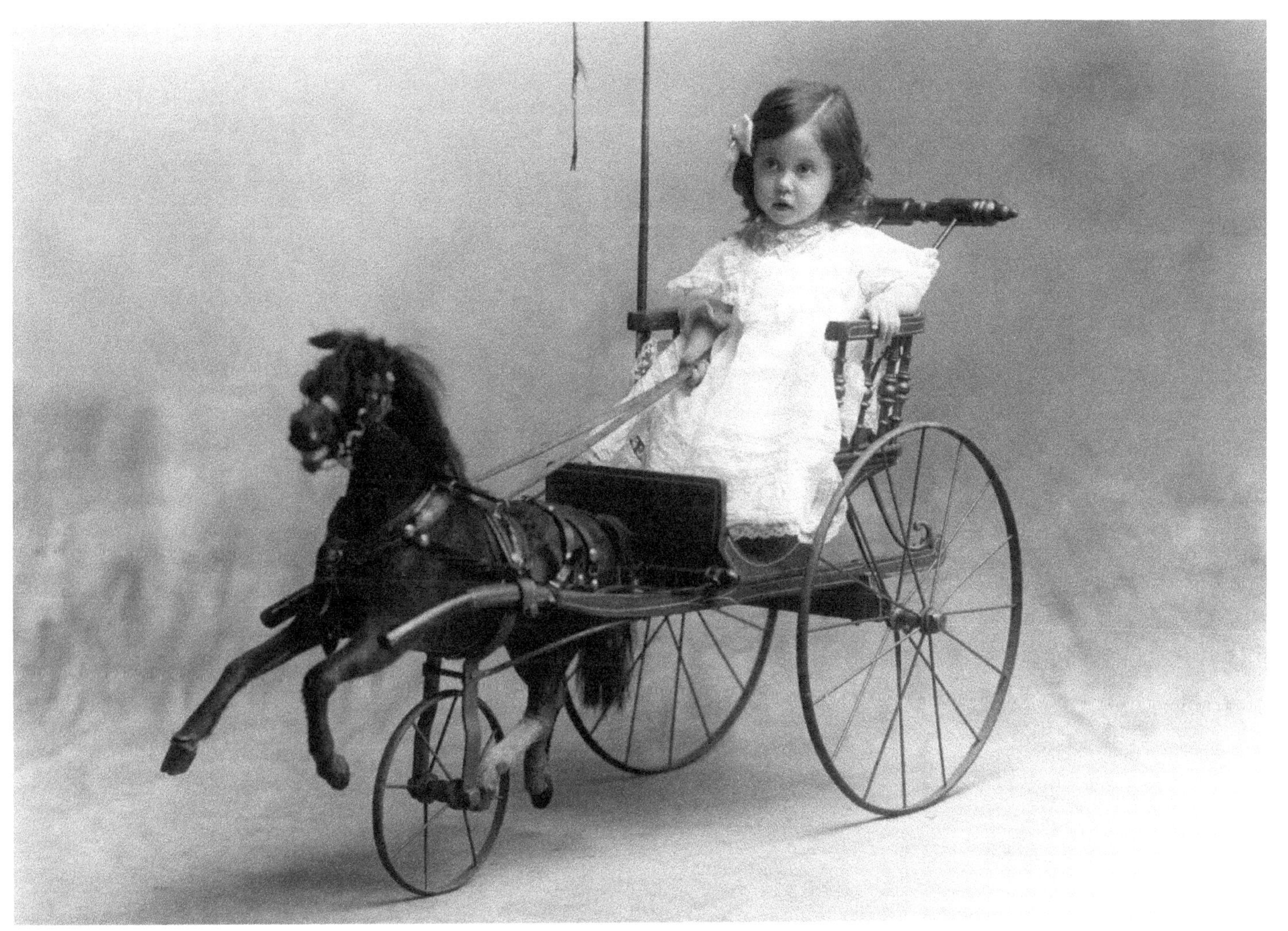

Today, photographers use all sorts of props in their portrait work, especially with children. That was no different in days gone by, as shown by this child sitting atop a toy horse and cart.

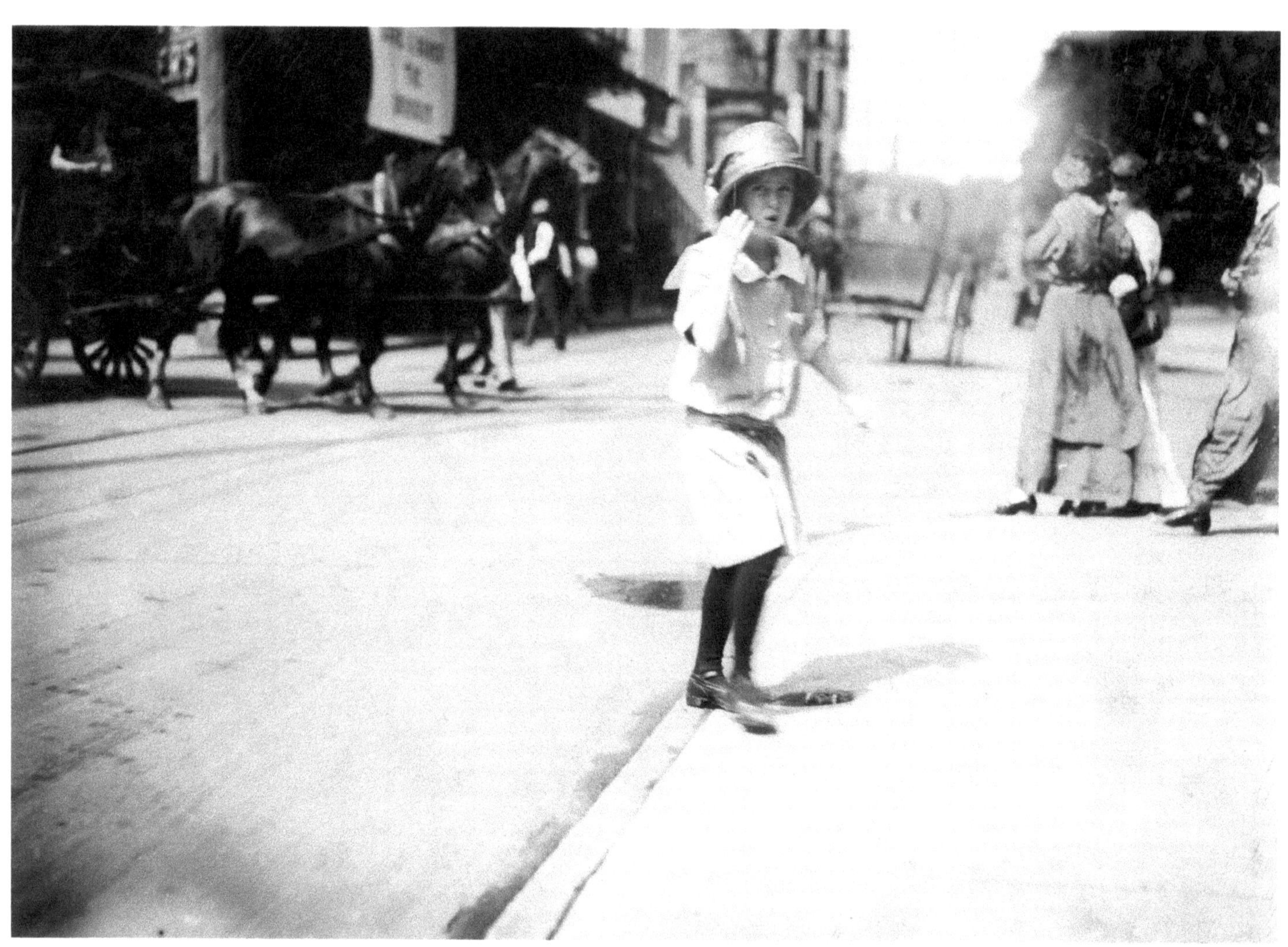

A Gayfer's Department Store "cash girl," October 1914. Lewis Hine reported that she was only nine years old.

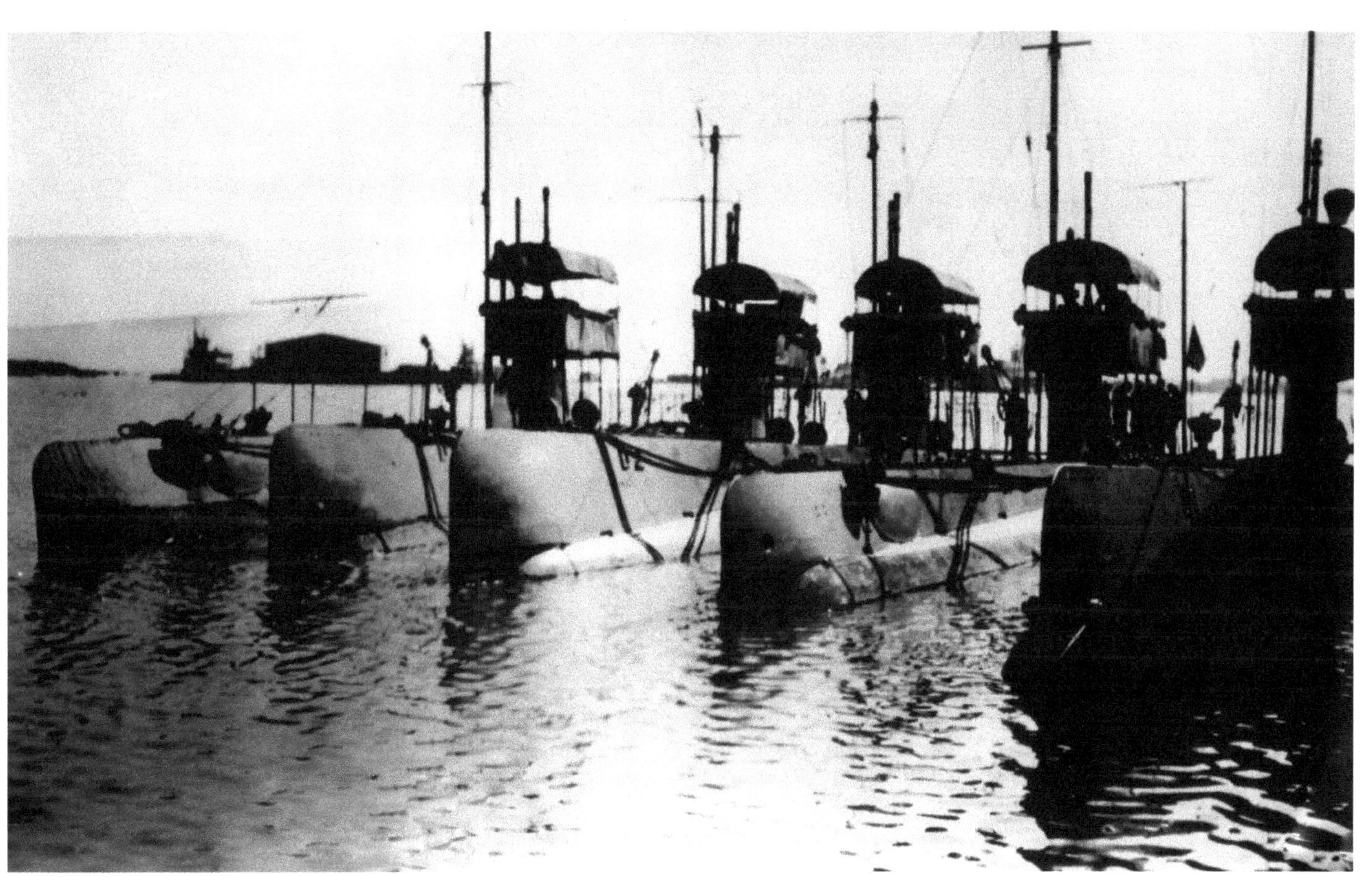

Vessels often make it a point to come to Mobile during the Mardi Gras season. In this image from 1914, five U.S. submarines have docked for just that reason.

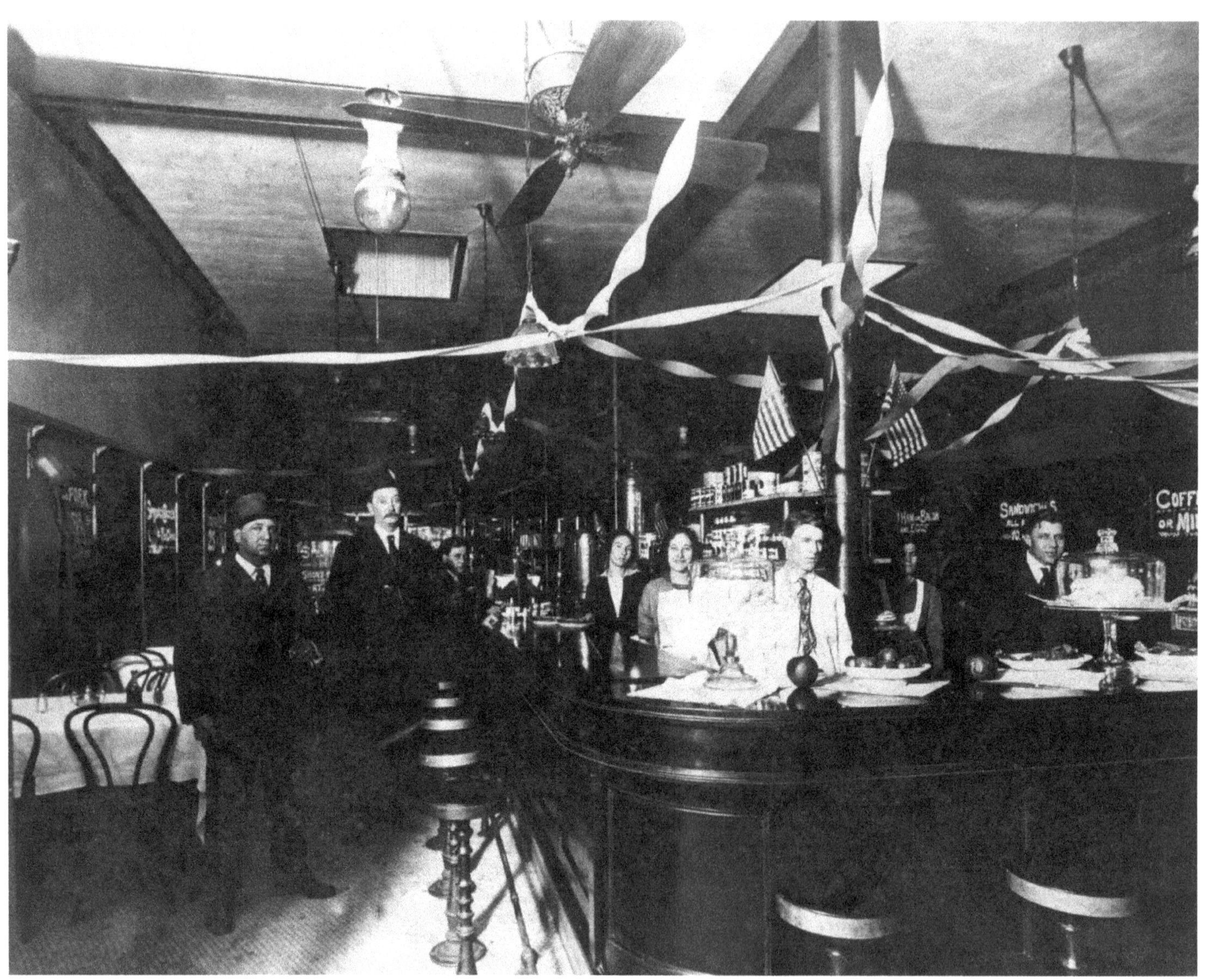

The interior of the Carlisle Café on South Royal Street in 1915.

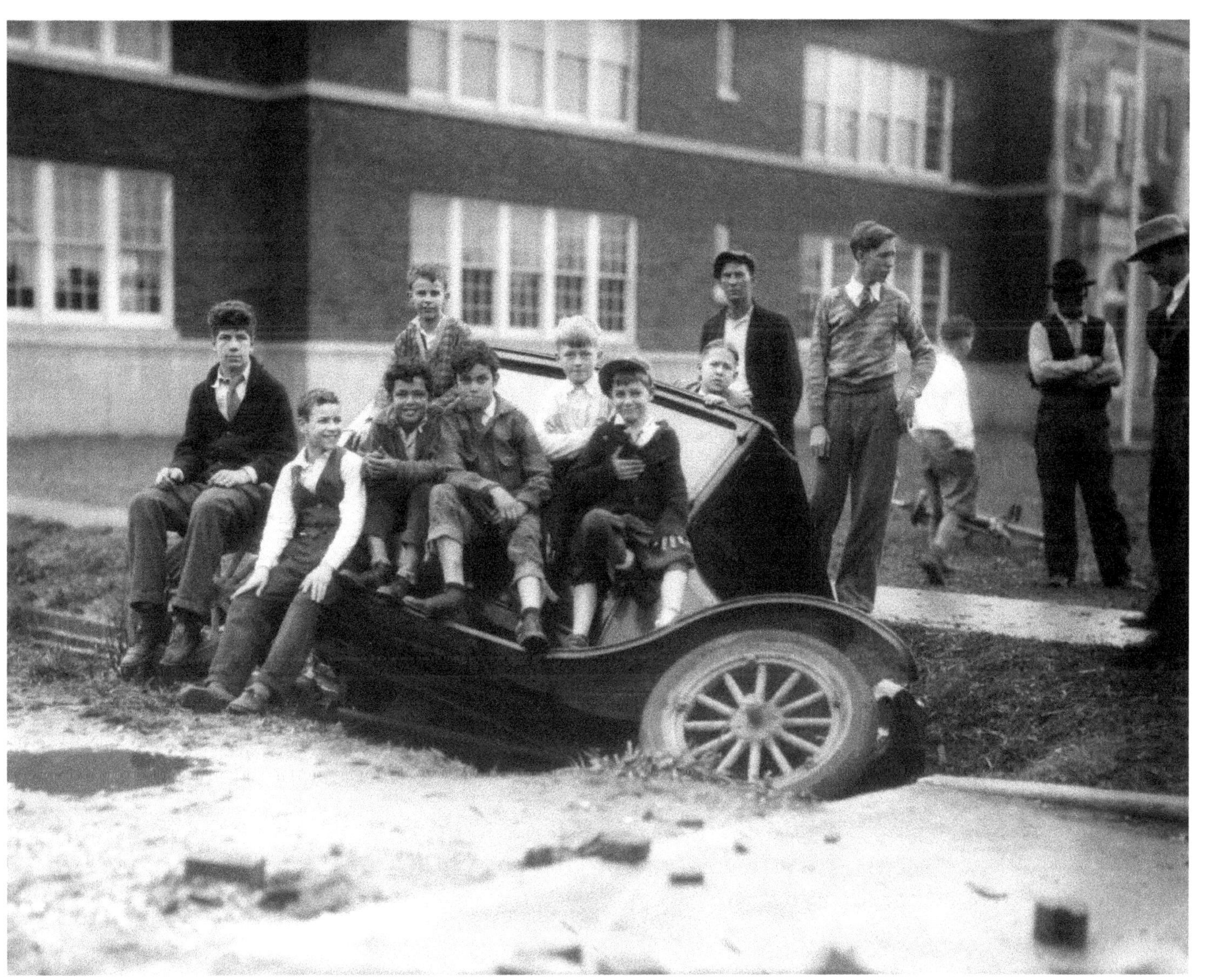

Children sit atop an overturned automobile, something quite novel for its time (ca. 1915).

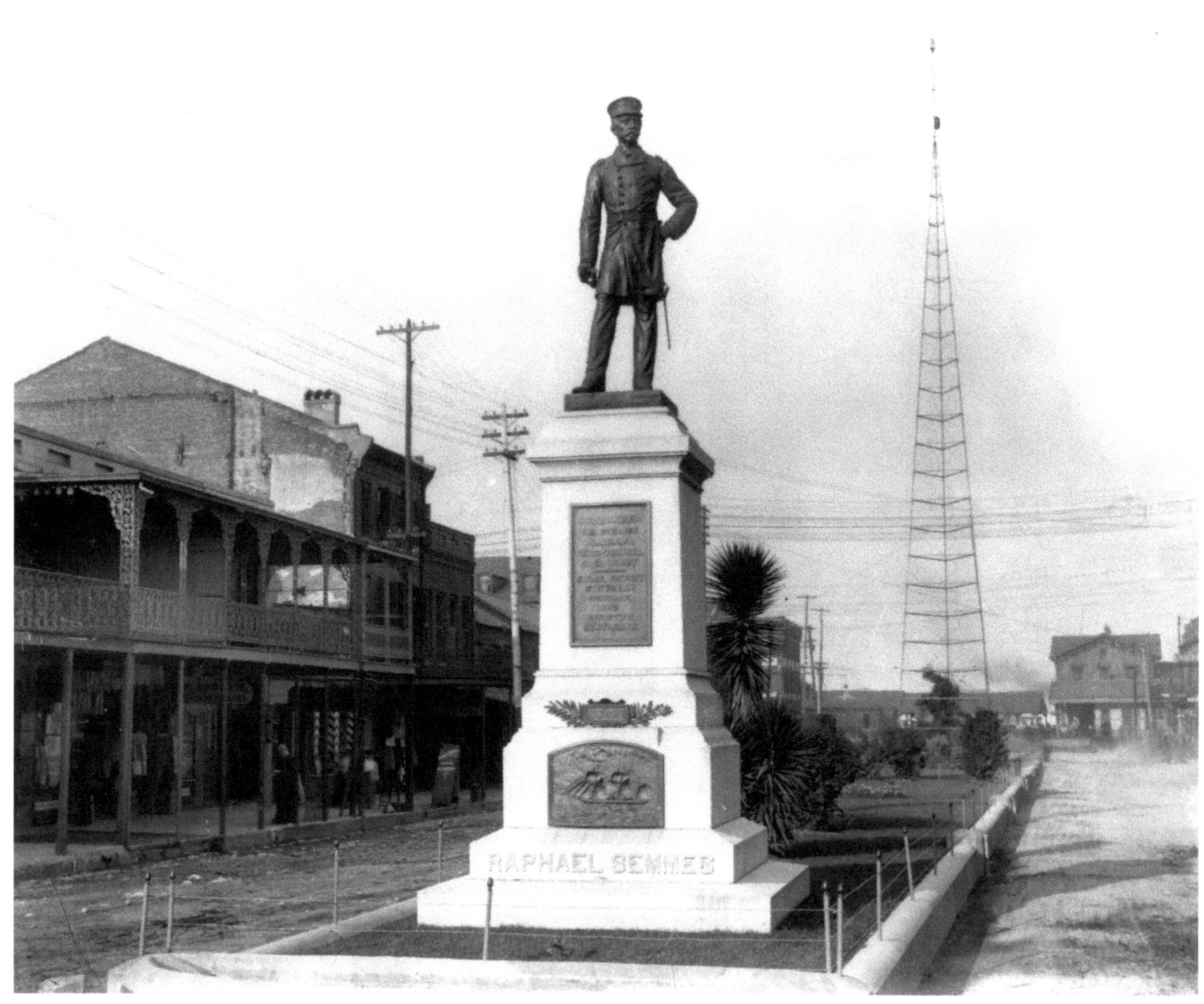

In memory of Admiral Raphael Semmes, captain of the CSS *Alabama* during the Civil War, Mobilians dedicated this monument in 1900. Semmes had been noted for his ability to harass Union shipping. His war service included being wounded and having his ship sunk by the USS *Kearsarge* in a duel off the coast of France in 1864. After the war he worked as a teacher and newspaper editor, later moving to Mobile to pursue a career as an attorney. He died in Mobile in 1877.

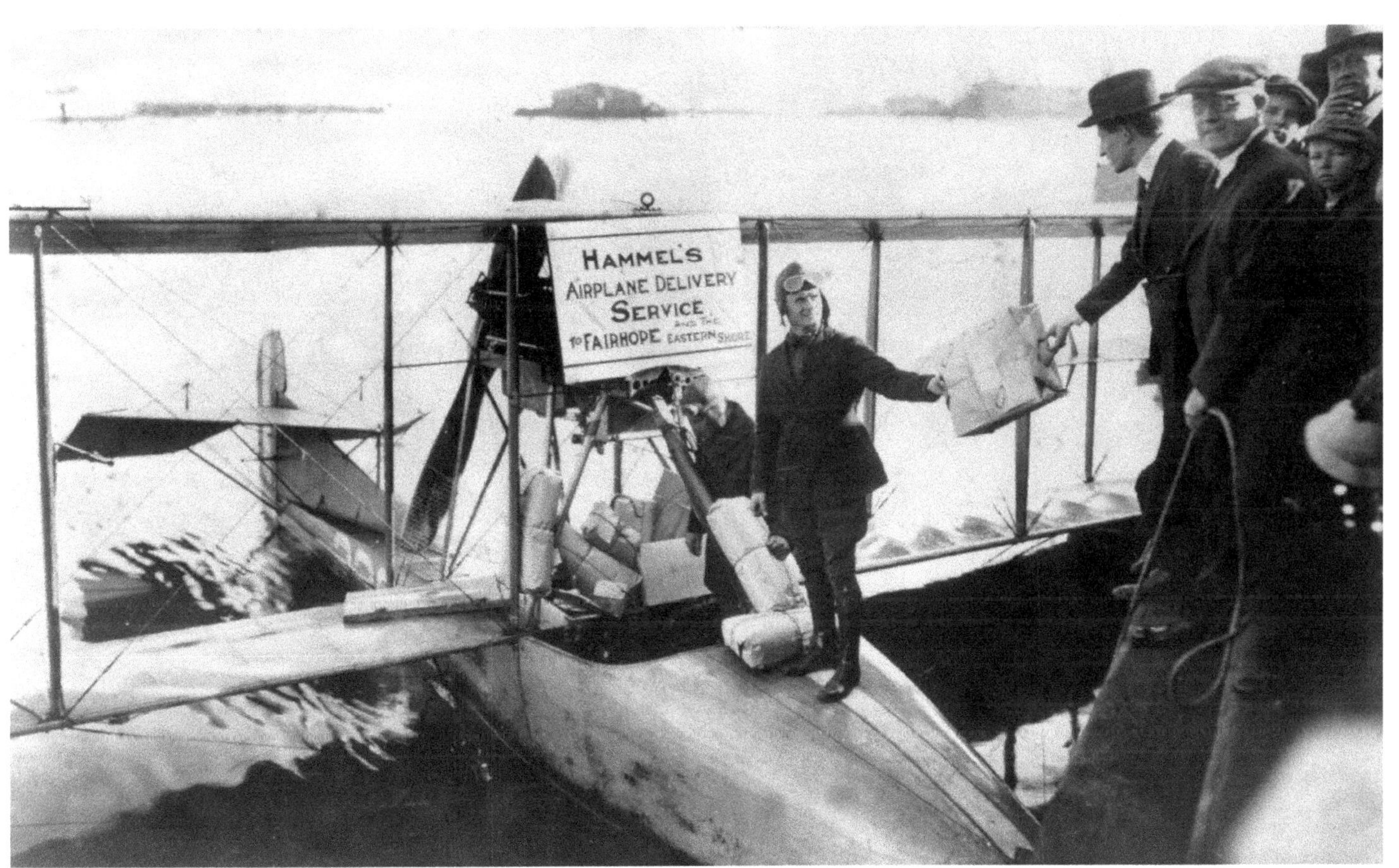

With no bridge to get across Mobile Bay, Hammel's Department Store improvised, using this hydroplane to make special deliveries in 1919.

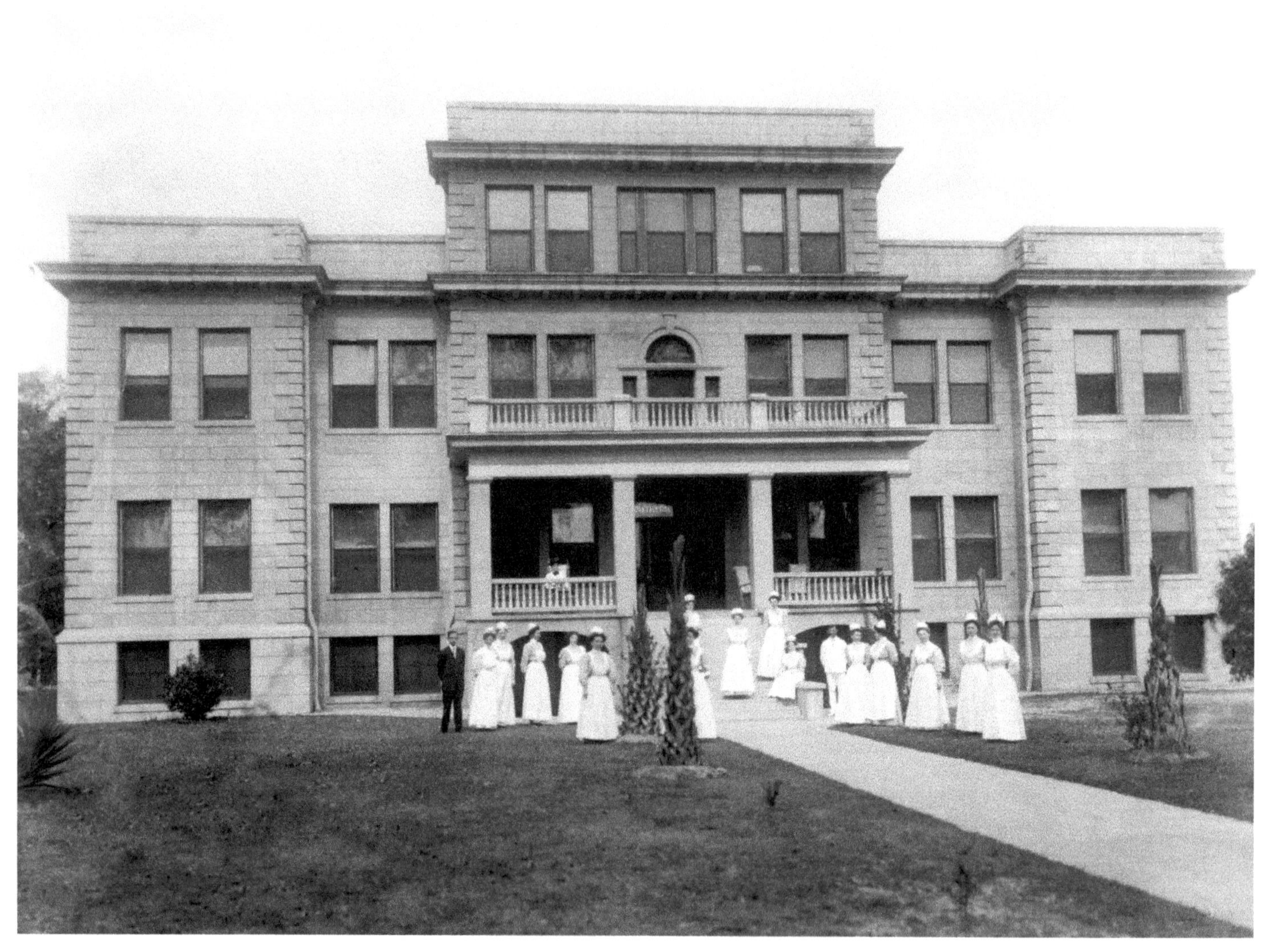

Nurses pose outside the Southern Infirmary on Saint Stephens Road.

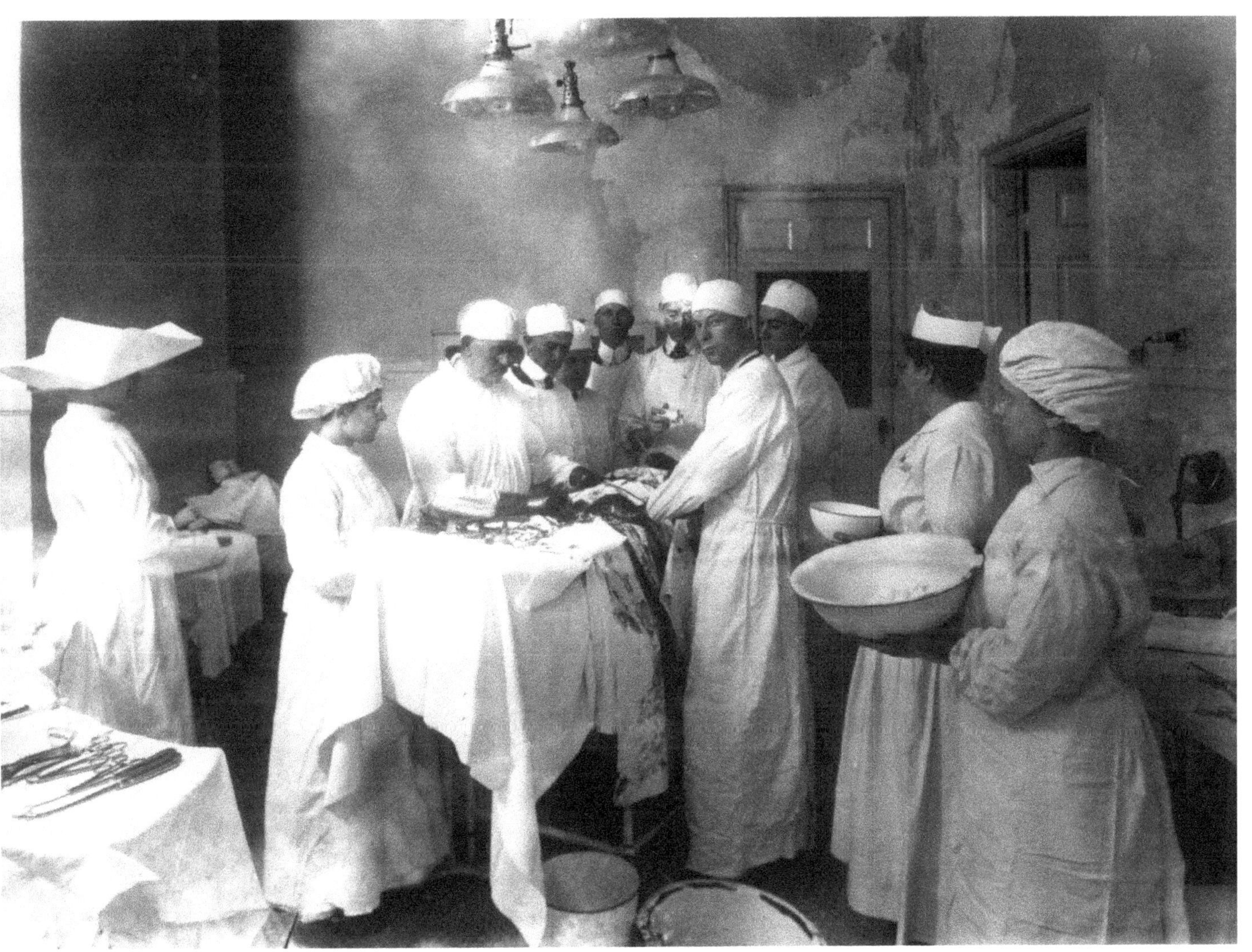

Medicine was still crude in the early twentieth century. This is a rare view inside the operating room of the Mobile City Hospital during a procedure in 1915.

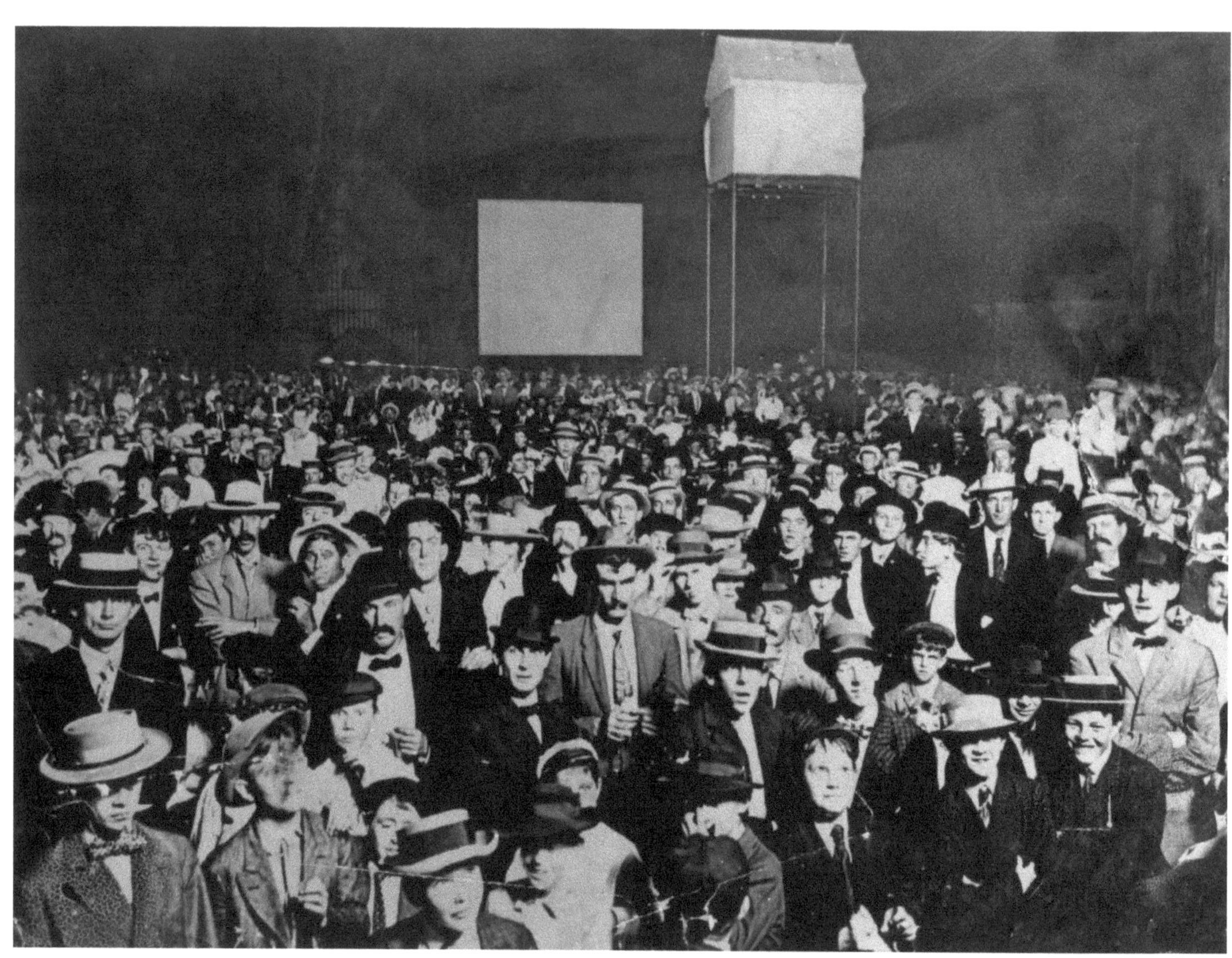

A crowd attends an event at the outdoor theater at Monroe Park around 1910. The park was destroyed in the hurricane of 1916.

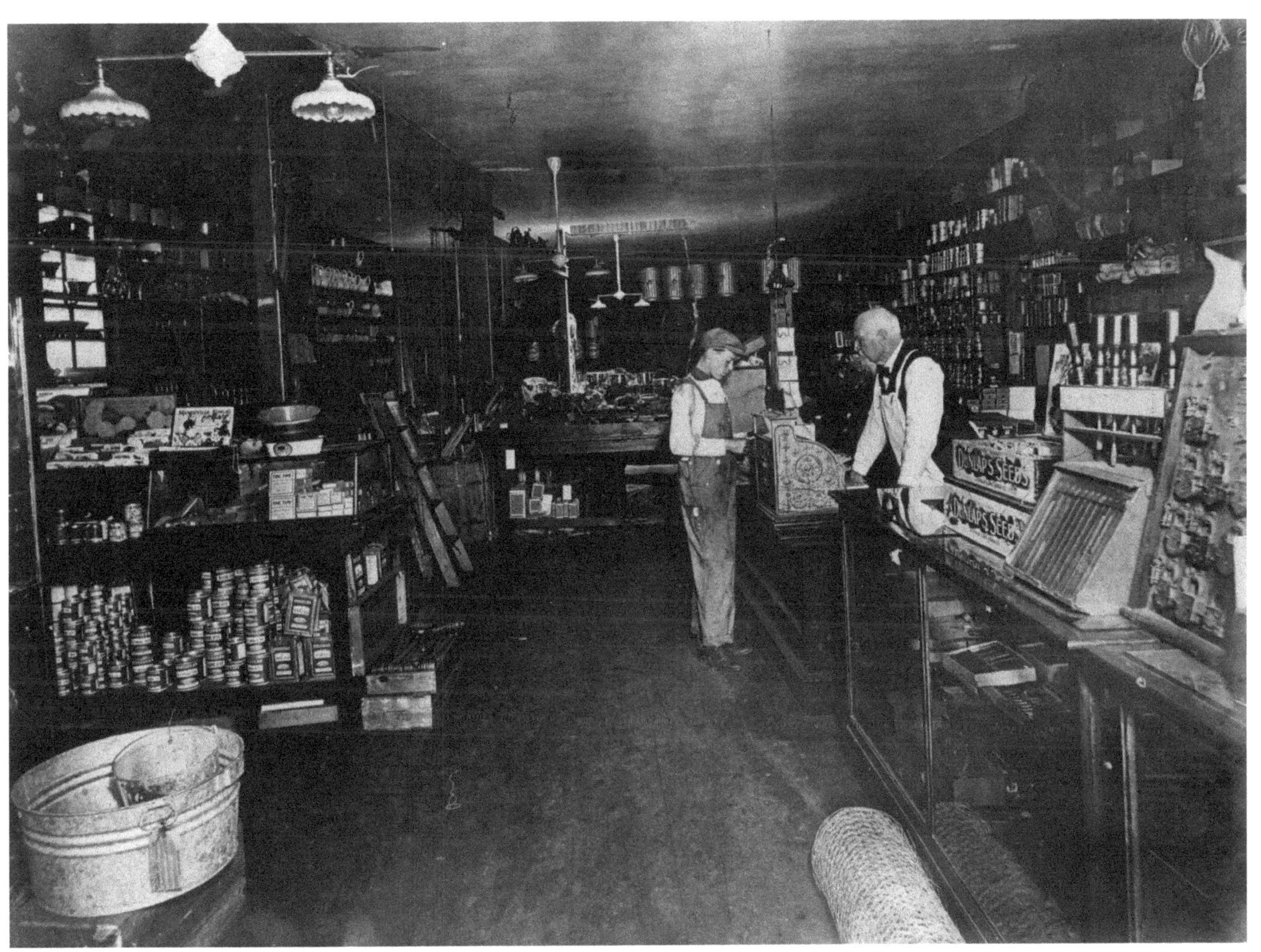

To satisfy their customers, general stores, like the one in this 1919 photo, had to carry a variety of goods, from seeds and spark plugs to crockery, galvanized buckets, and tire tape.

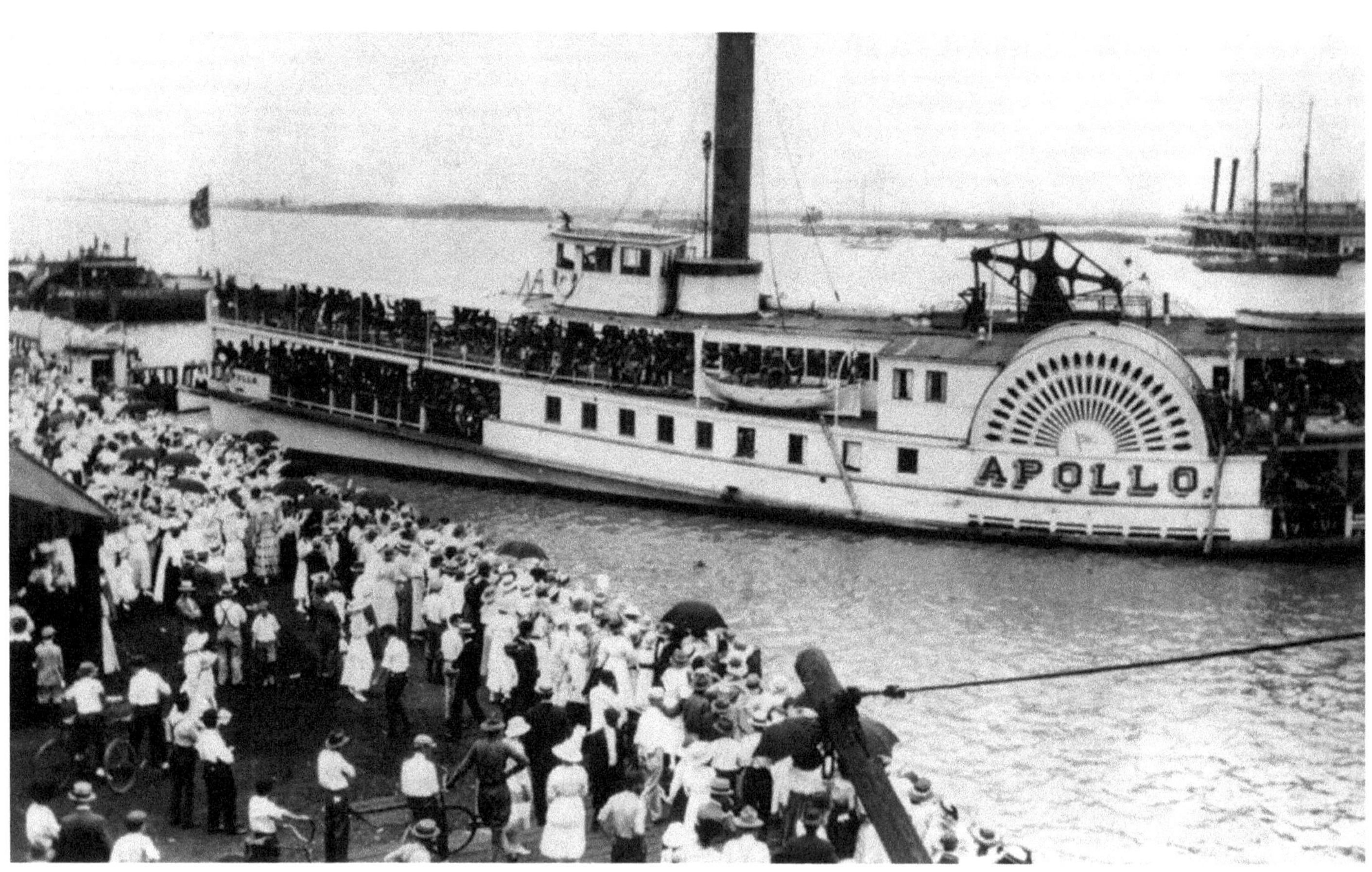

The 161-foot *Apollo* was a popular excursion boat. Built in 1864 for use in Boston Harbor and brought to Mobile in 1904, *Apollo* remained an active source of transportation until the 1916 hurricane impaired its ability to sail.

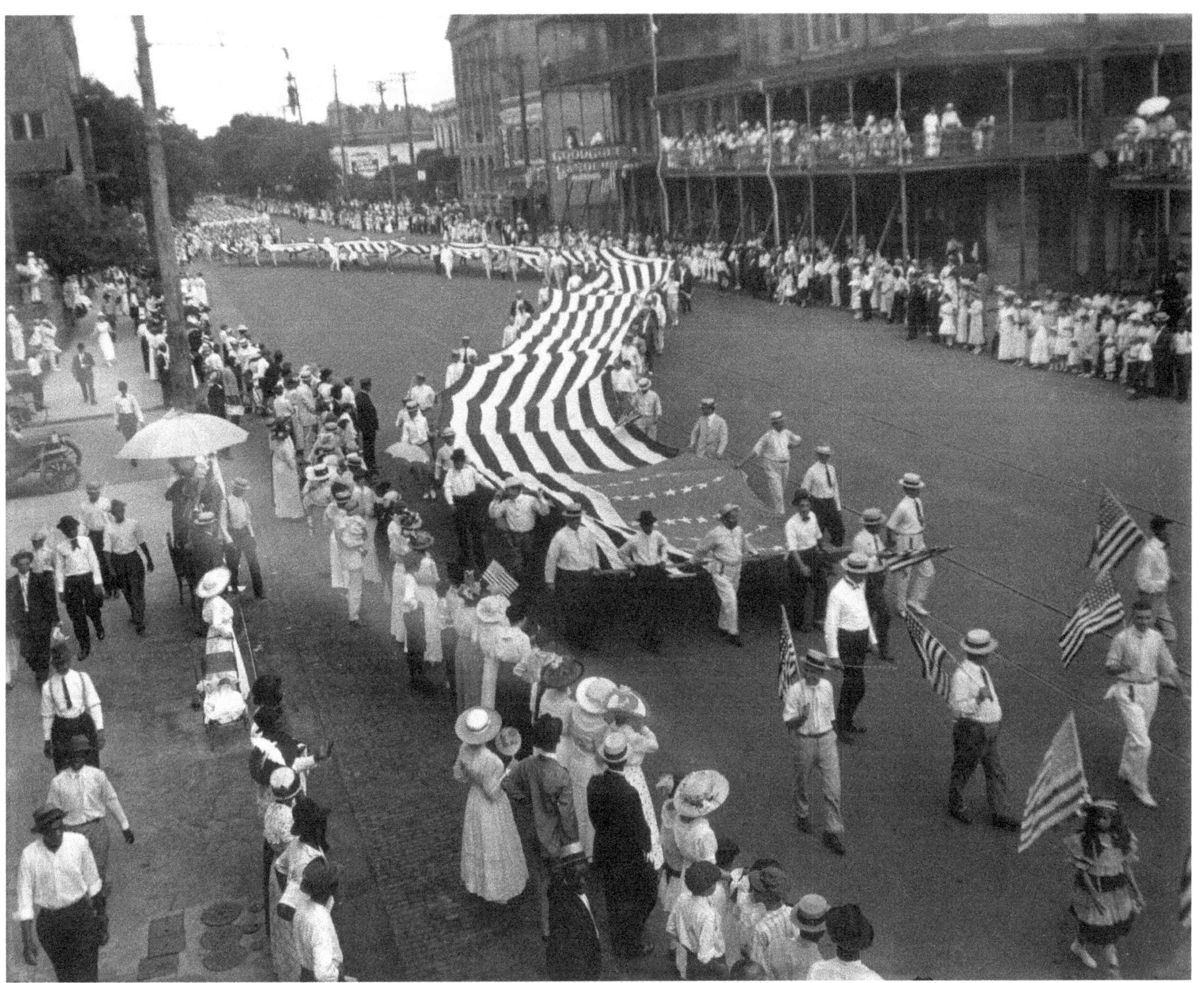

This July 4, 1916, preparedness rally down Mobile's Government Street was said to have shown off the longest American flag in history. Unbeknownst to these celebrants, a hurricane would hit the city the next day.

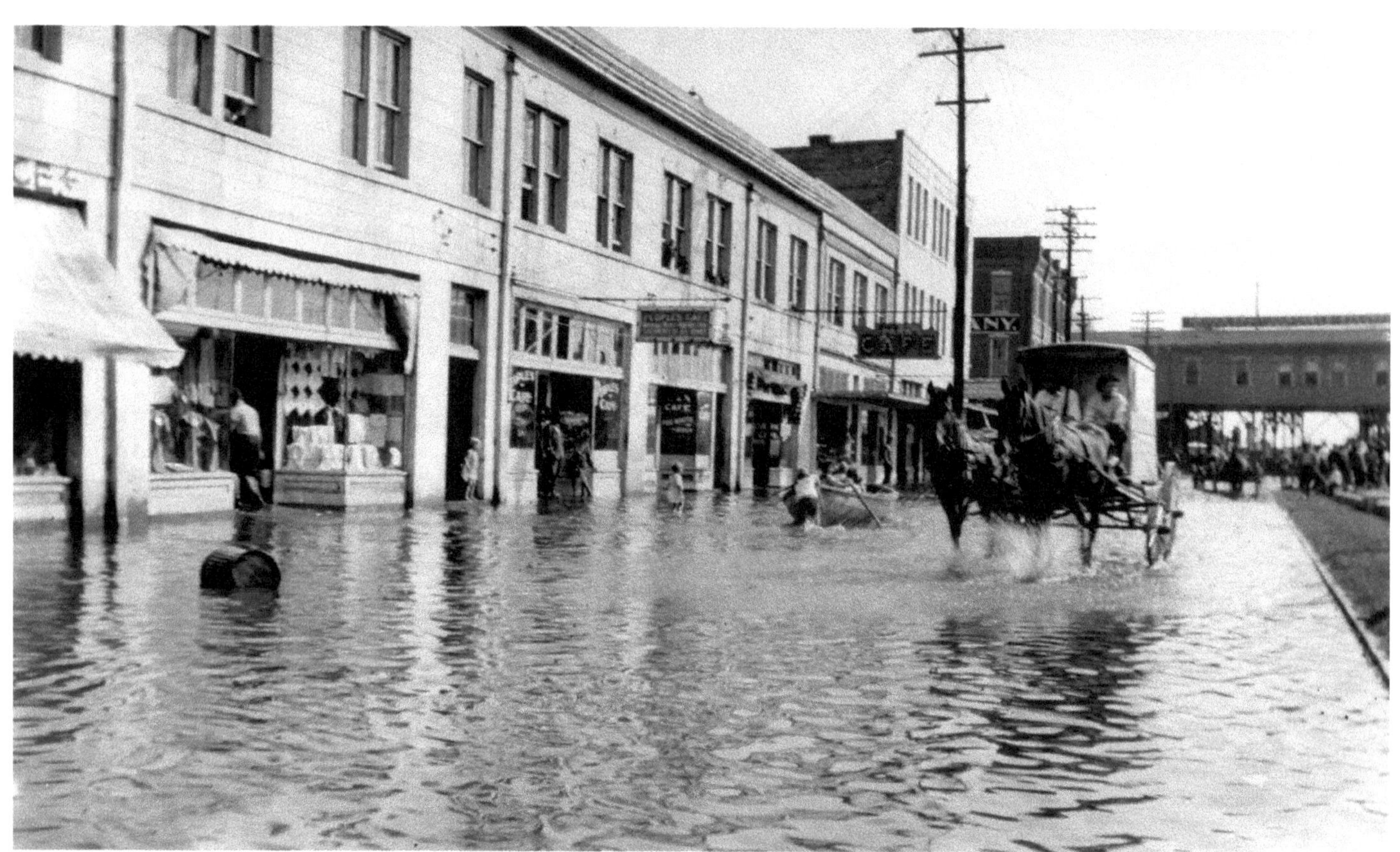

The next day's aftermath. The storm that hit Mobile on July 5, 1916, first formed in the Caribbean Sea on June 29. It was the first storm of the Atlantic hurricane season. The gale skirted the coast of Honduras and made landfall in Gulfport, Mississippi, only 75 miles from Mobile. The powerful rains and winds from the storm flooded streets and damaged businesses near Mobile's waterfront.

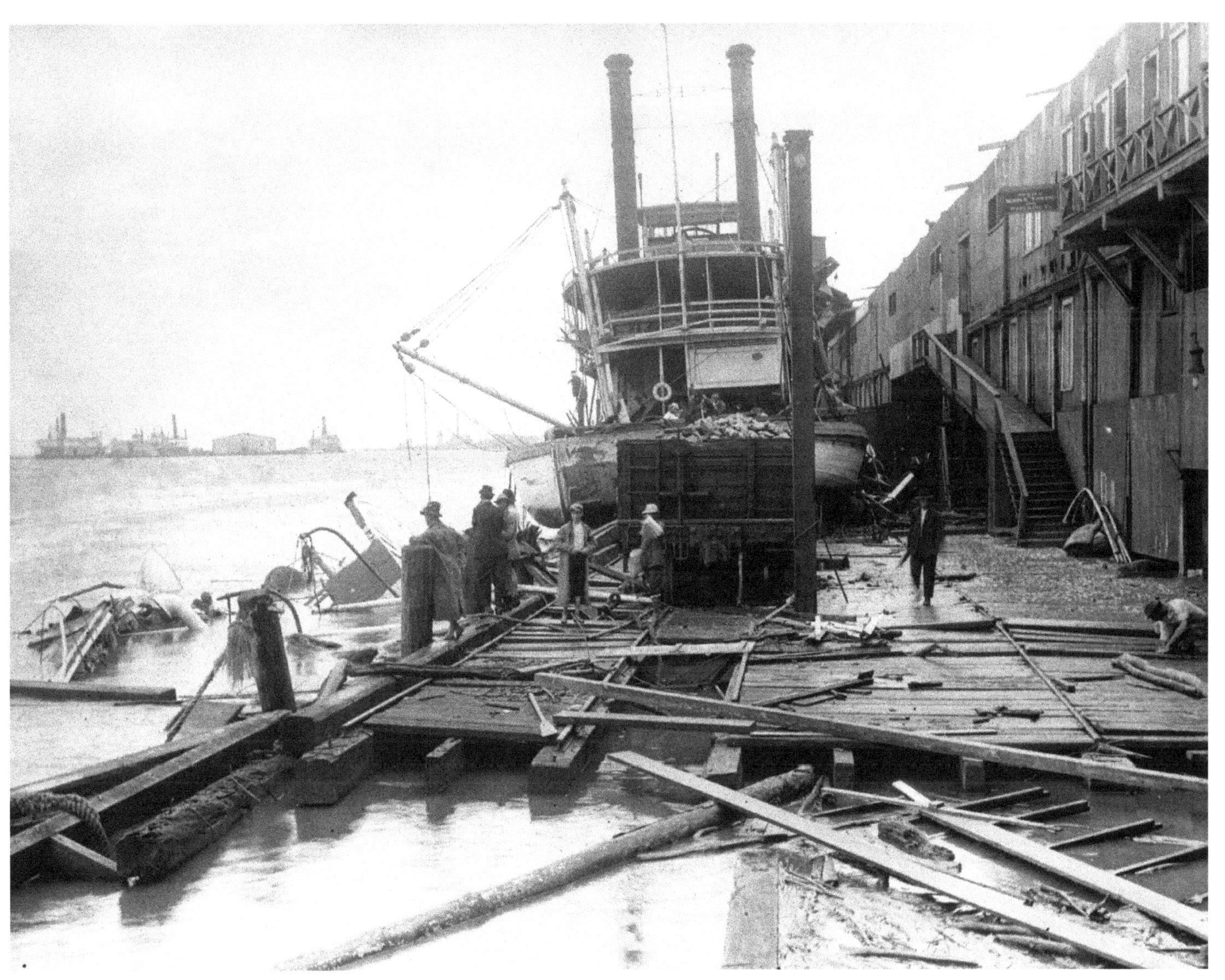

The Mobile & Ohio pier, located at the foot of Dauphin Street, was heavily damaged by the 1916 hurricane.

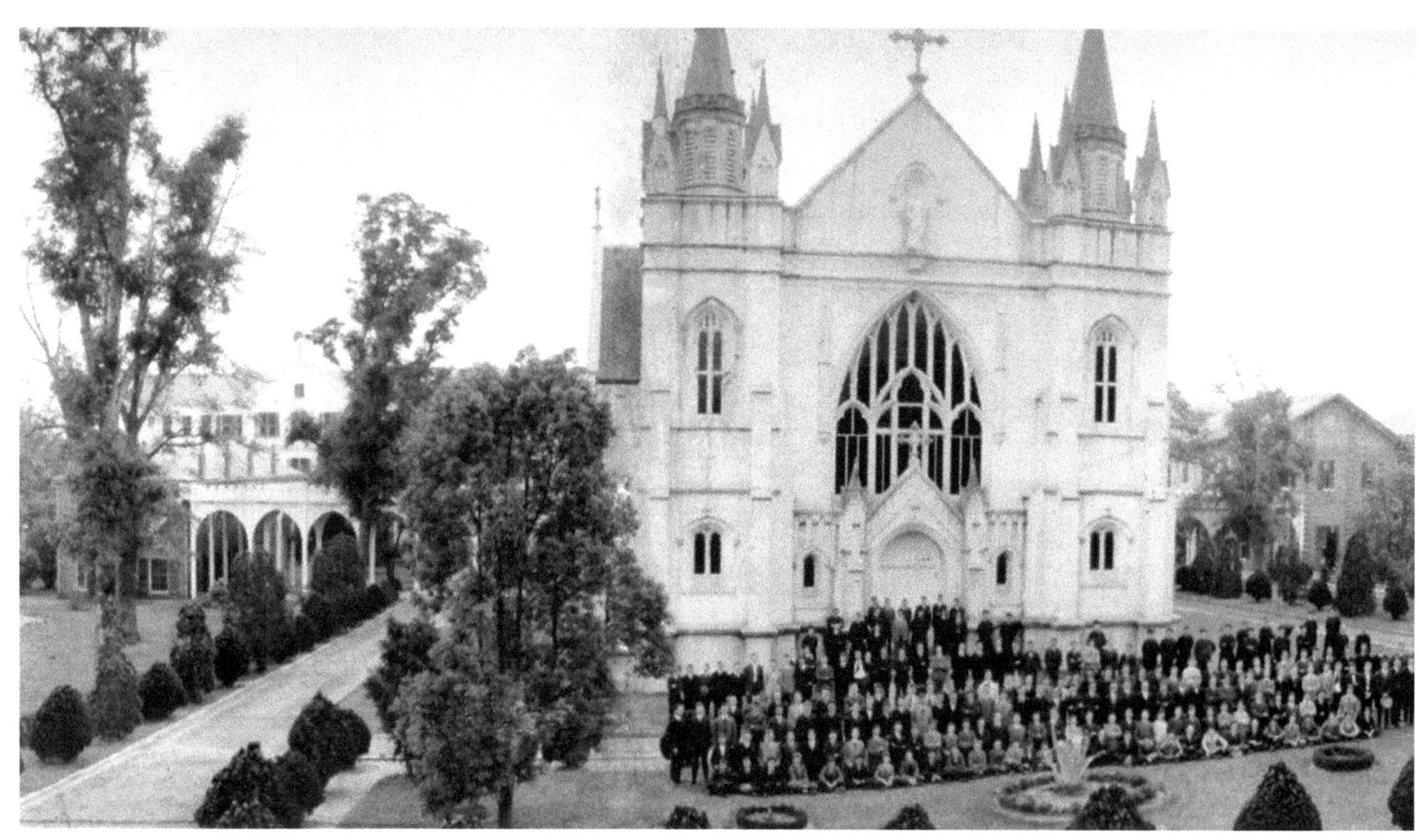

The grounds of Spring Hill College in 1918. Saint Joseph's Chapel is on the right.

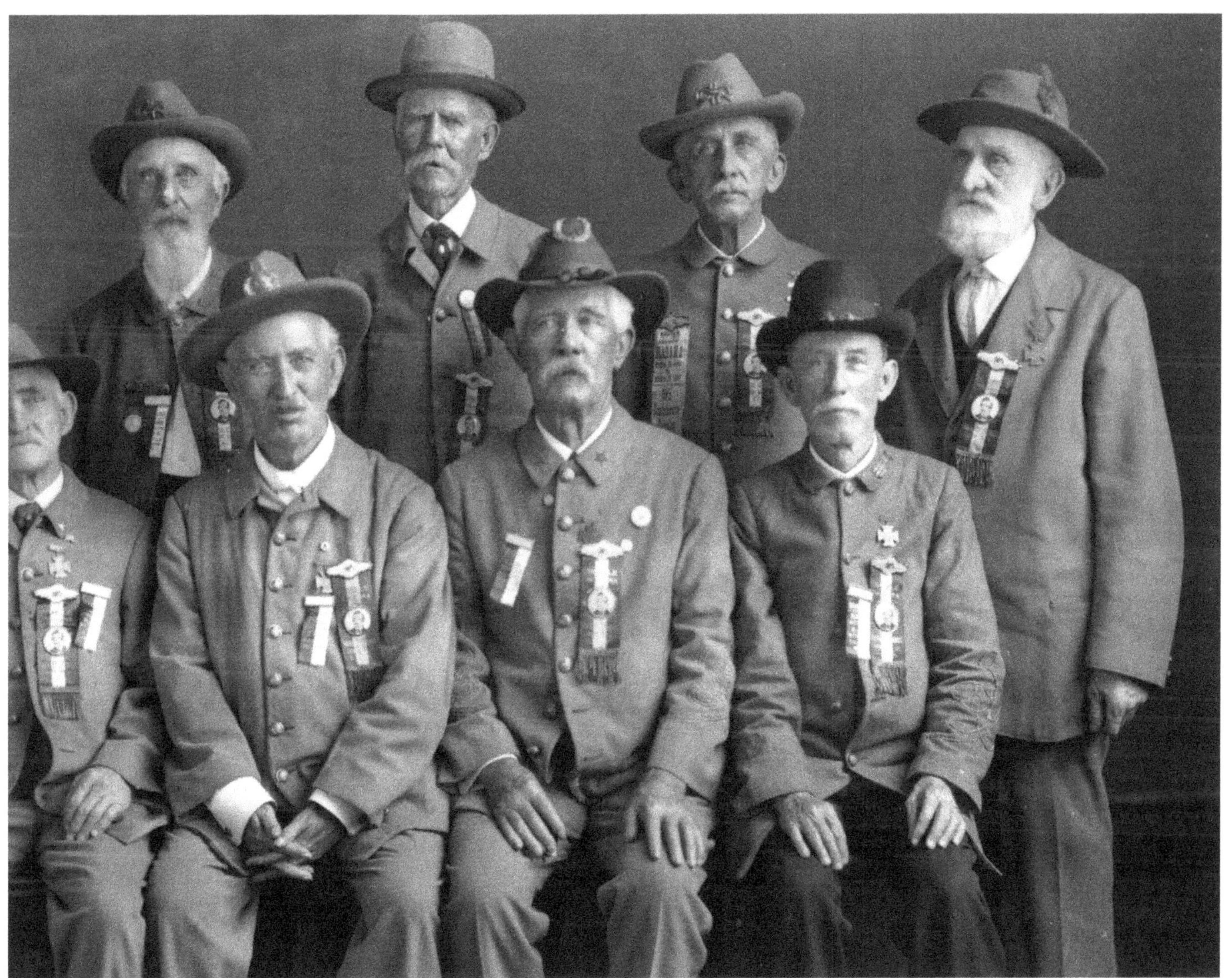

Members of the Raphael Semmes Camp of the United Confederate Veterans took time out from their 1918 reunion, held in Mobile, to sit for this group portrait. On the bottom row, from left, are Fremont Sterling Thrower, Thomas O'Rourke, Michael Thomas Judge, Sr., and Robert Edward Daly. Thrower left Spring Hill College at the age of 17 in 1862 to join the 92nd Alabama Partisan Rangers, which became the 56th Alabama Cavalry. Michael Judge hailed from Ireland. He came to the United States in 1852, moved to Mobile, and enlisted at the age of 16 in 1864 and served until the war's end. He and two of his sons would go on to become master brick masons. Judge once ran for mayor, losing by fewer than 300 votes. He died in 1932, some 14 years after this photo was taken. The men on the top row remain unidentified.

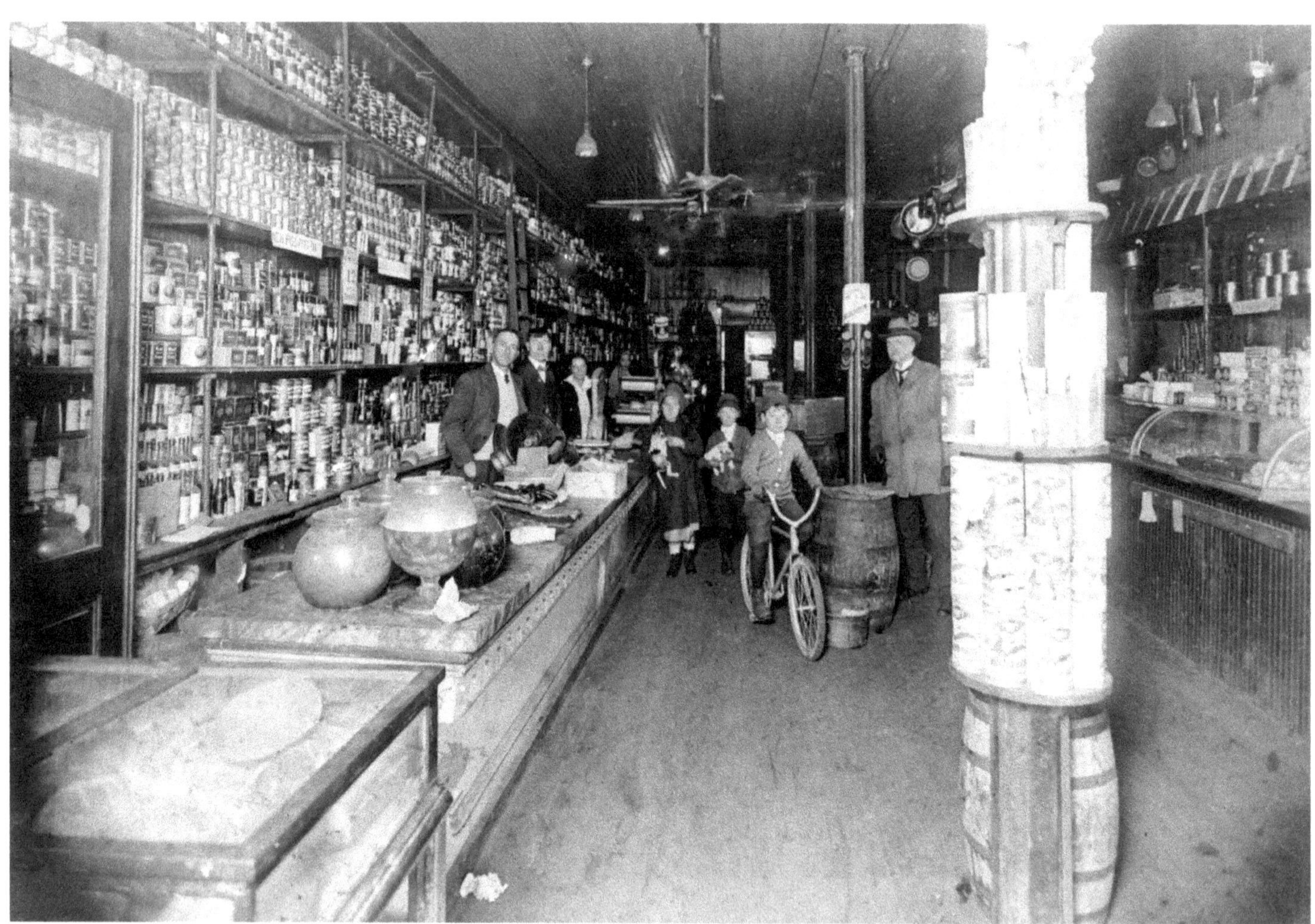

Members of the Meyer family pose in their grocery store on Dauphin Street in 1918. At that time, the store offered full service. Customers gave the clerk a grocery list, and he or she gathered all the items together. The store was located at Dauphin and Scott streets. Henry C. Meyer and his family lived on the top floor of the building and offered several rooms on the second floor for rent. Four murals covered the outside of the building, enticing passersby to come inside and shop. Twelve years after this photo was taken, the store was remodeled for self-service, reflecting the further commercialization of industry in Mobile.

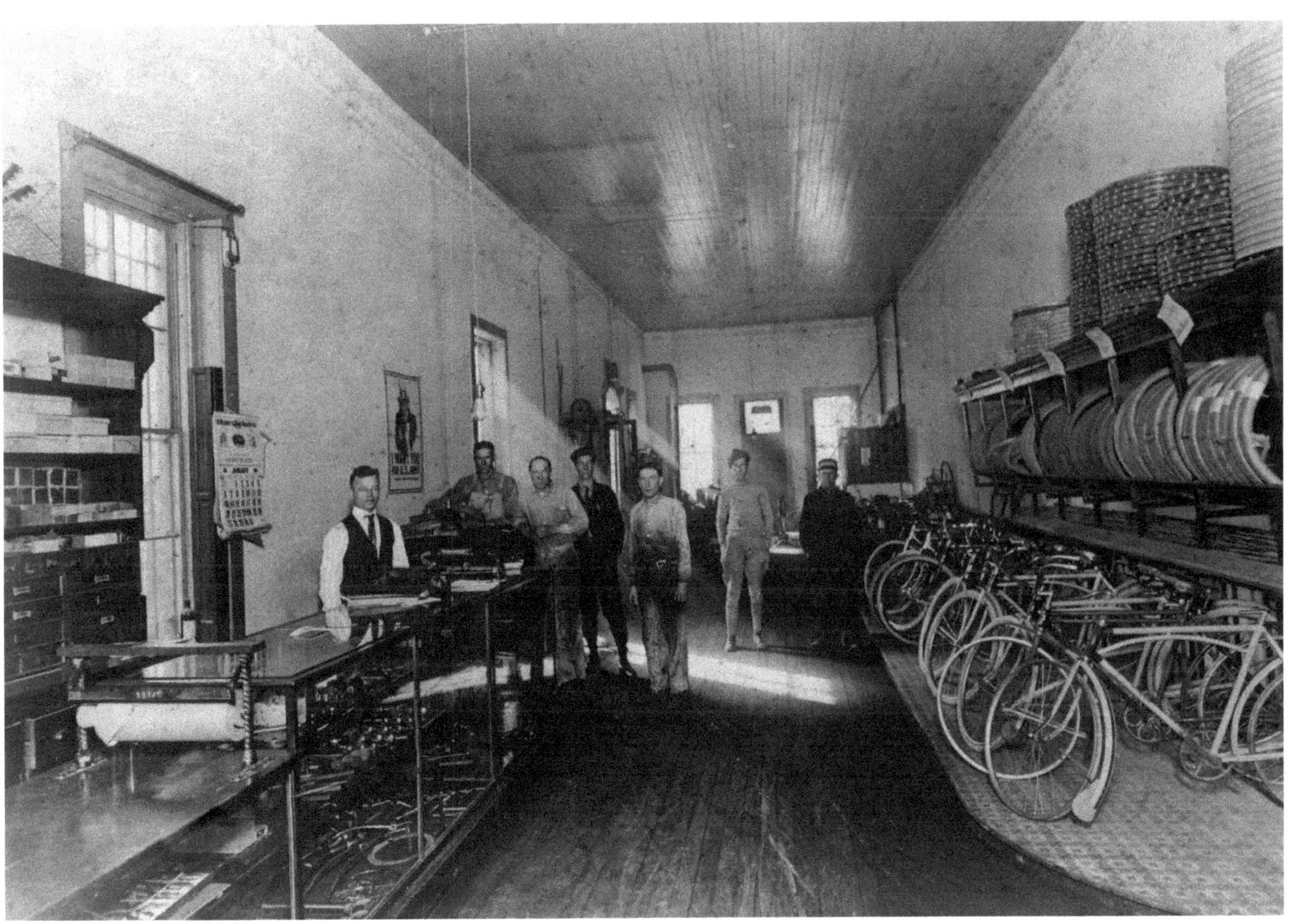

The Gulf City bicycle shop in January 1918. Their grease-stained clothing renders two mechanics conspicuous. In James Montgomery Flagg's famous war poster, on the wall at left, Uncle Sam recruits Americans for military service.

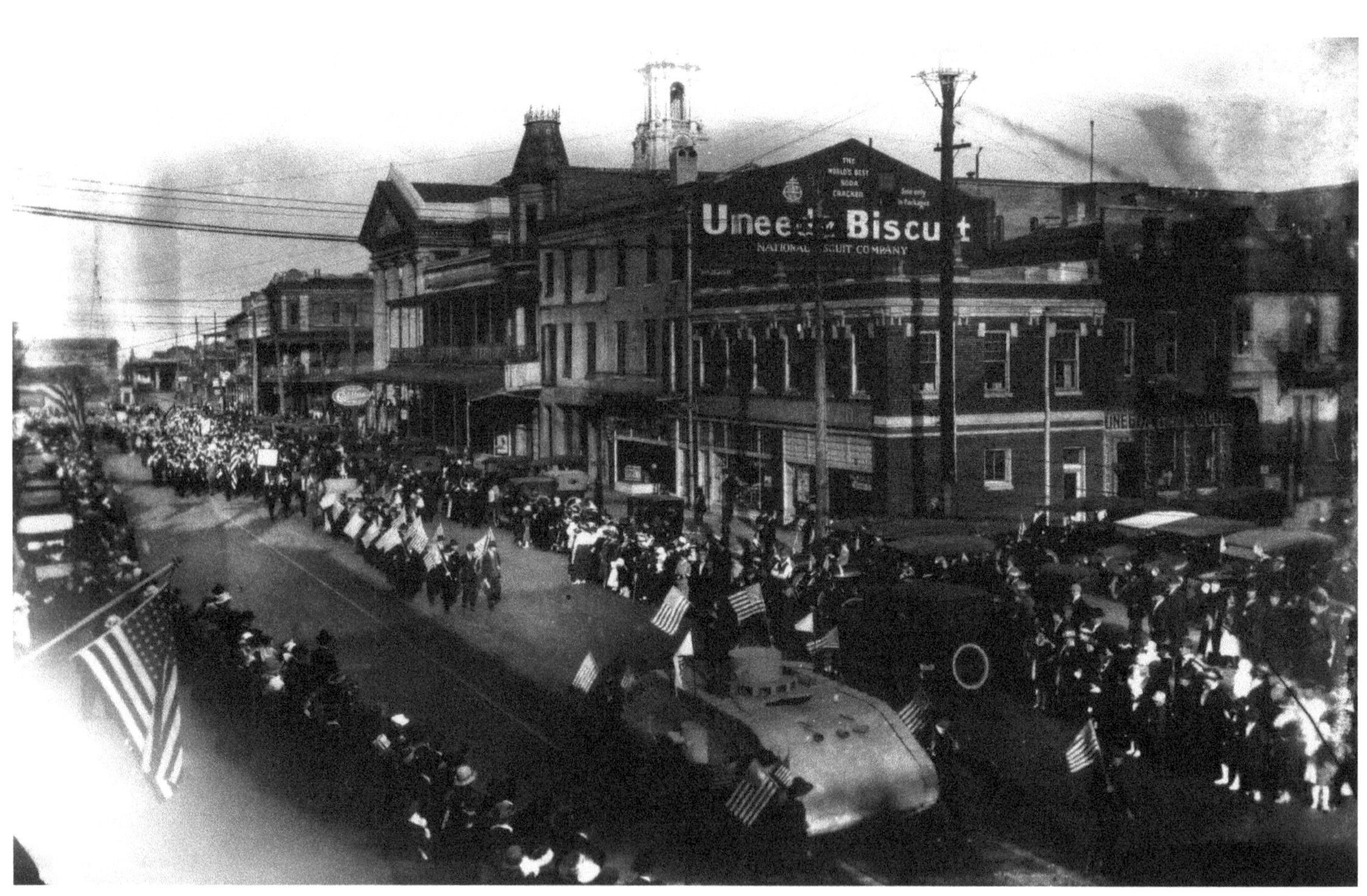

When America entered World War I, Mobilians supported the effort with several well-attended bond rallies, like this one on Government Street in 1918.

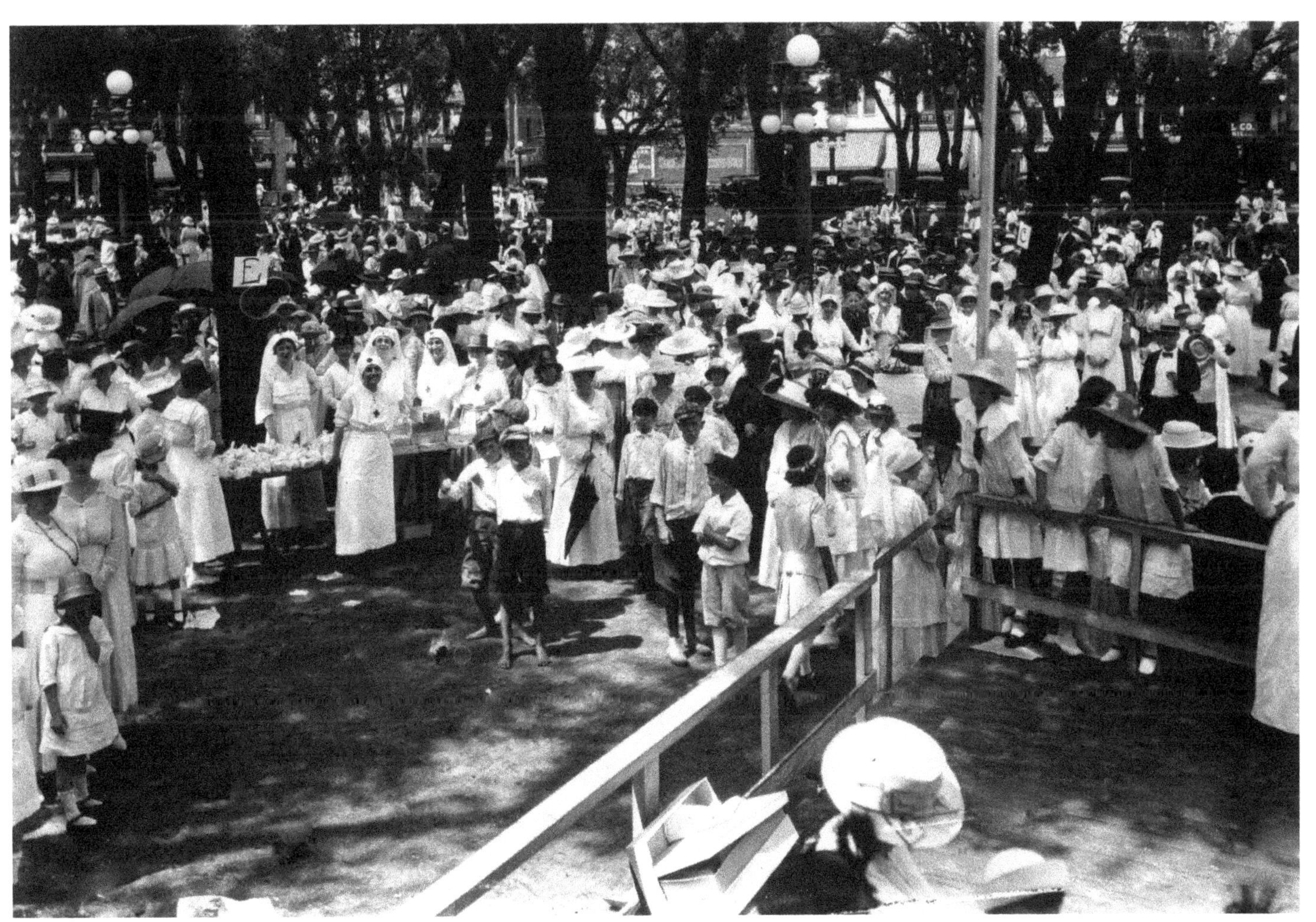

So many people filled the streets of downtown Mobile to celebrate the official end of World War I after the signing of the Versailles Treaty in June 1919 that the Red Cross had to set up an aid station in Bienville Square.

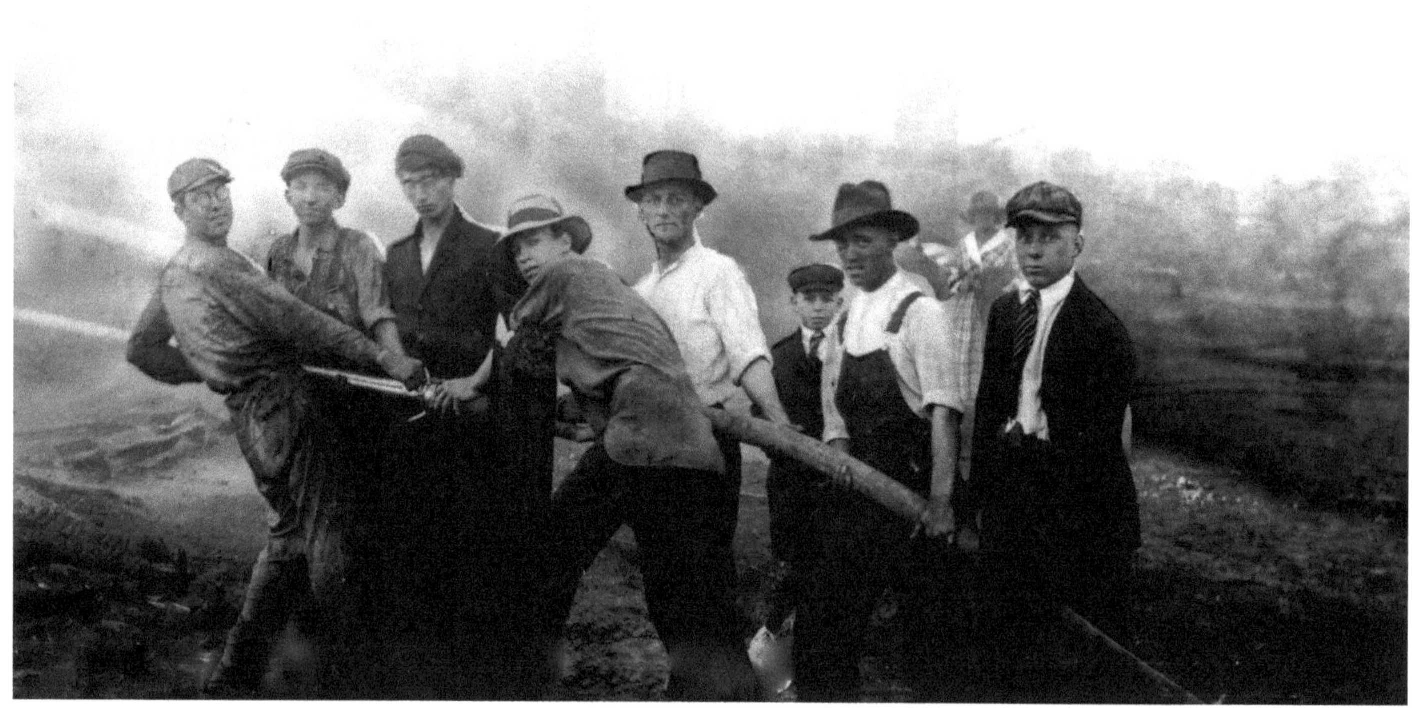

Fire fighters battle a blaze in Mobile in 1919. Remnants of burned downtown buildings can be seen in the background.

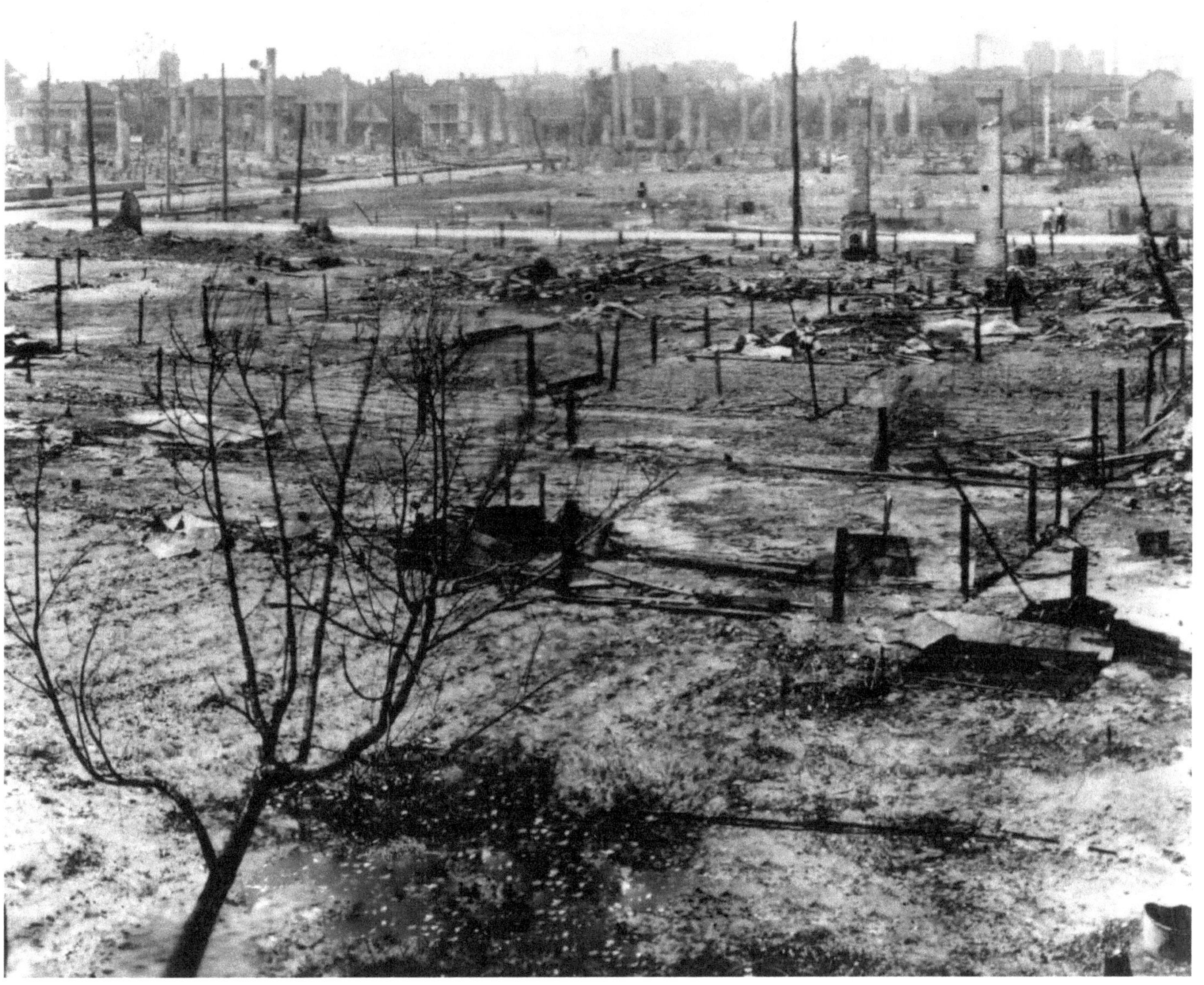

Fires devastated Mobile in the nineteenth and early twentieth centuries. The May 1919 fire destroyed 200 homes and businesses. Insurance estimates of the damage were $500,000.

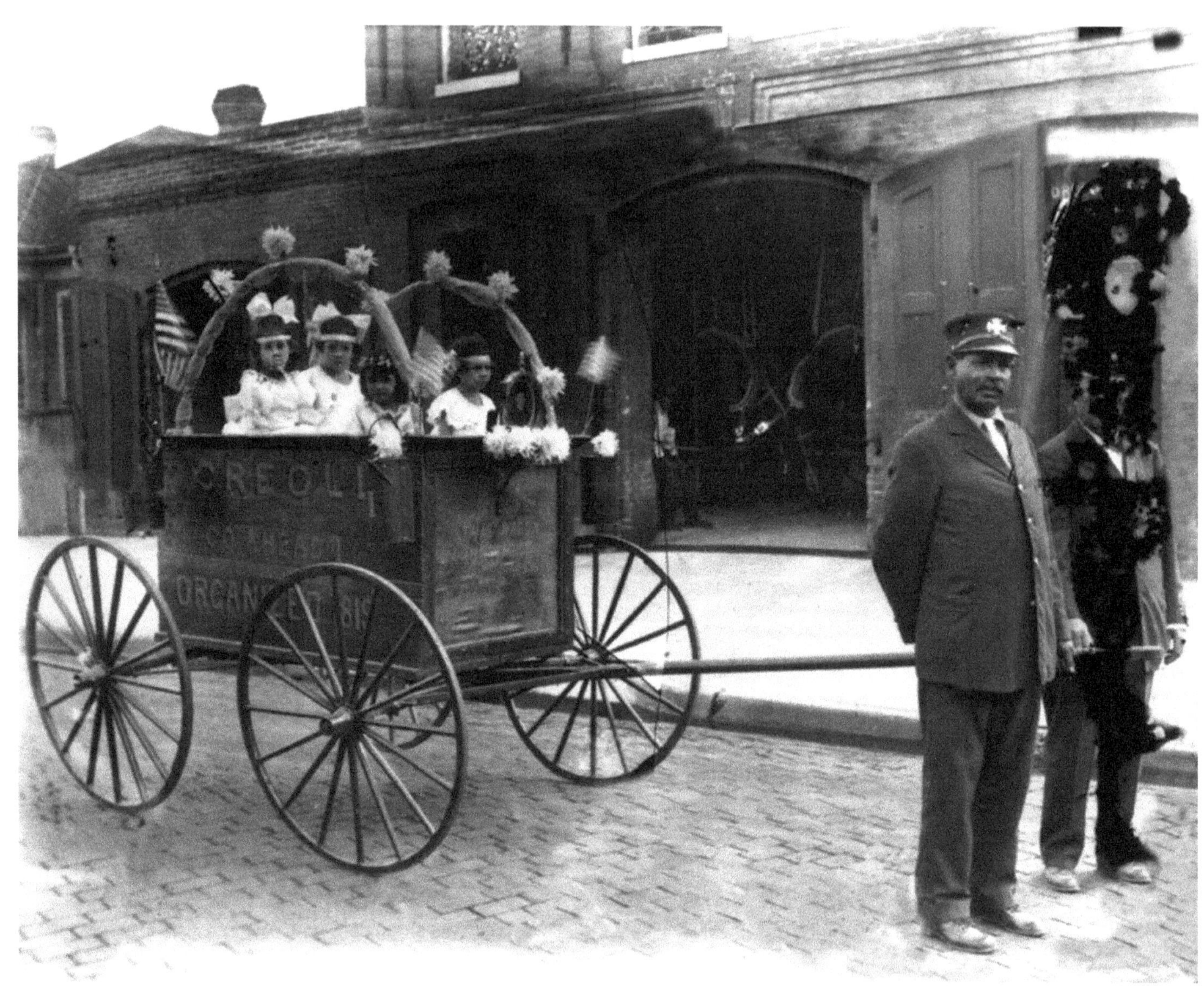

During the 1919 Mardi Gras season, these members of the Creole Fire Department and their families also celebrated their 100th anniversary by dressing up and decorating, and marching in that year's parade.

The Roaring Twenties

(1920–1929)

The 1920s "roared" in Mobile through a combination of large-scale civic projects and port expansion. Following the shipbuilding boom brought about by World War I, several industries invested heavily in Mobile's economy by building factories along the waterfront. In 1923, the efforts of local businessmen and other boosters to strengthen Alabama's investment in the Port City were rewarded when the Alabama legislature established a state dock. Four years later, Mobilians and Alabama Governor Bibb Graves dedicated the Cochrane Bridge, a ten-mile structure that spans five rivers to connect Mobile to the Eastern Shore. The bridge allowed for easier automobile access to and from the city and provided economic and civic improvements.

Several traditions and well-known institutions of the city began in the 1920s. In 1924, Mobilians welcomed Babe Ruth and the New York Yankees for the first of three exhibition games. The stately Saenger Theatre opened in 1927, adding to Mobile's rich social scene. The public library relocated to its present site on Government Street a year later. Two Mobile social traditions began in 1929. That year, the Junior Chamber of Commerce sponsored the city's first Azalea Trail. In the summer, the first fishing tournament in what would become the Alabama Deep Sea Fishing Rodeo attracted sportsmen from several states. The latter event remains an integral part of Mobile's annual calendar.

The 1920s were also a decade of growing political awareness for minorities. In November 1920, female Mobilians voted for the first time. In 1925, John LeFlore, a young postman weary of racial injustice—and arguably one of the South's most prolific civil rights advocates—reorganized the local chapter of the National Association for the Advancement of Colored People and was elected secretary, a position he held until 1956.

Between 1920 and the October 1929 stock market crash, Mobile's economy expanded. The depression that followed curbed the industrial boom that had characterized the city earlier in the decade. Despite looming economic hardships, Mobilians took part in Mardi Gras and other civic events with a sense of heady optimism, counting on the traditions of the past to see them through a bleak future.

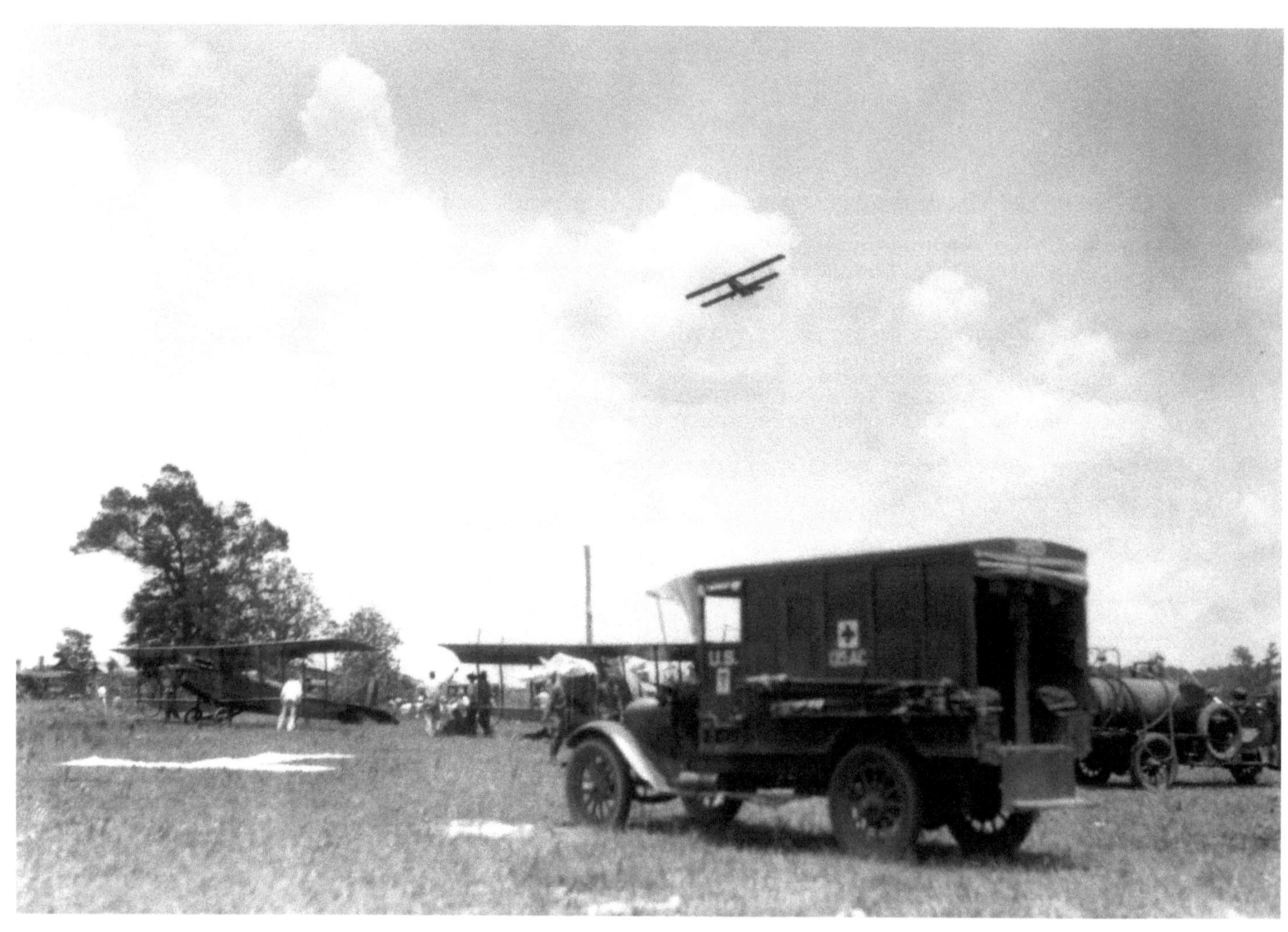

The two forms of modern transportation that the twentieth century brought Mobilians, airplanes and motor vehicles, are combined in this photo from around 1920.

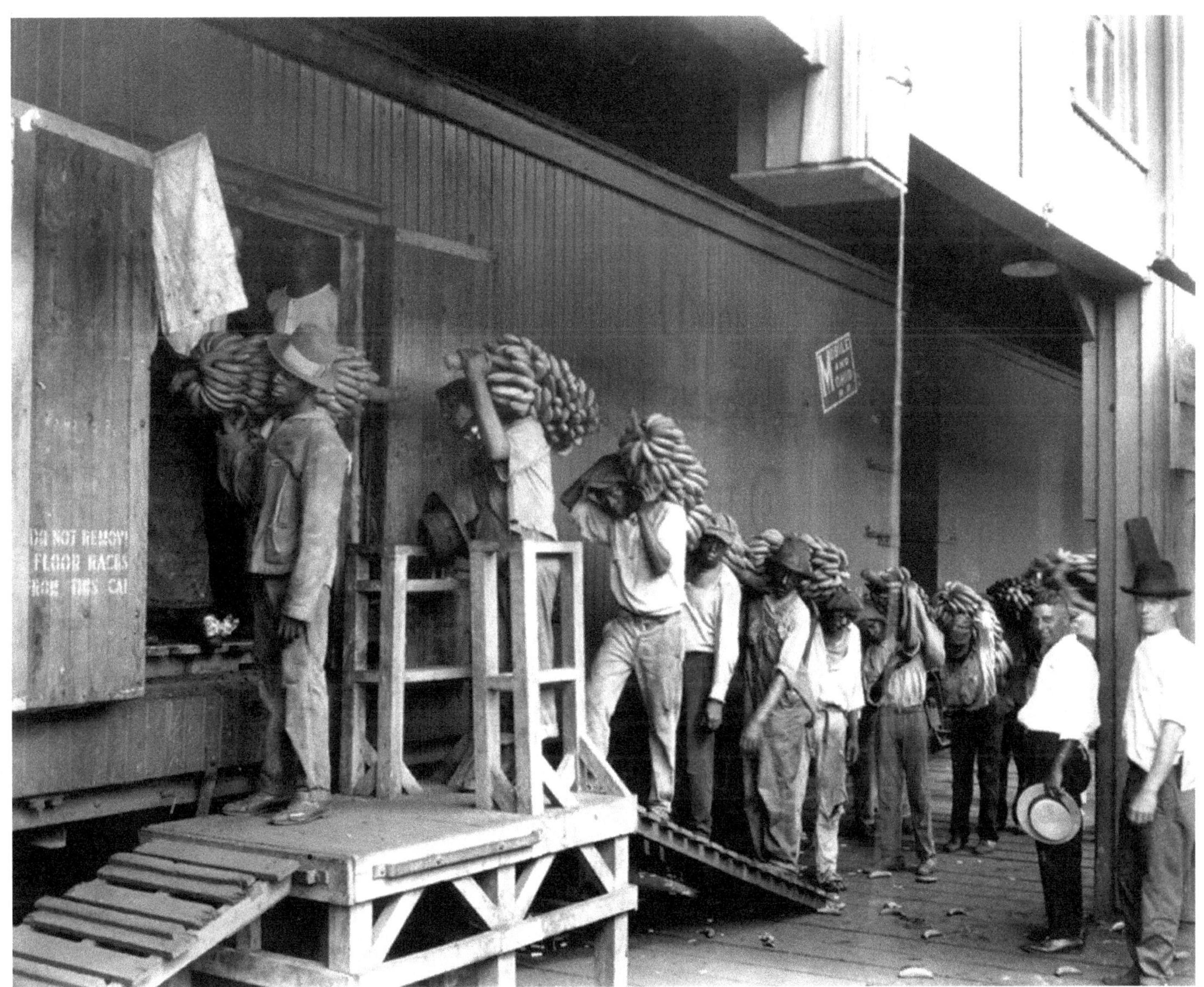

As the importance of cotton declined, the South American banana trade grew in significance. These African-Americans are loading bananas onto railroad cars.

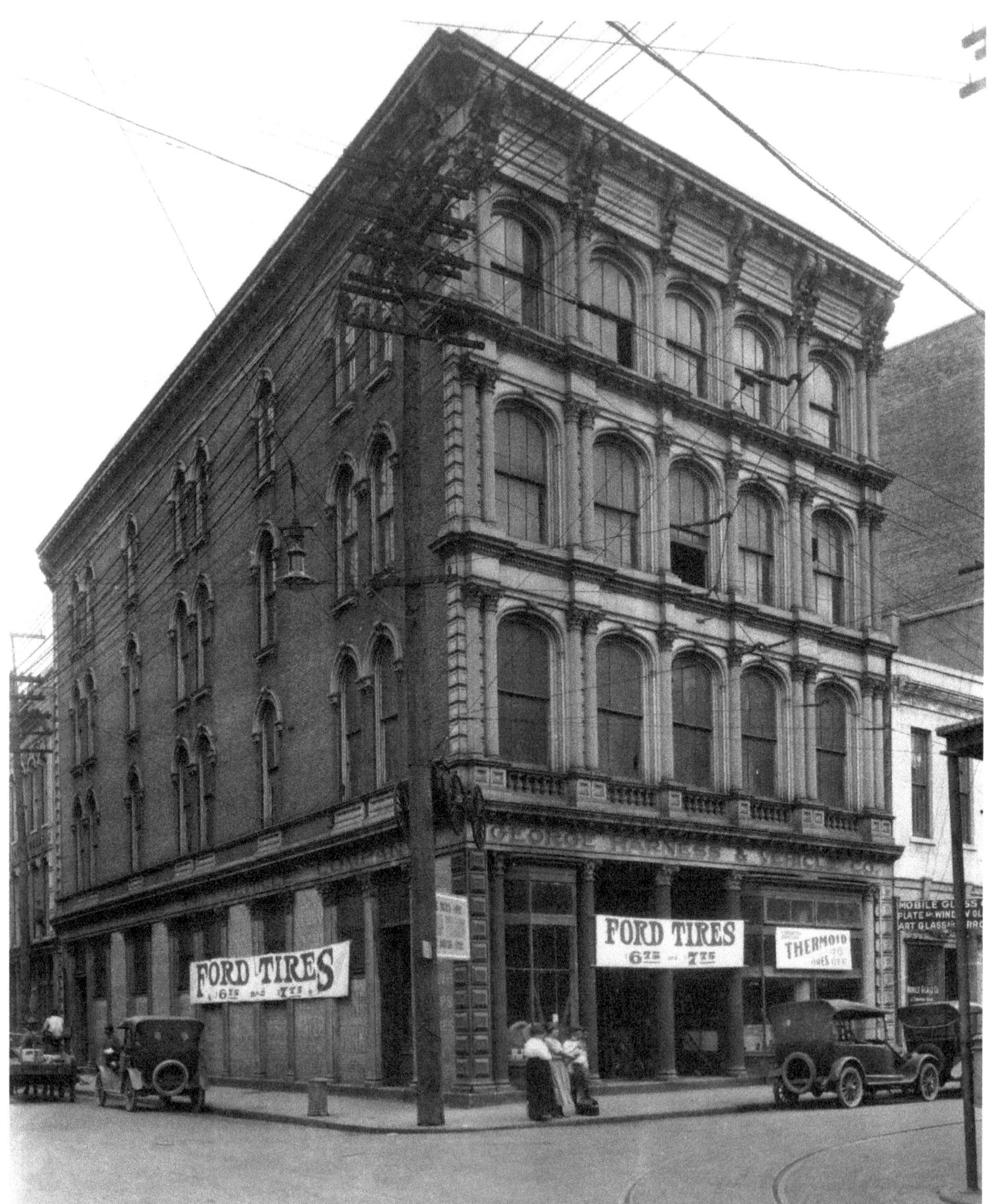

The George Harness & Vehicle Company building, located on the southwest corner of Dauphin and Water streets (ca. 1920), featured a cast-iron facade.

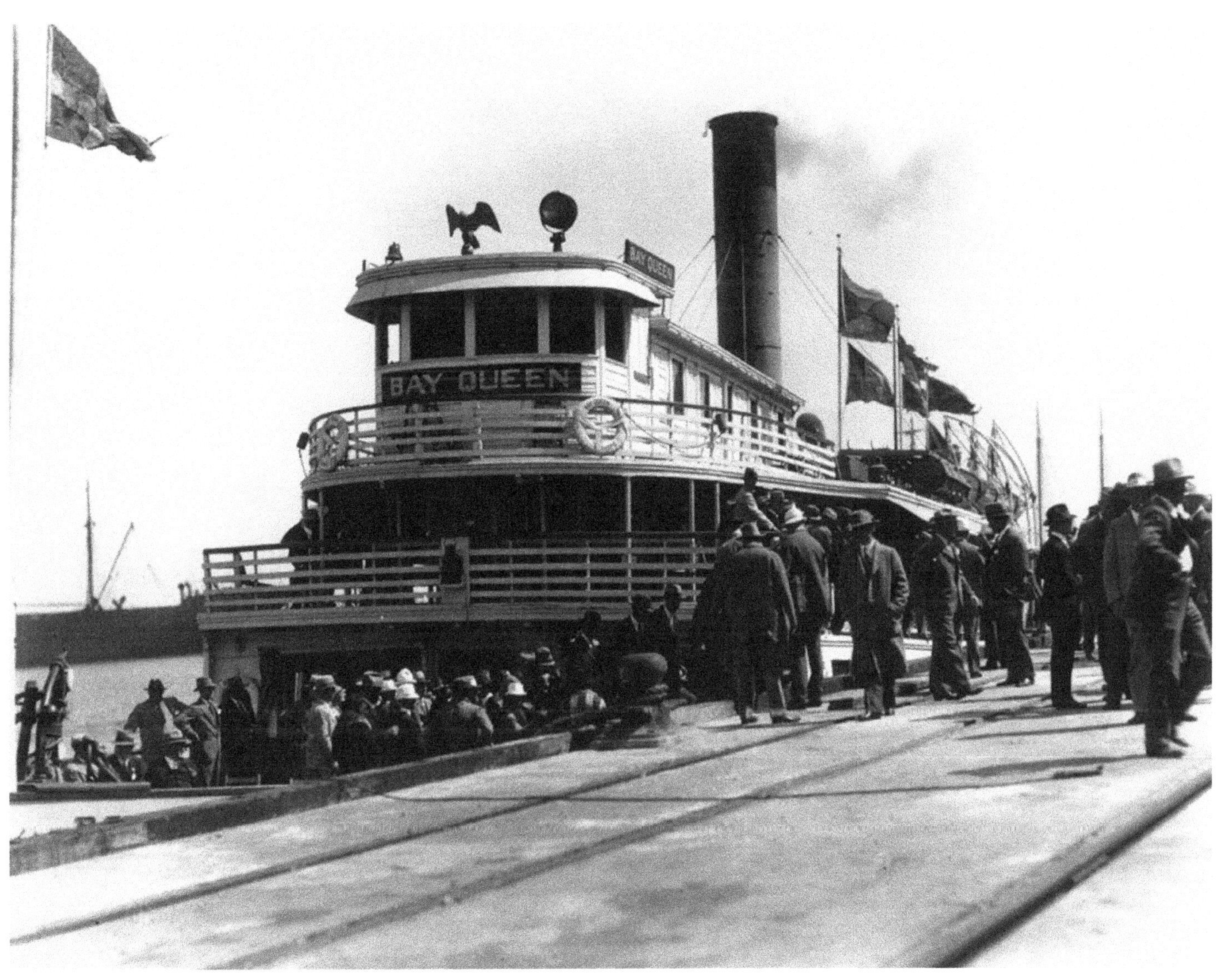

The *Bay Queen,* one of the many boats that plied the waters of Mobile Bay.

This young woman prepares to christen the *City of Mobile* at the Chickasaw shipyard in 1920.

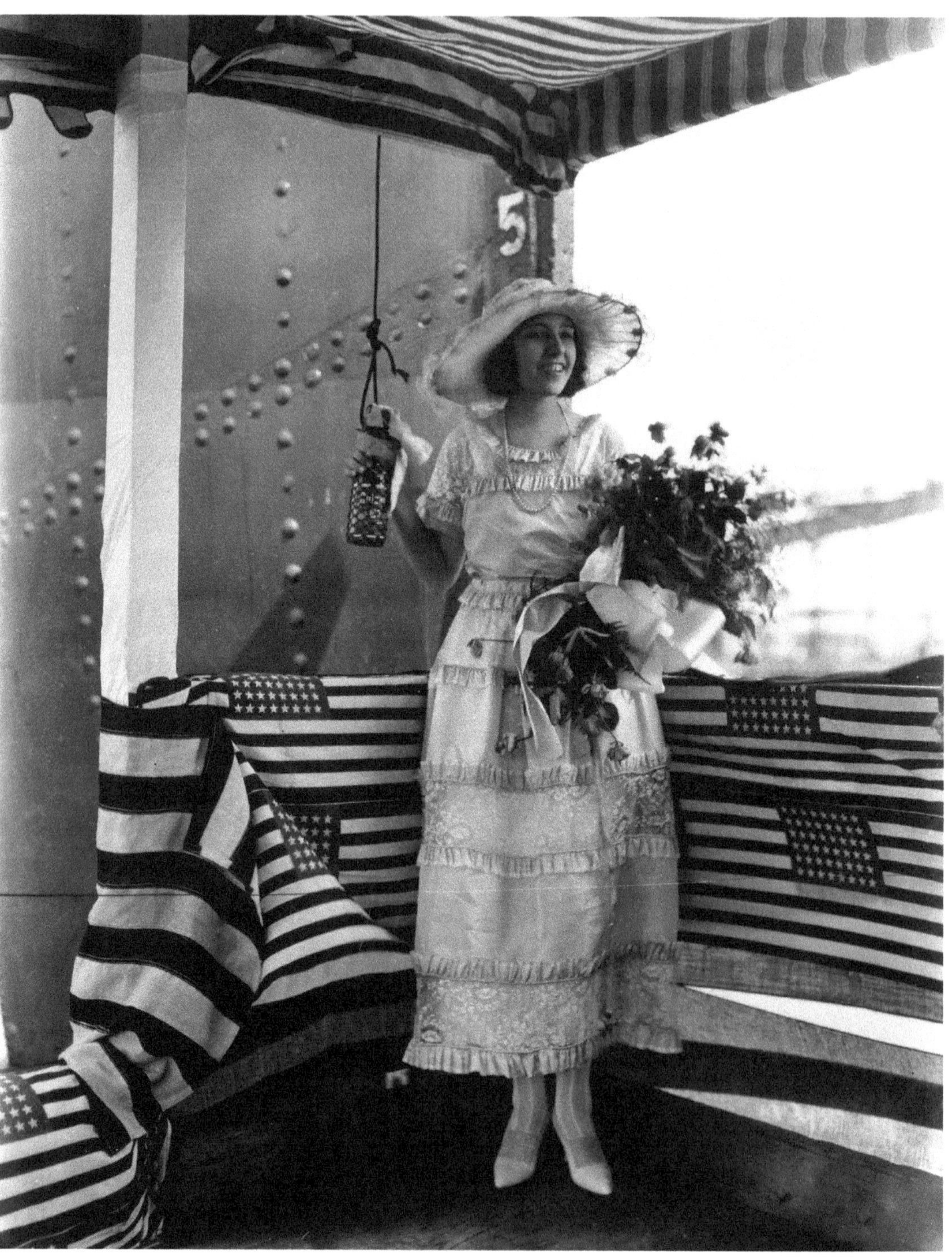

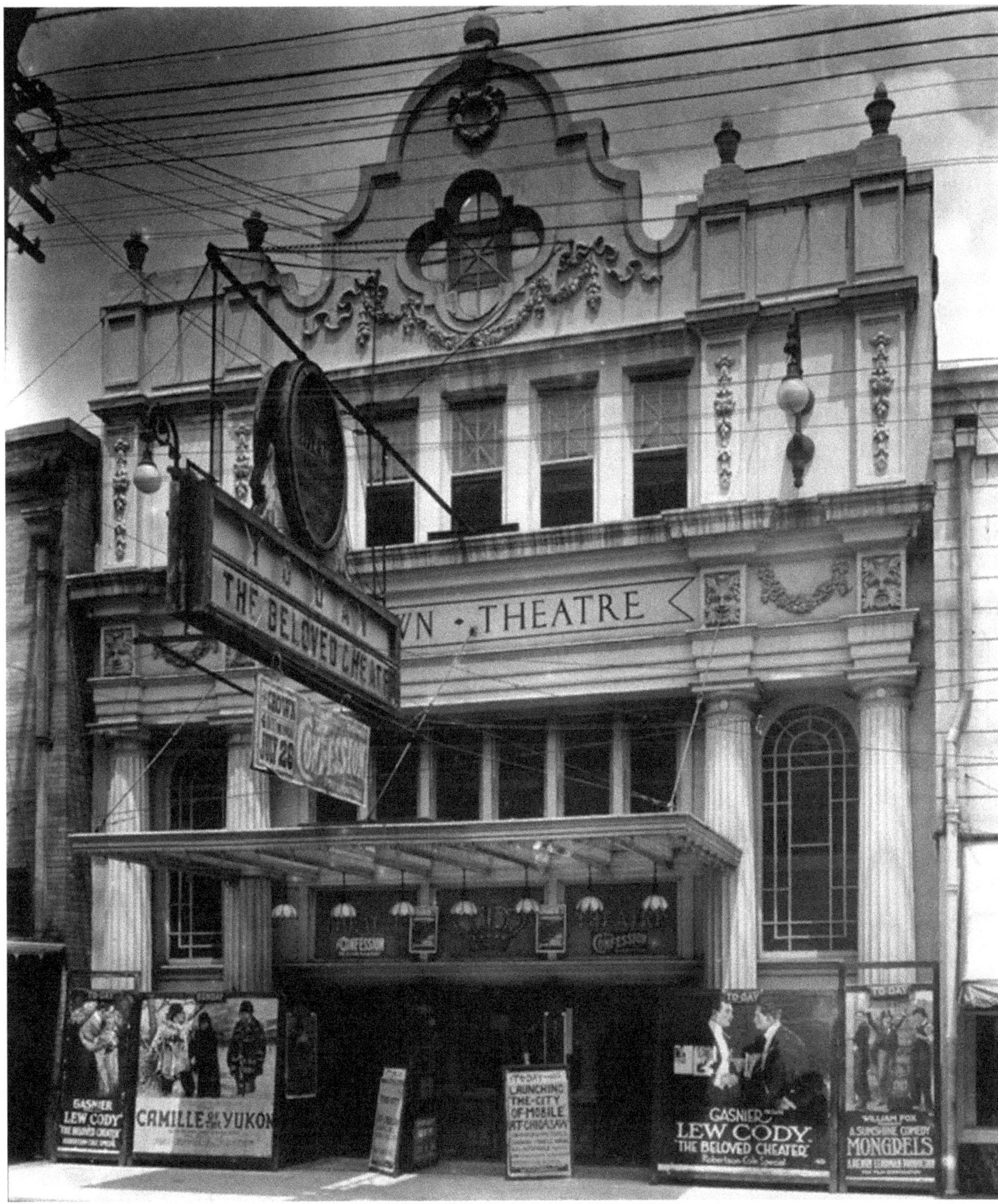

Mobilians could go to the Crown Theatre on Dauphin Street and watch footage of the *City of Mobile* launching from the Chickasaw shipyard, and, as the sign proclaims, an automobile parade and "other interesting scenes."

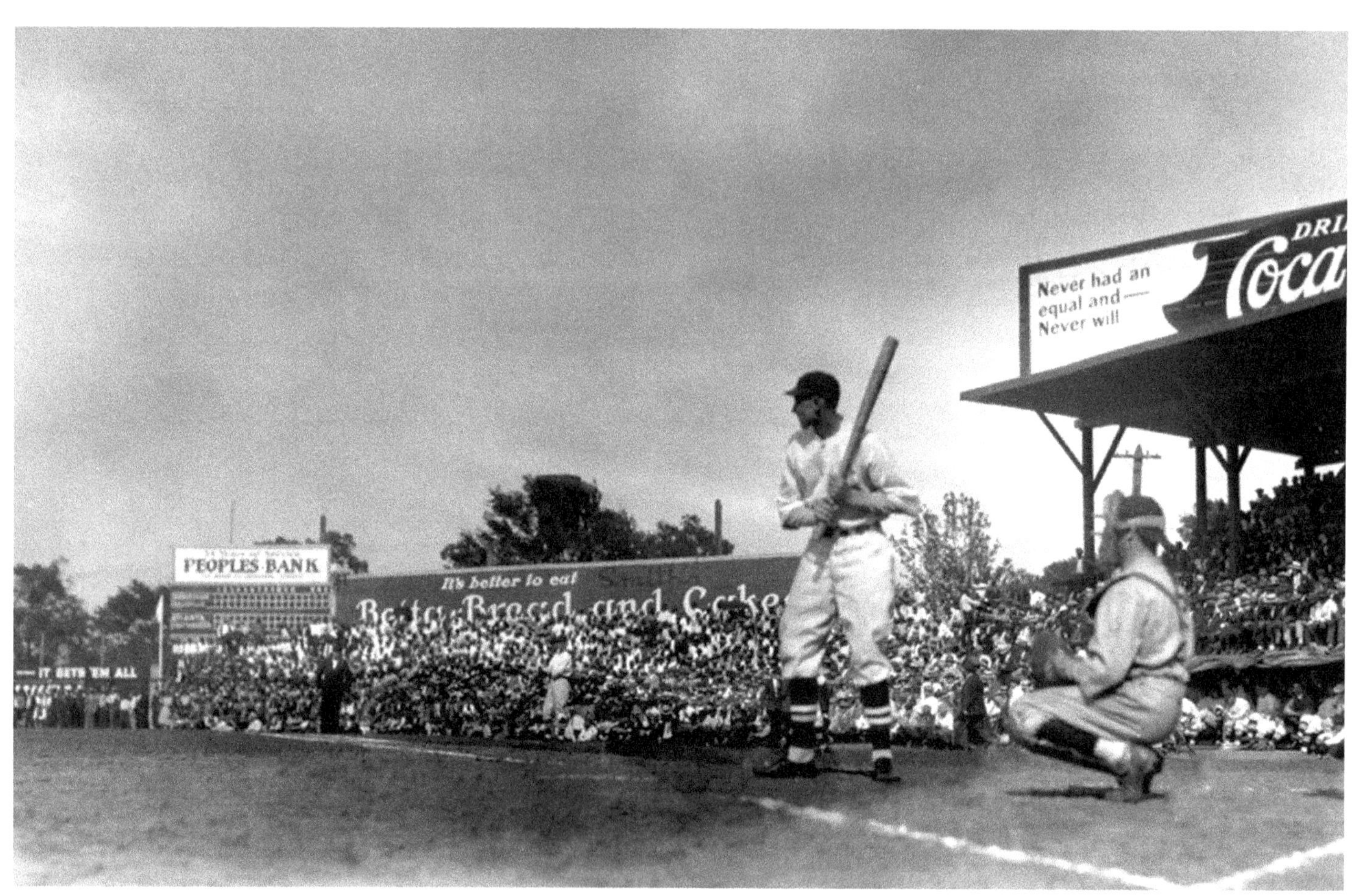

Mobilians enjoy a leisurely afternoon baseball game in Monroe Park. The park was destroyed during the 1926 hurricane and replaced with Hartwell Field, named in honor of Mayor Harry Hartwell, in 1927.

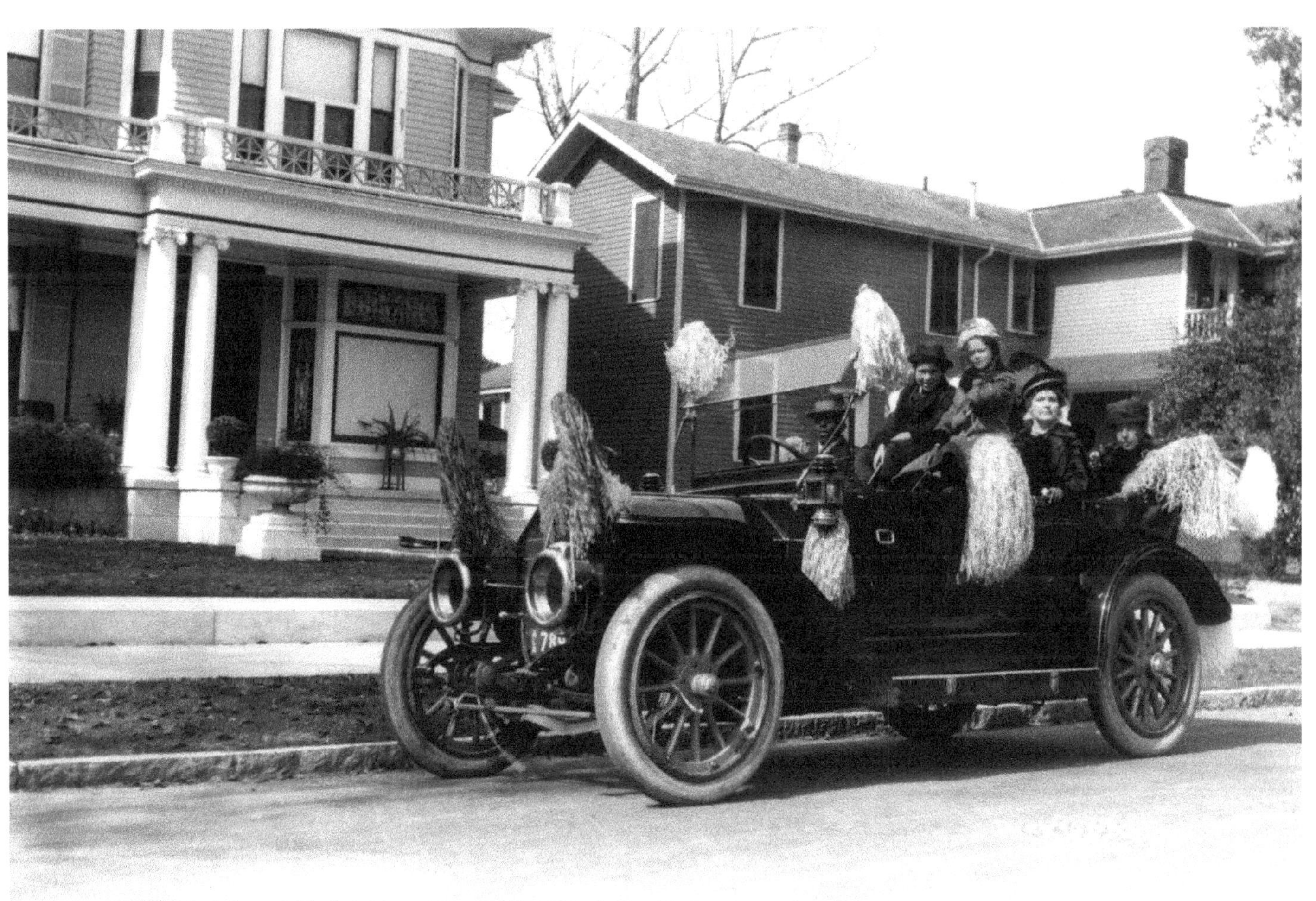

Bessie Morse Bellingrath—wife of local businessman and entrepreneur Walter Bellingrath—and relatives are seated in a car in front of their Ann Street home. Bellingrath's niece Alice Sackhoff (wearing the white hat) is seated behind her.

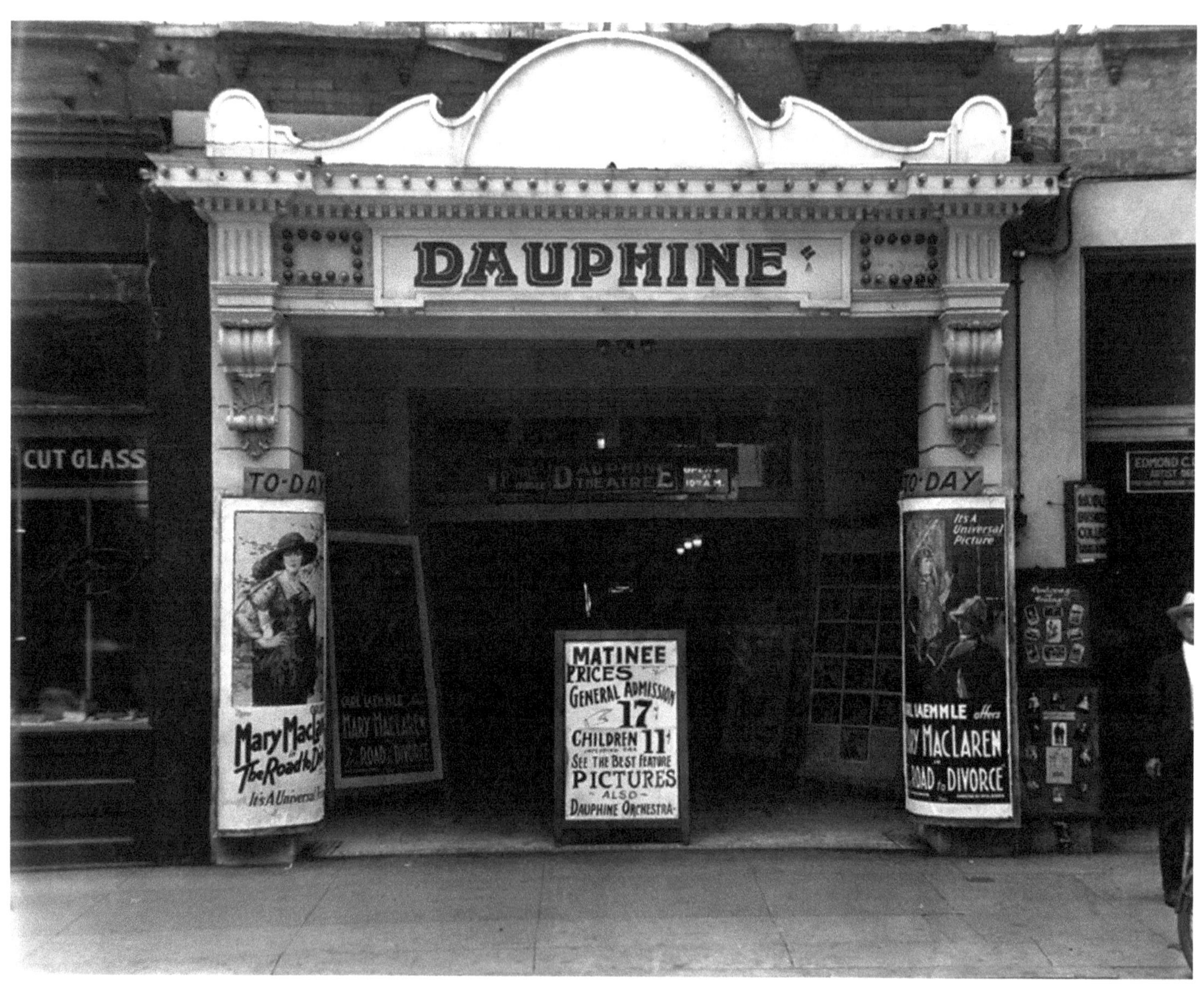

The entrance to the Dauphine Theatre, 1920. The theater underwent several name changes. In 1918 it was the Majestic and in 1922 it became the Bijou. Imagine paying 17 cents to see a movie! Mobile Business College stood to the immediate right.

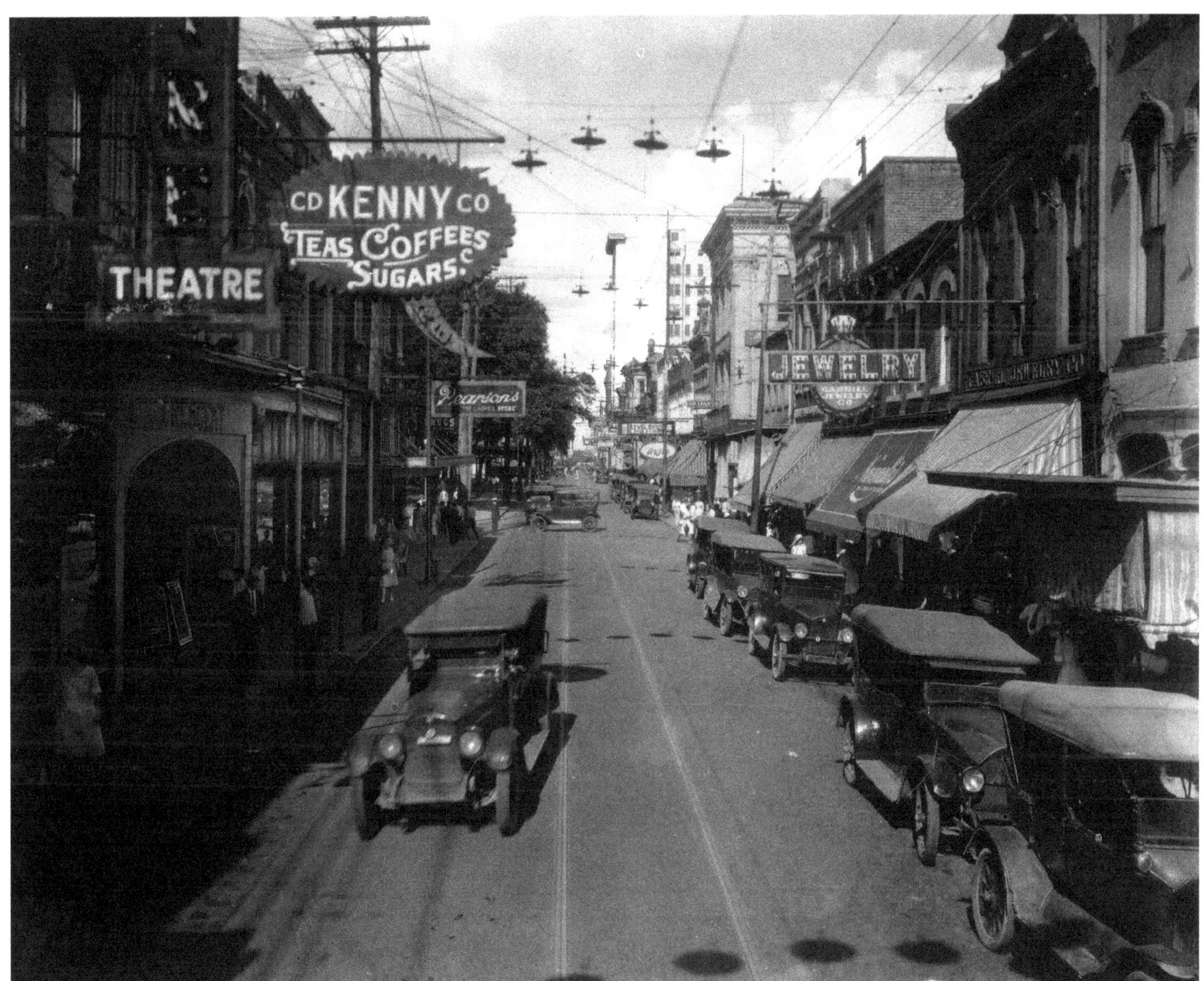

This image shows Dauphin Street to the east, between Joachim and Conception streets, about 1922. It was once the city's retail center. Farther down the street, on the right, were at least three shoe stores, including Simon's Shoes and Level Best Shoe Store.

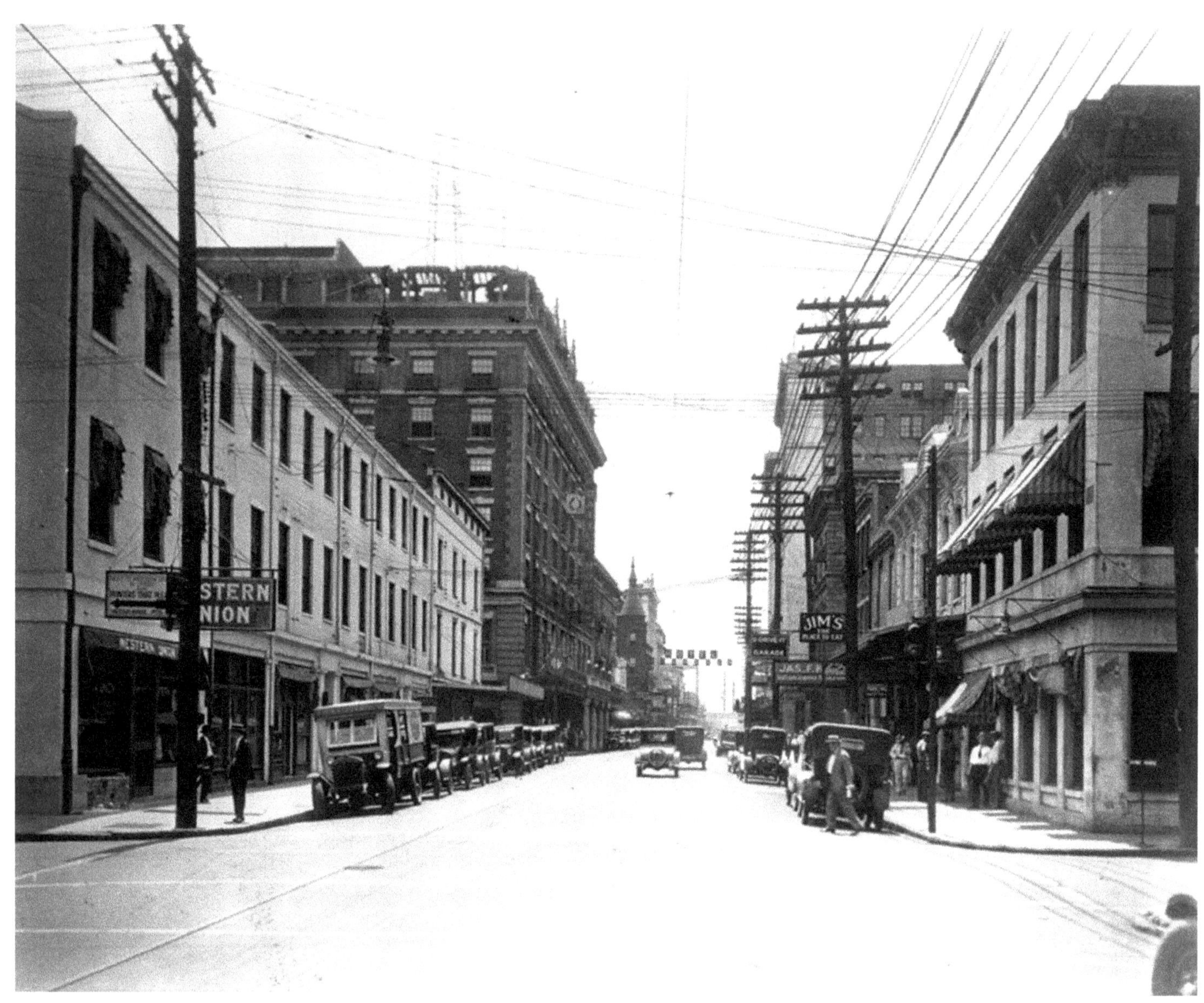

Royal Street viewed to the south shows the Western Union office, the Battle House Hotel, and Jim's Restaurant, "The Place to Eat."

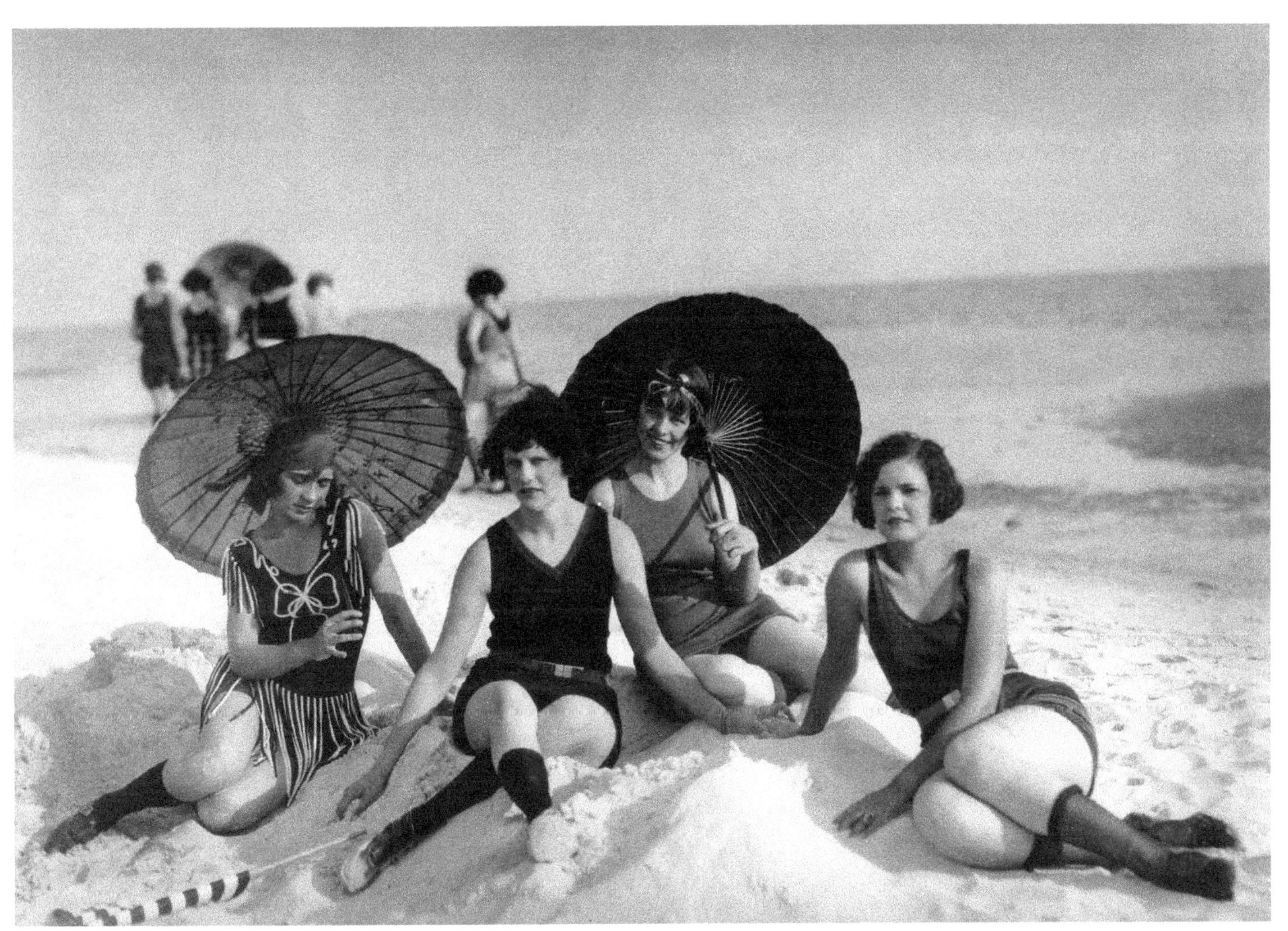

Eric Overbey was Mobile's preeminent photographer and captured images not only of the city but also of the surrounding area, including these 1923 beauty pageant contestants on Biloxi Beach.

The Curtis Feed Company cleverly used the checkerboard theme of the Ralston Purina Company to highlight its business (ca. 1920).

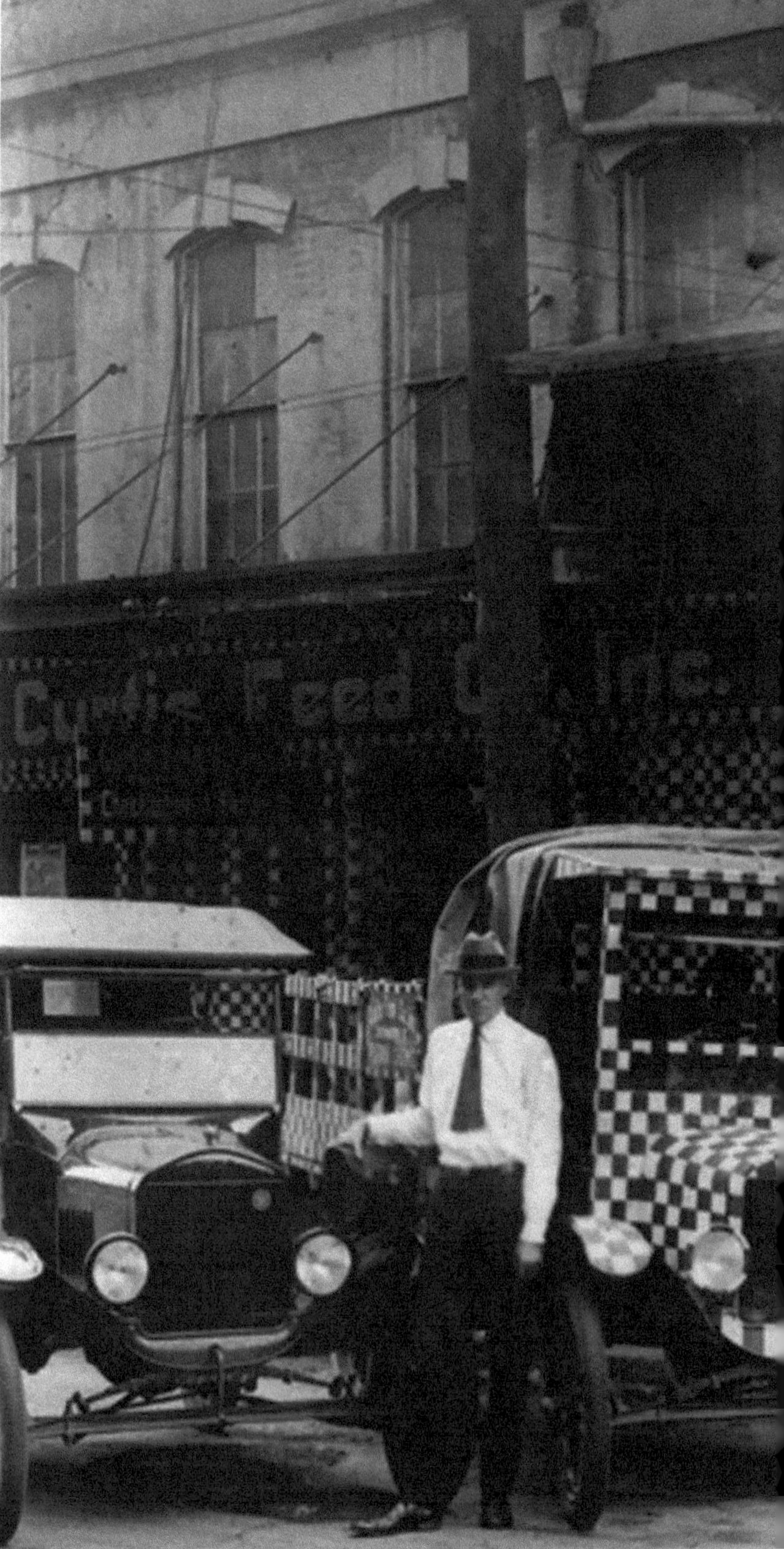

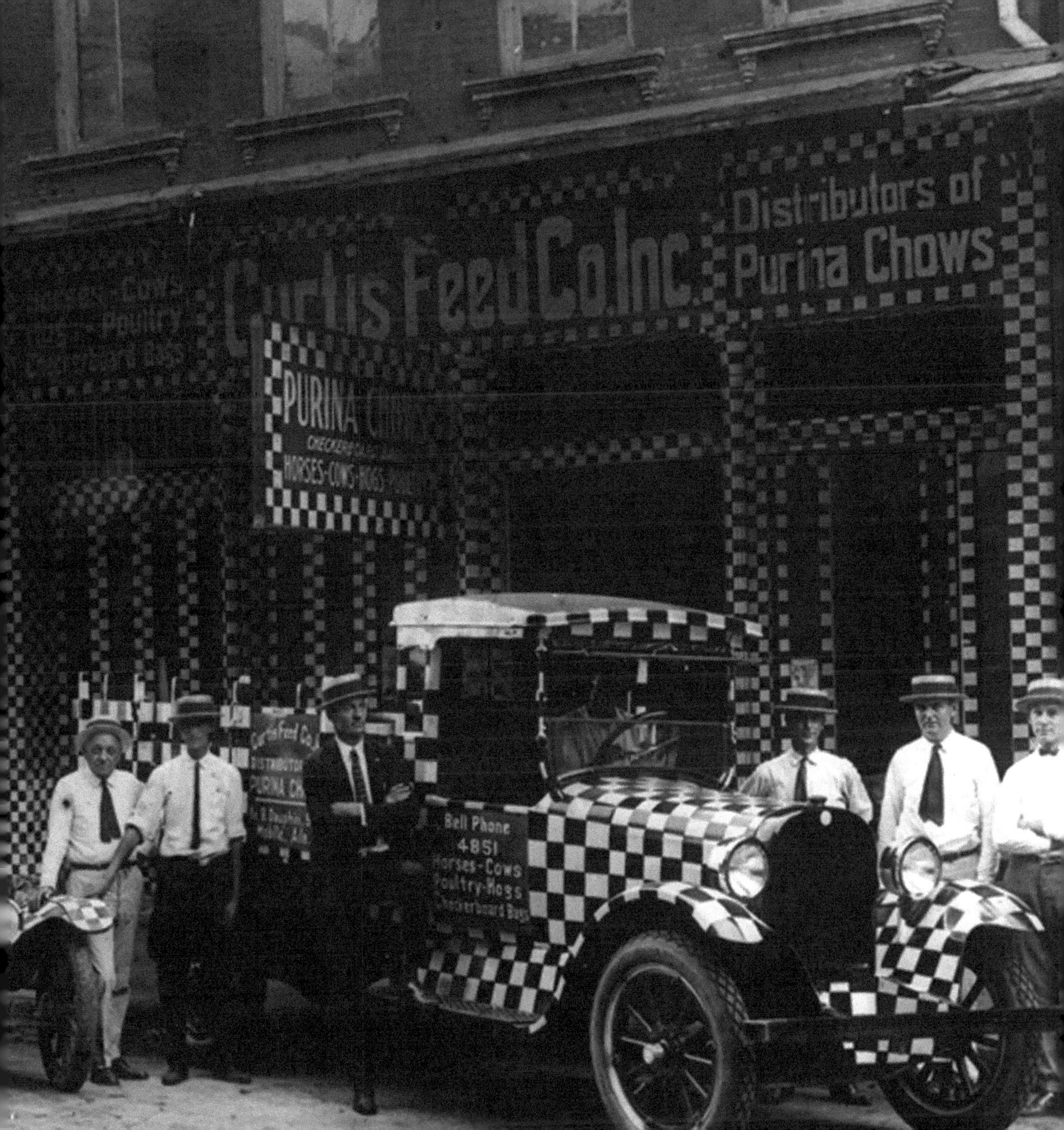

Distributors of
Purina Chows
Feed Co. Inc
Bell Phone
4851

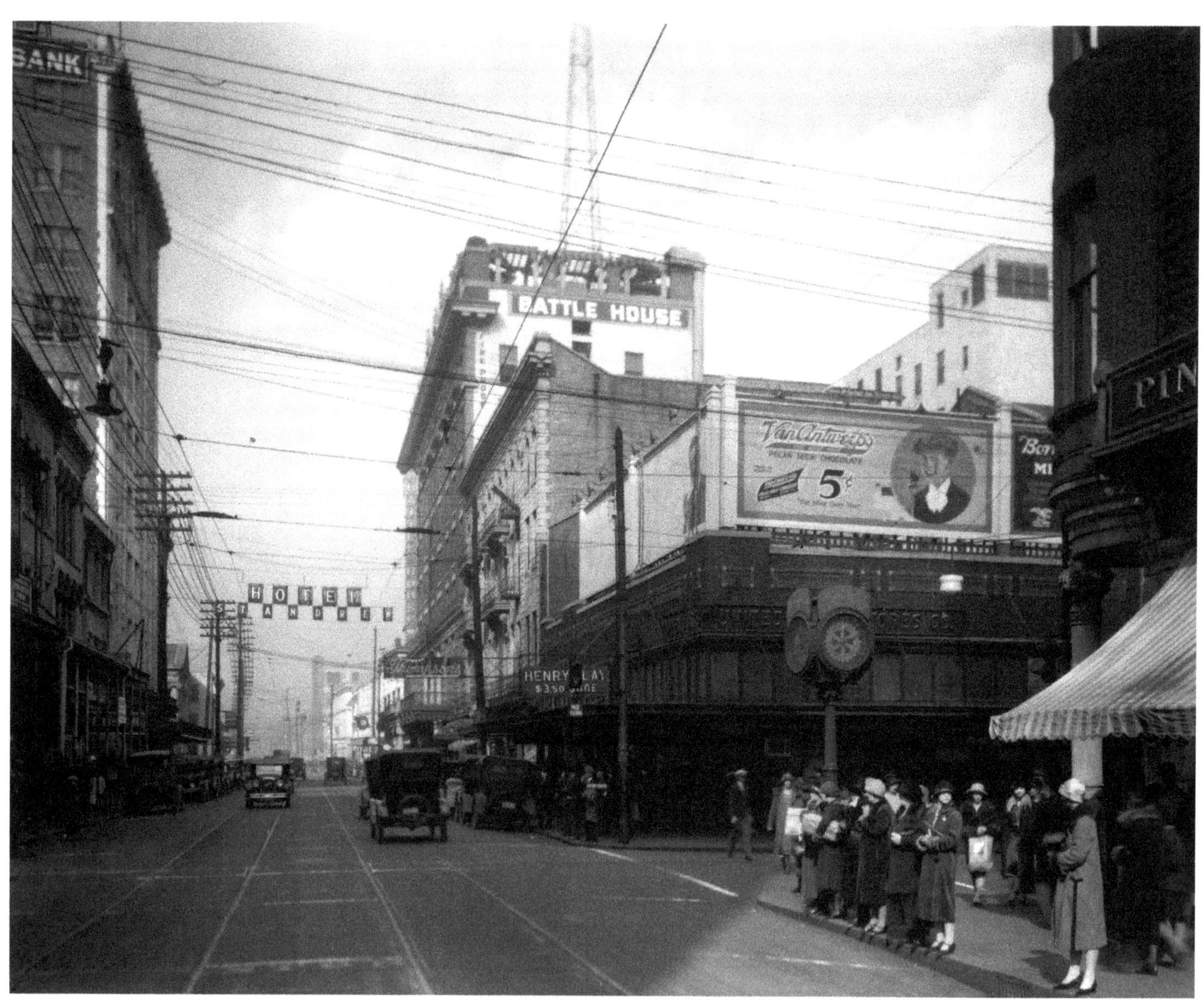

Royal Street at Conti, looking north (ca. 1925).

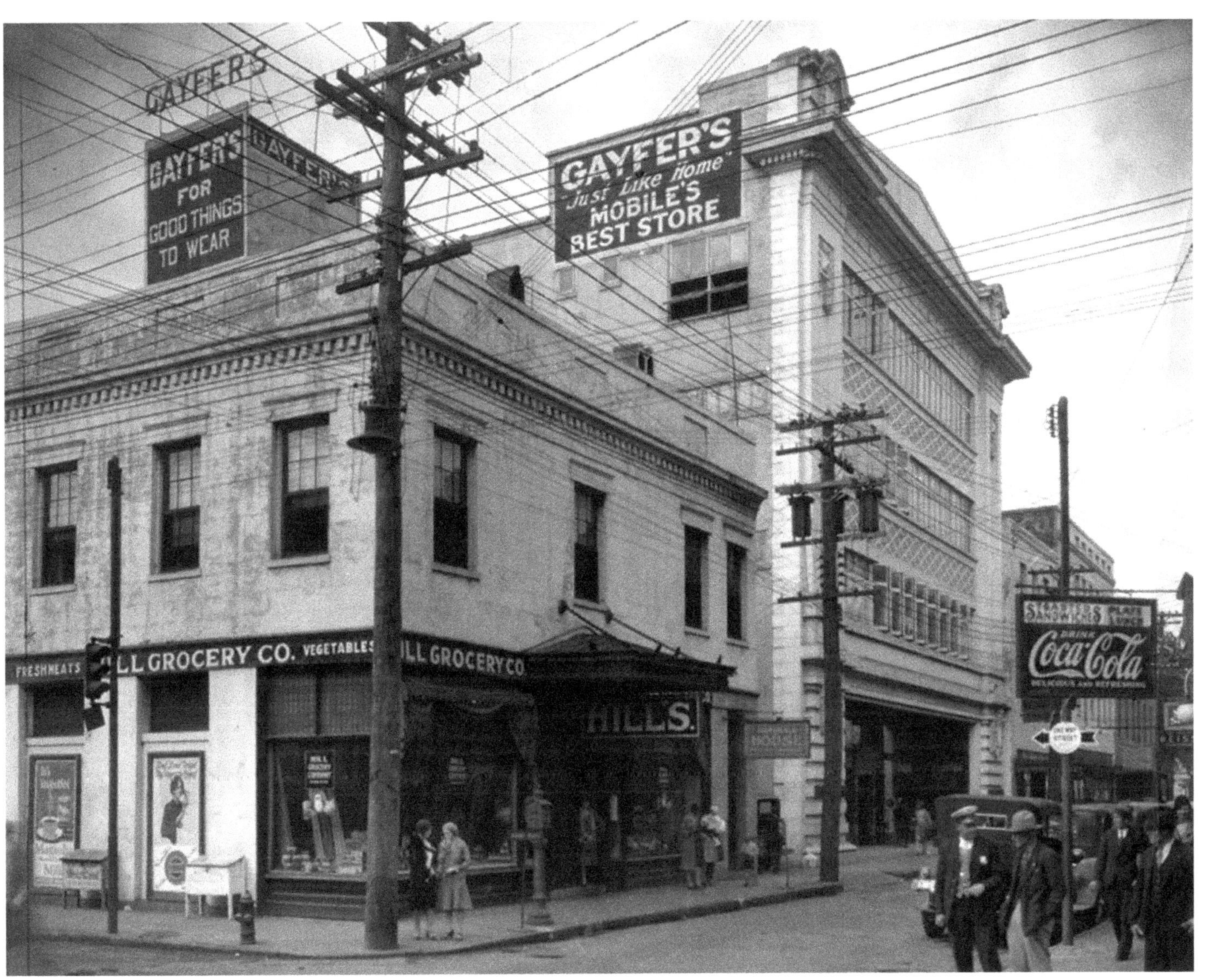

Saint Emanuel Street, looking north to Dauphin from Conti in 1929. Hill's Grocery Company is on the corner, just south of the homegrown Gayfer's Department Store.

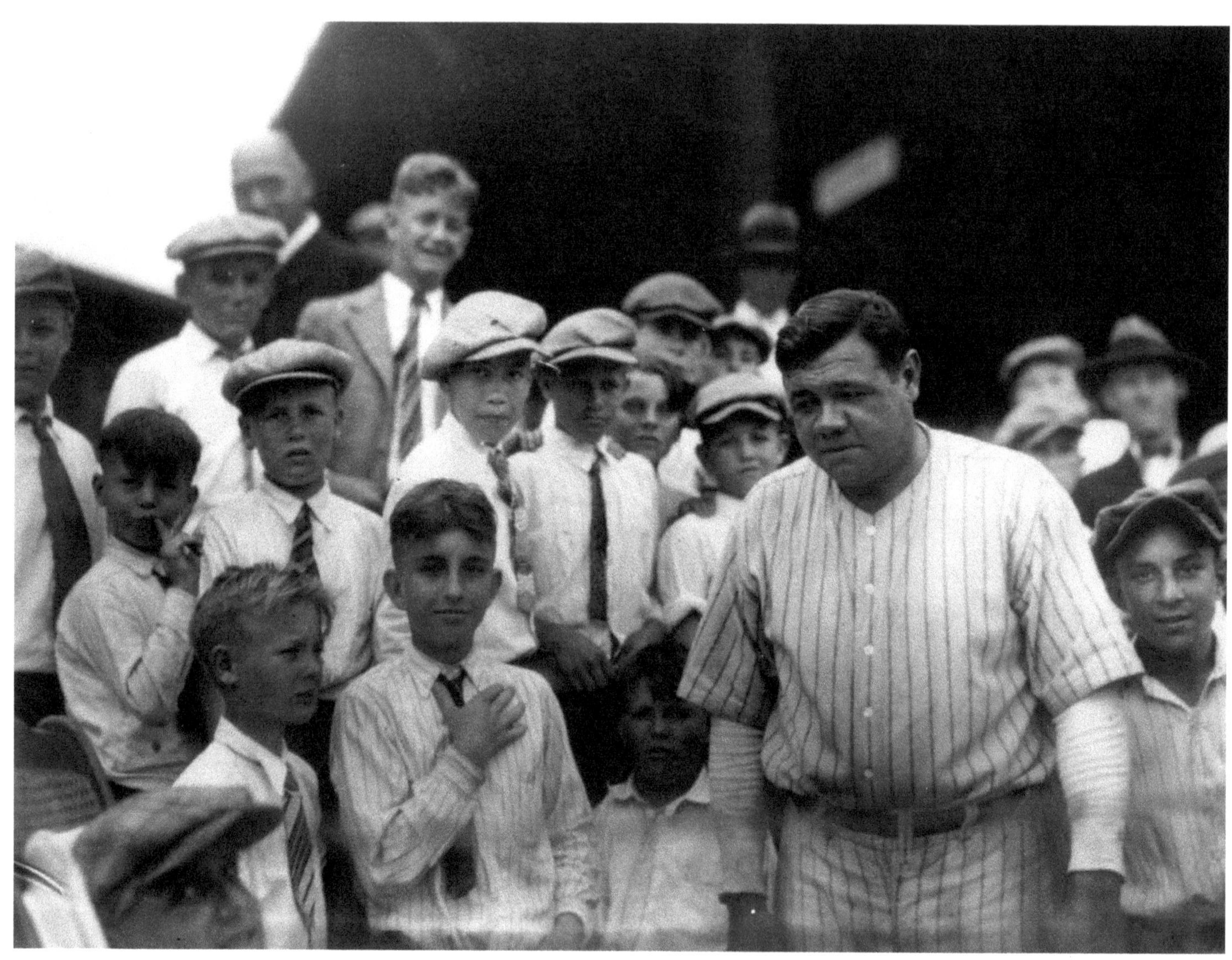

Babe Ruth and the New York Yankees came to Mobile several times in the 1920s to play exhibition games. Here, the "Sultan of Swat" meets some of his younger fans. An orphan himself, Ruth usually took time out of his schedule to visit the local Catholic Boys Home.

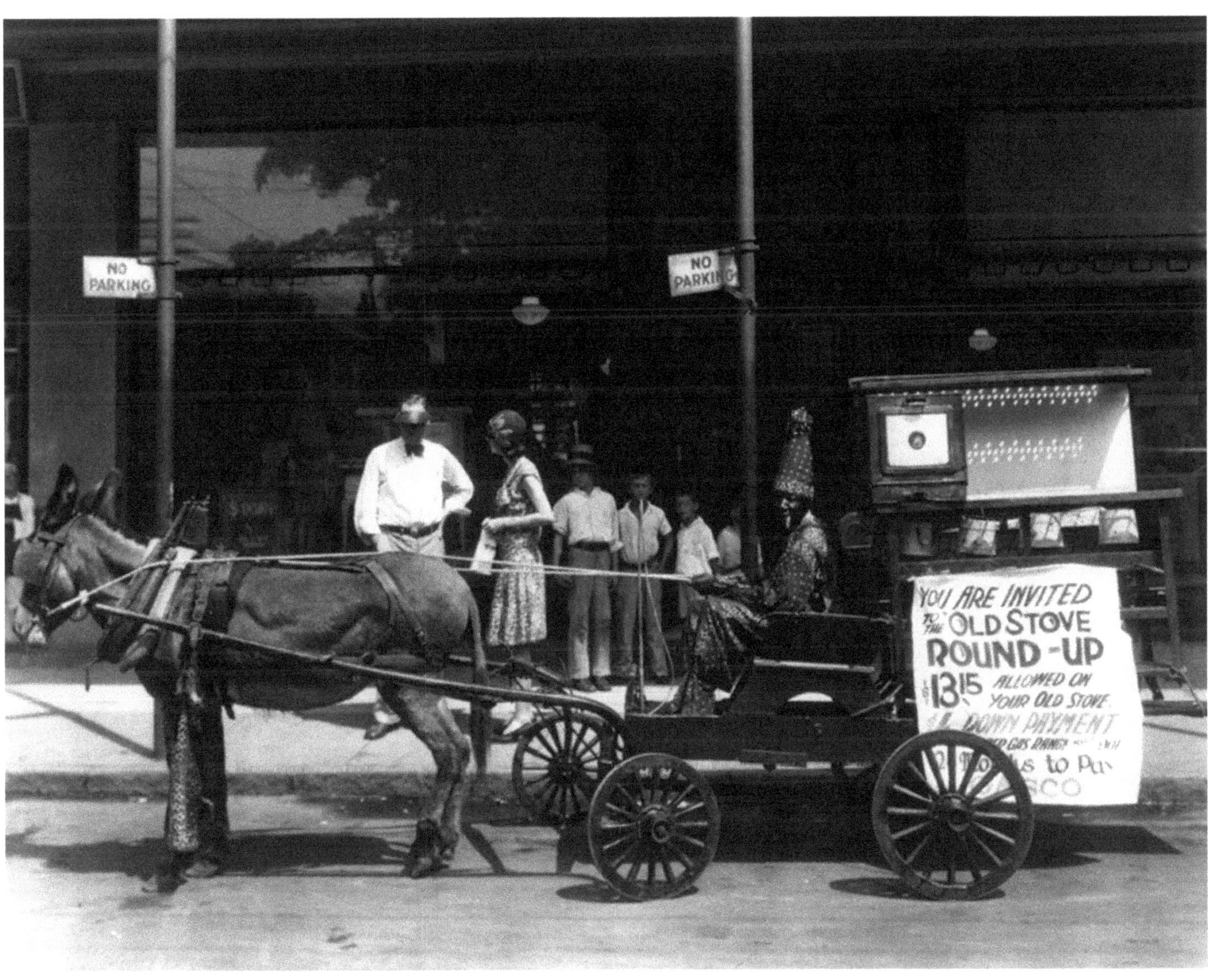

The annual "old stove round-up" was a promotional parade and sales event sponsored by the Mobile Gas Company. This one most likely took place in the 1920s. A clown driving a mule-drawn carriage draws a sign reading "You are invited to the Old Stove Round-Up. $13.15 allowed on your old stove. $1 down payment . . . 12 months to pay."

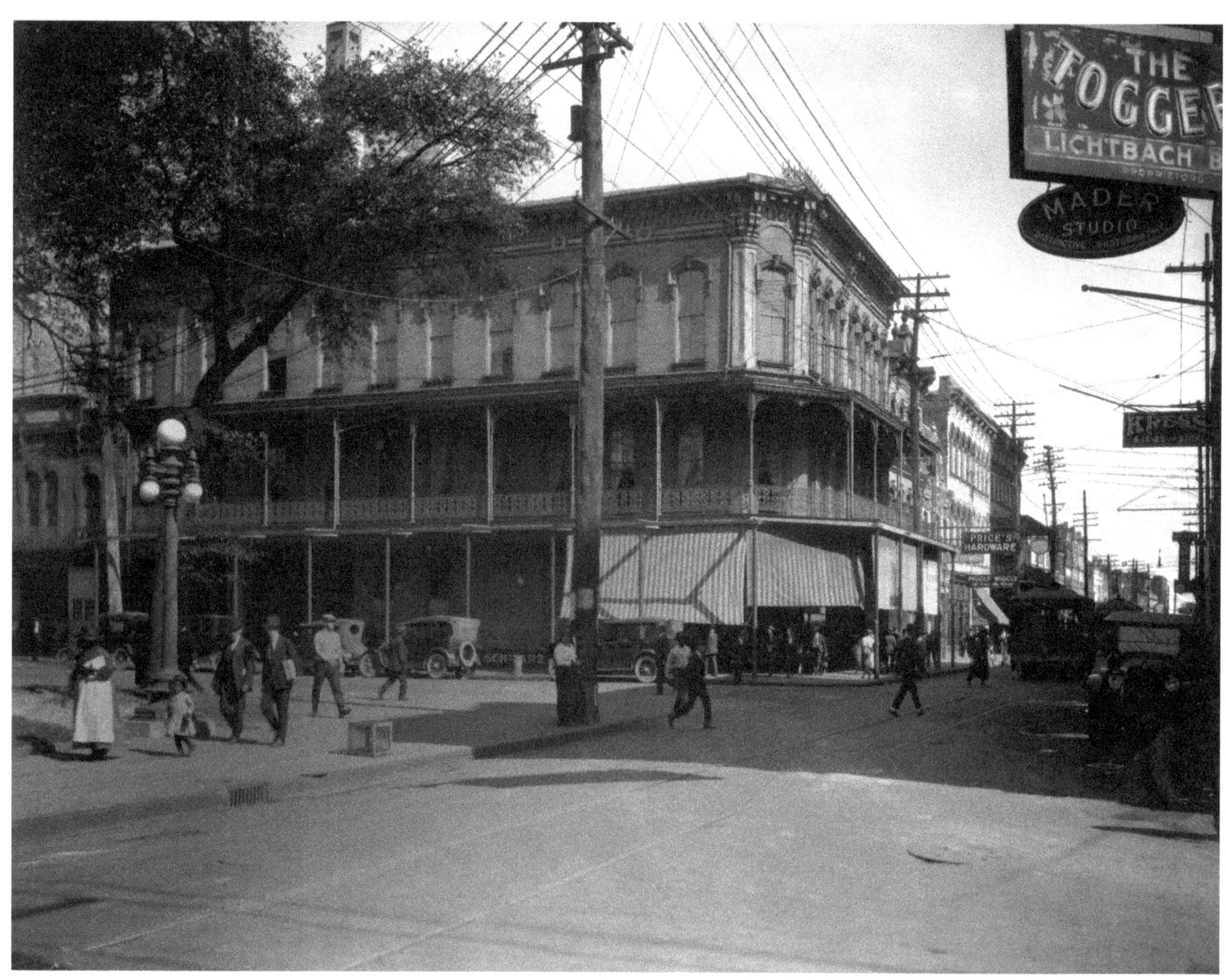

Dauphin Street at St. Joseph, looking east about 1920. A corner of Bienville Square is visible at lower-left.

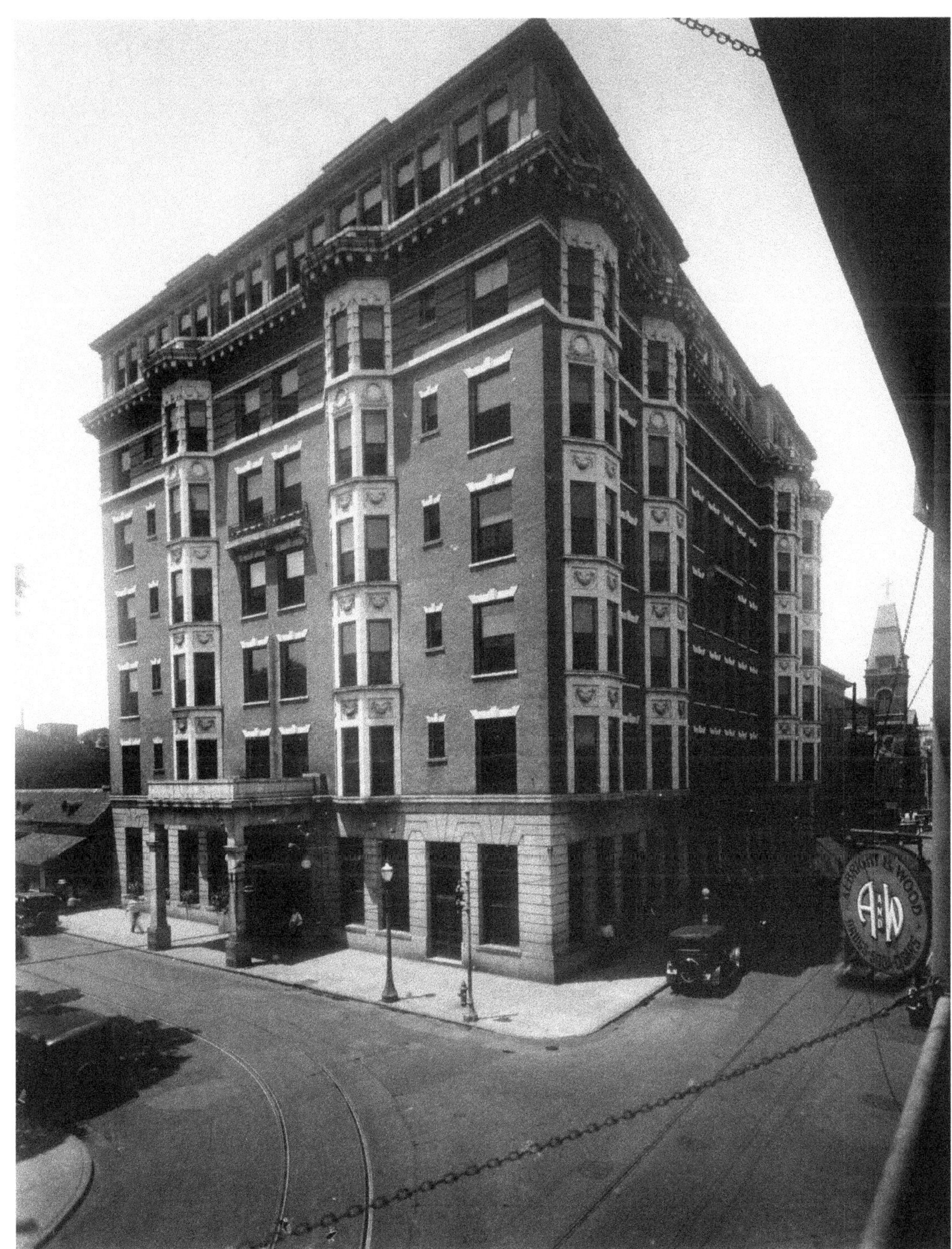

The Cawthon Hotel was built in 1906 using a steel frame and reinforced concrete. Atop the hotel was a glass-enclosed garden for dances and banquets. In 1927—about the time this image was taken—the celebrated evangelist Billy Sunday stayed at the hotel while holding a series of religious revivals.

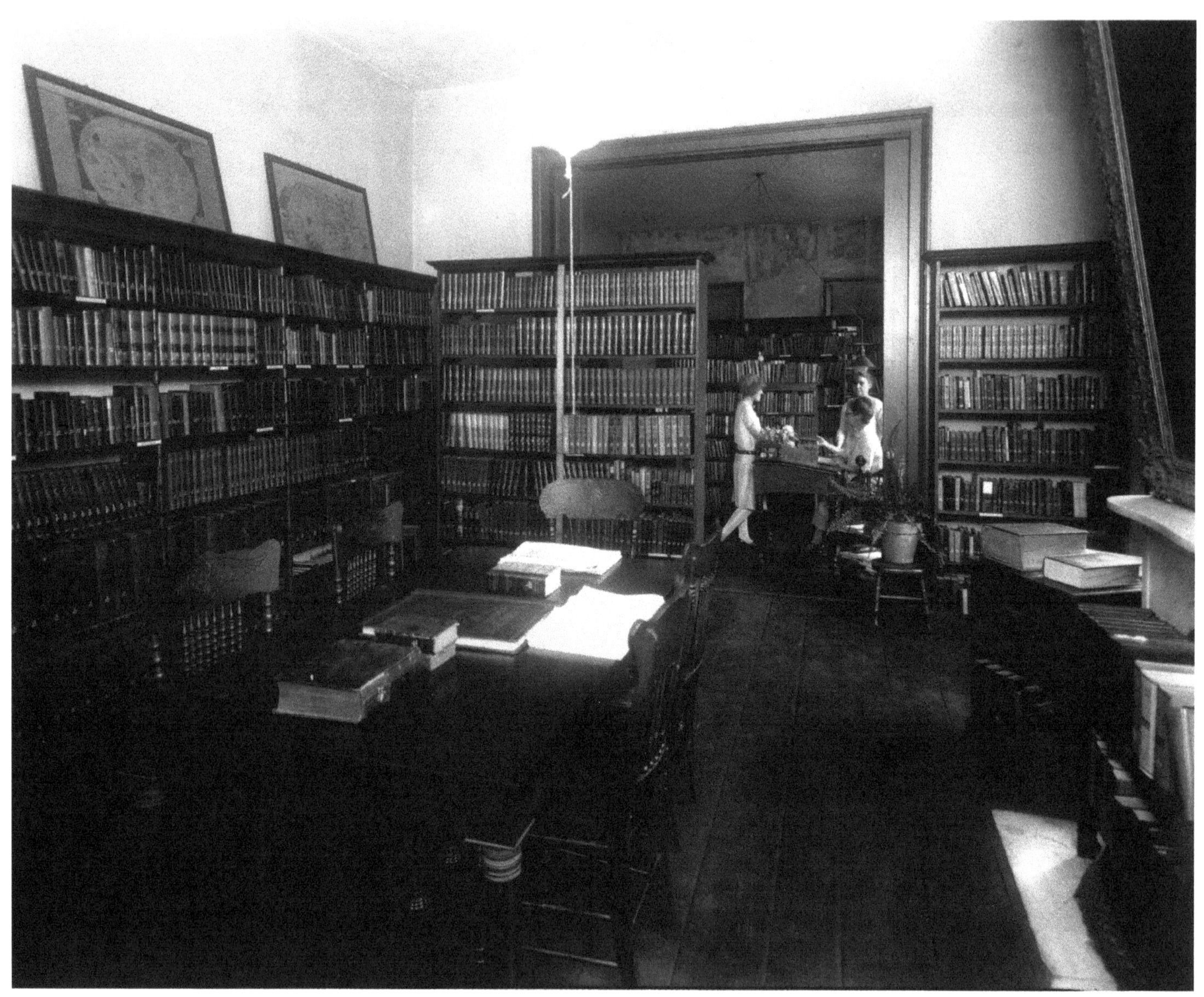

The interior of the old Mobile Public Library, which stood on Conti Street until the present building was constructed in 1928.

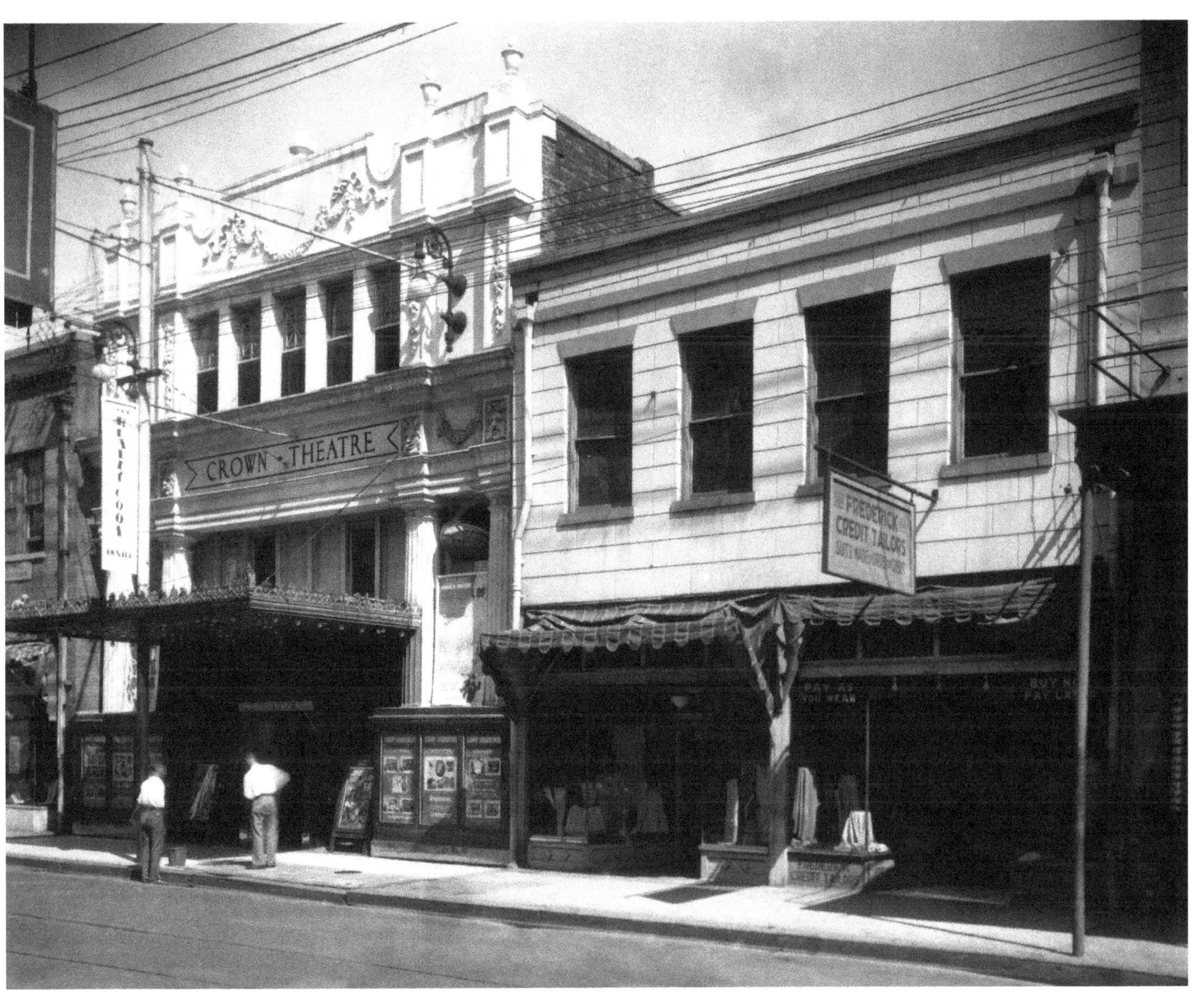

The north side of Dauphin Street between Joachim and Jackson in 1928. The Crown Theatre, shown on the left, enticed moviegoers inside with a sign reading "It's really cool inside."

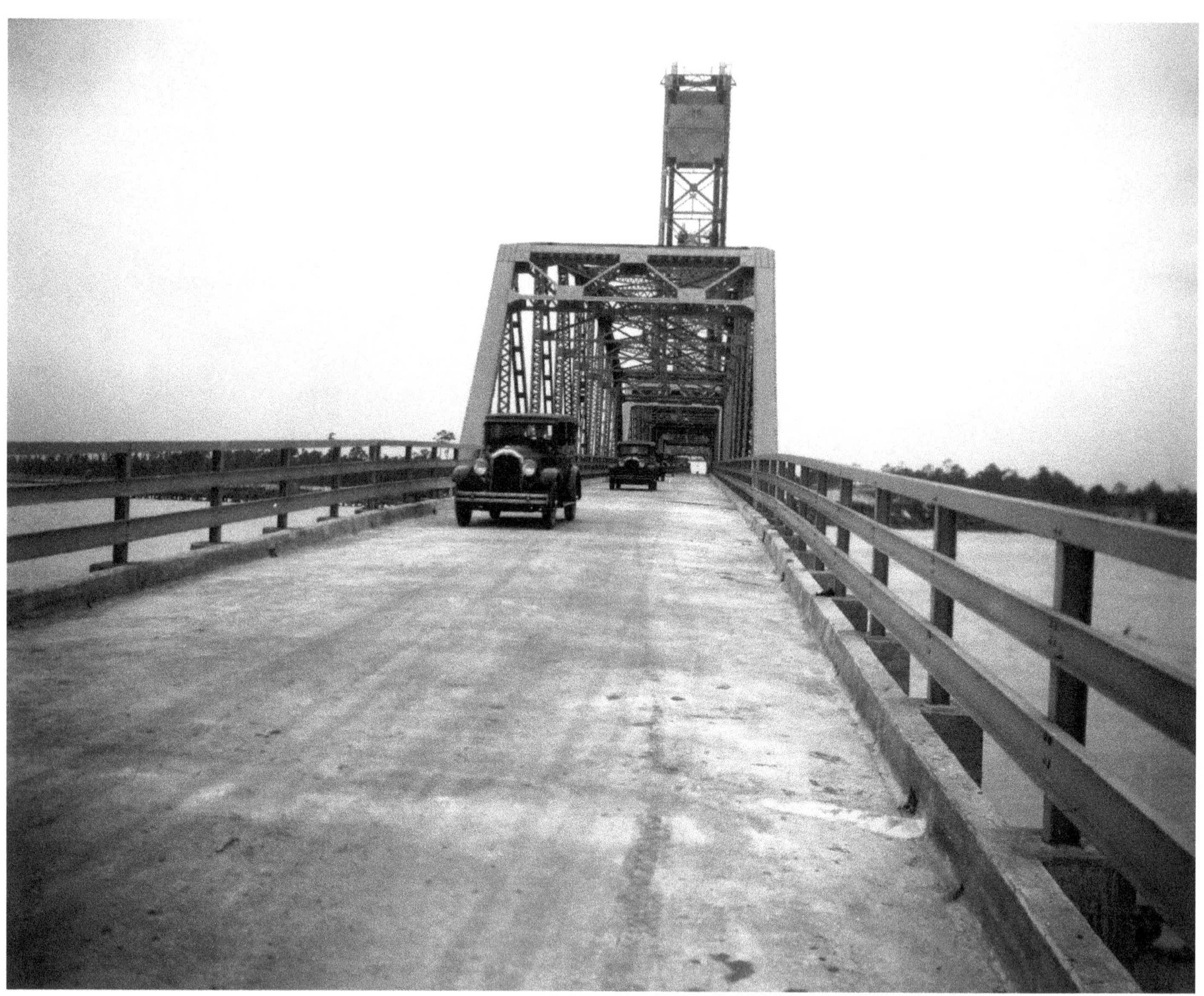

Cars crossing the Cochrane Bridge around 1928. Before it was completed in 1927, the only way across the Mobile River and to the Eastern Shore of Baldwin County was by boat.

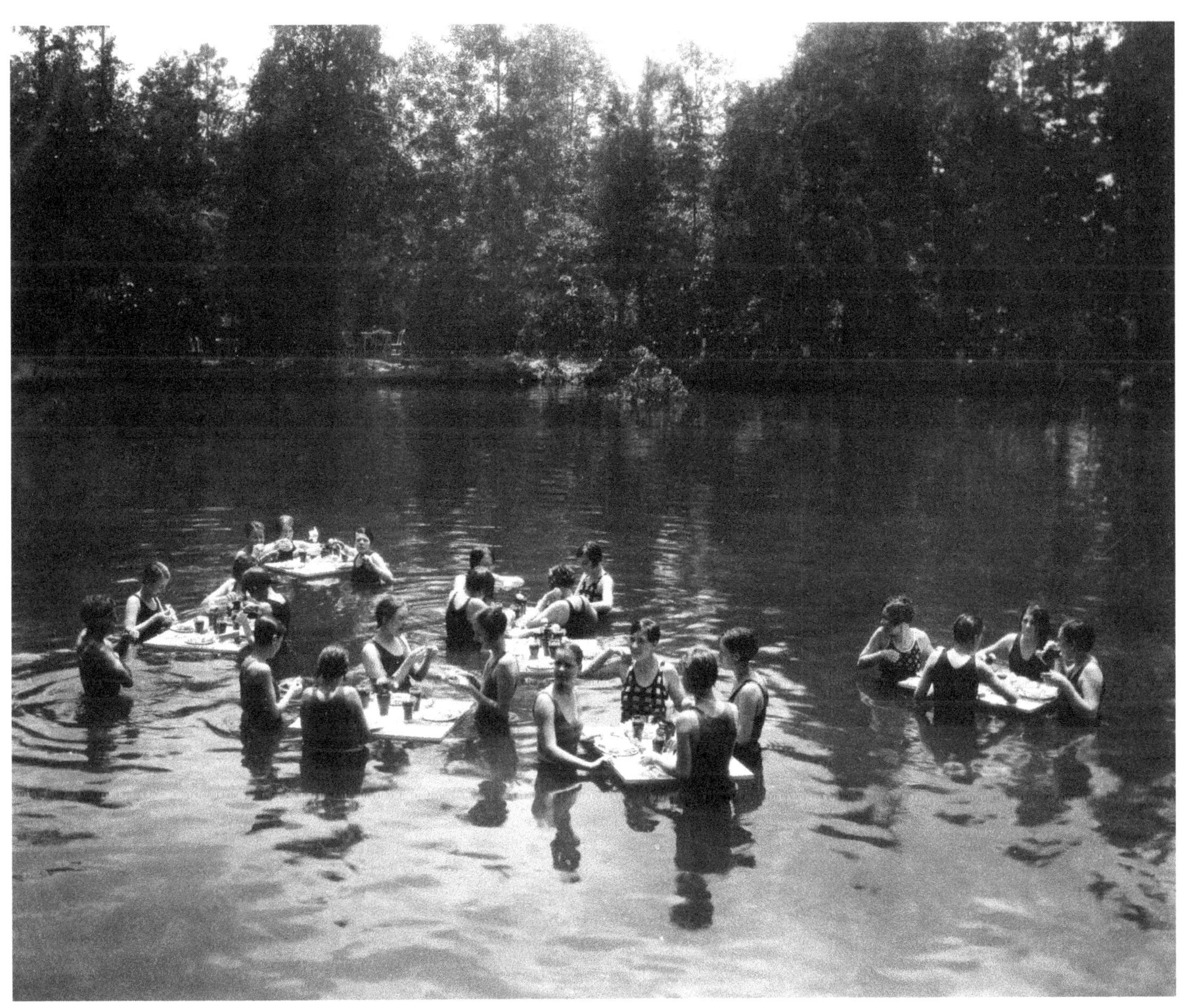

In 1926, people found creative ways to beat Mobile's hot summers. Why not throw a party at the same time?

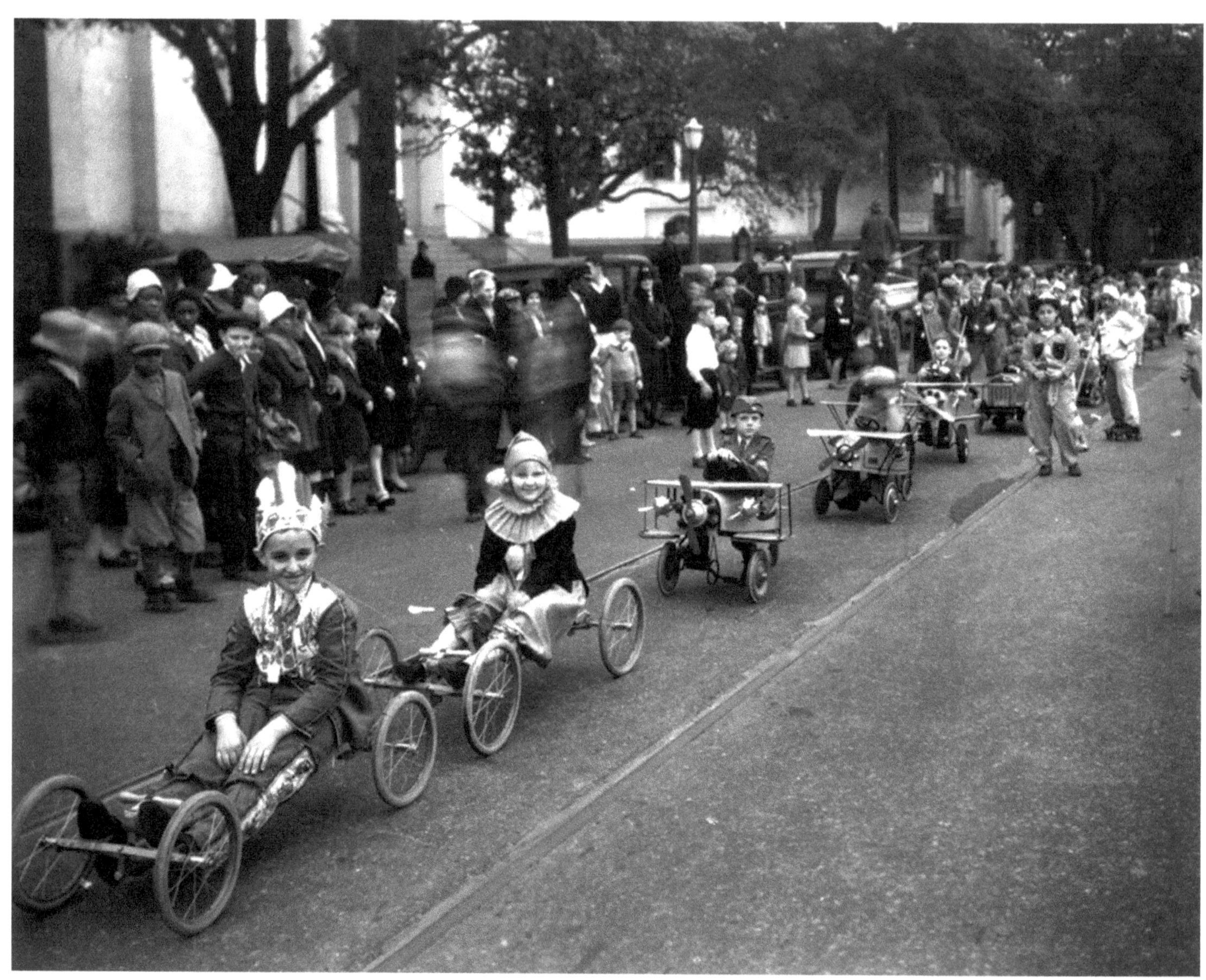

As a means of advertising and promotion, the Reiss Mercantile Company sponsored this holiday parade in 1927, which featured children riding the latest in toys.

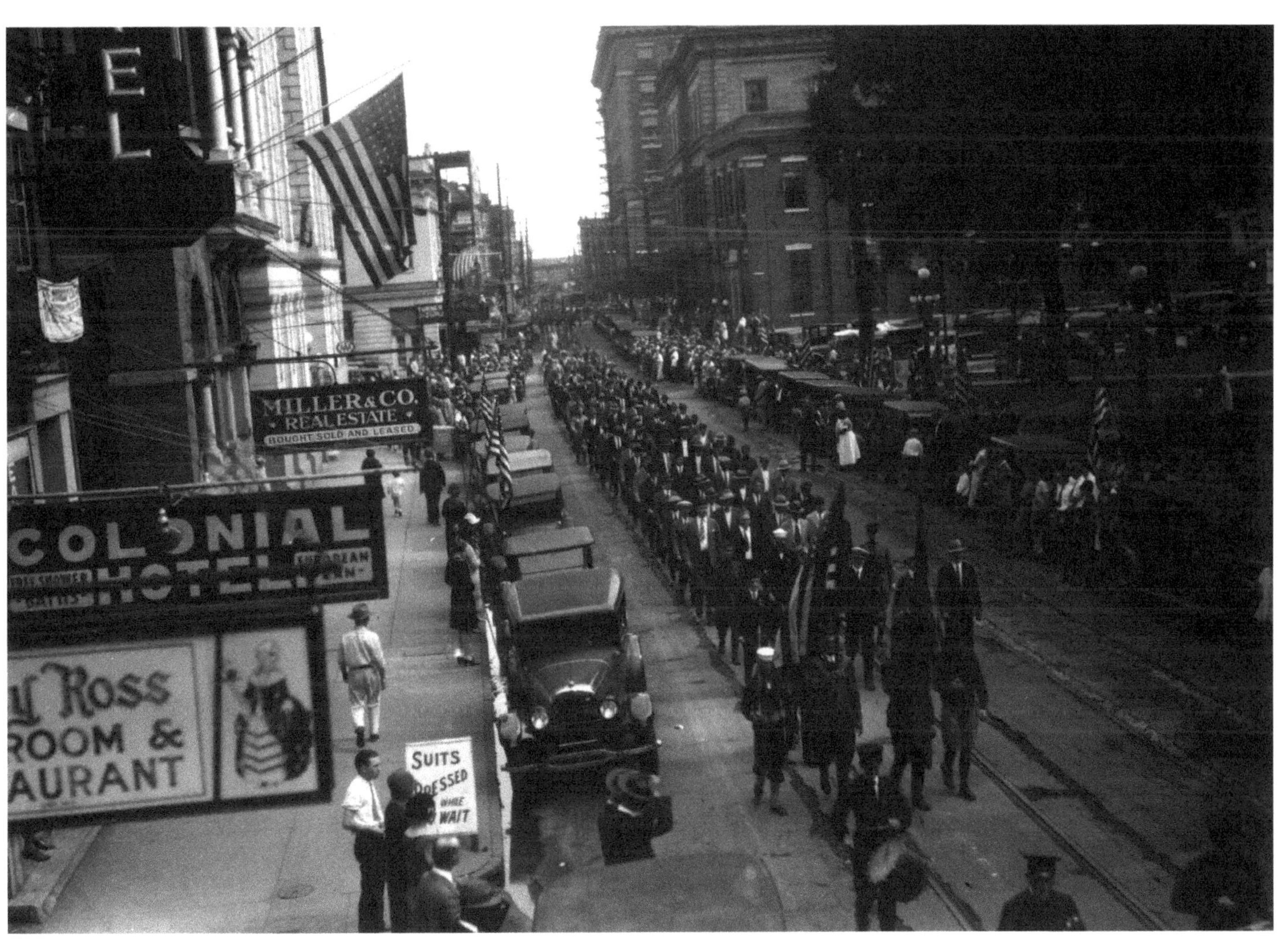

Marchers parade up St. Francis Street as a crowd looks on (ca. 1928). The reason for the procession is unclear, but it may have been a July 4th event featuring veterans of the Great War.

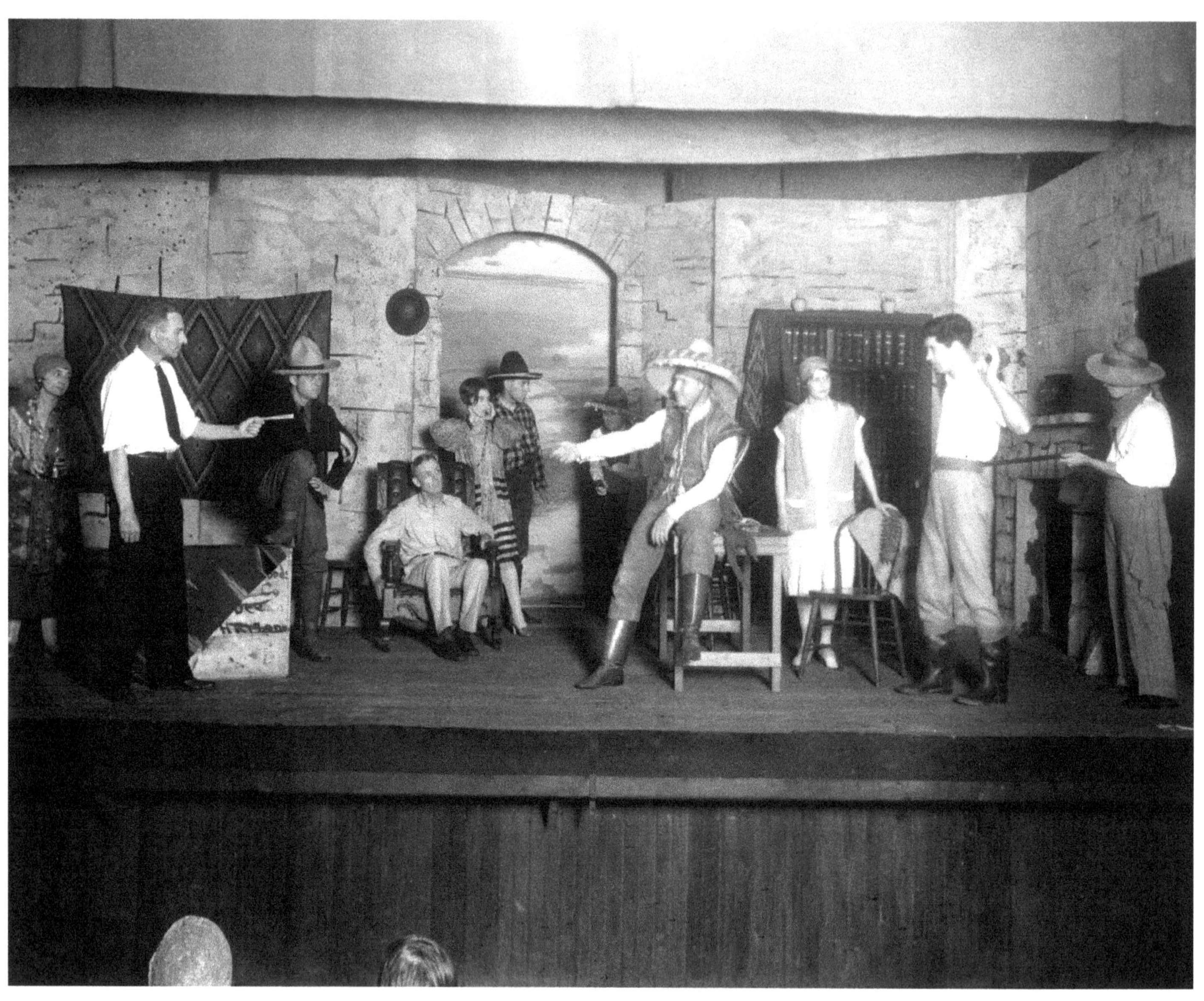

The Little Theatre, predecessor of the Joe Jefferson Players, performing the play *The Bad Man,* a Porter Browne story about a Mexican bandit.

New Deal Mobile

(1930–1939)

As the 1930s opened, Mobilians, like citizens of every other place in America, faced hard times. Many people lost jobs or could not find work. Those least able to withstand the financial loss—the city's African-Americans—were usually the first to be dismissed. Families were forced to economize, to share living space, to tighten their belts, and to grow their own food. Sadly, as the decade wore on, Mobile lost more than jobs. Its people dismantled the charming ironwork that adorned homes and businesses and sold it off as scrap metal to the nations that they would soon face in World War II.

All was not bleak, however, either for the city's whites or its blacks. In 1934, the Southern Association of Colleges and Schools accredited all-black Mobile County Training School. This accomplishment was unique in the South and successful largely through the efforts of Benjamin Baker, the school's principal. Economically, Mobile fared better than some other cities. For one thing, its principal commodities—cotton and timber—were not as vulnerable to market forces as were steel and automobiles. For another, the federal government, under the direction of Franklin Roosevelt, stepped in with "alphabet-soup programs"—so called because they became known by letter abbreviations such as CCC—to help many in the city. One of those programs, the Works Progress Administration, built the Bankhead Tunnel (begun in 1938), cleared Three Mile Creek, and constructed Fort Whiting Auditorium (completed in 1938). Through the WPA, men and women were put to work making toys, clothes, and mattresses, all to be distributed to needy families.

Other bright spots appeared on Mobile's horizon as well. By 1936 travelers no longer had to pay the toll to cross the Cochrane Bridge, which increased traffic—economic and otherwise—between the city and points east. Boosters like Walter Bellingrath and John Waterman devoted themselves to building a first-class steamship line, which for a time would be the nation's largest. International Paper Company, which had opened some years before, employed more Mobilians than any other business until the shipbuilding boom of World War II in the next decade.

Despite these positive efforts, money was tight and times were tough. Something had to change. And it did. The looming war did for Mobile what it did for other American cities: propelled it out of the Great Depression.

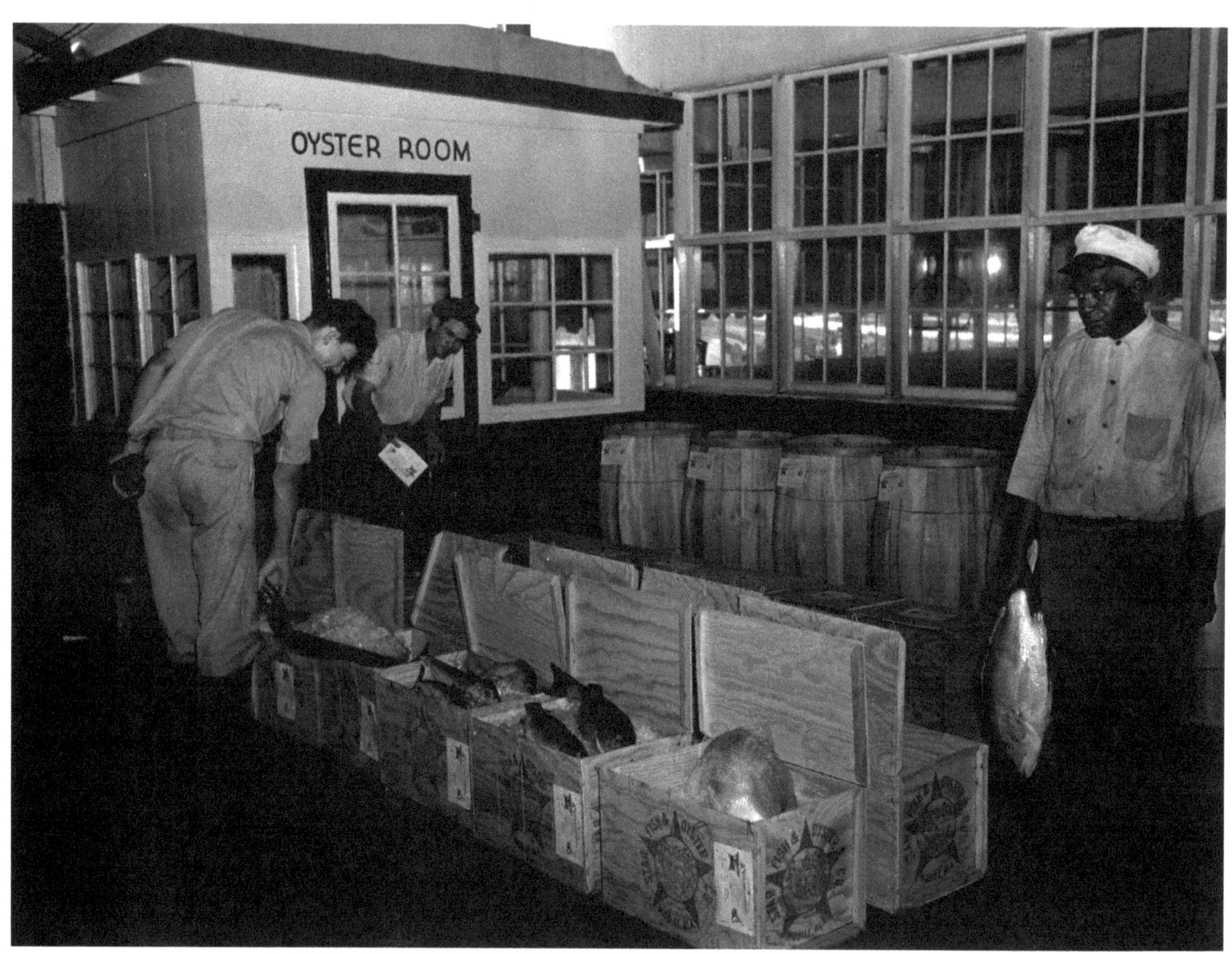

Men pack seafood with ice outside the Oyster Room at the Star Fish and Oyster Company about 1930. The company was founded in 1900 by Sebastian Gonzales and became one of the most successful commercial fishing concerns in the United States, running a fleet of schooners that brought in for sale each year hundreds of thousands of pounds of red snapper and other seafood.

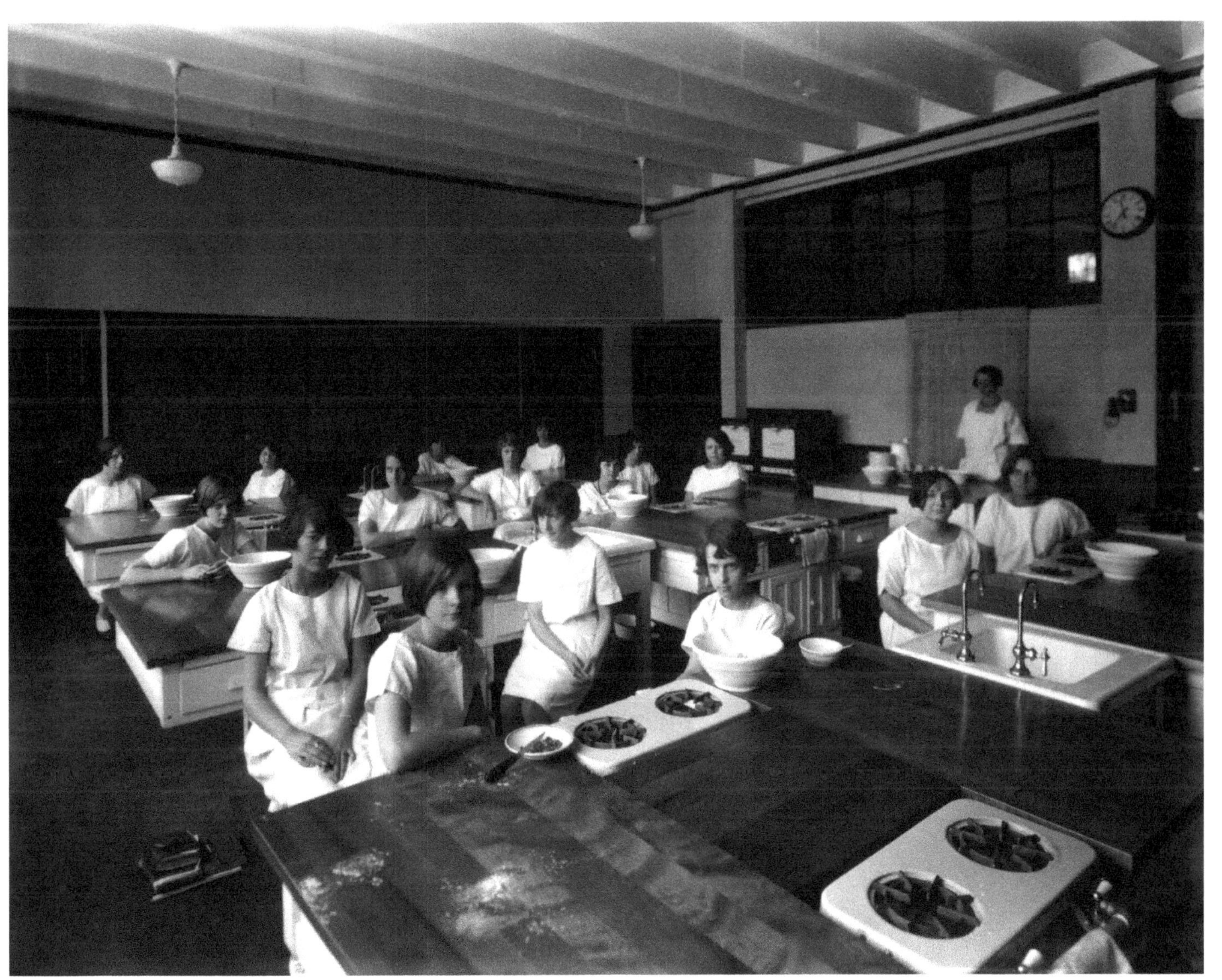

A home economics class at Mobile's Murphy High School.

Thick, black smoke billows skyward as the Alabama Naval Store at South Water and Virginia streets burns.

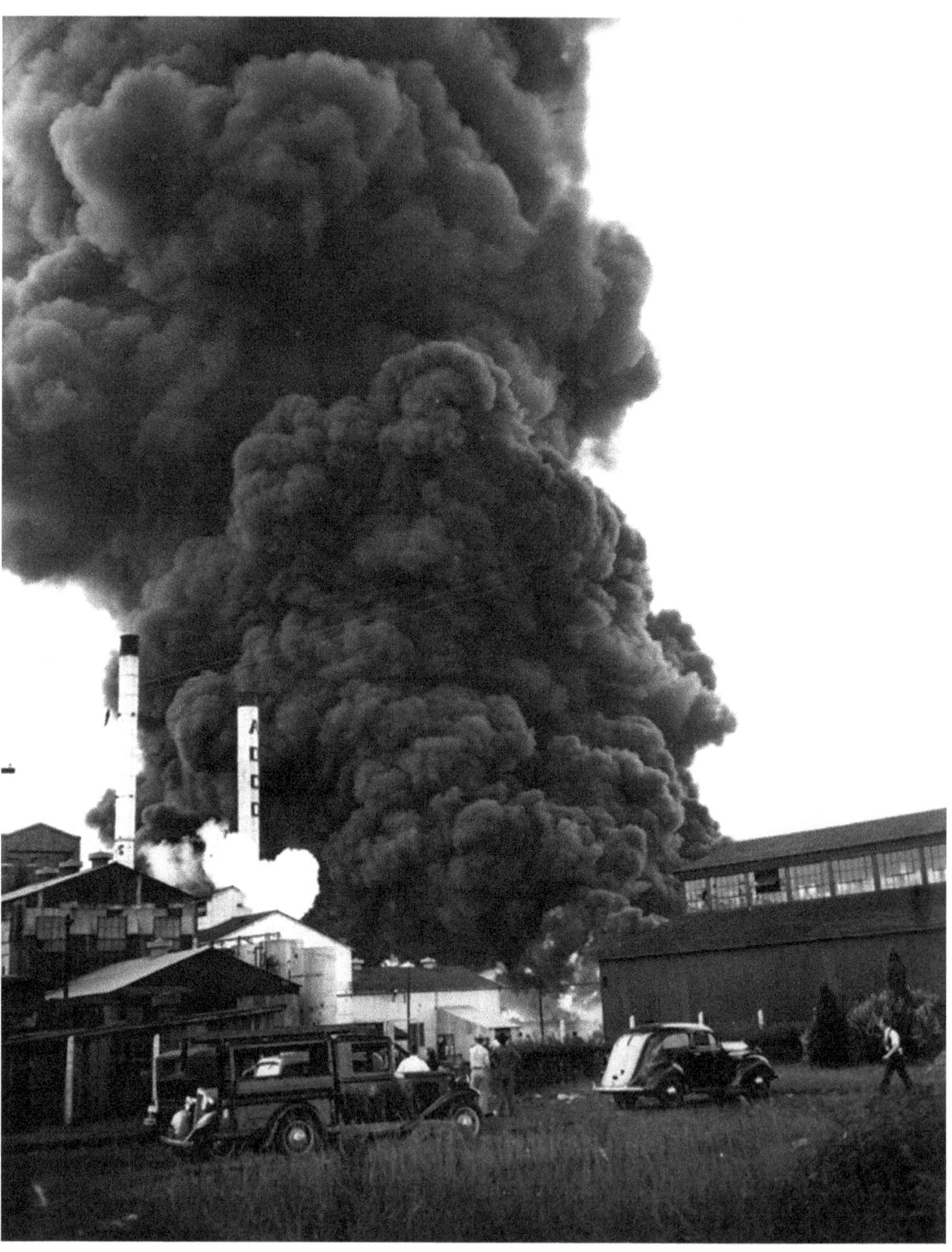

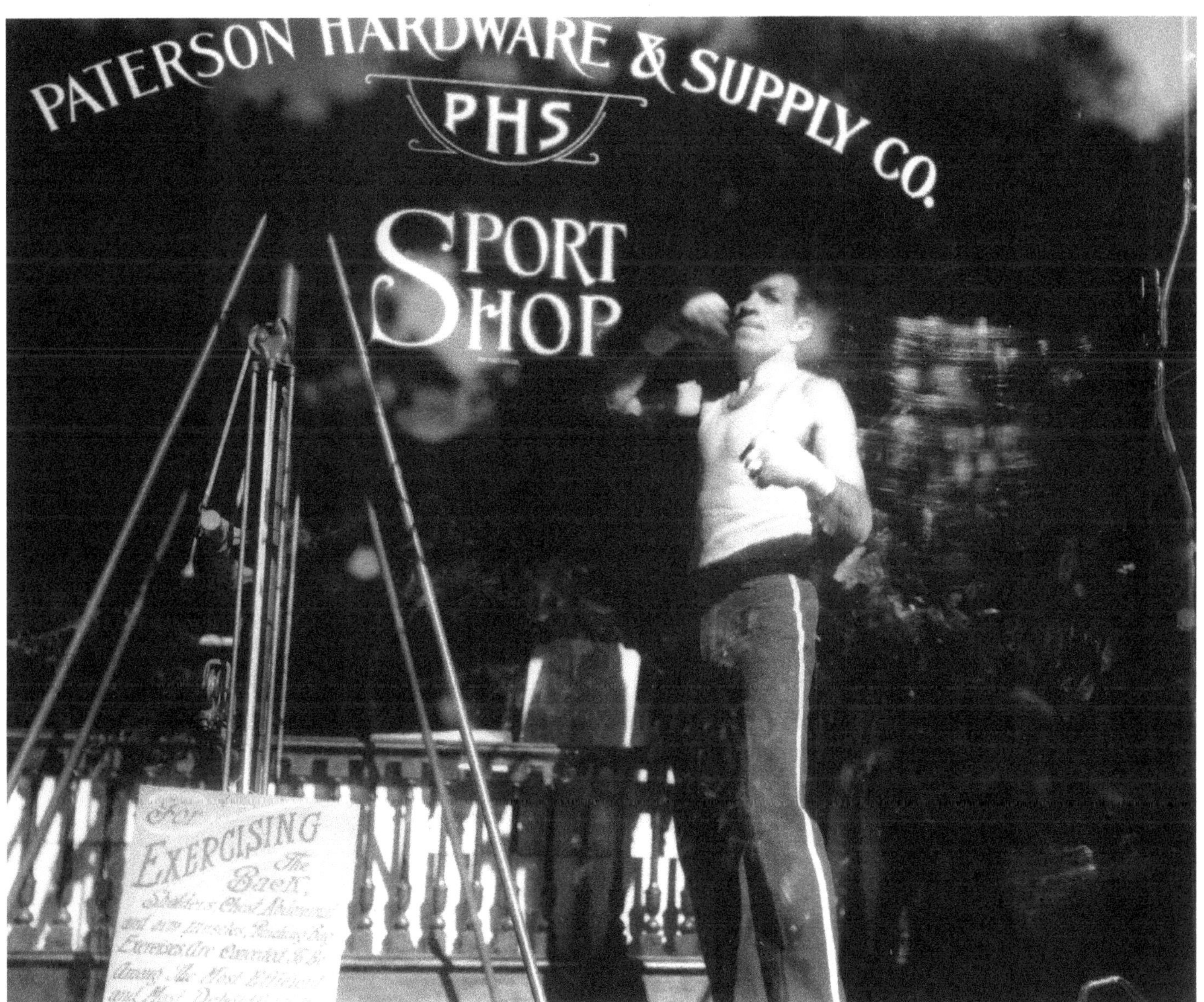

Sam Impastato, also known as Tommie Littleton, was a middleweight boxing champion. Mobile crowds used to come and watch him fight on the wharves. This image shows Littleton in the early 1930s, hitting a punching bag in the window of a local sporting goods store, which he did for 24 straight hours! That landed him in *Ripley's Believe It Or Not.*

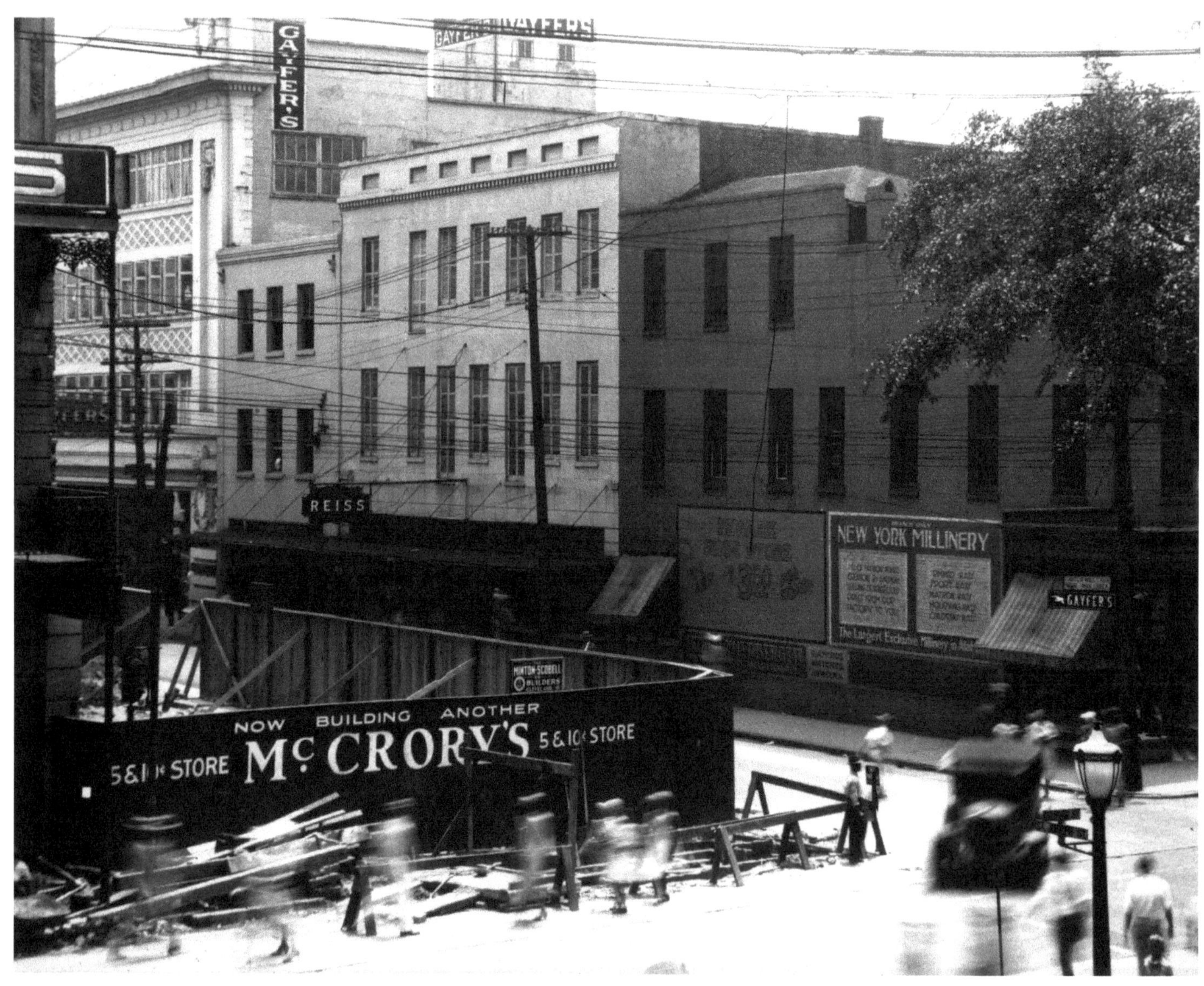

Saint Emanuel Street to the south, 1930, with a second McCrory's Five and Dime Store under construction and the "new" Gayfer's Department Store in the background.

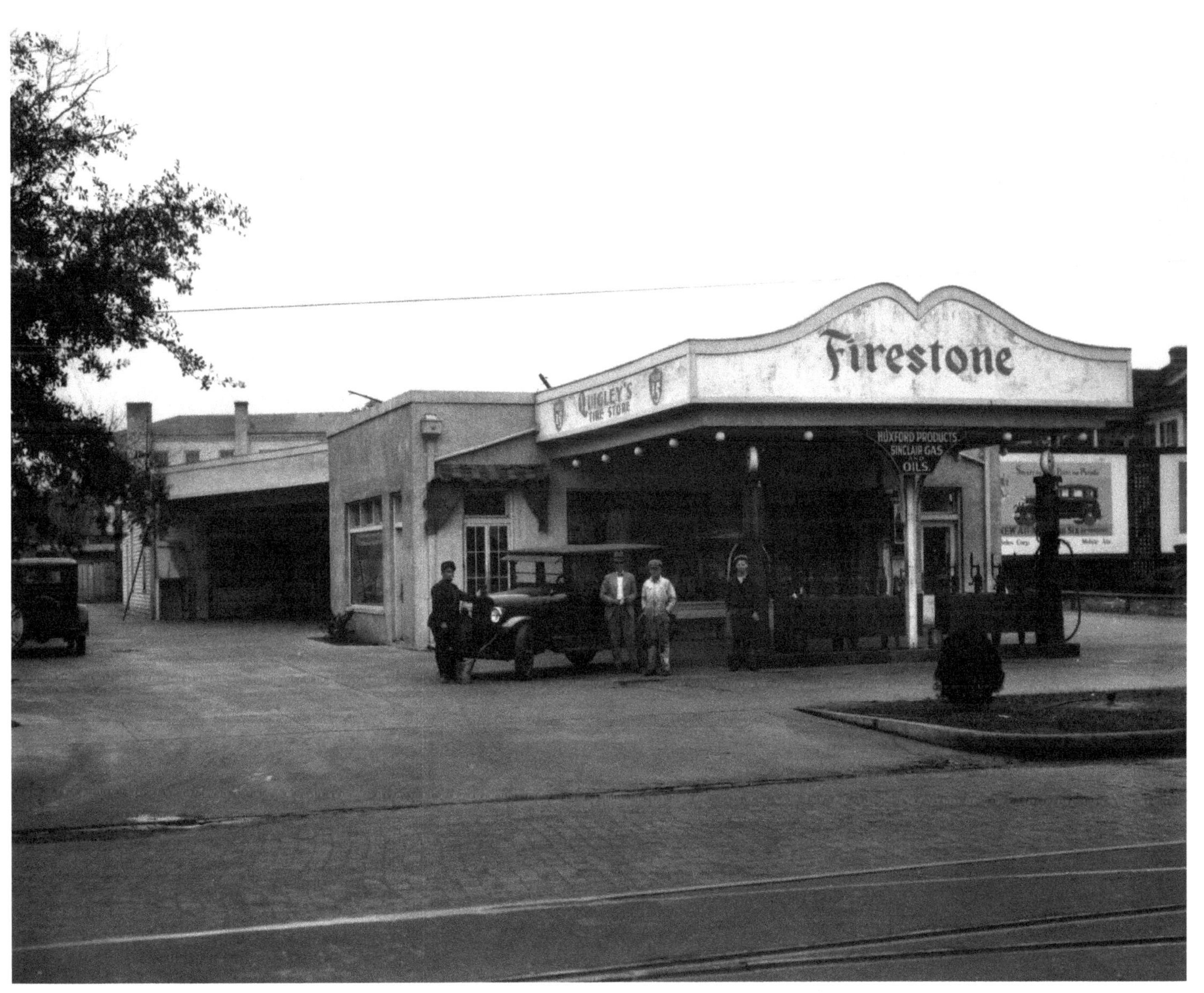

Huxford Oil Company's gas station on Broad Street in Mobile around 1930.

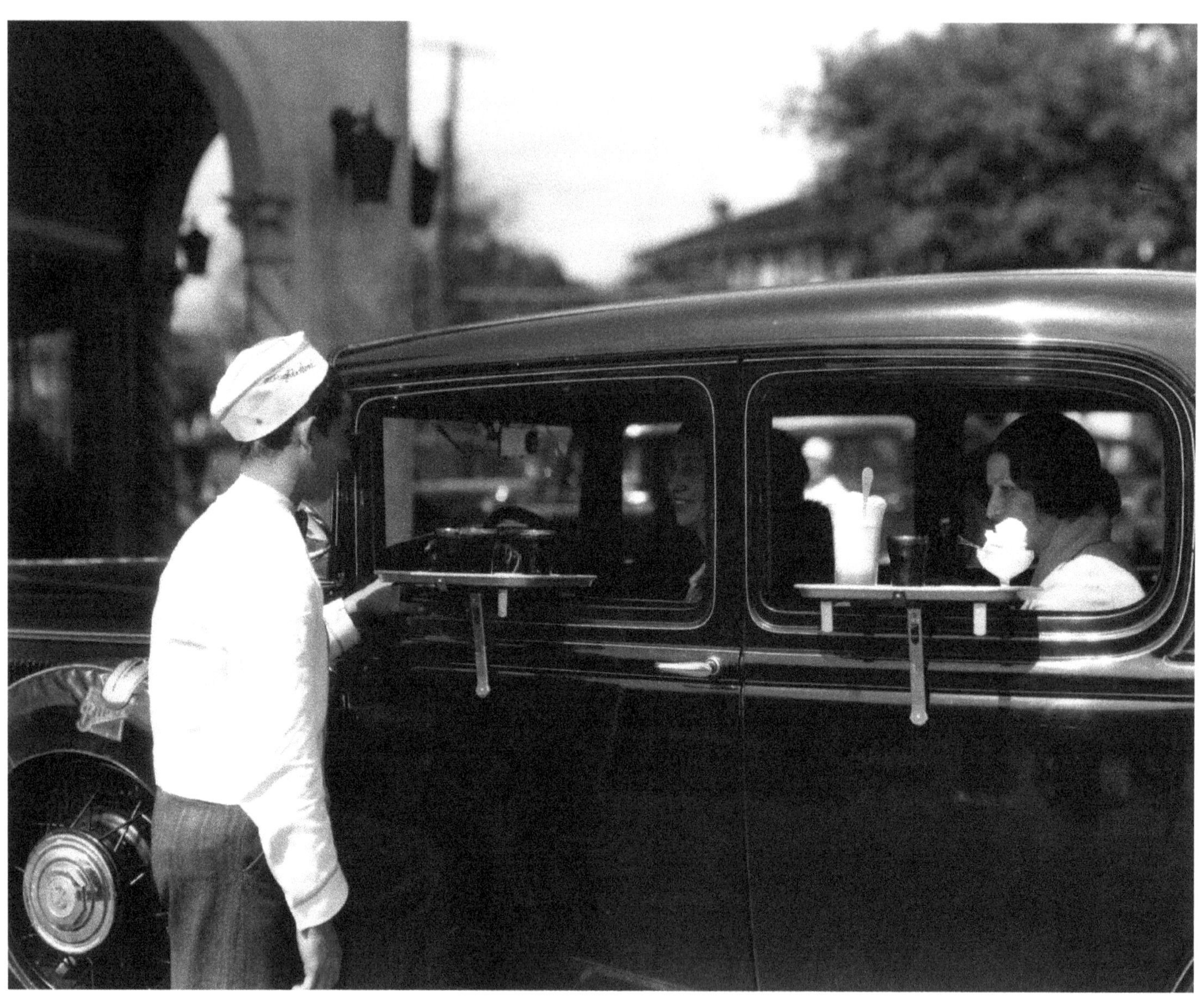

Two unidentified women enjoy refreshments served to them by an Albright and Wood carhop. Albright and Wood once had a chain of drug stores operating in Mobile. This image was taken in 1931.

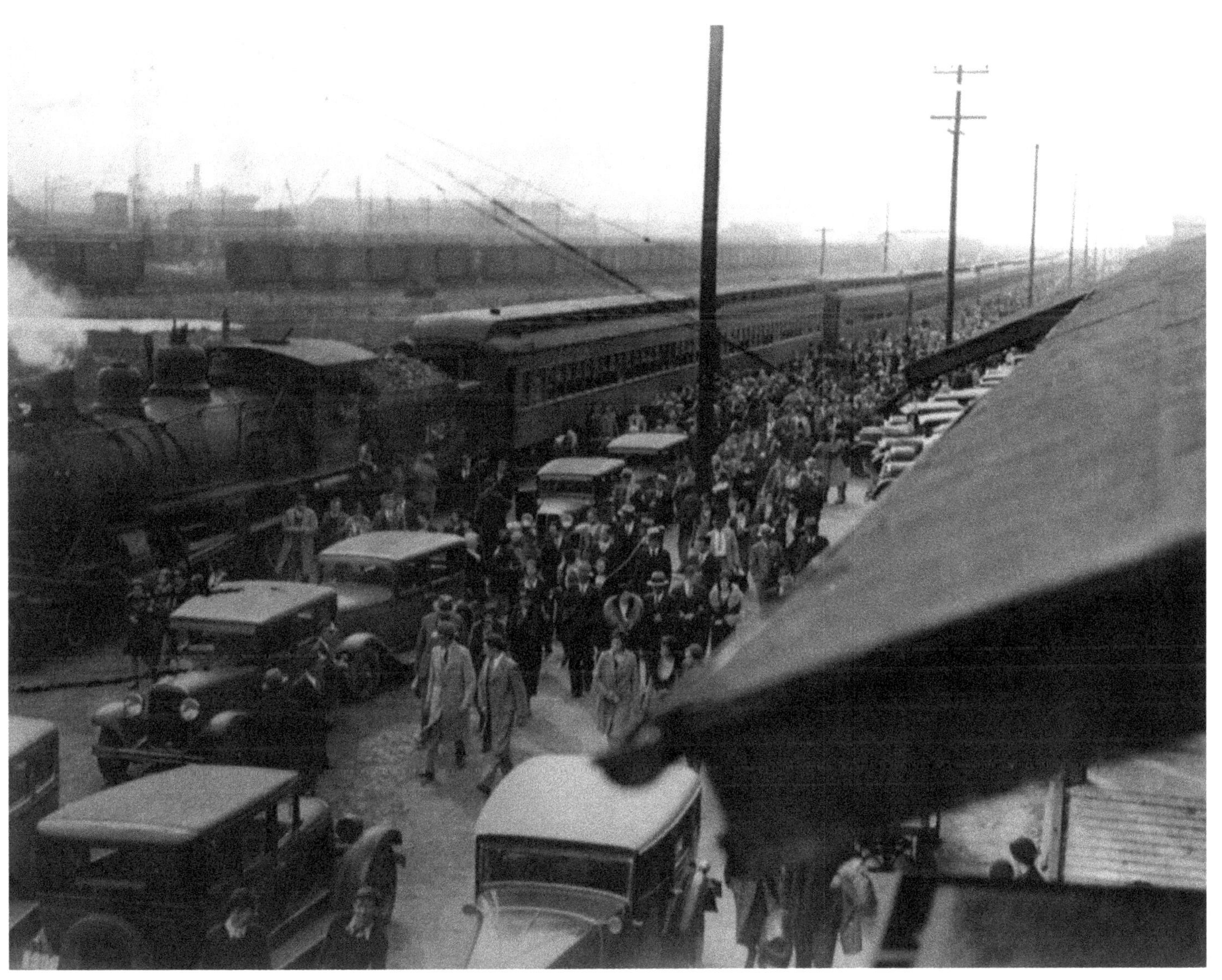

In the 1930s railroad travel was a popular and necessary means of transportation. These passengers are loading and unloading from the Louisville and Nashville depot at the foot of Government Street on January 12, 1932.

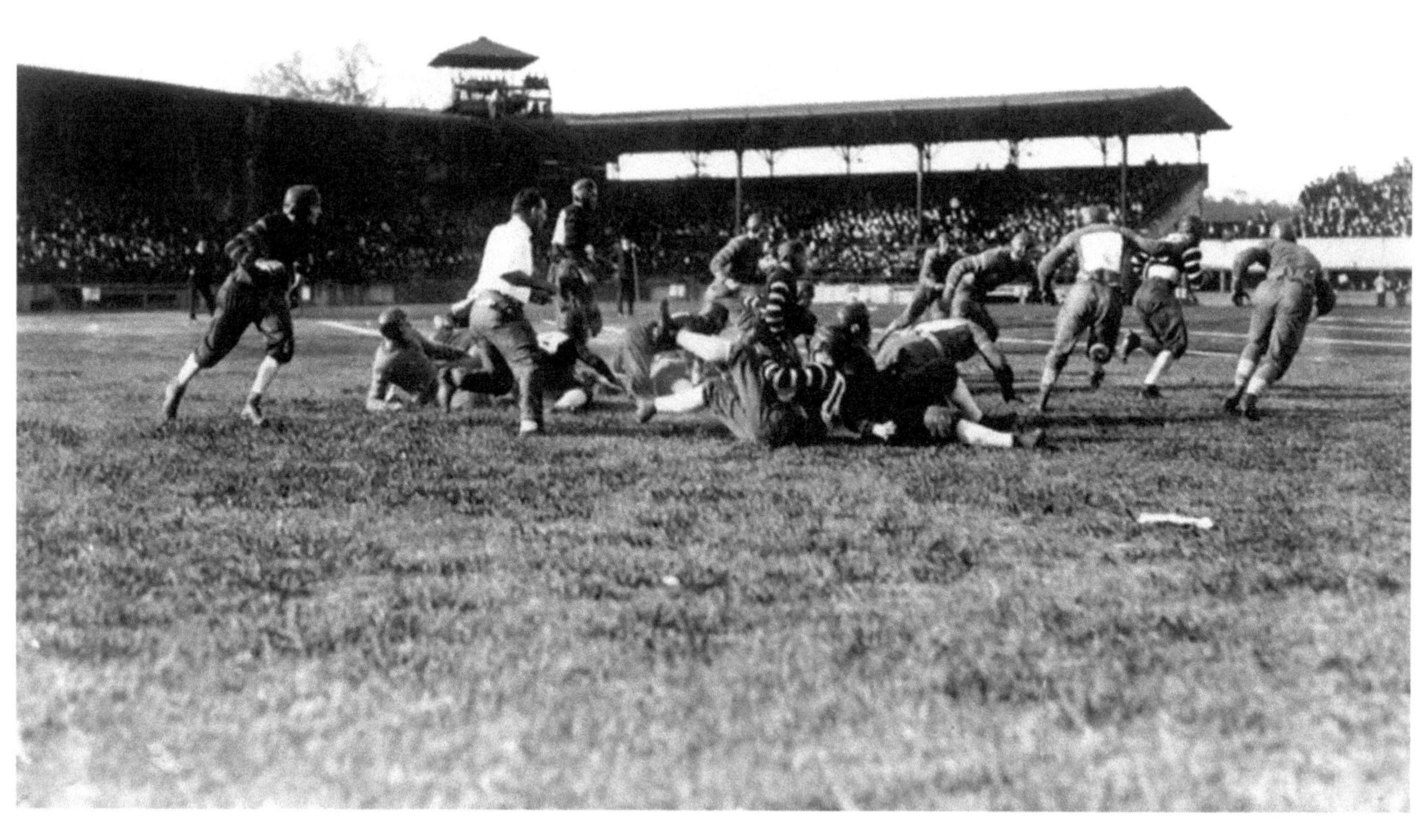

An unidentified group of men play football in the 1930s at the old Hartwell Field, which was located at Tennessee and Ann streets.

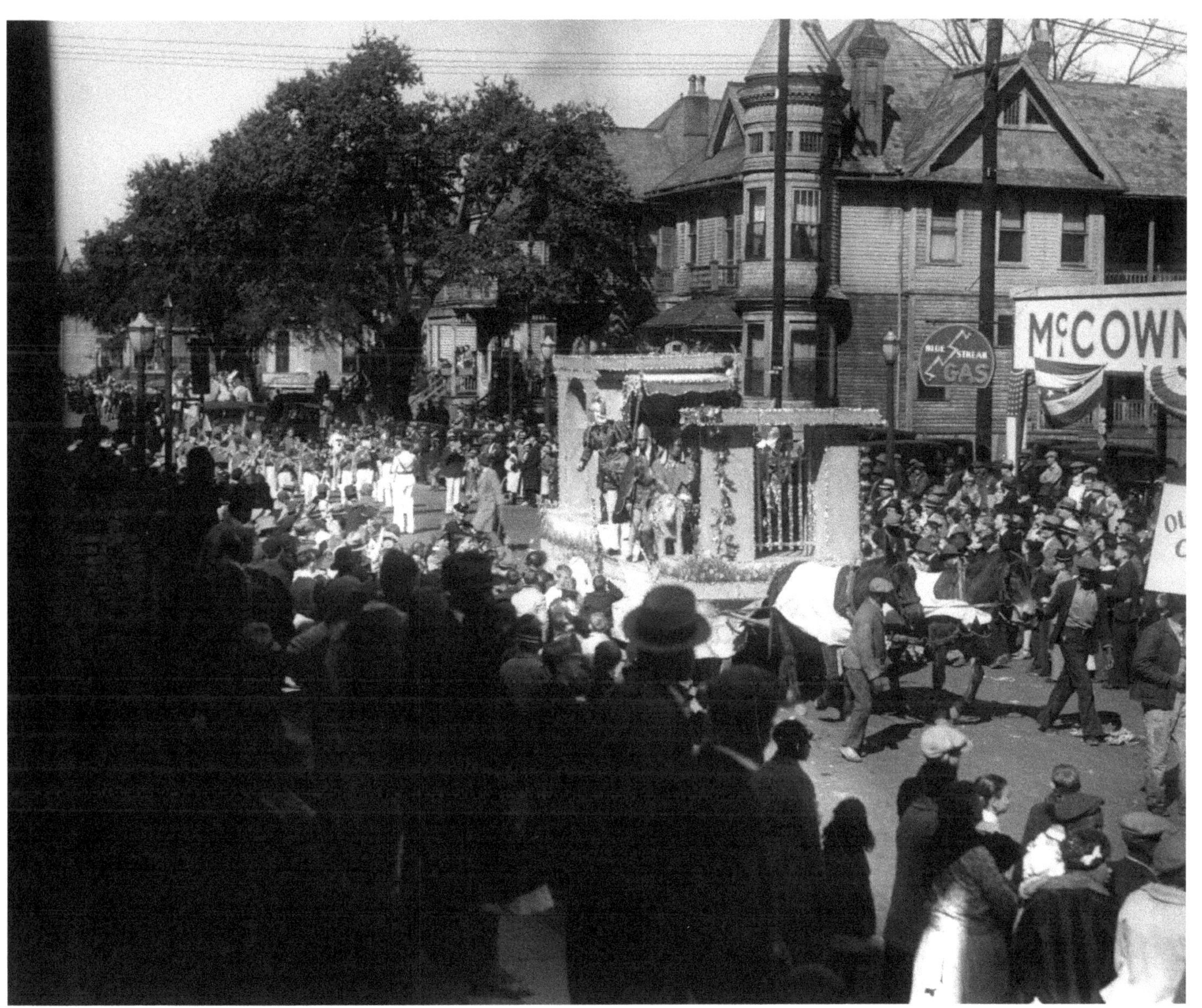

A crowd at the intersection of St. Joseph and St. Louis streets watches as a Mardi Gras float rolls by (ca. 1933).

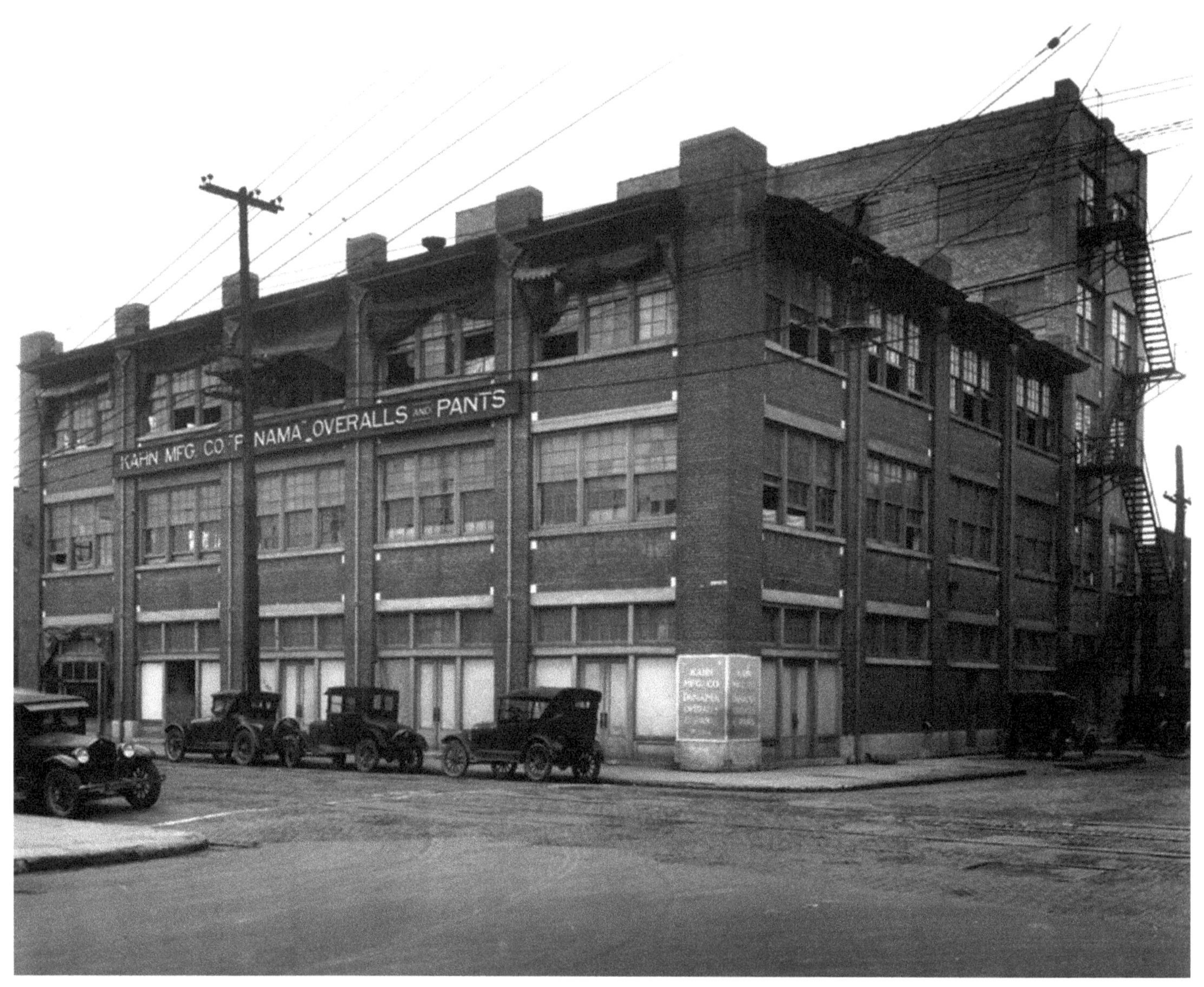

Kahn Manufacturing Company, located between St. Louis and State streets.

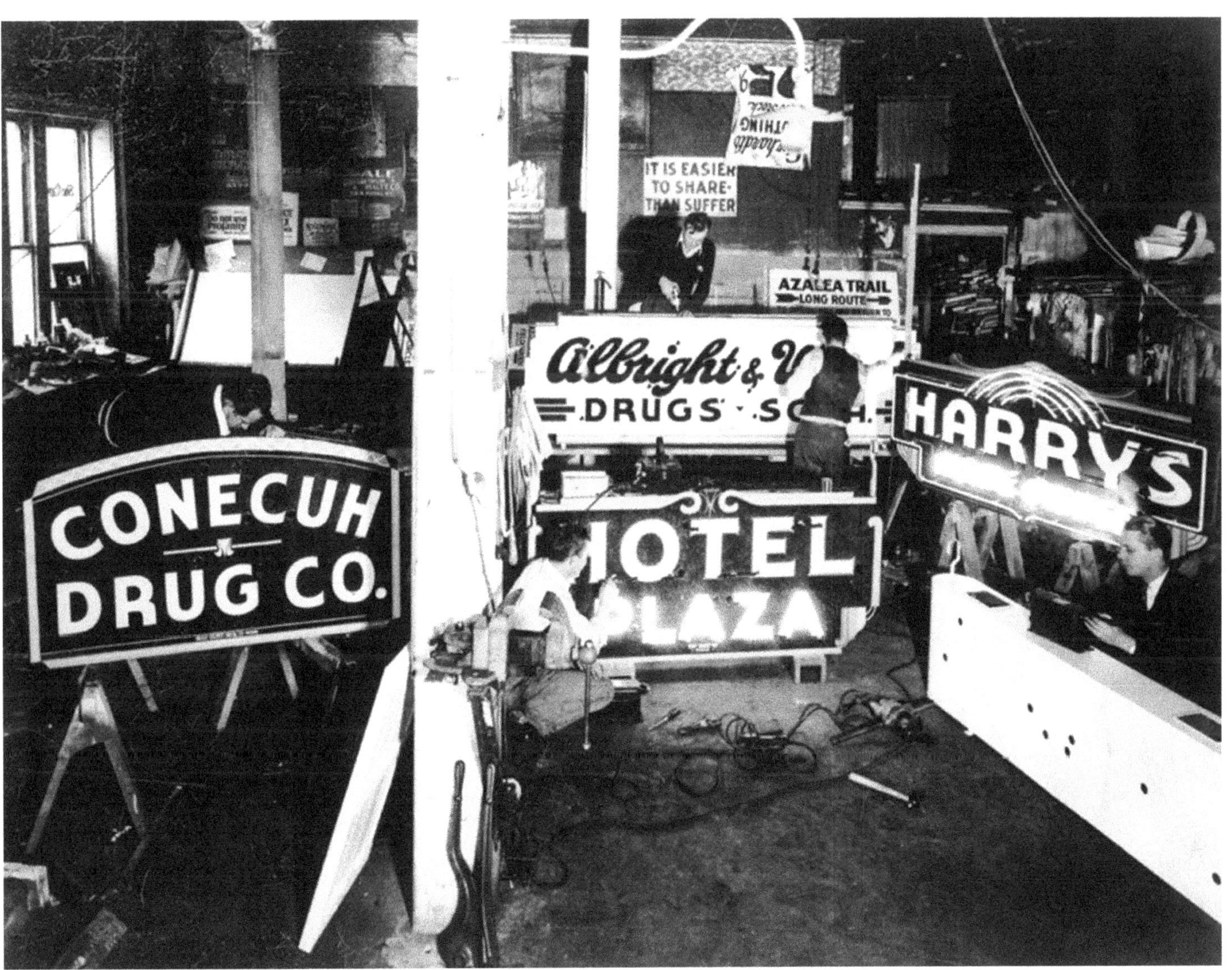

The interior of the Gulf Coast Sign Company, showing workers creating signs for the Conecuh Drug Company, Harry's, the Hotel Plaza, and Albright and Wood Drug Store (ca. 1935). One sign in the background reads, "It is easier to share—than suffer." Another says, "Do not use profanity."

An employee with the Malbis Bakery stands outside as the photographer catches his image. Using $200,000 borrowed from a bank in Chicago, Jason Malbis, a Greek immigrant, established the business in 1927. Since Malbis was competing with a more well-established bread company, the going was tough at first, but within ten years the mortgage was paid off.

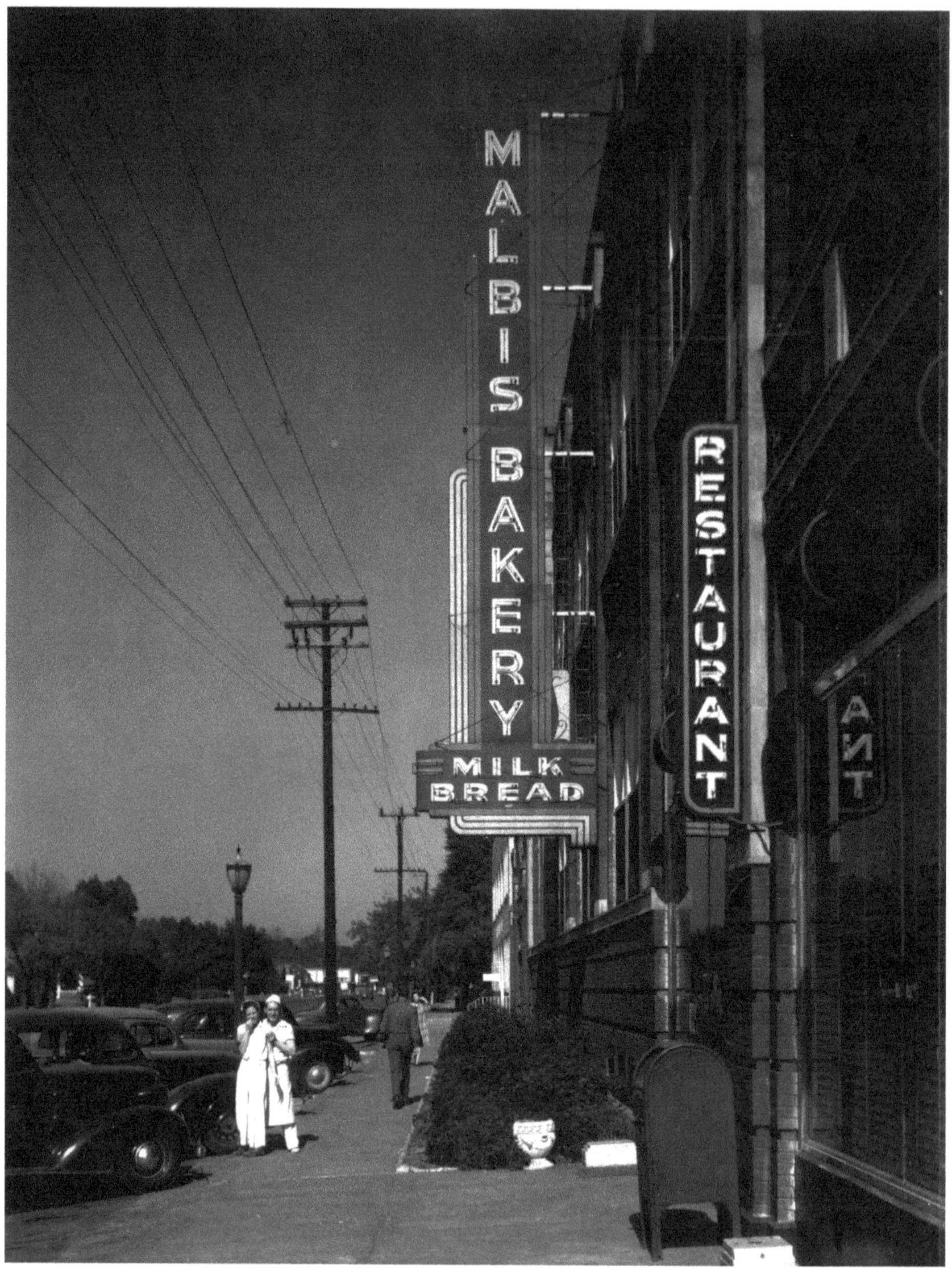

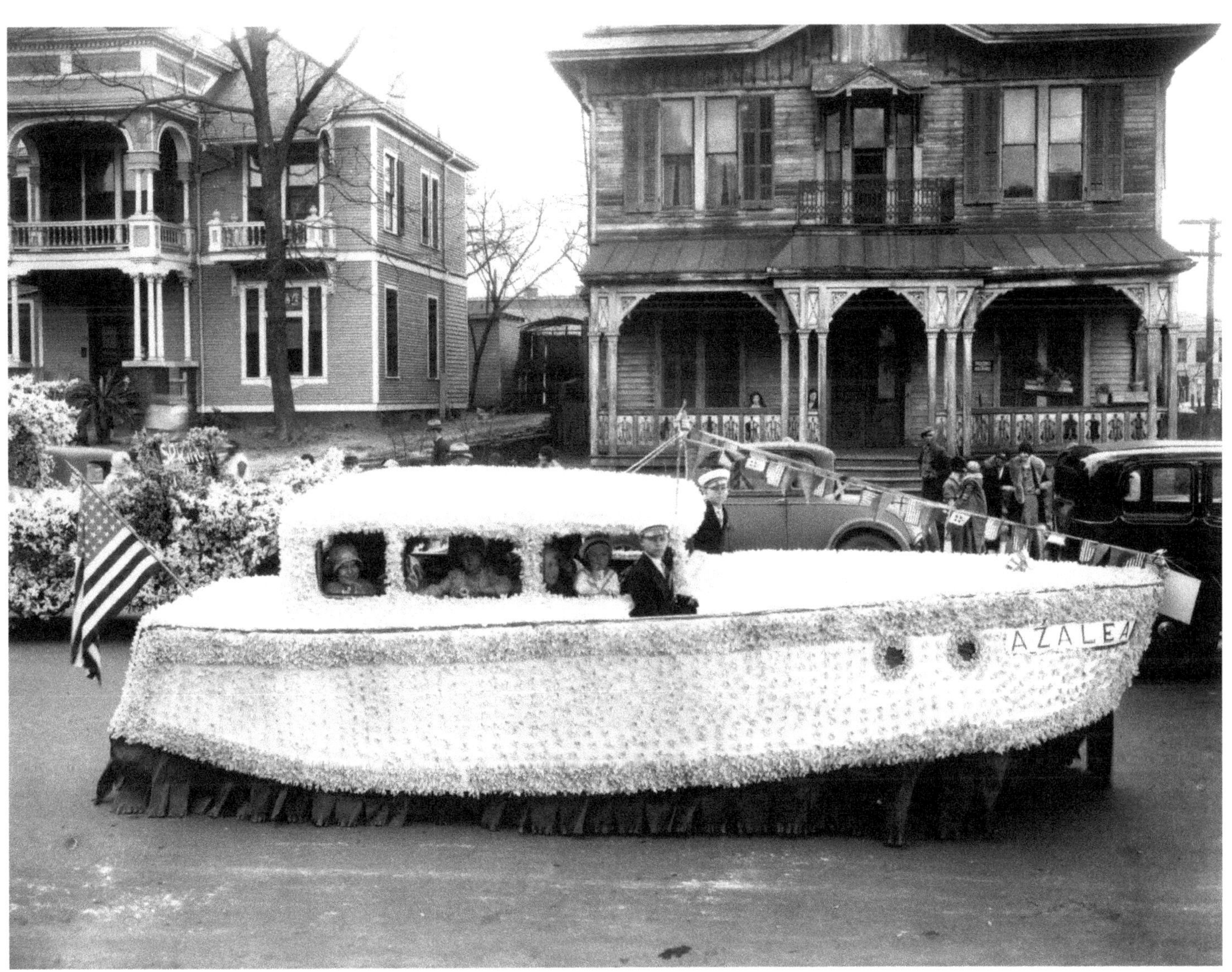

This beautifully decorated car, which the family dubbed the "Azalea," is all decked out for the annual Mardi Gras Floral Parade (ca. 1935).

The old Trinity Episcopal Church, which was located at St. Anthony and Jackson streets. The cornerstone for the building was laid on April 8, 1853, by the Right Reverend Nicholas Hamner Cobb, first Episcopal bishop of Alabama. In 1946 the parish moved to its present location on Dauphin Street.

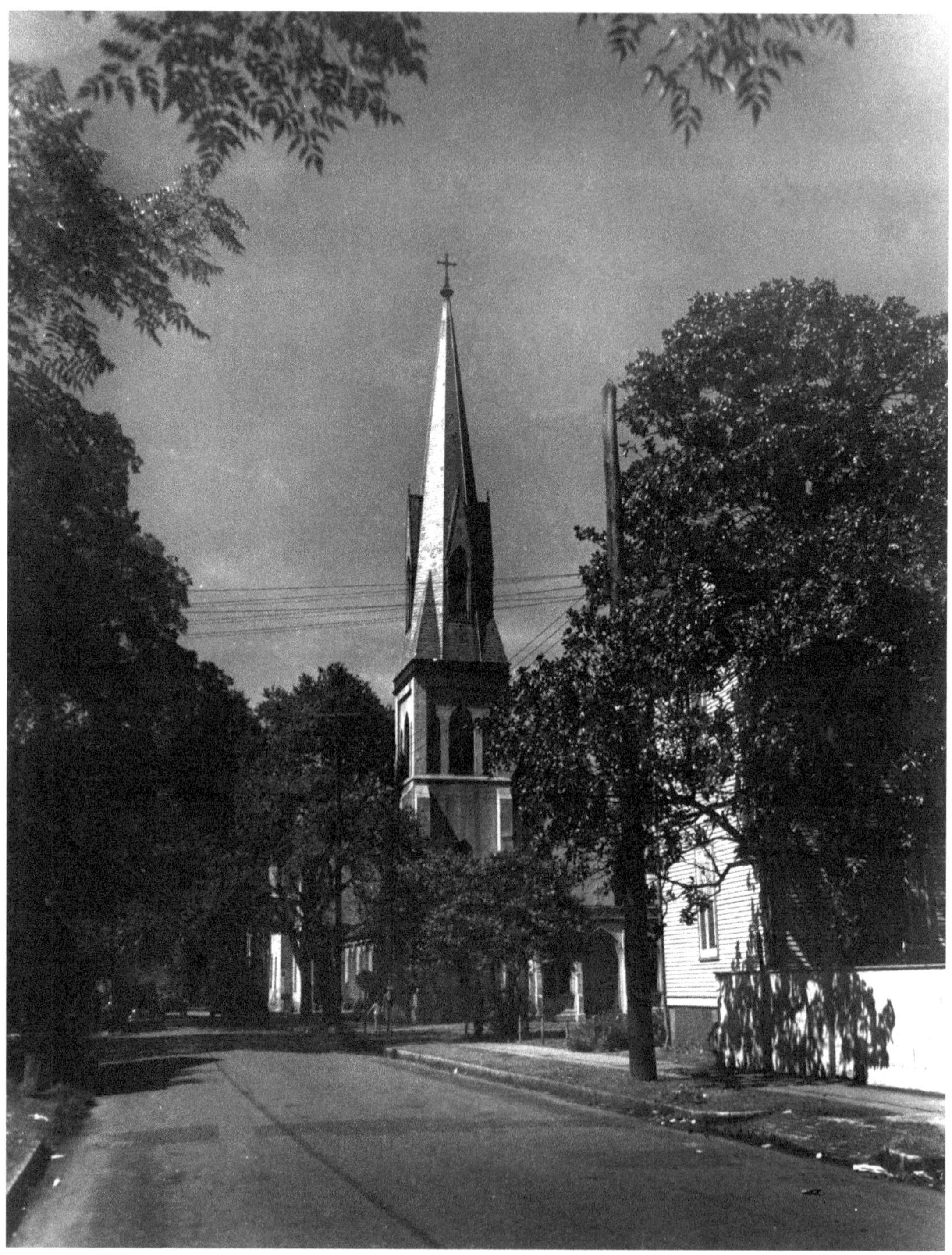

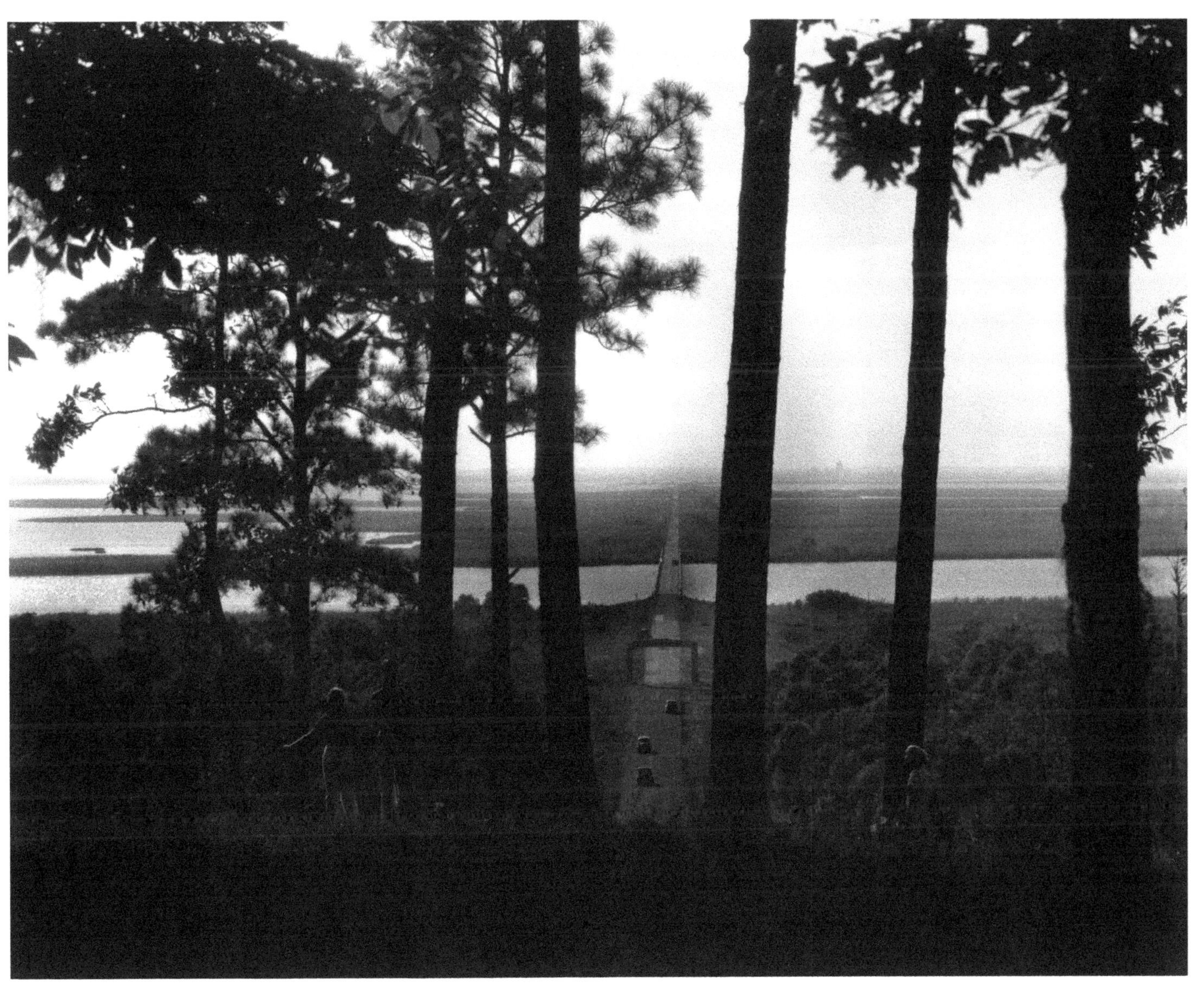

Looking down from Spanish Fort toward Mobile around 1930.

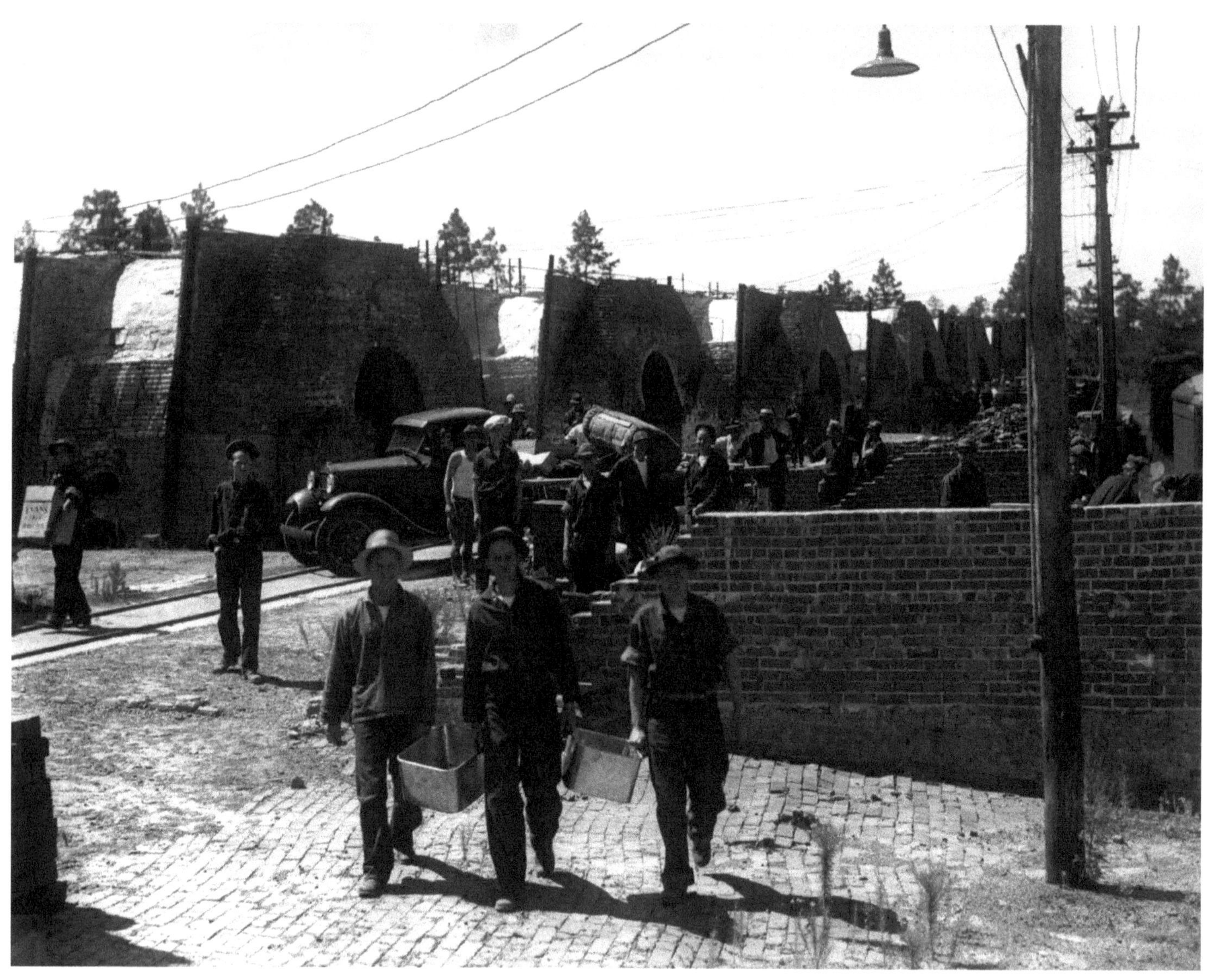

Civilian Conservation Corps workers load items into brick kilns at a brickyard somewhere between Kushla and Chunchula, Alabama, around 1933.

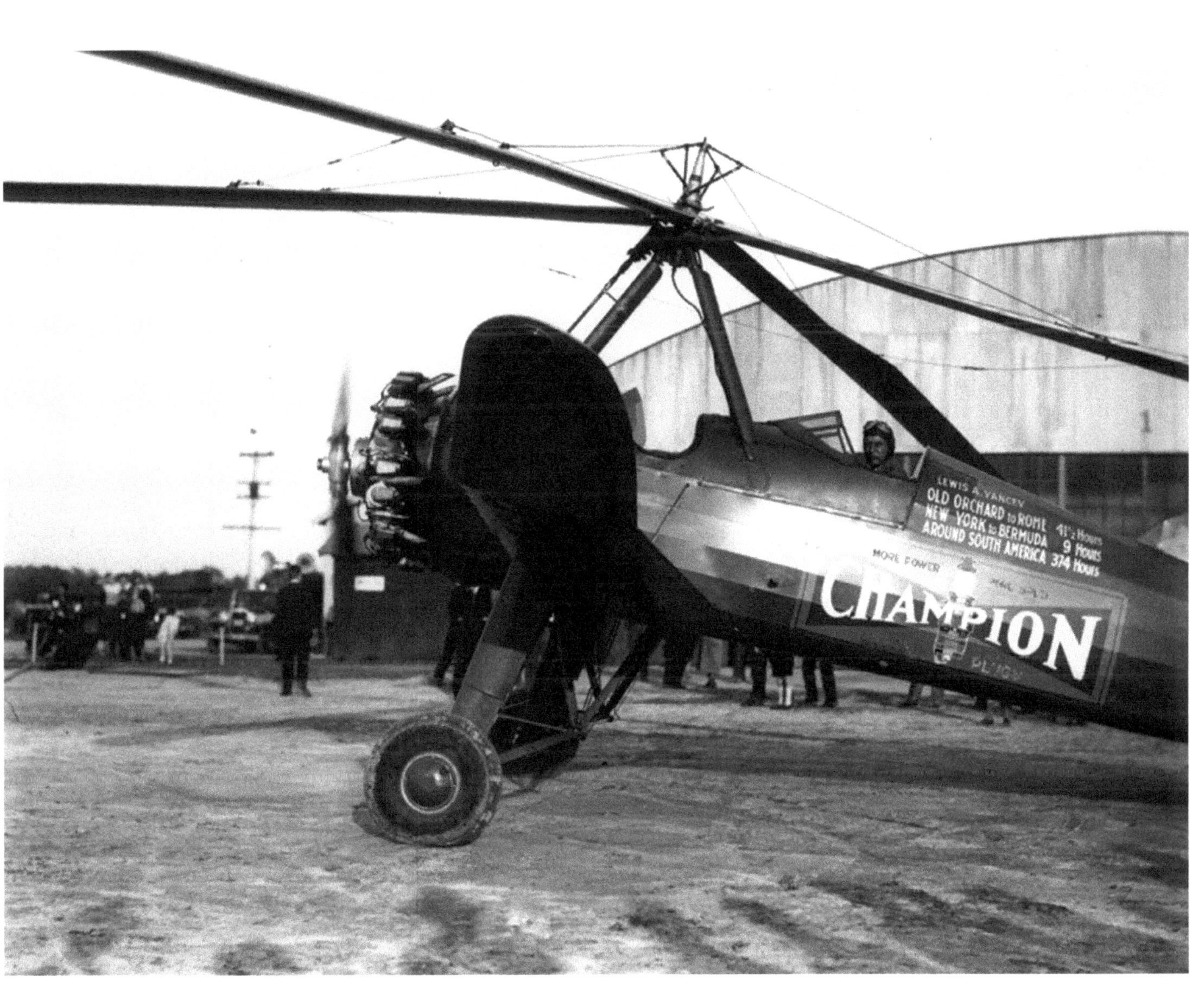

In 1936, this autogiro, a predecessor of the helicopter, came to Mobile to promote Champion spark plugs. The craft landed at Bates Field and offered rides to several Mobilians, including the proprietor of McGowin-Lyons Company, the largest local seller of Champion products. The pilot is Lewis Yancey.

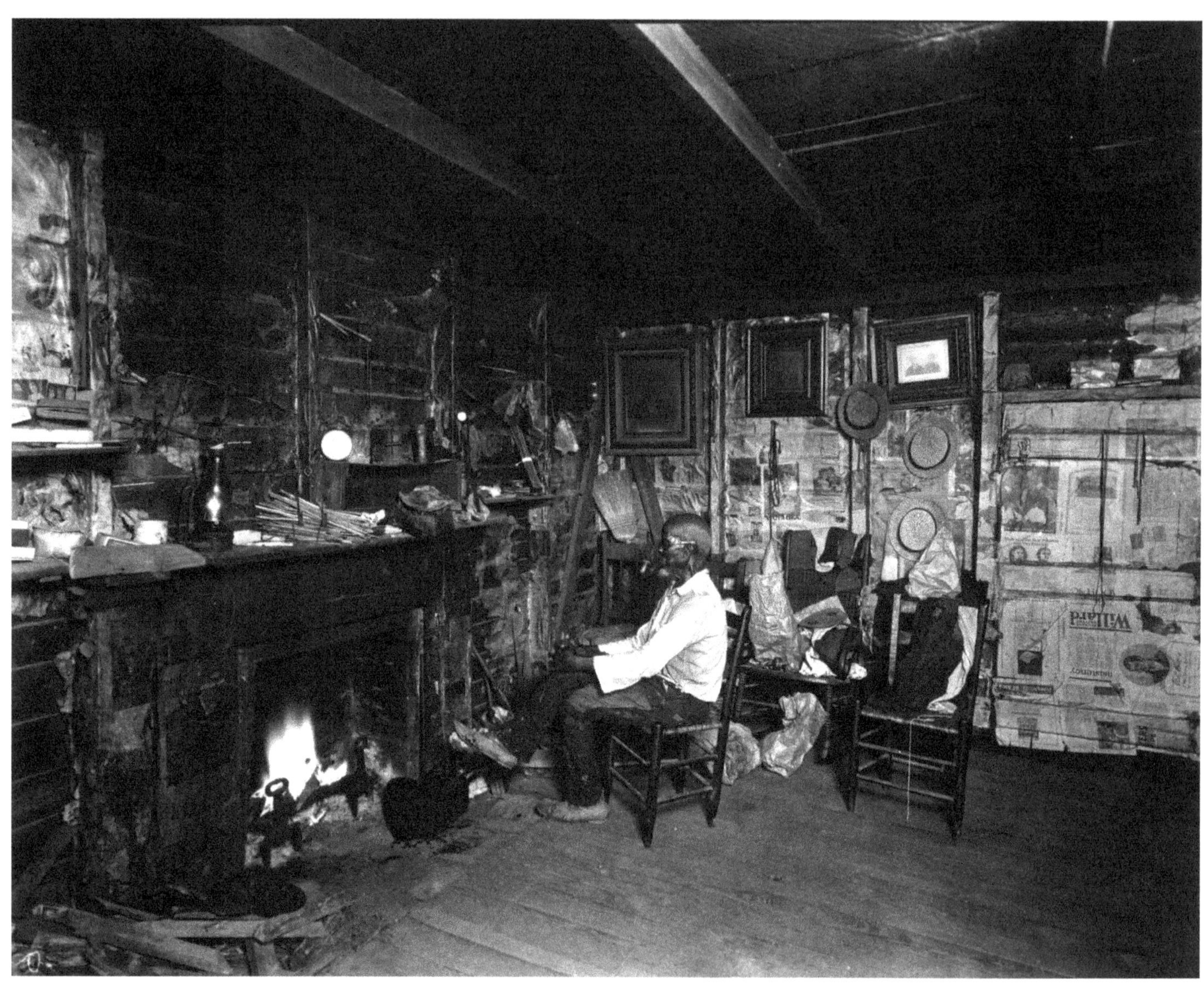

Cudjo Lewis in his home in the 1930s. He was one of a number of Africans that Timothy Meaher and Captain William Foster conspired to illegally smuggle into Mobile in 1860. They were brought from the coast of the African continent to the United States, landing in the Plateau/Magazine Point district north of the city. After the Civil War many of the Africans returned to that area and established a settlement they called Africatown. Cudjo became their spokesman.

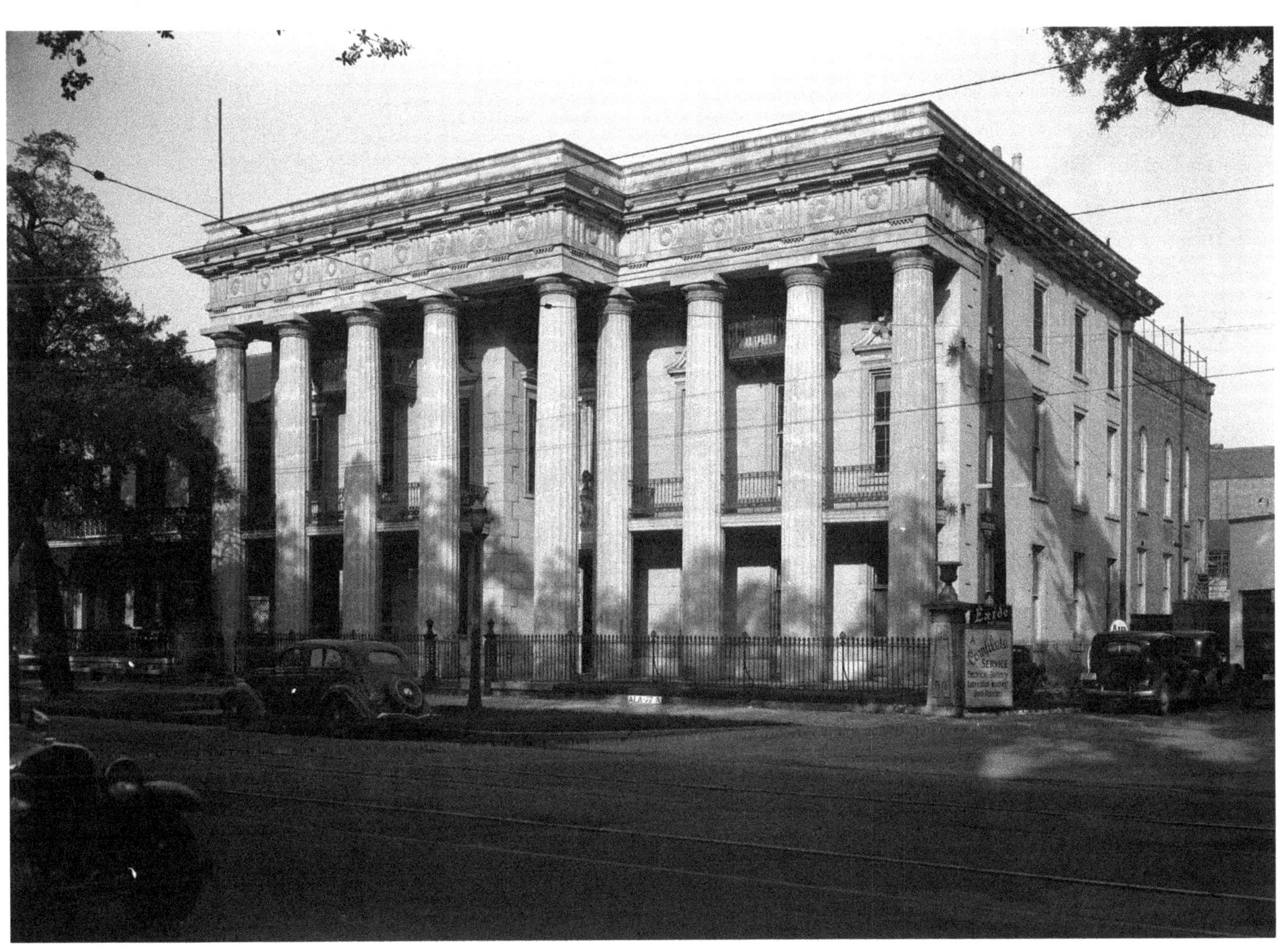

McGill Institute, a high school for Catholic boys, was constructed in 1896 and named for Arthur McGill, the owner of a shoe store who had bequeathed in his will the money necessary to build the structure. Until 1952 the school was located downtown, on Government Street. Due to increasing enrollment, it moved to its present location on Old Shell Road between Catherine and Lafayette. In the 1970s it combined with Bishop Toolen High School to become McGill-Toolen.

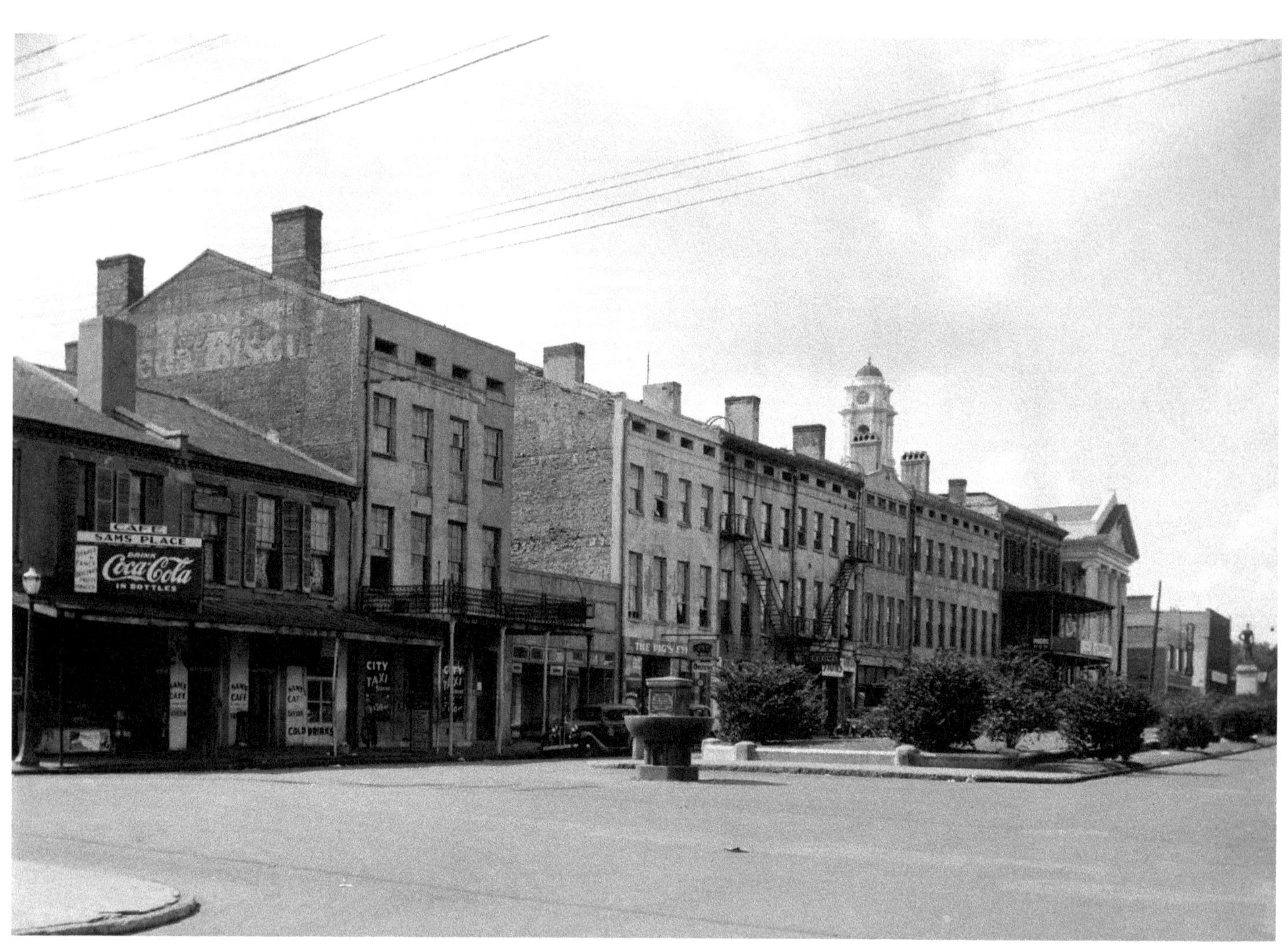

A view of Government Street in 1935, between Water and Royal streets. The block included Sam's Café, the City Taxi Service, the International Seaman's Union, and Pigs Eye Beverages.

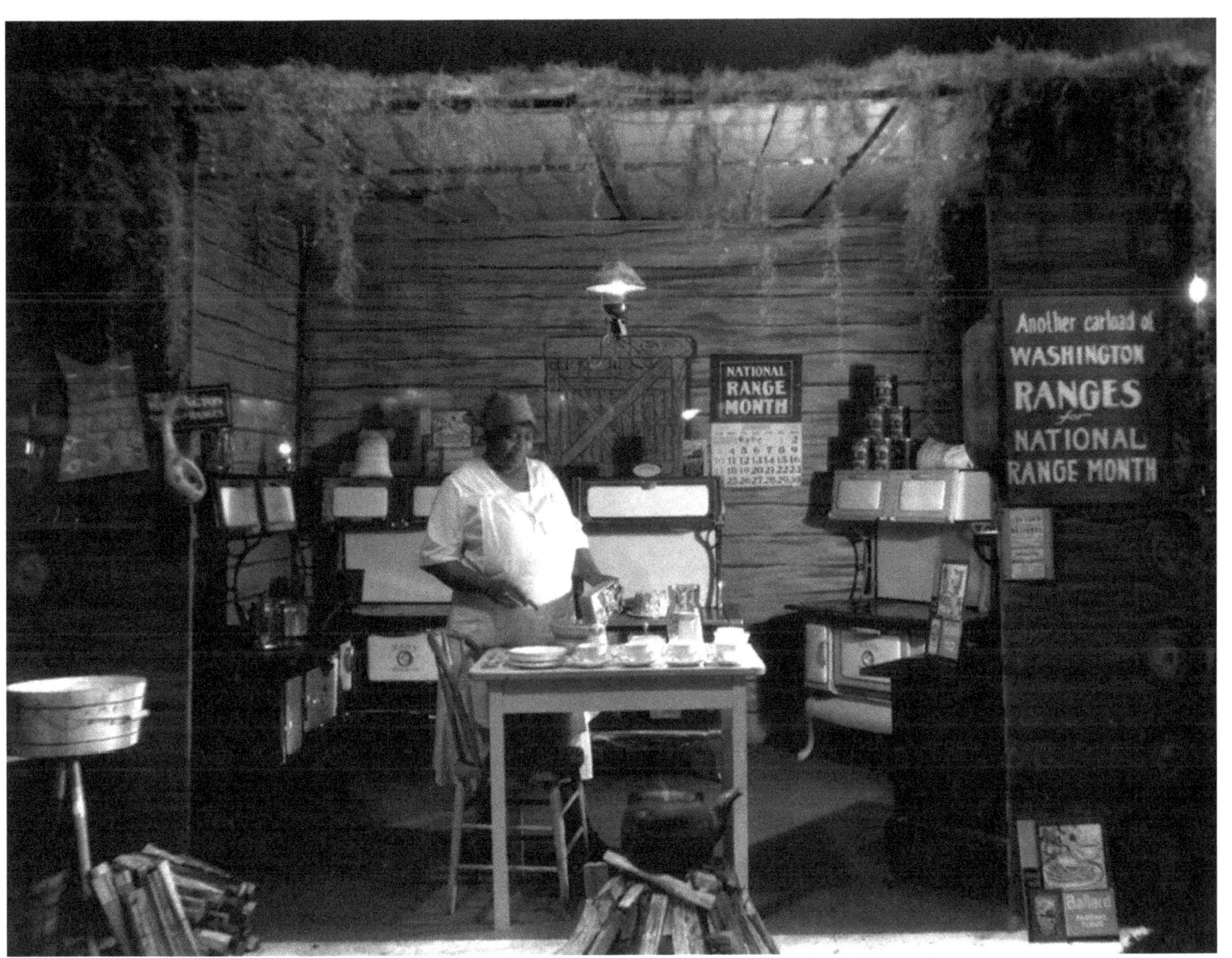

An African-American woman pours Ballard Pancake Flour into a bowl during a promotional event for National Range Month, probably sponsored by the Mobile Gas Company. The woman is meant to appear as if housed in an authentic log cabin.

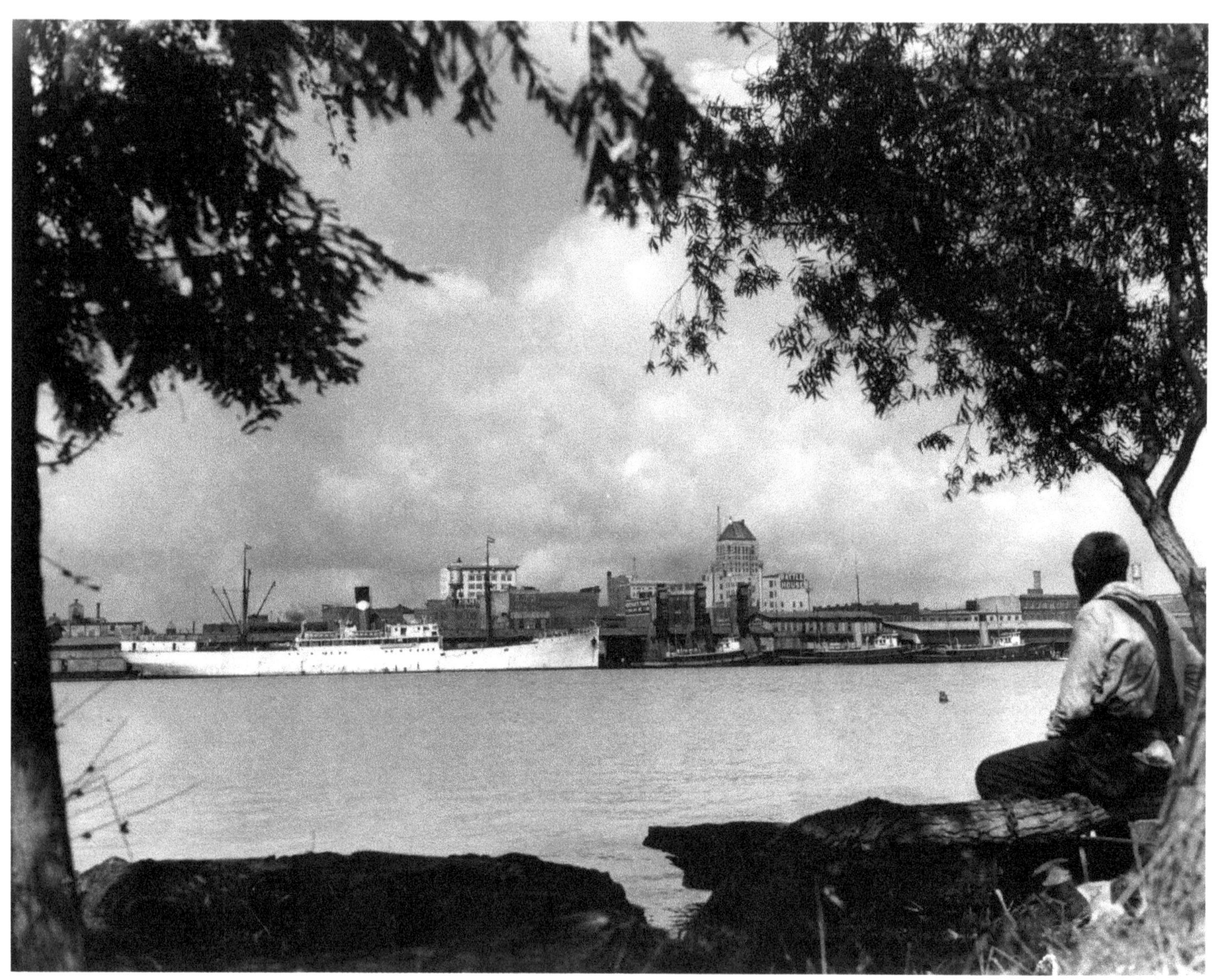

A view of the Mobile skyline taken from Pinto Island about 1935.

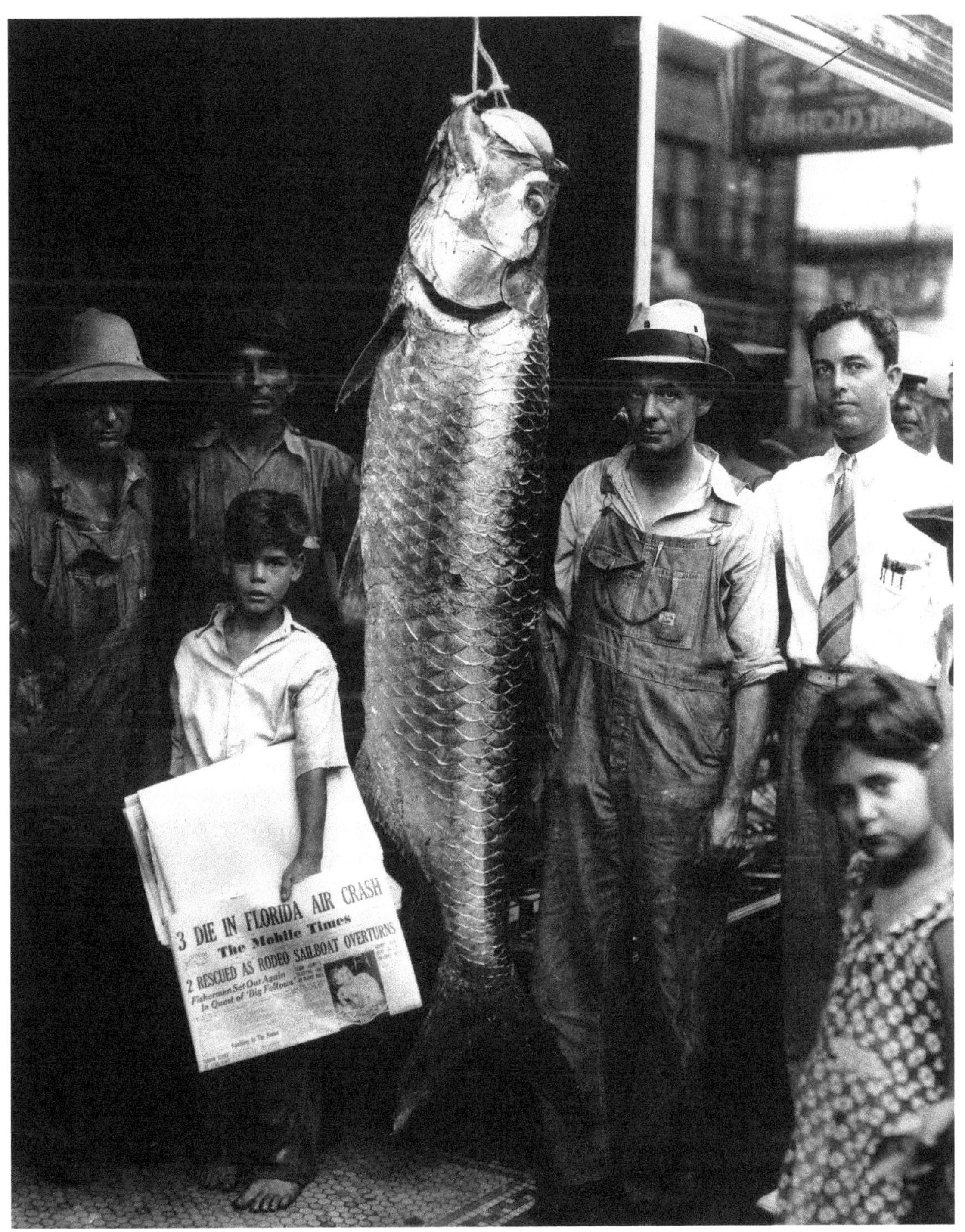

Two stories surround this photograph, which was taken in 1937. One says that the three men in overalls caught the huge tarpon. All three worked for the L&N Railroad. Another story has it that Jim Hare caught the fish and, because he was full-blooded Cherokee, stood silently in the back as the image was taken. It is said that all of Mobile turned out to see the big fish. Left to right (back row): M. Copeland, Jim Hare, A. F. O'Neal, and Eugene Thoss, Jr. The newsboy and the girl remain unidentified.

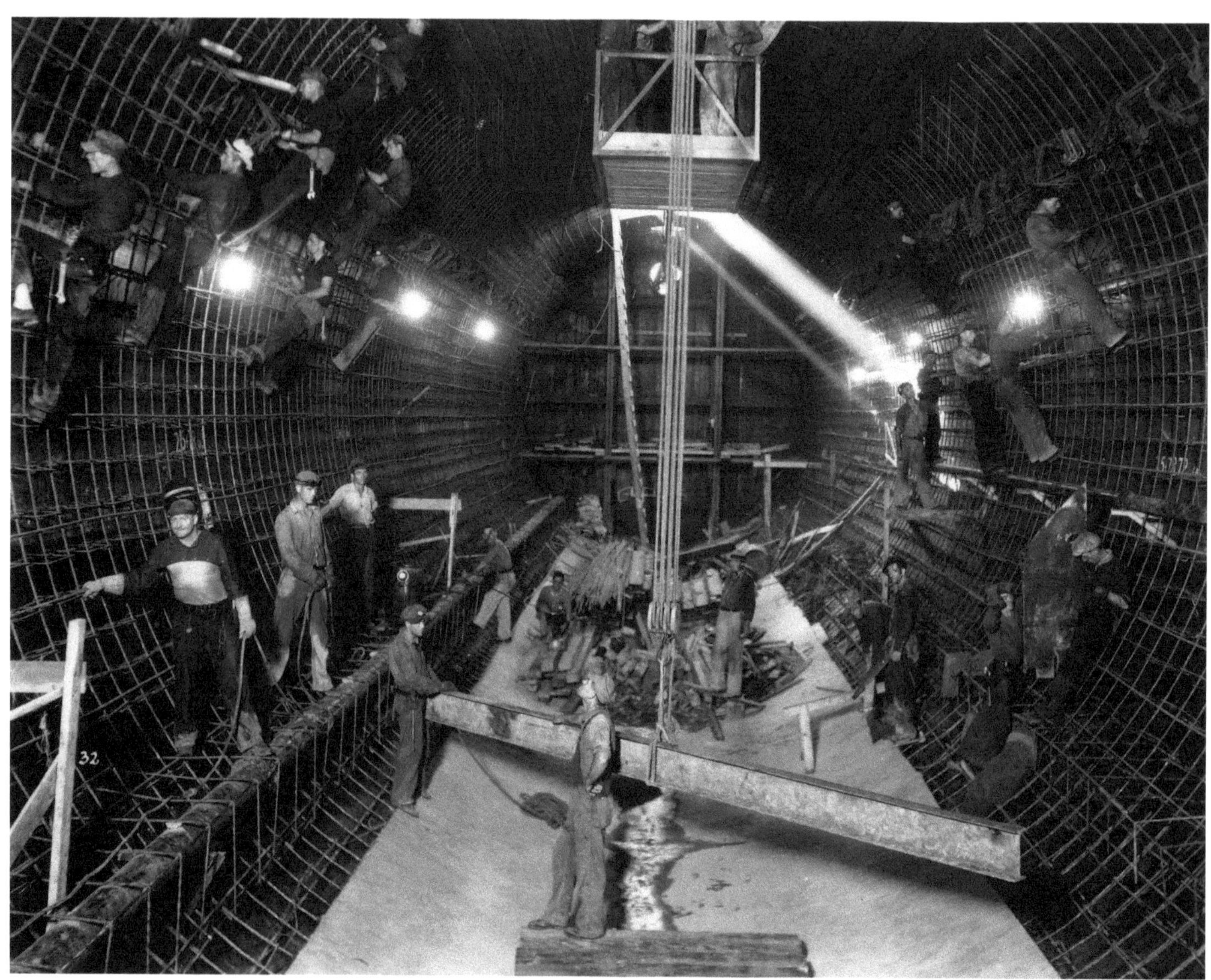

These men are working on a section of the Bankhead Tunnel, which allows traffic to pass under the Mobile River to points east of the city. The tunnel was a Works Progress Administration project begun in 1938 and completed in 1941. It cut seven miles off the previous route traveled over the Cochrane Bridge. After this tube section was finished, other men sunk it into the Mobile River and dragged it to its intended position.

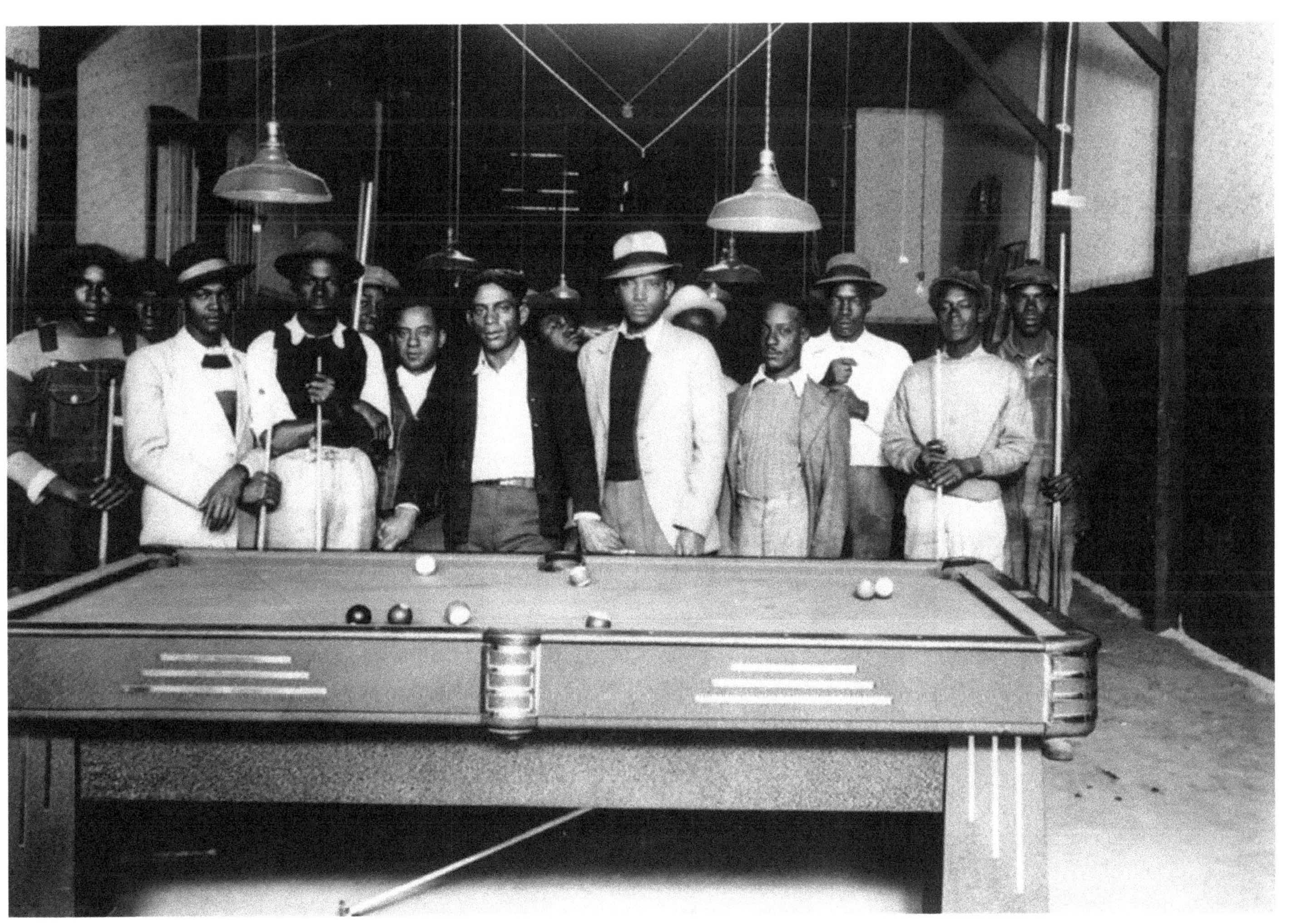

A group of pool players inside Jim's Billiards on Davis Avenue poses for a group shot in 1939.

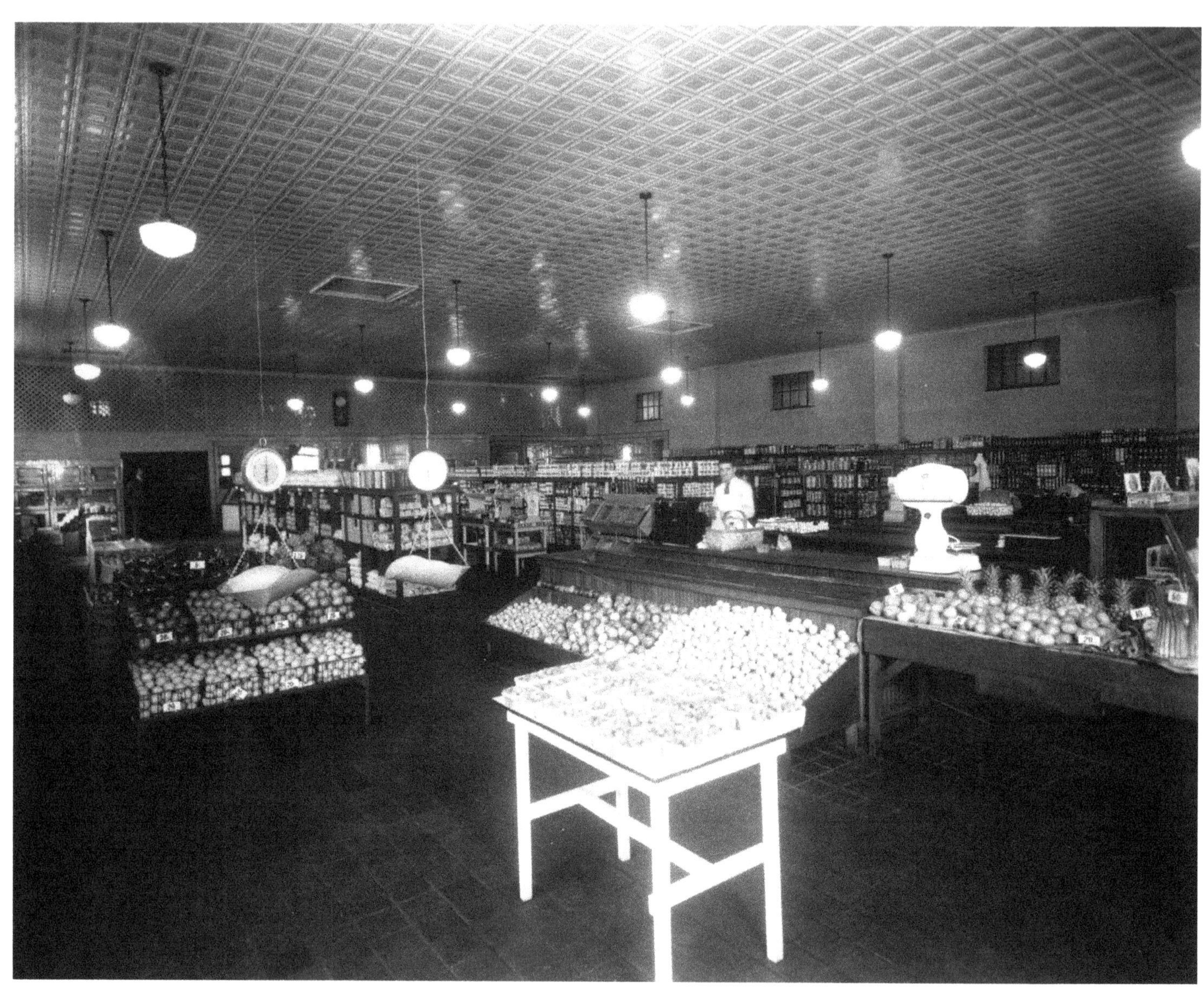

Interior of a Delchamp's Grocery Store in Mobile around 1930.

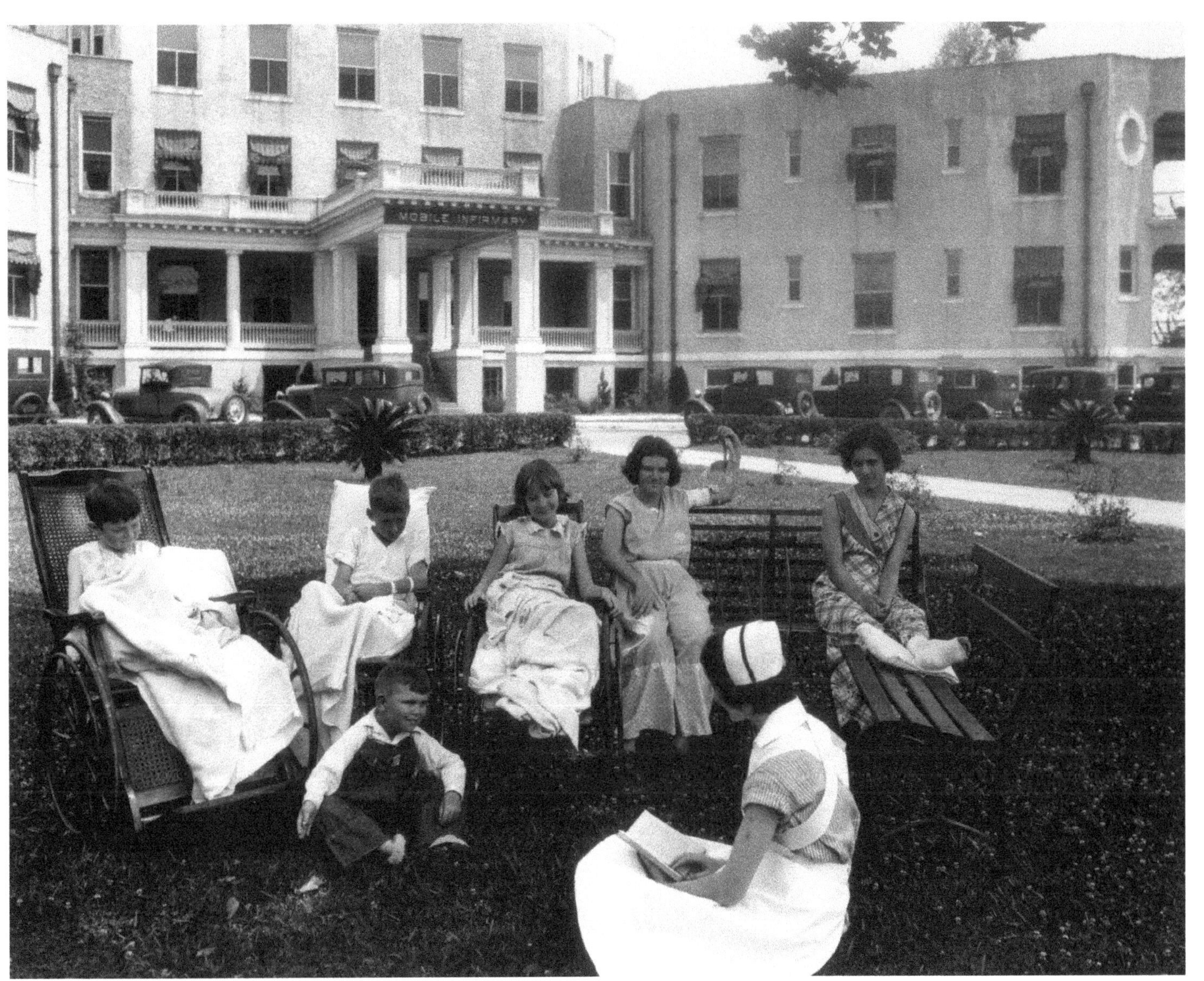

A nurse reads to young patients outside the Mobile Infirmary.

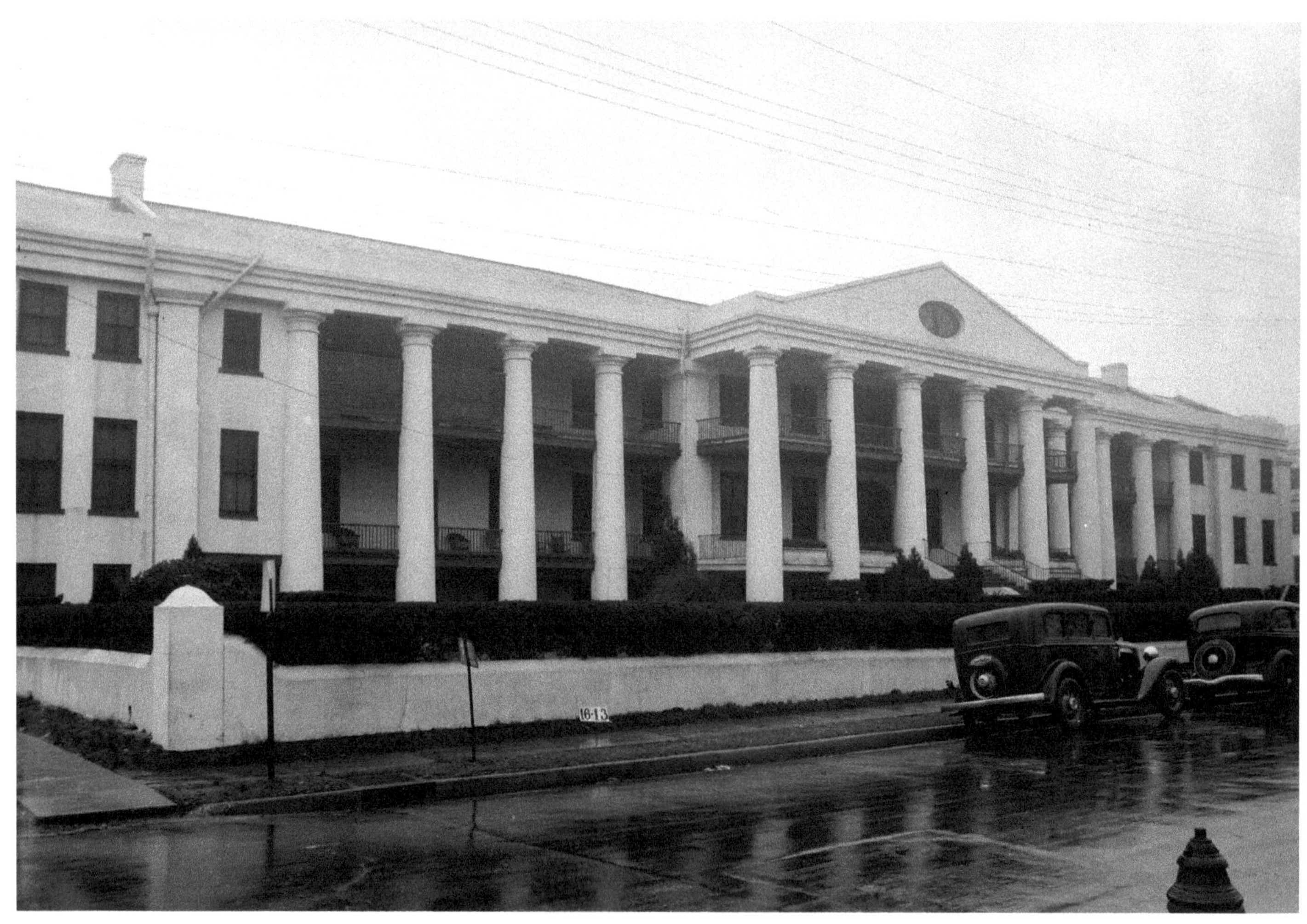

The old City Hospital, constructed in 1833, was the first Greek Revival building to be built in Mobile. The end bays, seen in this image from 1934, were not a feature of the original building. Today it houses the Mobile County Health Department.

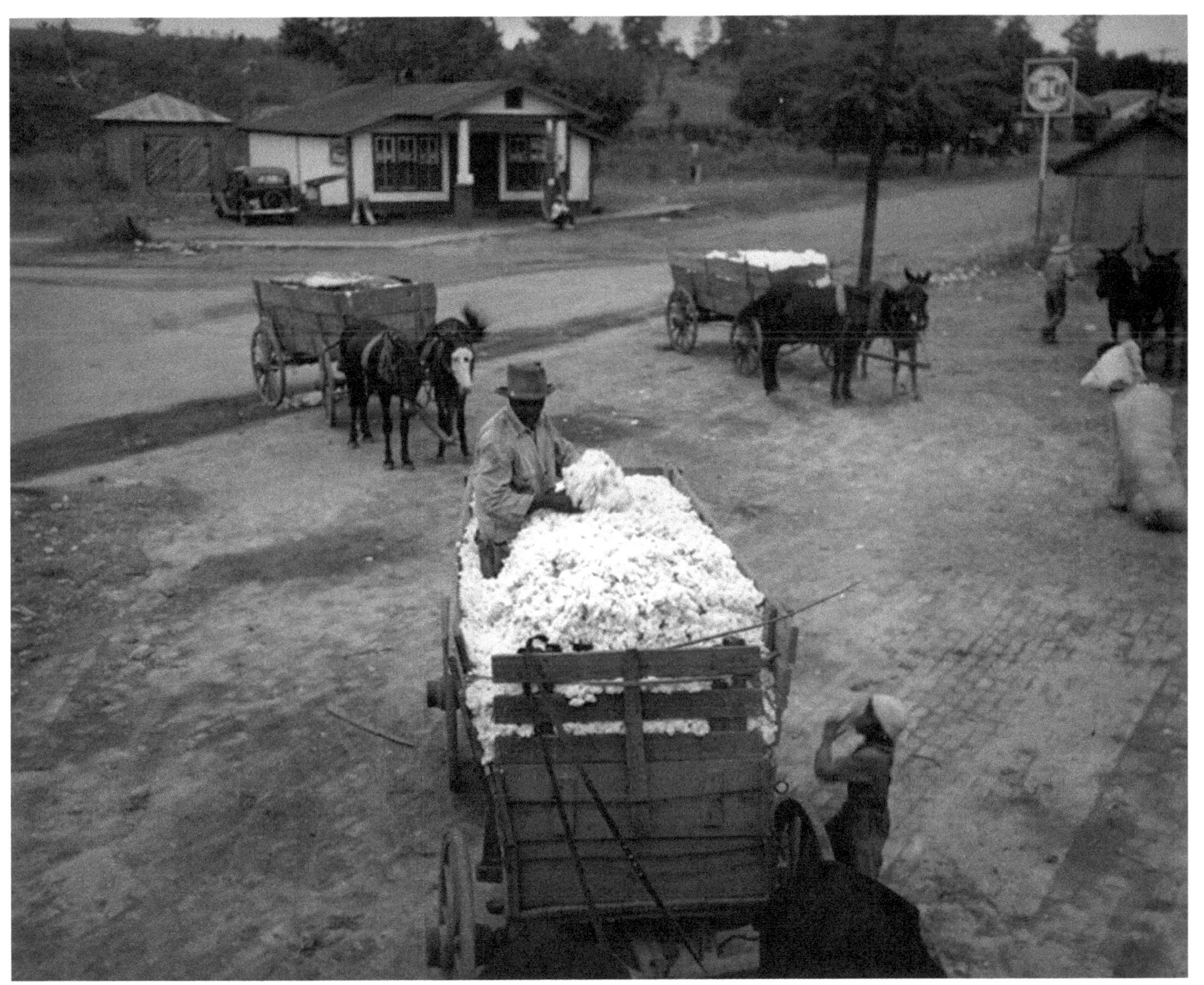

Even into the 1930s, residents in parts of rural Mobile used mule-drawn carts to transport cotton and other produce to market.

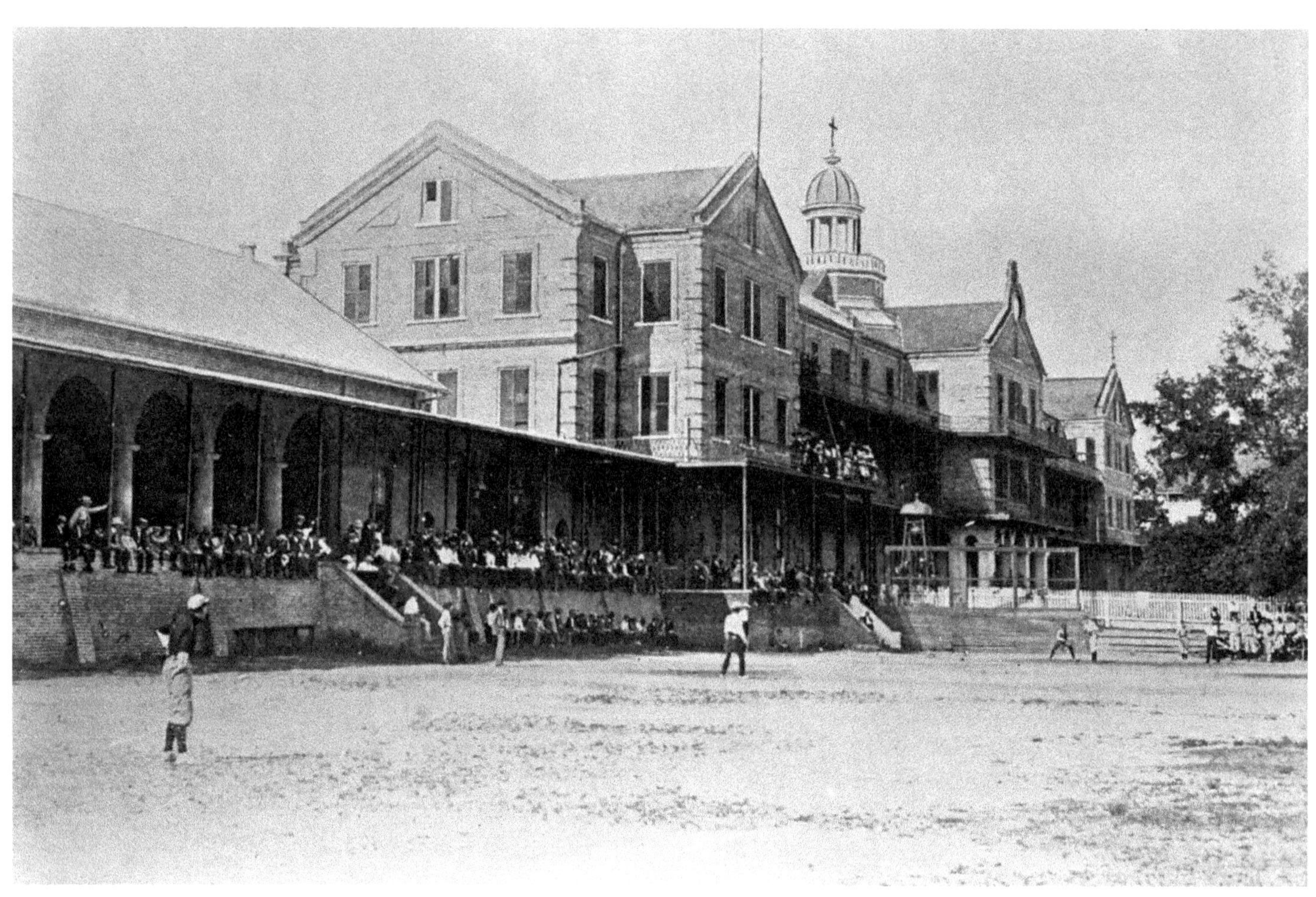

Established in 1830, Spring Hill College is one of the South's oldest universities. In this 1936 photograph, students interrupt their studies to enjoy a baseball game.

World War II and Beyond

(1940–1949)

Mobile would never be the same after the 1940s. Those ten years brought the city both economic benefits and economic despair. With the American economy heating up for war, there was a boom in employment early in the decade. The Alabama Dry Dock and Shipbuilding Company ran three shifts, 24 hours a day. Thousands of people from the state's interior came to the Port City to take the jobs ADDSCO offered. Overcrowding became so bad that single men often had to take turns sharing sleeping quarters. Families were forced to set up housekeeping in shacks or tents. Because of a shortage of classrooms, many schoolchildren prowled the streets during the day. Conditions were so poor in Mobile during World War II that the social revolutionary John Dos Passos called it a city "taken by storm." Despite the hardships associated with living in a place that had grown so large, so fast, people were grateful to have jobs.

As American men fought and died overseas, Mardi Gras took a five-year hiatus. But the city's perennial "whoop-de-doo" was back in full-swing by 1946. By then, shipyards were laying off their workers. There was one bright economic spot: through the efforts of local U.S. congressman Frank Boykin, Brookley Field maintained its prewar workforce. In fact, it surpassed ADDSCO as the city's largest employer.

For African-Americans, the 1940s were not unproductive years. The civil rights protests in Montgomery, Birmingham, and Selma were still years away, but one local leader, John L. LeFlore, attacked Jim Crow in Mobile on all fronts, from job discrimination to voting rights to interstate travel. And the people who ran Brookley Field, because it was a U.S. air base, were required to treat black workers equally.

Despite the enormous growth in population Mobile had experienced and the other changes the city had gone through during the 1940s, city leaders had failed to entice new industry or provide its citizens with other social benefits like an art museum or civic auditorium. Brookley was so large, they were sure it would provide all the employment the city needed. That lapse in judgment would soon come to haunt City Hall.

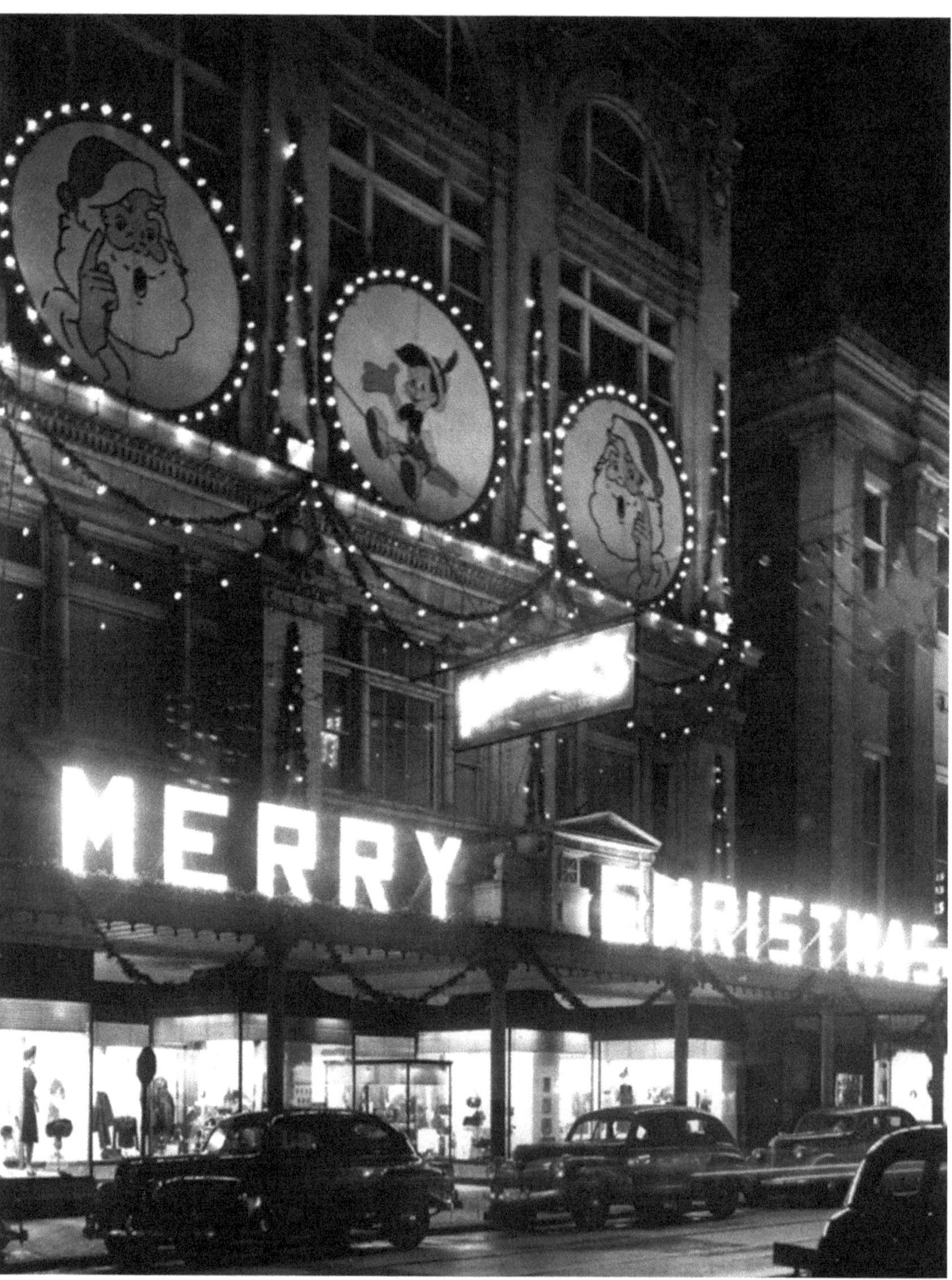

The outside of Hammel's Department Store, decorated for the Christmas season in 1948.

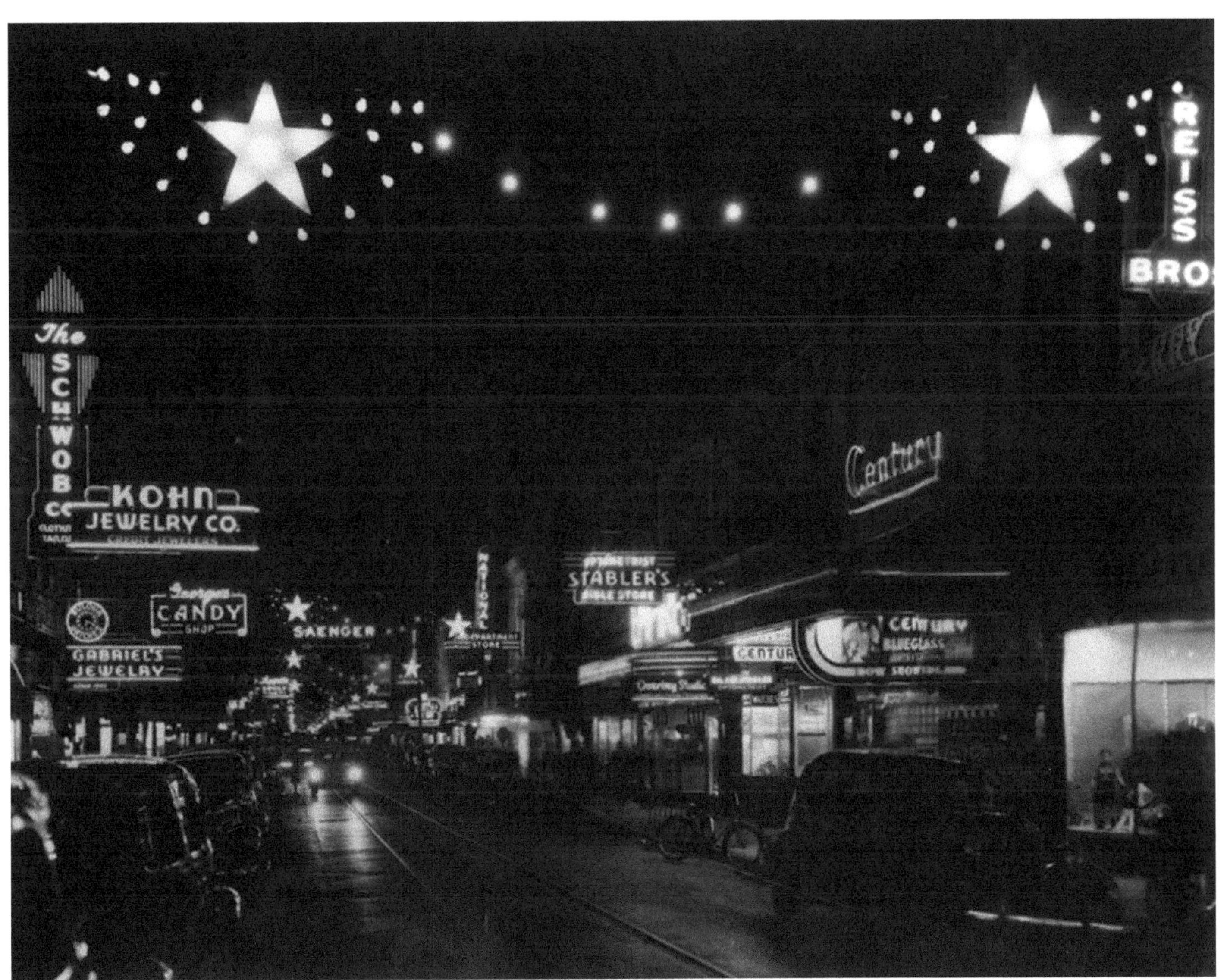

Dauphin between Conception and Joachim, lit up for the holidays (ca. 1940).

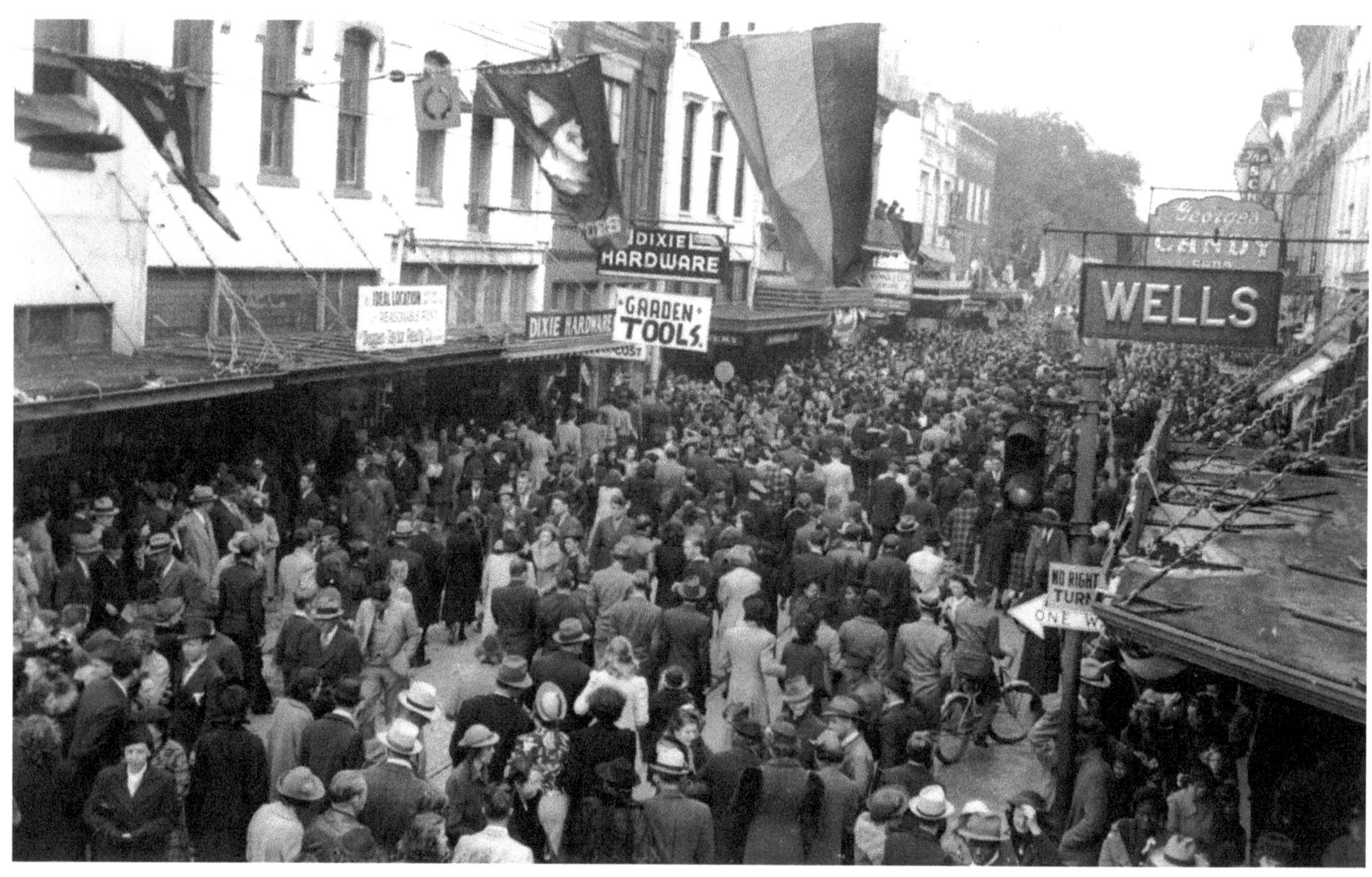

A crowd streams down Dauphin Street toward Bienville Square, probably during the Carnival season (ca. 1940).

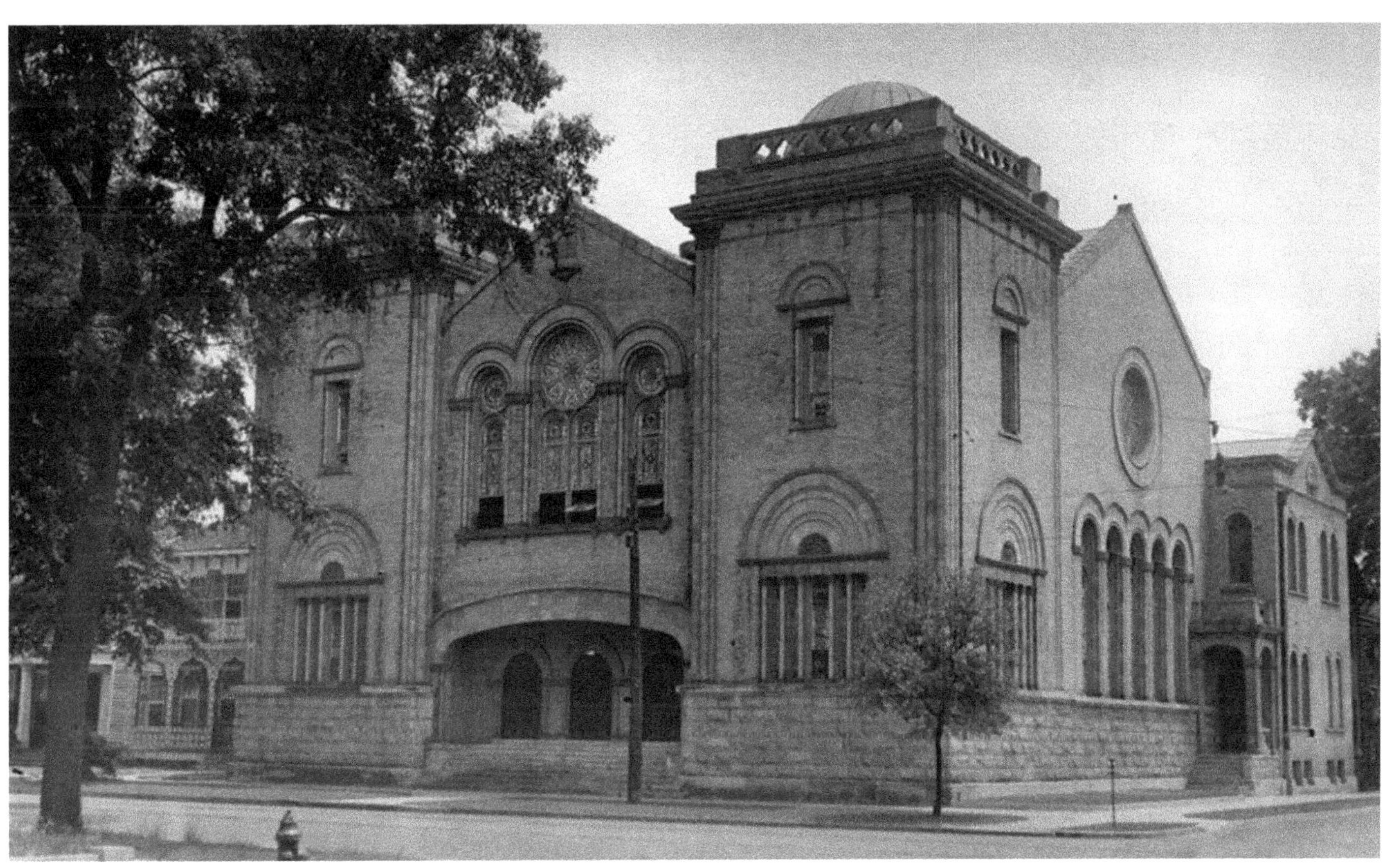

The Sha'arai Shomayim Synagogue on Government Street. Alfred G. Moses, who had served as the congregation's rabbi since 1901, was succeeded by Dr. Sidney Berkowitz in 1940. The next few years would see rapid changes in leadership as Berkowitz and his successor, Bertram Korn, left for military service.

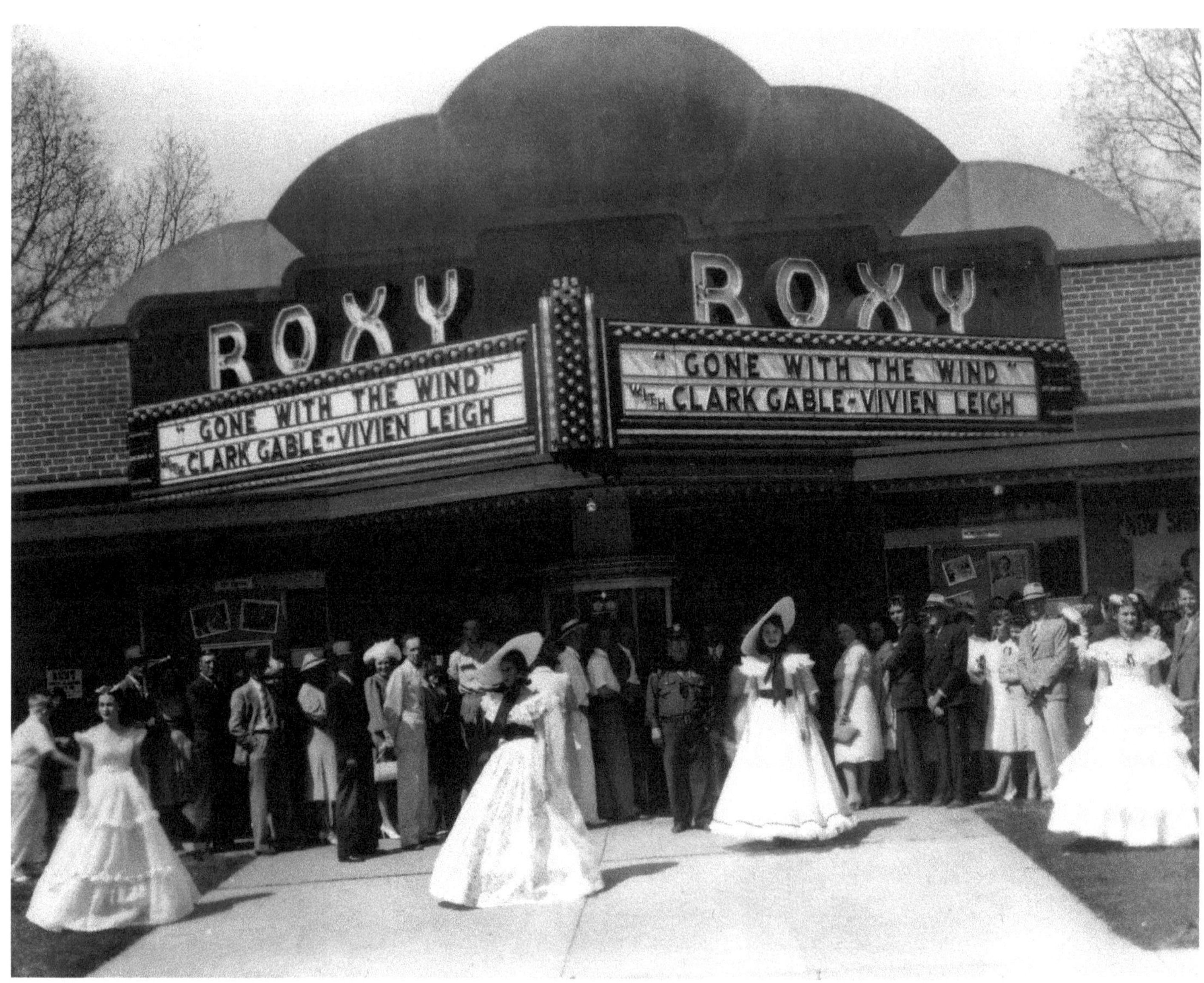

Like other Americans, Mobilians were taken with the movie *Gone with the Wind.* The winner of ten Academy Awards, the film eventually made its way to Mobile. In this 1941 photo, Azalea Trail maids pose in front of a crowd waiting to get into the Roxy Theater.

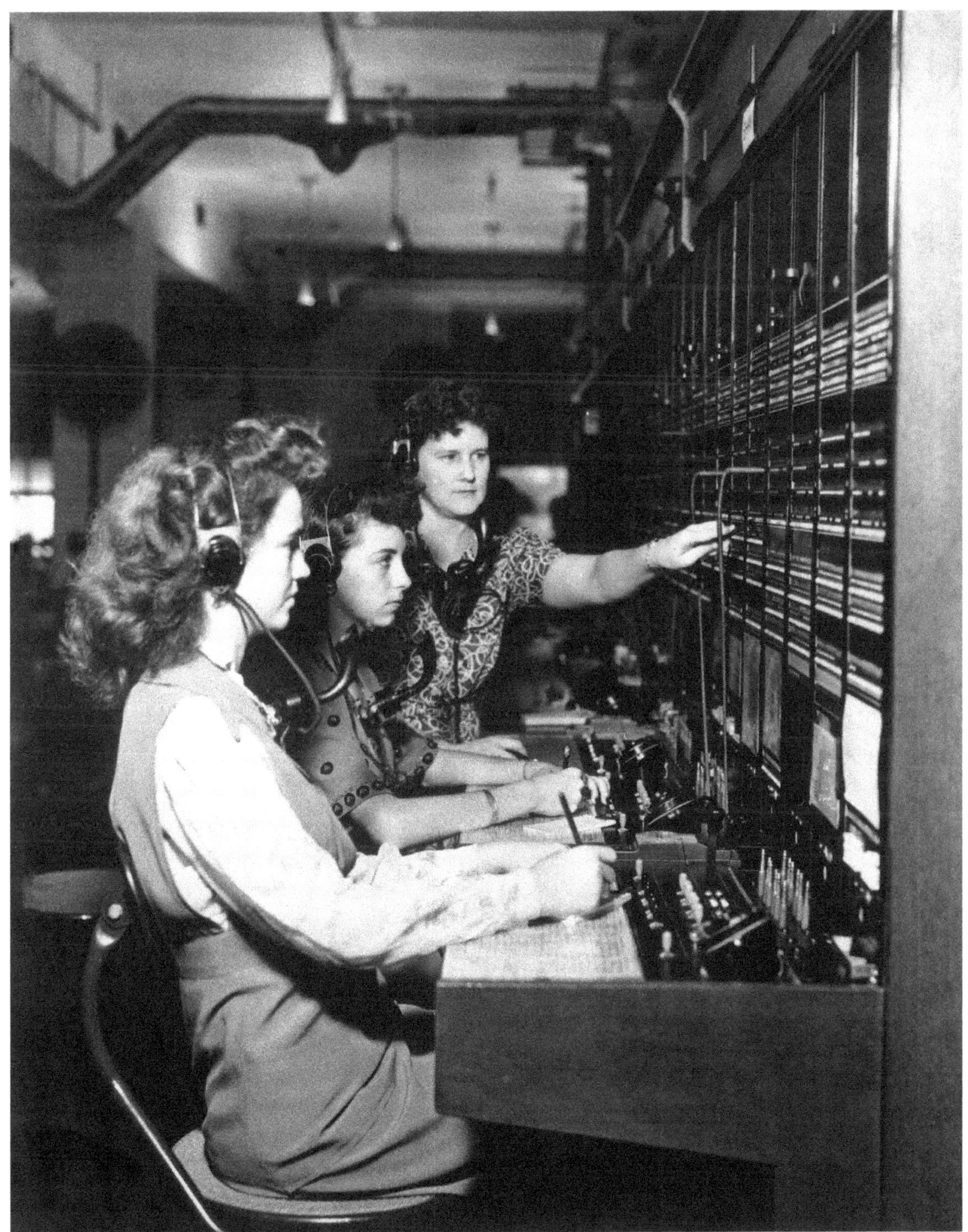

A supervisor with the Southern Bell Telephone Company instructs two women on how to connect phone calls, 1942 style.

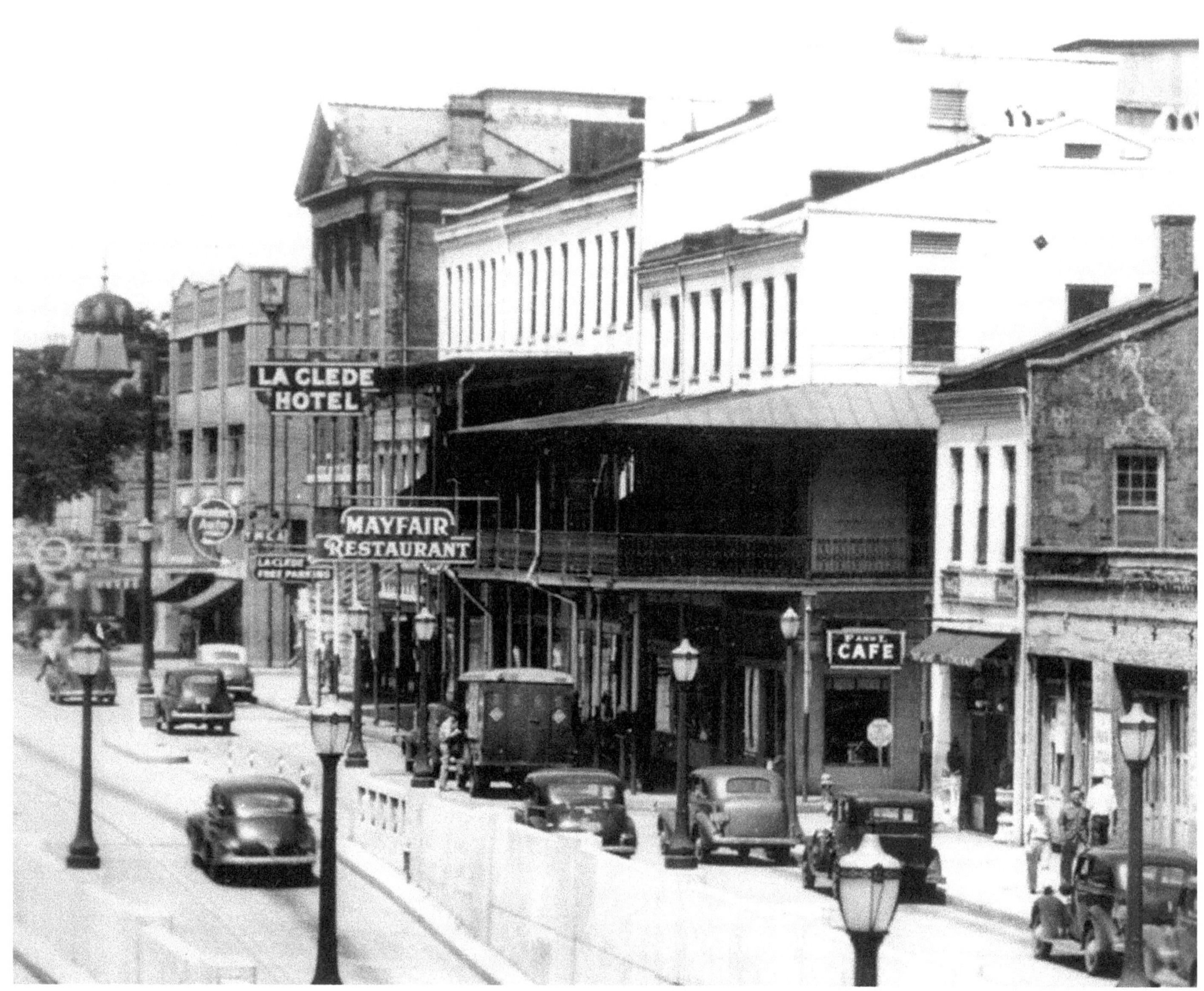

This photo from 1941 shows Government Street at the Bankhead Tunnel, looking west toward the La Clede Hotel and beyond.

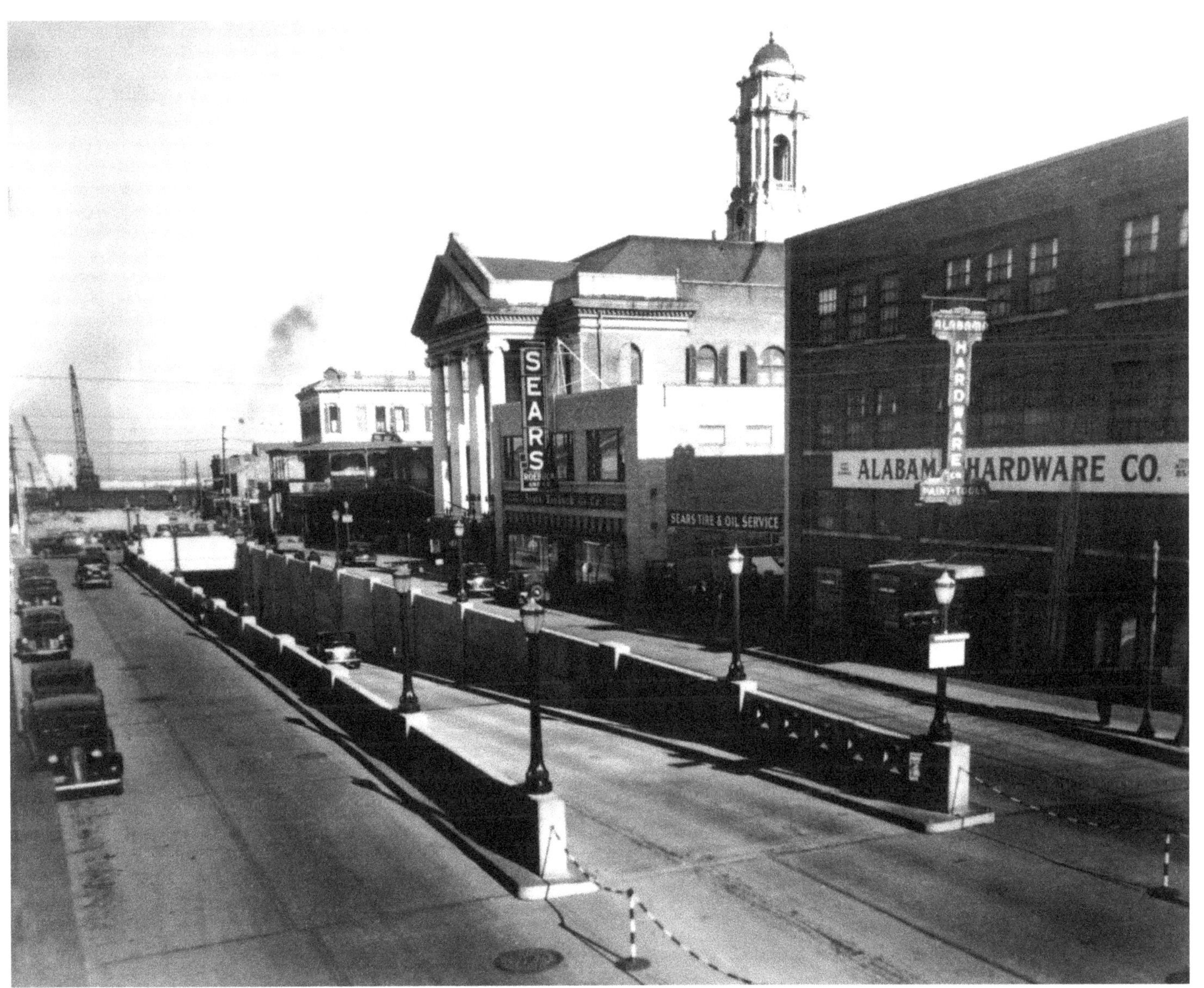

Government Street, looking east from the entrance to the Bankhead Tunnel (ca. 1942).

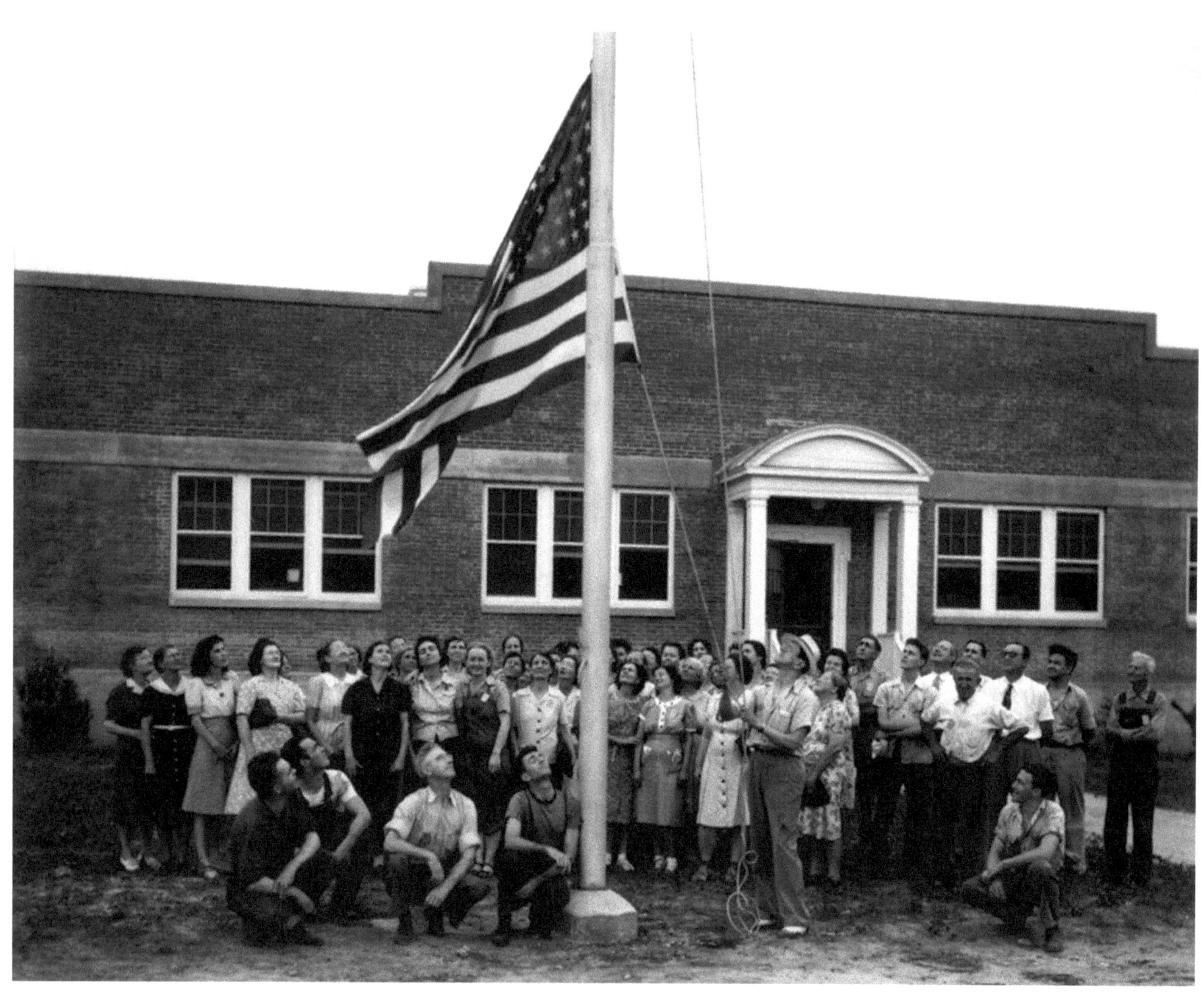

An employee of Bemis Brothers Bag Company raises the nation's flag as his fellow workers look on, May 5, 1943.

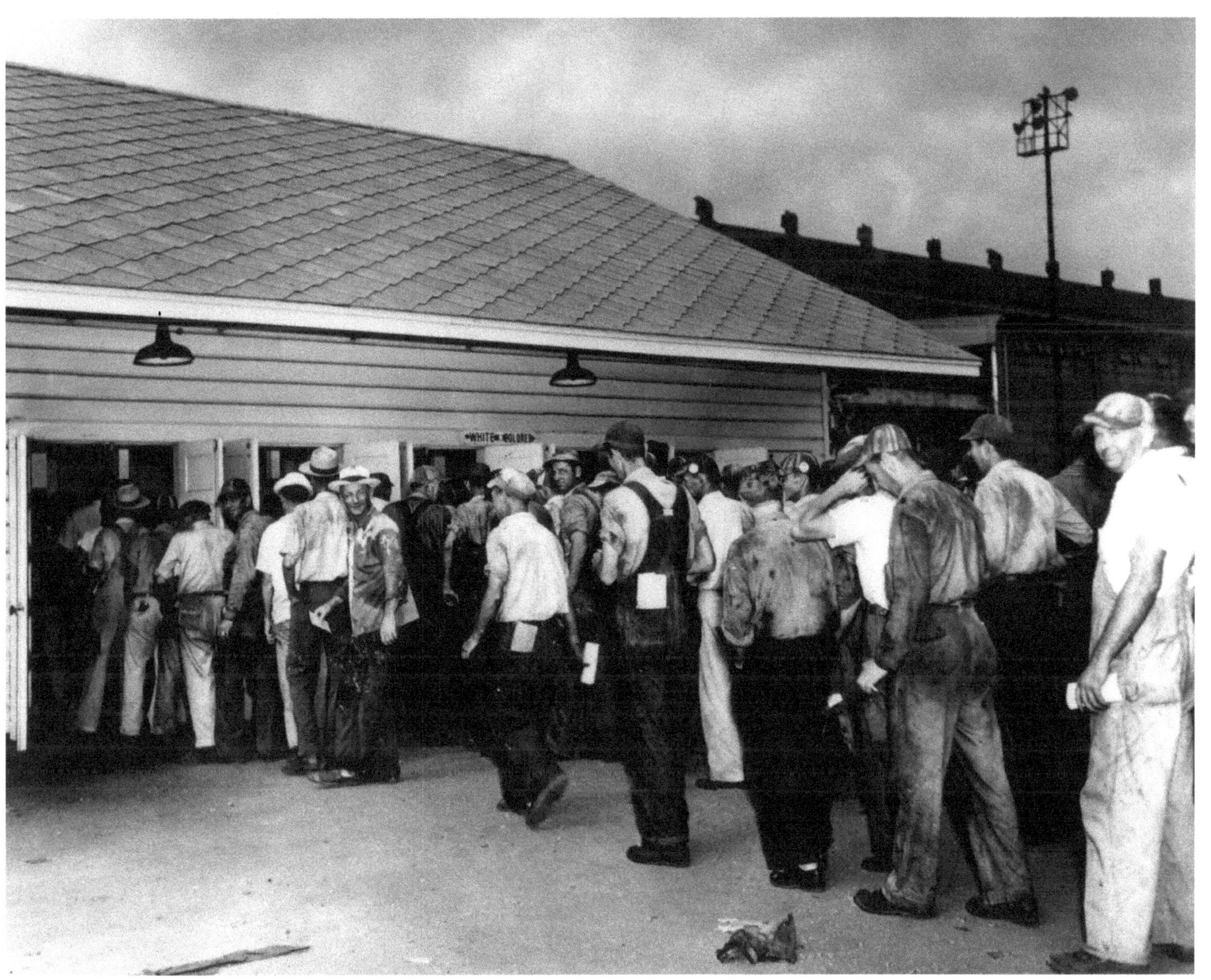

Shipyard workers at Alabama Dry Dock and Shipbuilding Company (ADDSCO) wait for their wages in the pay line around 1943. The sign on the clapboard siding is evidence of the days of segregation.

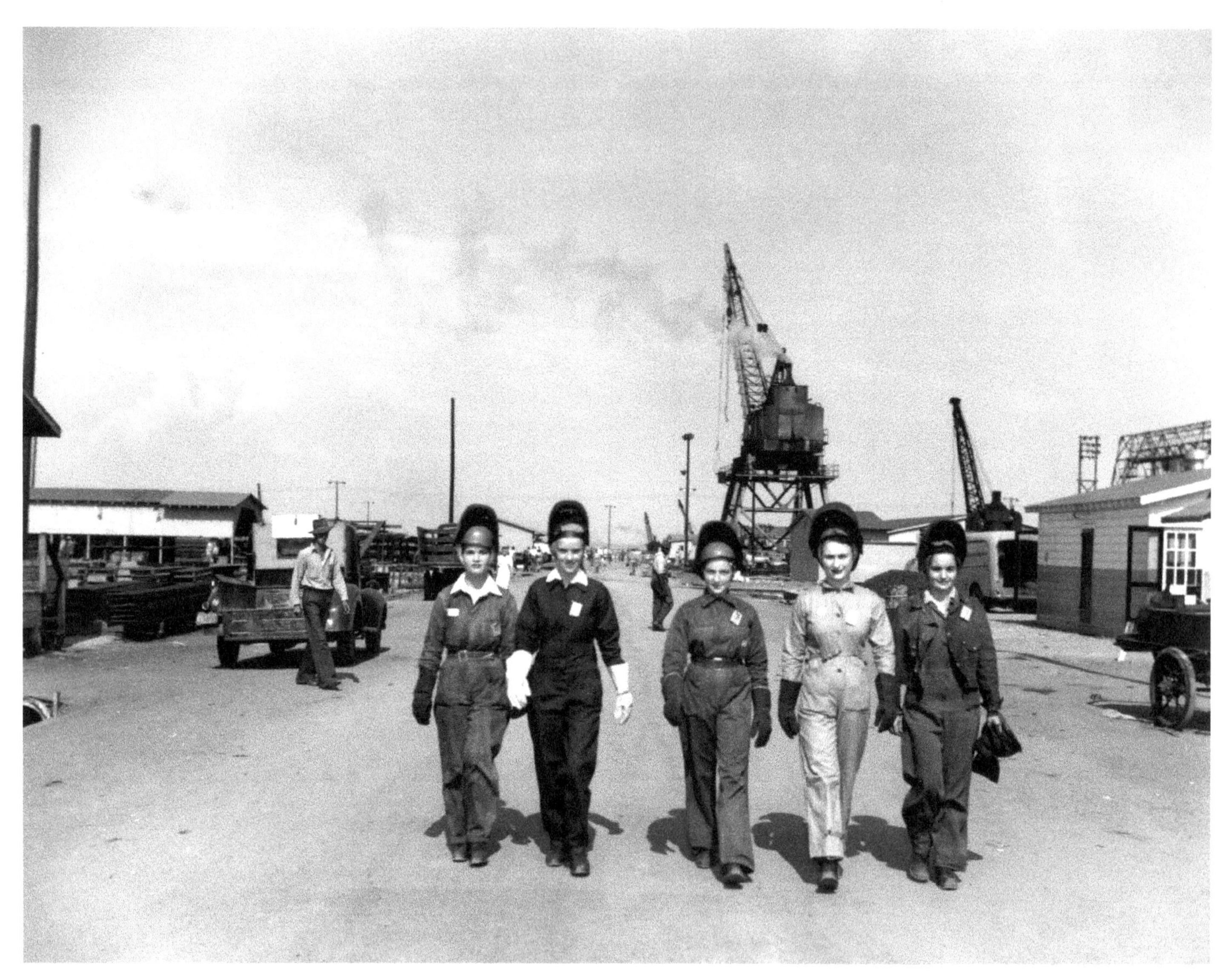

More than 60 women worked as welders at ADDSCO during World War II. These five women are representative of them.

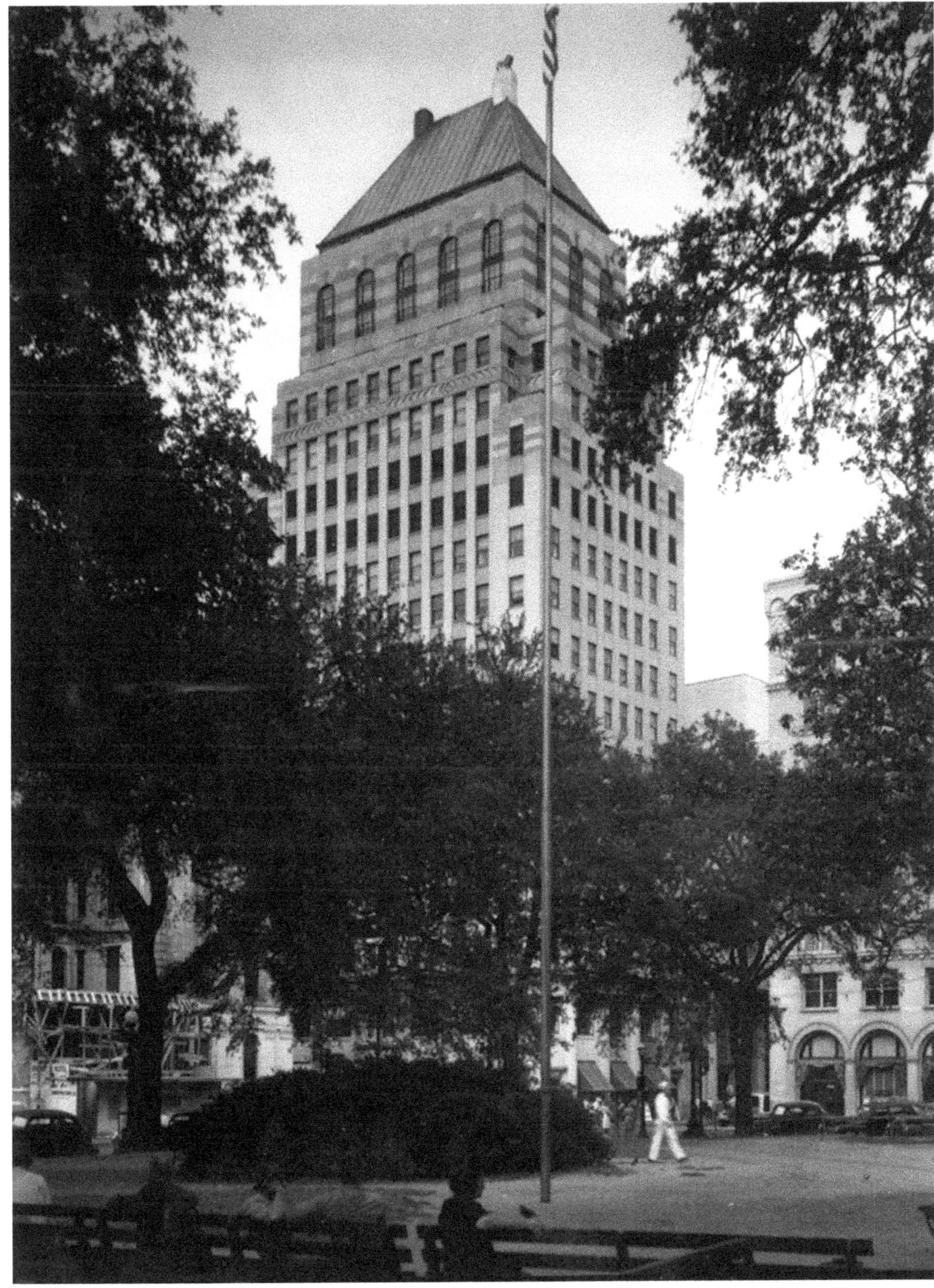

Built in 1929, the Merchants National Bank building looms over the scene as a sailor walks across Bienville Square around 1942.

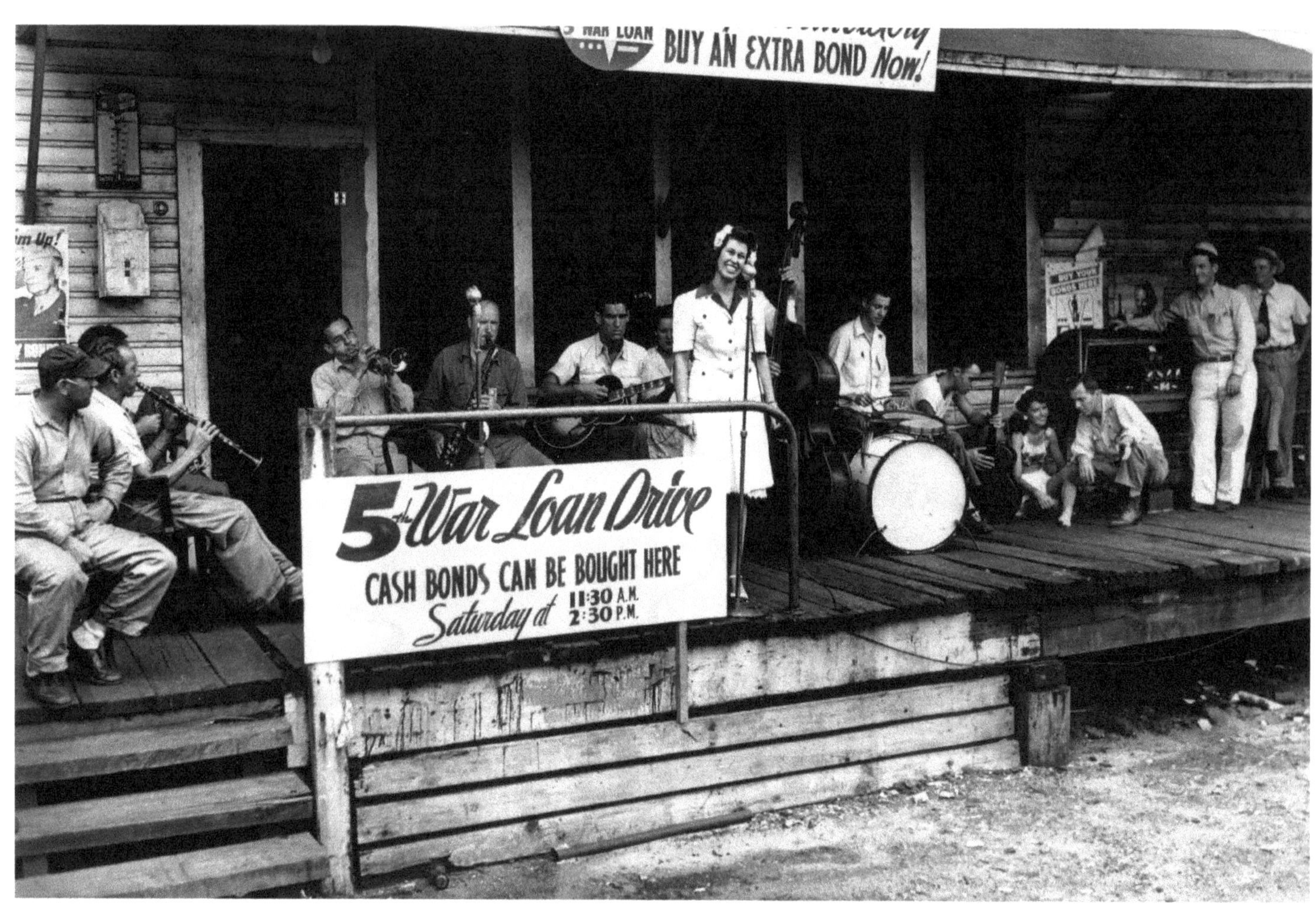

One of many bond rallies held at ADDSCO during World War II (ca. 1944). Such rallies were a common practice, helping to finance the conflict.

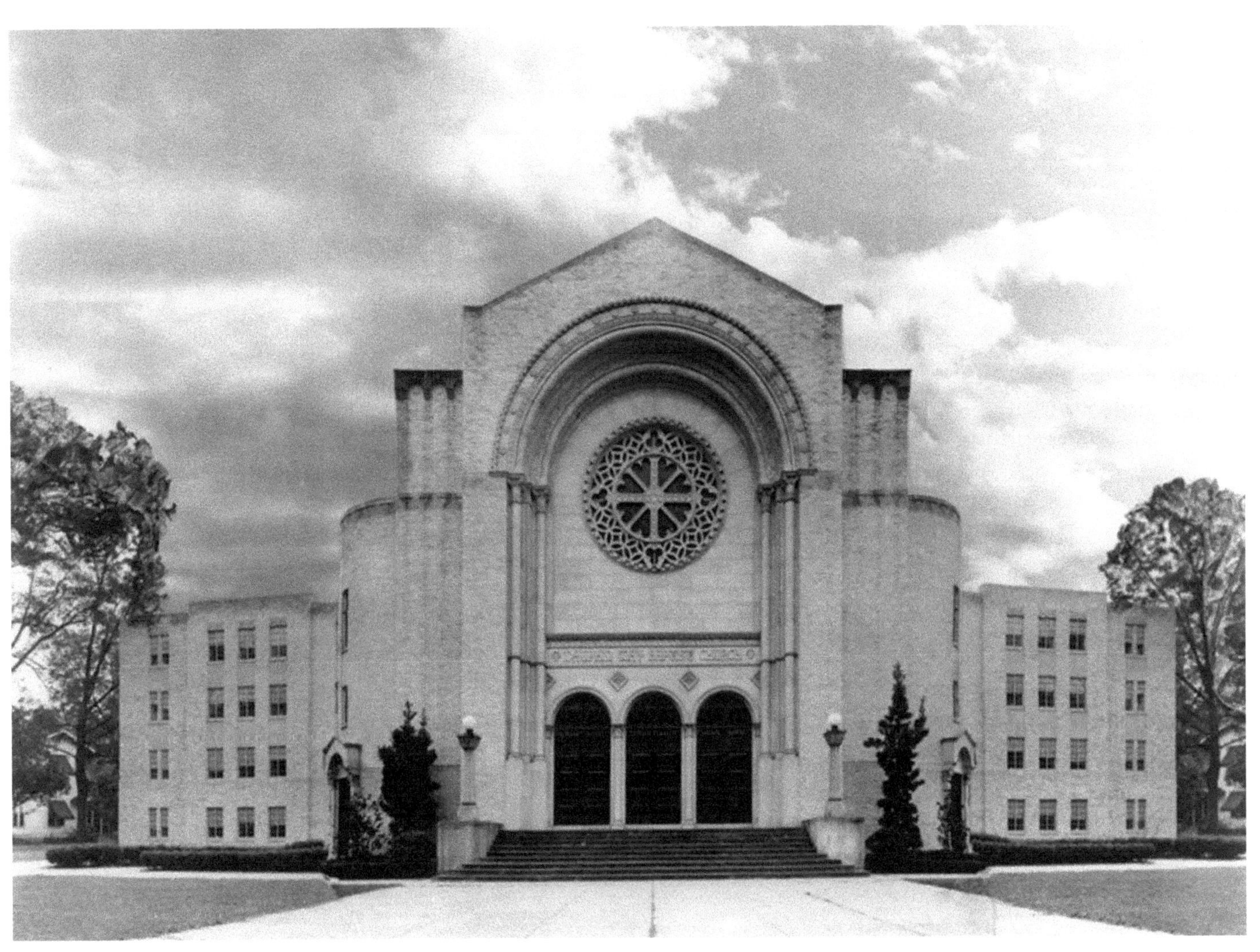

The old Dauphin Way Baptist Church on Dauphin Street. After the church relocated to West Mobile, the Alabama School of Math and Science moved into this building.

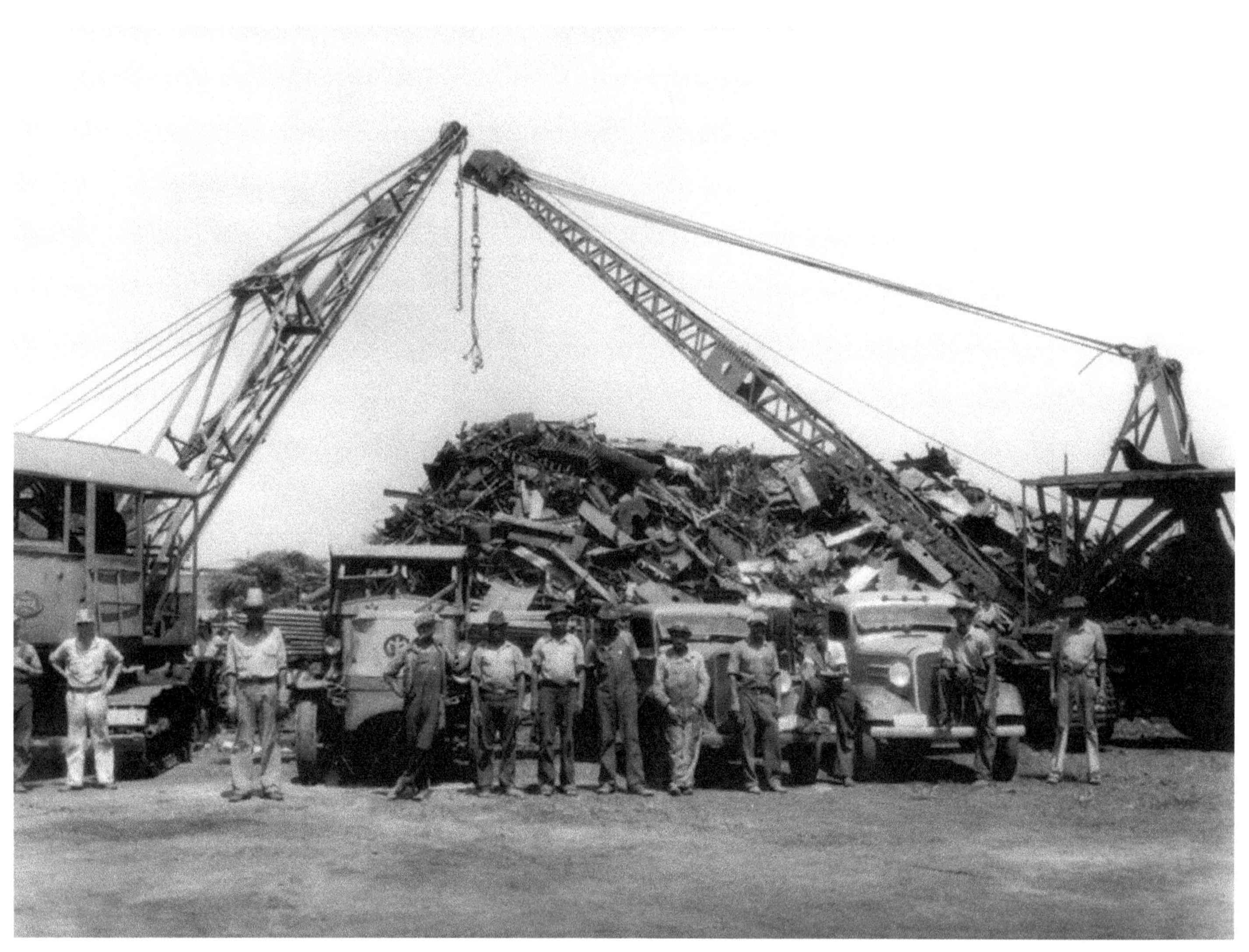

Workers stand in front of piled scrap metal as cranes hover in the background (ca. 1940).

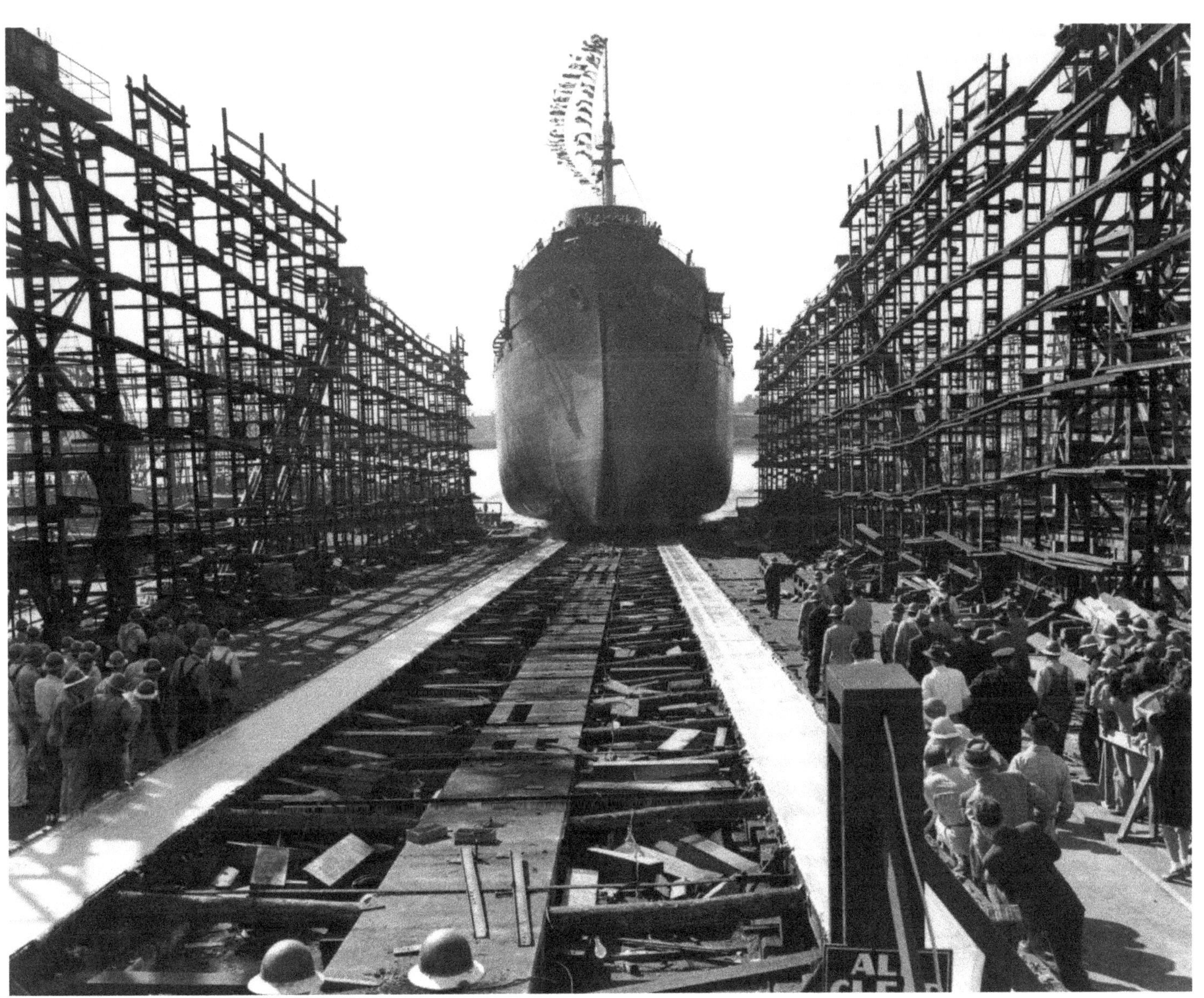

Mobile's shipbuilding industry has always been an important part of its economy. Here the tanker SS *Wyoming Valley* slides down the way on January 31, 1944. The ship was the 47th vessel built at ADDSCO during World War II, and was sponsored by the wife of city commissioner Charles Baumhauer.

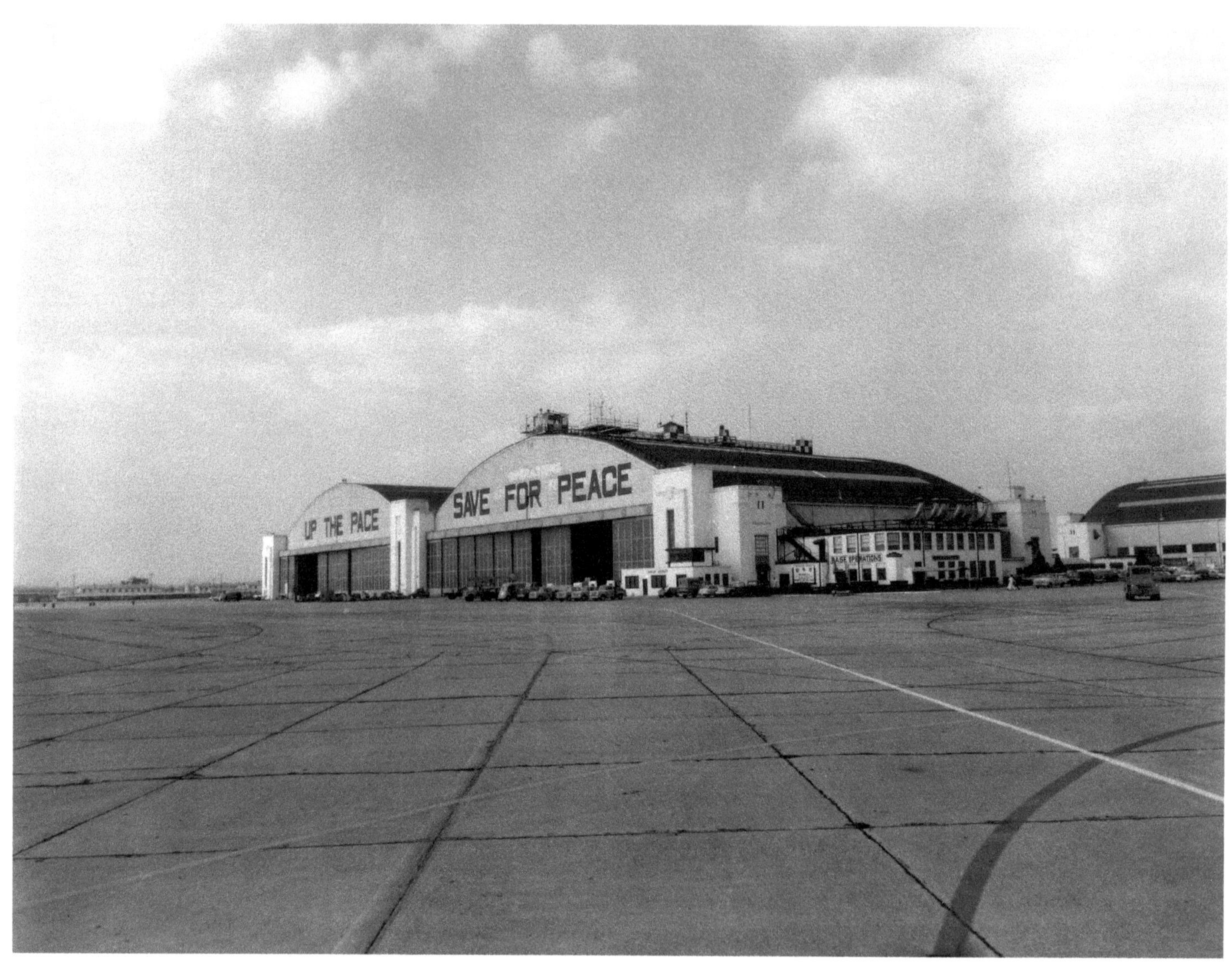

Through the efforts of local U.S. Congressman Frank Boykin, the federal government announced plans on July 13, 1939, to put a new air supply depot at Brookley Field. Located on the waterfront, the site was chosen for its deep water and rail access. Construction began on June 20, 1940. The first enlisted man arrived August 10, 1940, and the first plane landed on March 5, 1941.

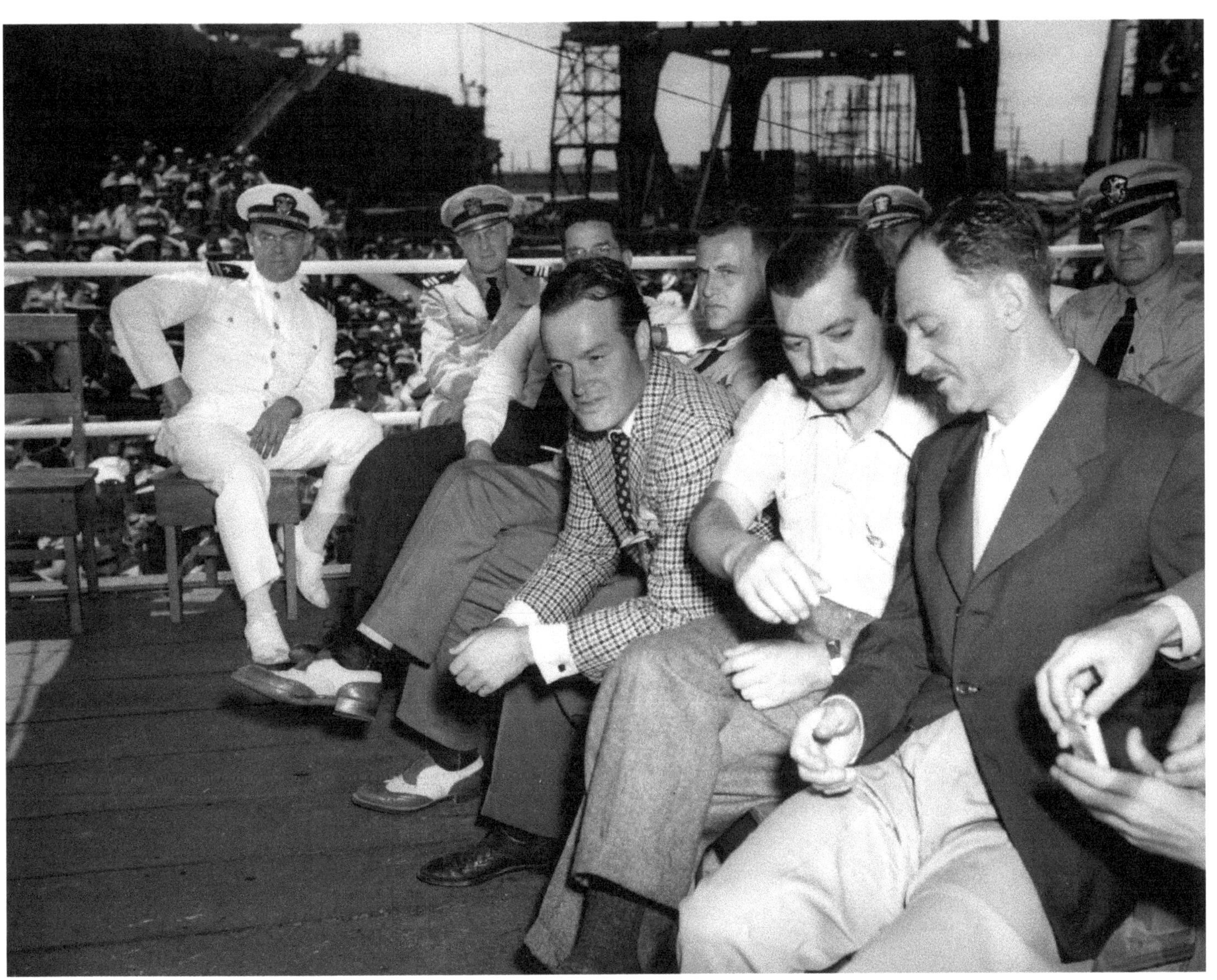

On March 1, 1944, Bob Hope, Jerry Colonna, and other entertainers came to Mobile to launch the SS *White River.* While here, Hope and his troupe entertained ADDSCO workers.

This elaborate Victorian building, constructed of brick and terra cotta, originally housed the Zadek Jewelry Company. In 1947, when this photo was taken, the Three Sisters clothing store occupied the site.

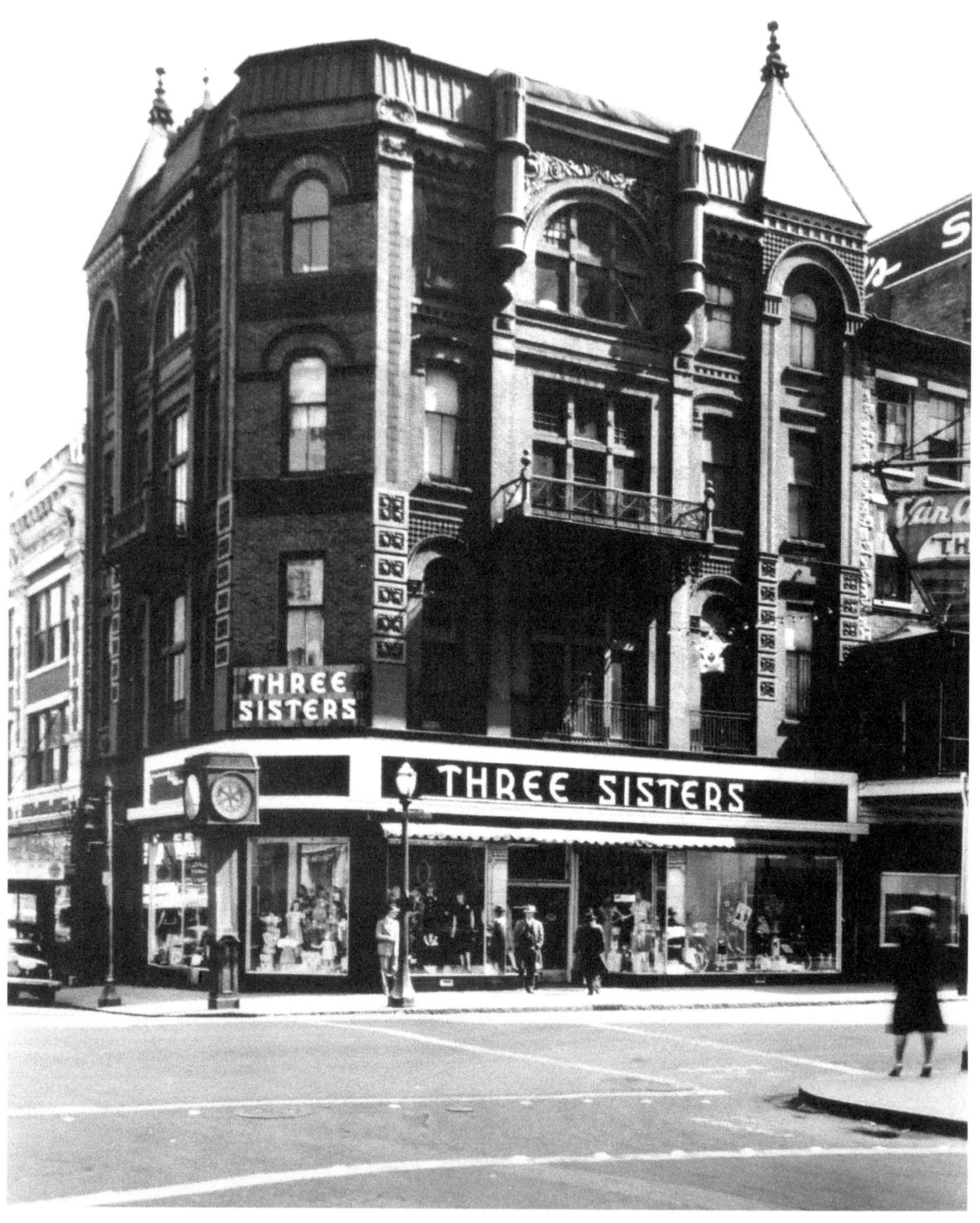

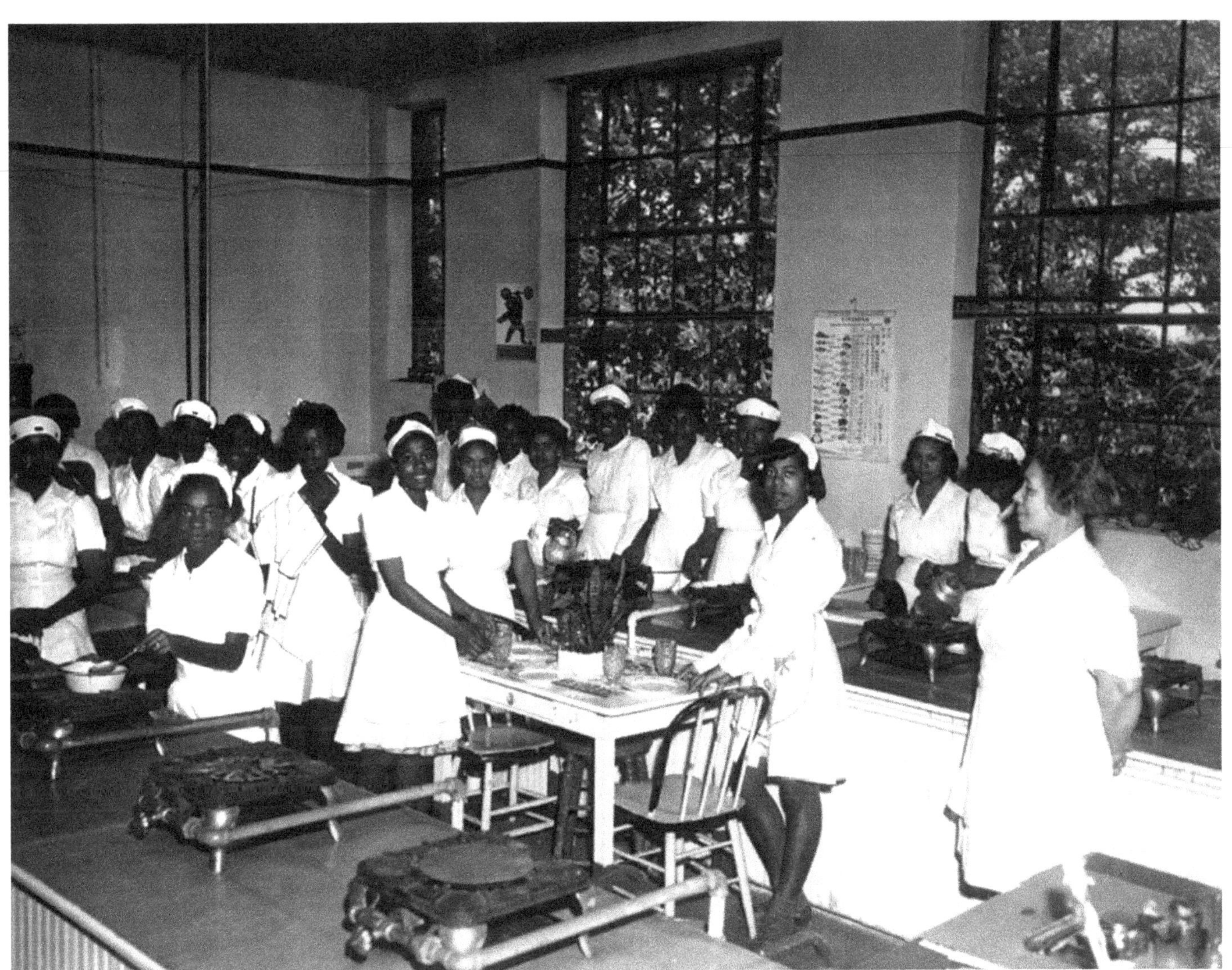

A home economics class at all-black Dunbar High School in 1946.

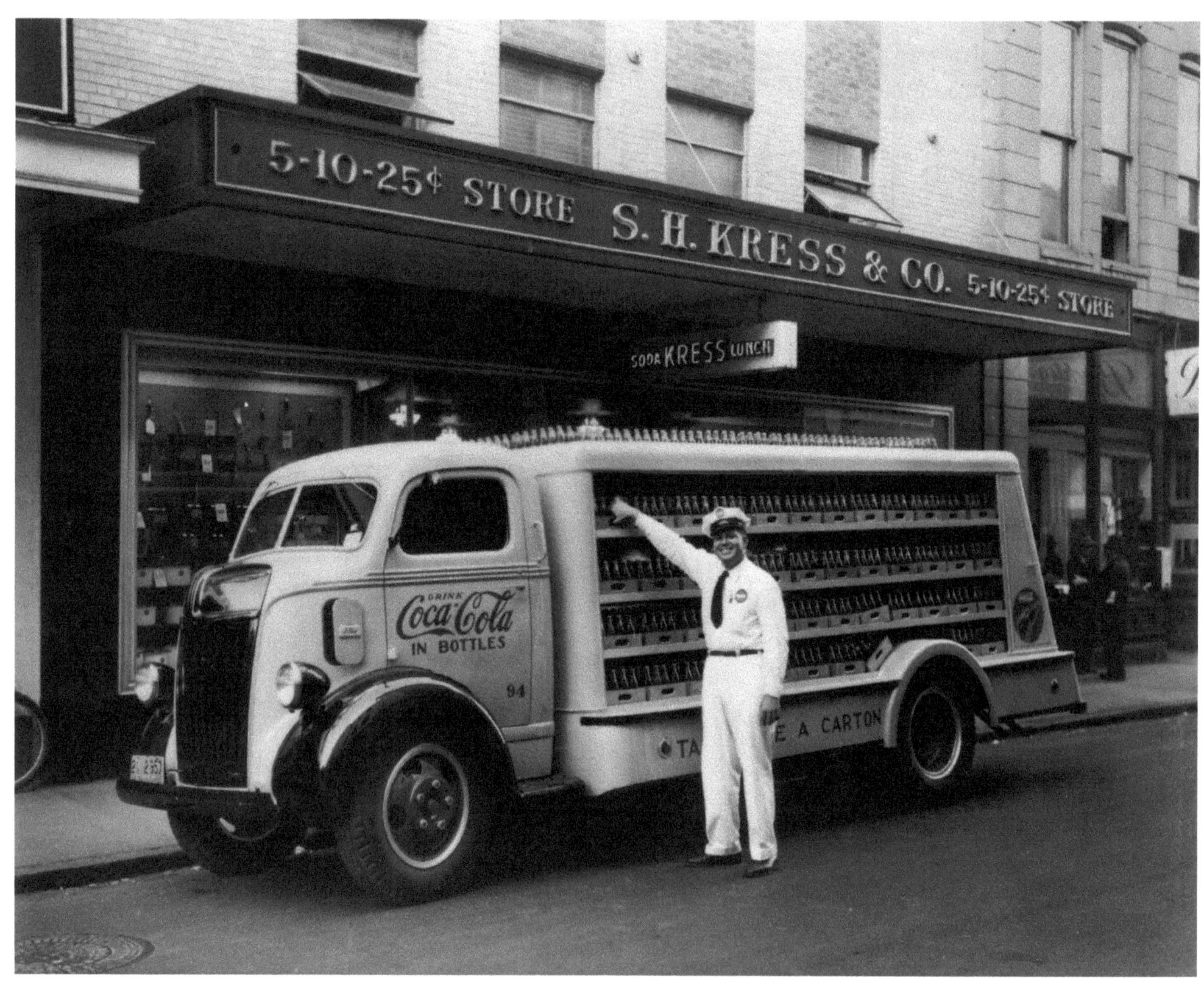

Driver Carlisle Dahmer stands in front of his Coca-Cola delivery truck outside the S. H. Kress dime store in the 1940s, when Coke was widely distributed in glass bottles.

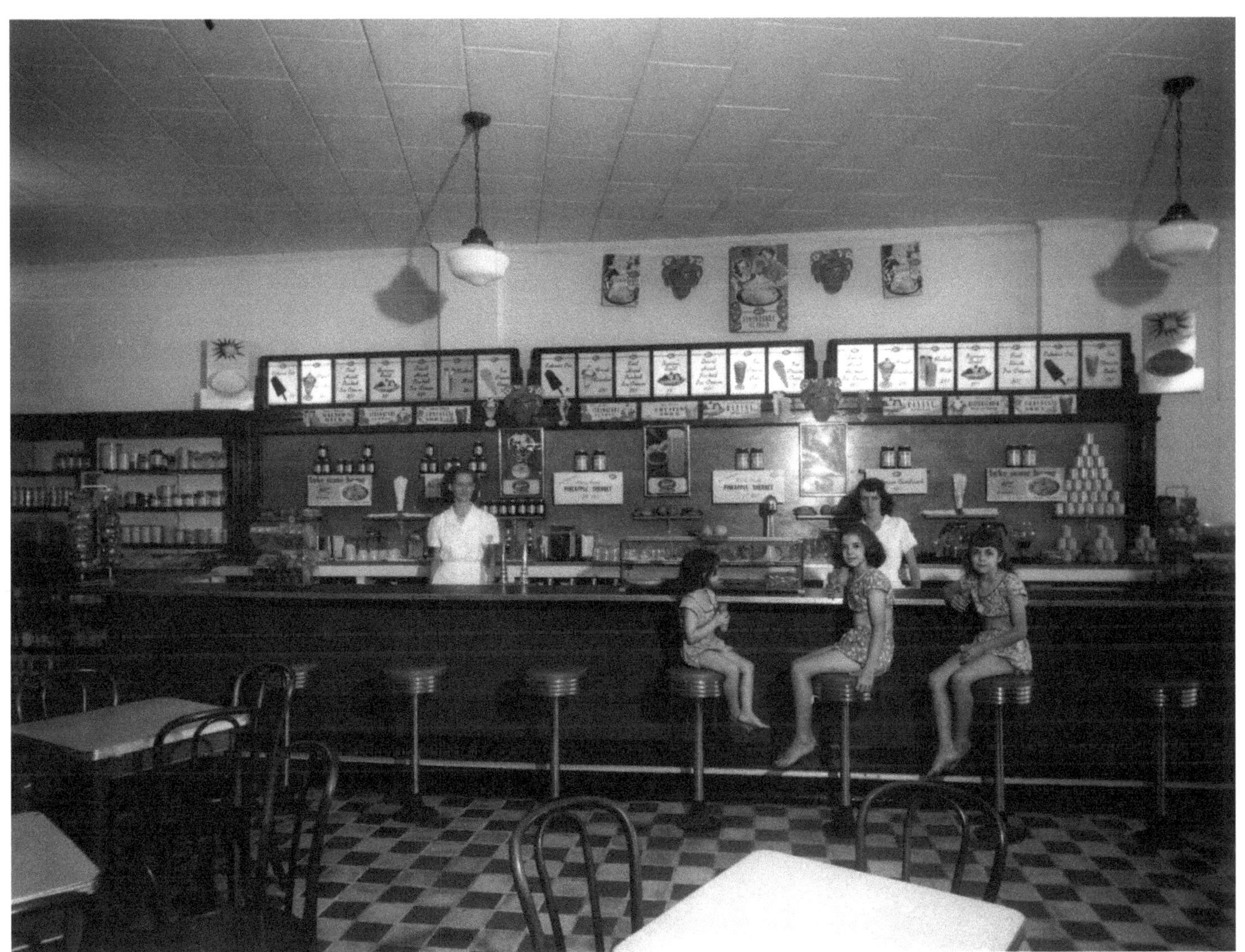

The soda fountain at the Toulminville Drug Store in 1948. It sold ice cream cones for a nickel and banana splits for thirty-five cents.

A youngster looks up from reading a comic book in the magazine section of a local grocery store. The smorgasbord of comics includes issue number two of *Marge's Little Lulu, Roy Rogers,* a number of pre-comics code titles, and *Walt Disney Comics and Stories,* at lower right, but few if any superhero titles.

From Opportunity to Stagnation

(1950–1979)

As Mobile entered the 1950s, it could sit back and enjoy the good life. Europe was in ruins and America was ascendant. Jobs were plentiful and conditions had improved. The city seemed to be doing well. Carnival not only continued, it grew. New mystic societies formed, and the celebration expanded until it became an event lasting a fortnight rather than a few days, as it had years before.

But problems were on the horizon. City leaders had historically been slow to seek new sources of revenue. They had relied on the port and the goods that moved through it and, since World War II, on the tax base provided by Brookley. A 1960 report finally aroused City Hall. It took Mobile to task for its industrial, social, and civic malaise and ranked it lower than New Orleans and Atlanta in nearly every category. Equally shocking, the federal government announced plans in 1964 to close Brookley. Now the city faced the prospect of losing a payroll that had reached $93 million in 1960.

Mobile seemed to be a town in the doldrums. Unlike New Orleans or Savannah, which preserved their historic buildings and charming ambience, Mobile fled its downtown. It toppled many of its most architecturally beautiful buildings. People rejected the old in favor of West Mobile or the Eastern Shore, movement made easy by the automobile and new interstate highway systems. To make matters worse, the city was devastated by Hurricane Frederick in September 1979, which caused two deaths and massive damage.

City leaders, however, rose to the challenges facing them. They attracted new industry, built an art museum, constructed a city auditorium, and made tourism a priority. Additional help came when the University of South Alabama was founded in 1963. It helped brunt the economic loss caused by Brookley's closing and is today one of the city's largest employers. African-Americans, too, progressed through the 30 years between 1950 and 1979. They launched a successful school desegregation suit and prevailed in a court case that eventually changed the city's form of government. They integrated golf courses, the police force, and lunch counters.

As 1980 approached, Mobile still seemed to be afraid of the future yet unwilling to embrace its past. Regardless, the city could look back on its long history and learn from it, knowing that it had withstood a civil war, natural disasters, an embarrassing bankruptcy, and civic complacency.

Dauphin Street at Conception, looking east, with a city bus in the foreground and the W. T. Grant Company in the background (ca. 1950).

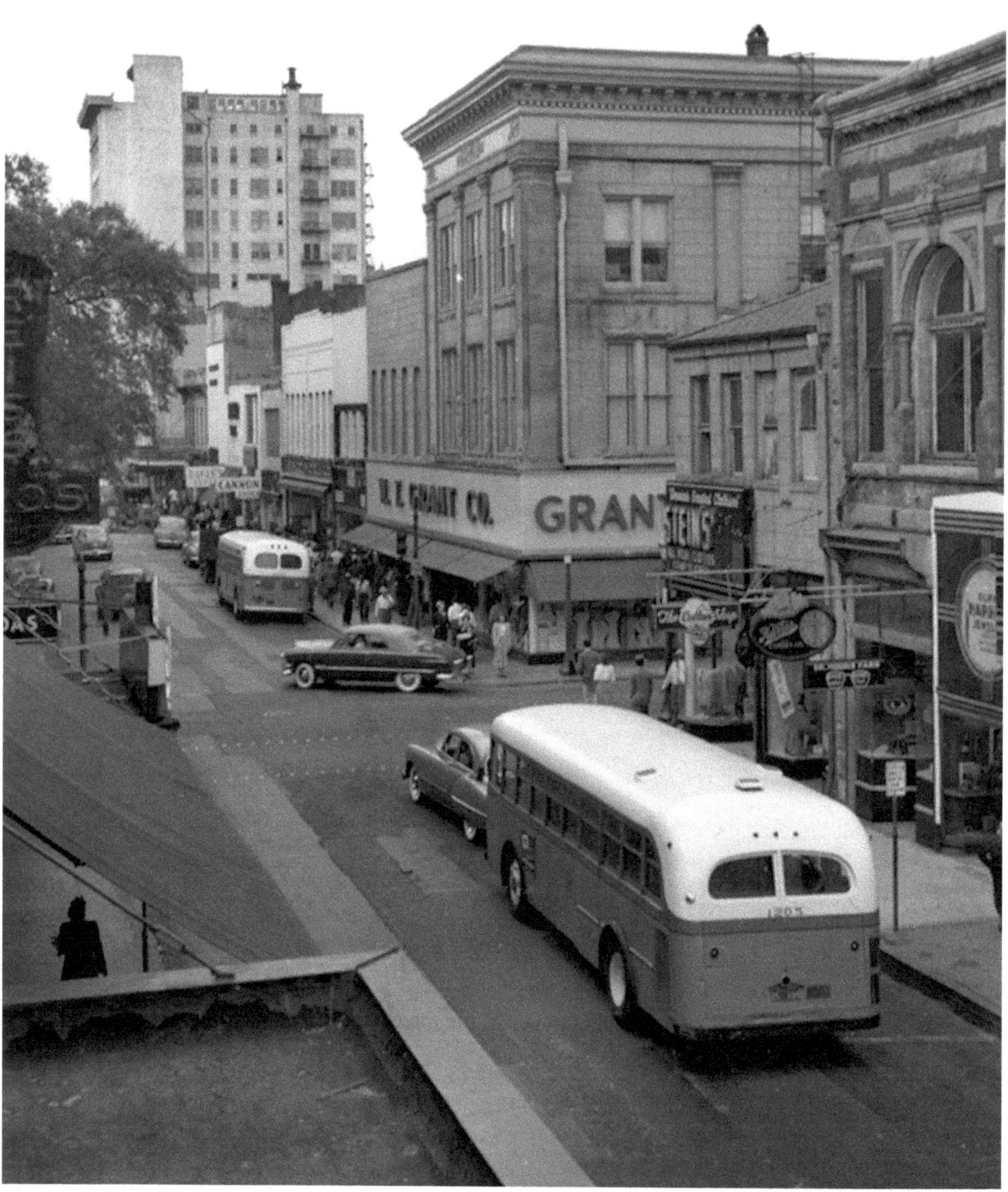

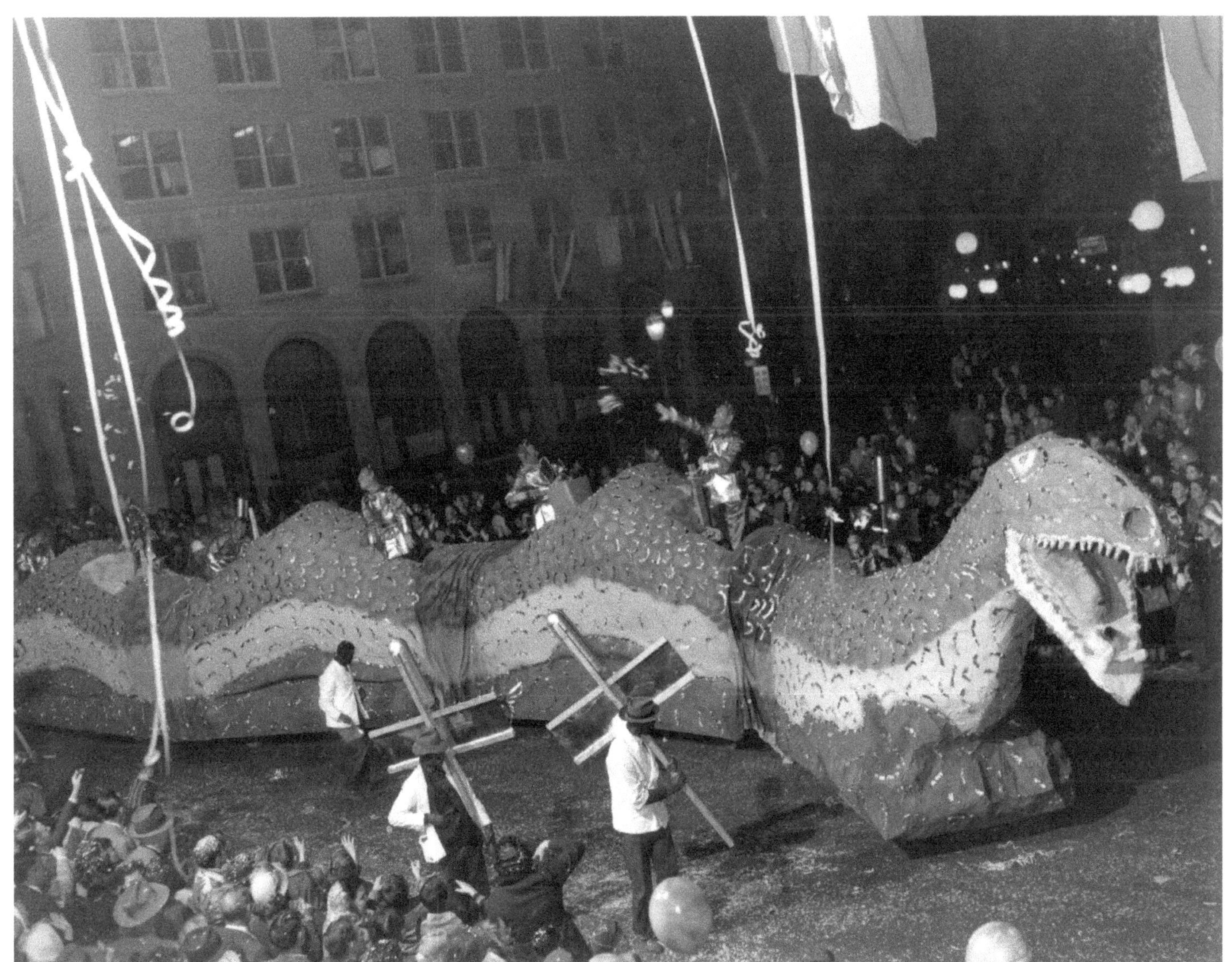

Vernadean—a combination of Verna and Dean—is the dragon associated with the Mystics of Time Mardi Gras society. It has been featured in their processions since the organization's first parade in 1949. Here she is in 1950, winding down the street as maskers throw trinkets to the crowd.

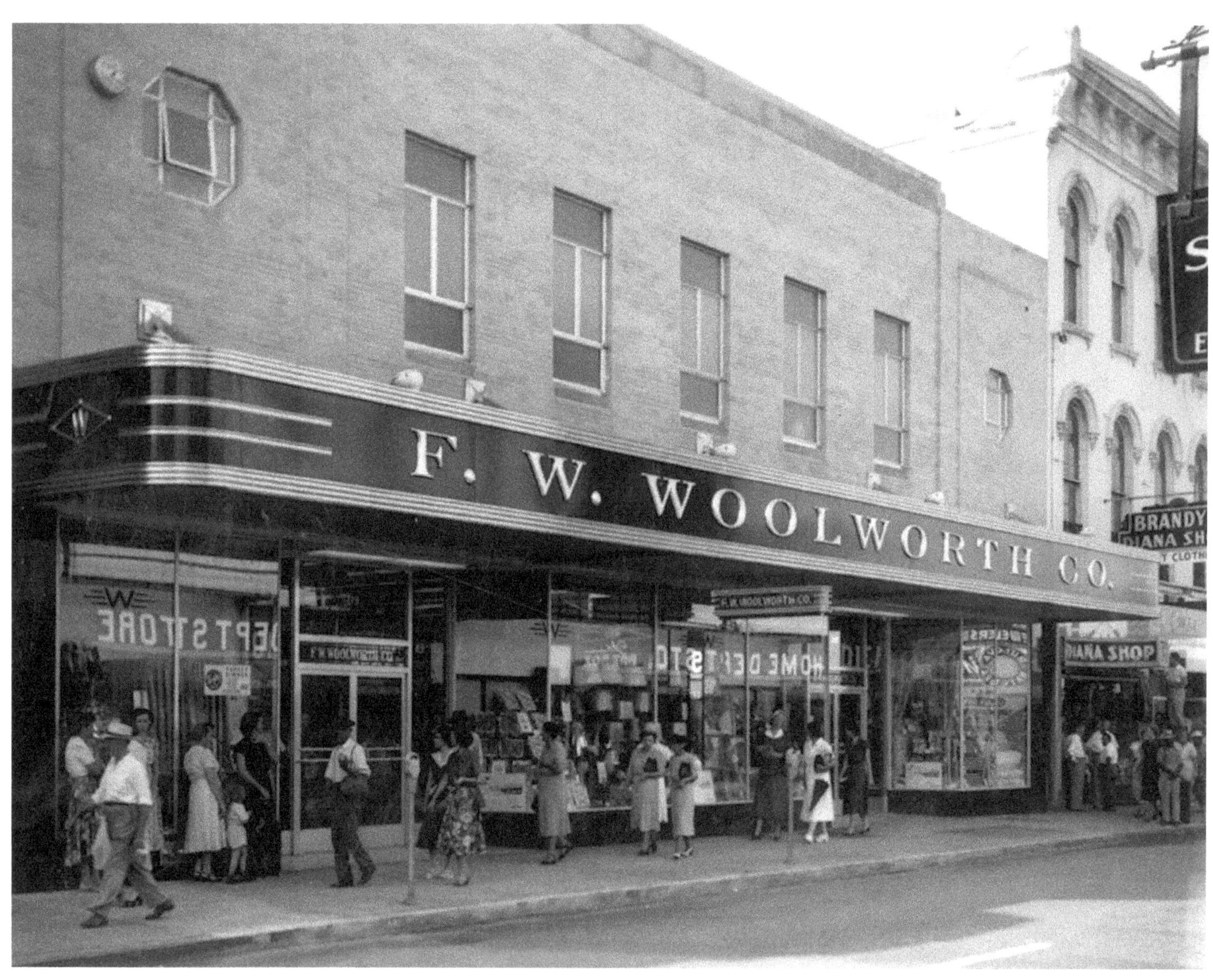

The exterior of Woolworth's Five and Dime in 1950, which was located then on Dauphin Street.

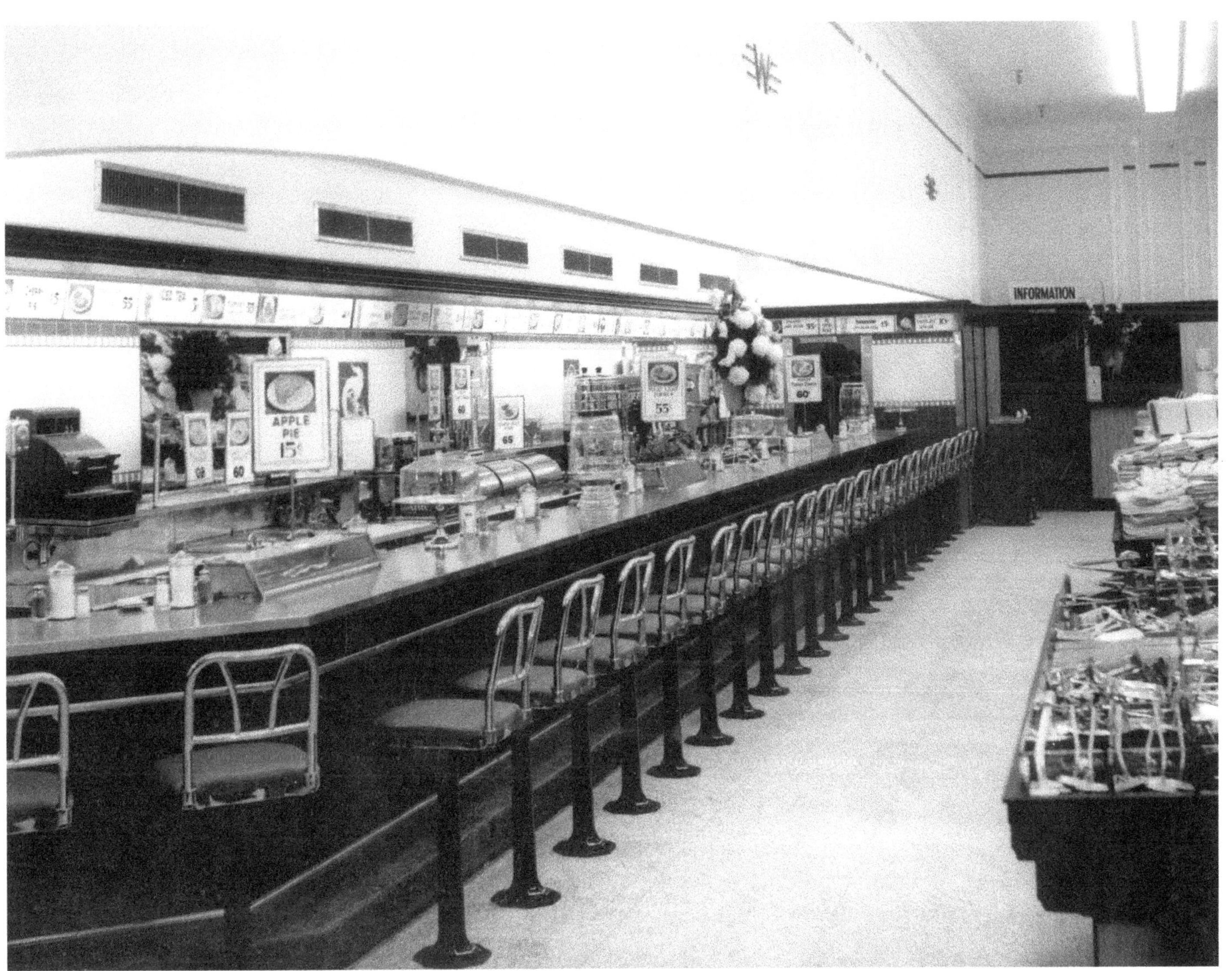

The lunch counter of the Woolworth's Five and Dime in 1950. One of the signs at the far end of the photo requests, "No Tipping Please."

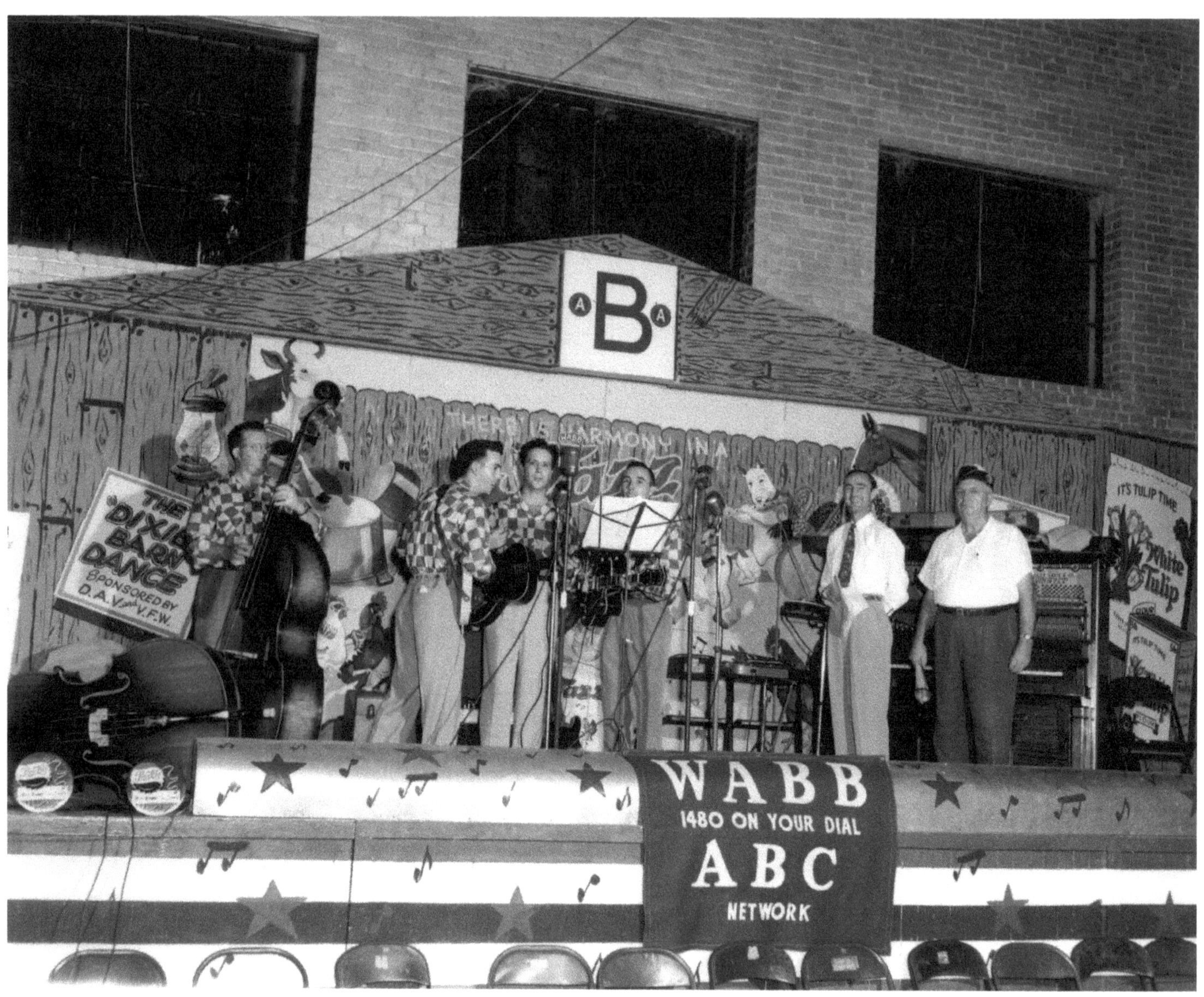

This September 11, 1952, dance was sponsored by the Disabled American Veterans and Veterans of Foreign Wars. It was probably held at Fort Whiting Auditorium. The band remains unidentified.

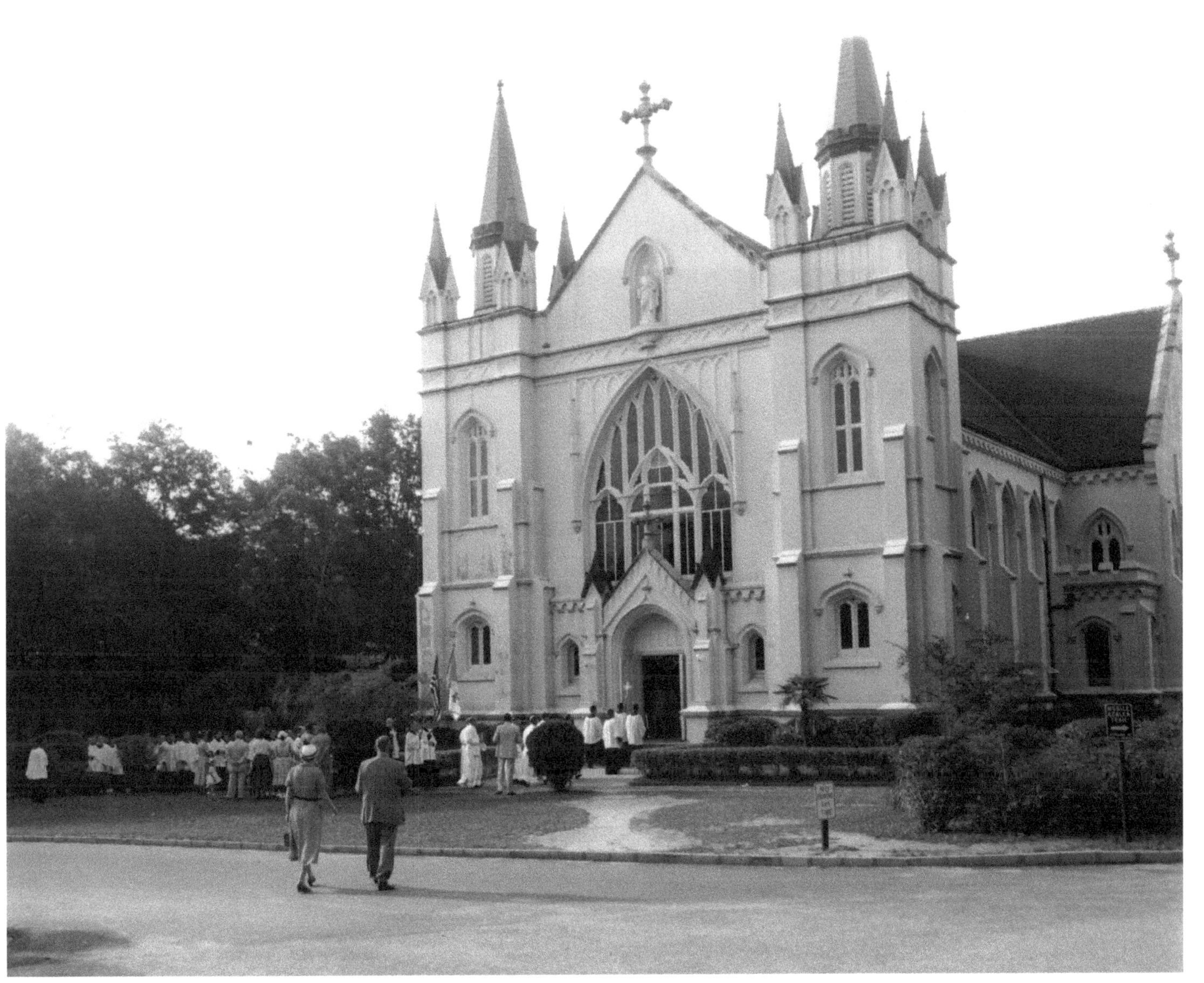

Ordination at St. Joseph's Chapel on the campus of Spring Hill College, June 16, 1954.

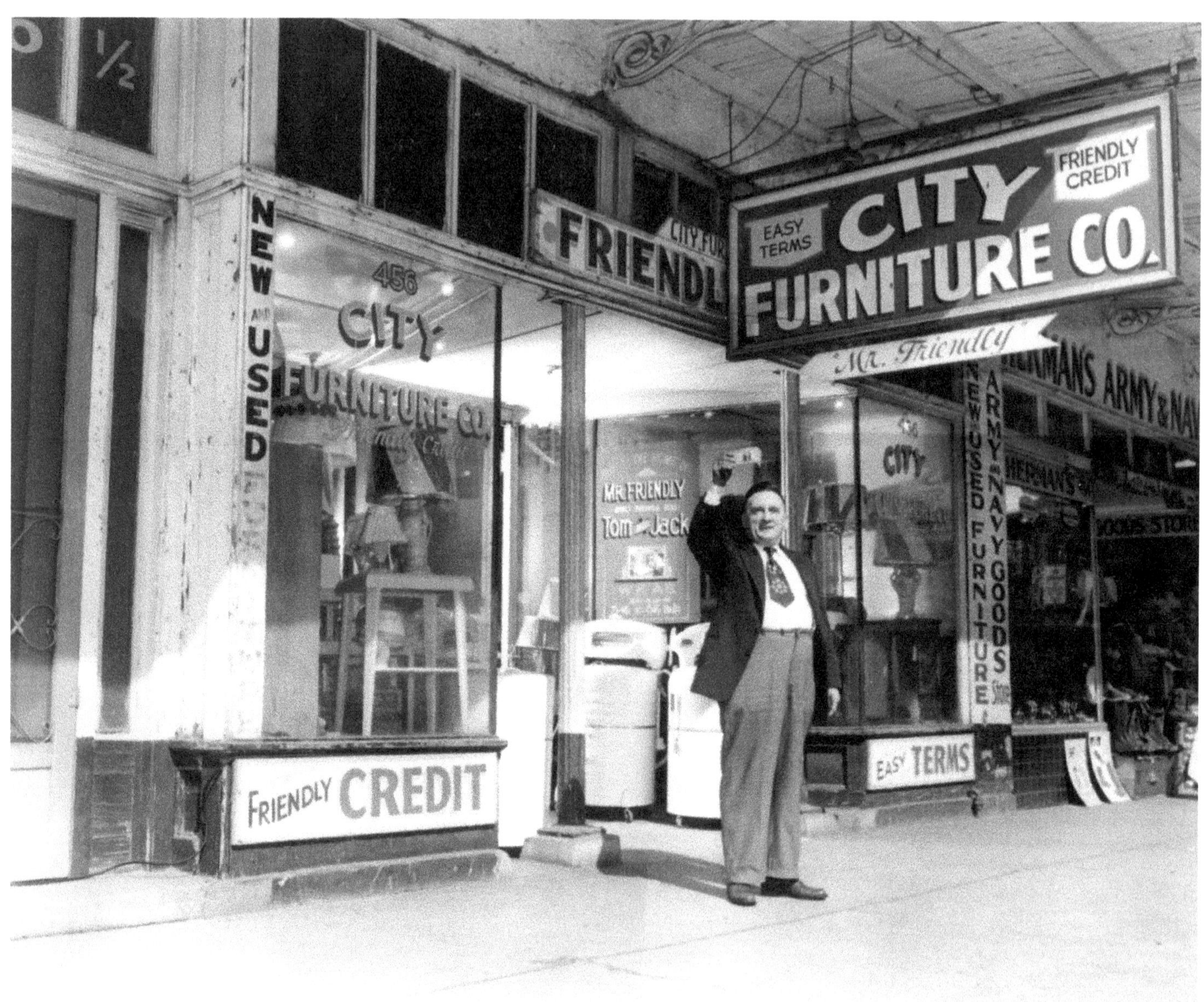

This happy fellow waving a dollar bill outside the City Furniture Company in February 1953 is probably "Mr. Friendly" himself. The business, located at 456 Dauphin Street, sponsored the Tom 'n' Jack show on WKAB radio. The February 1955 issue of *Cowboy Songs* magazine noted that Mobile recording artist Jack Cardwell's eight-room home had been completely furnished by the furniture store that had been his radio sponsor for seven years.

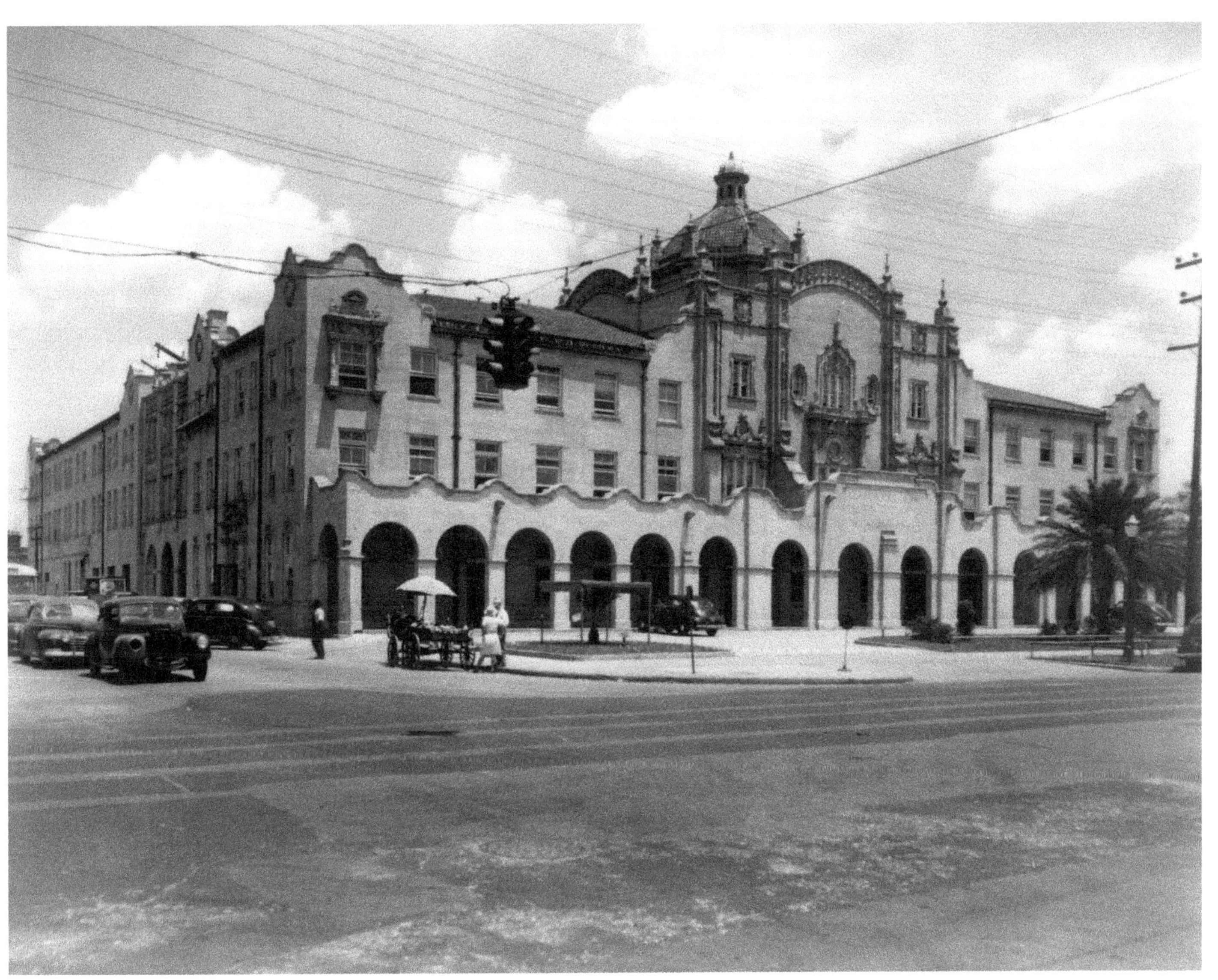

The Gulf, Mobile, and Ohio building as it looked around 1950. Fascinated with the Spanish Mission Revival style of architecture, Mobilians constructed the terminal in 1905. It is still in use as a transportation hub today.

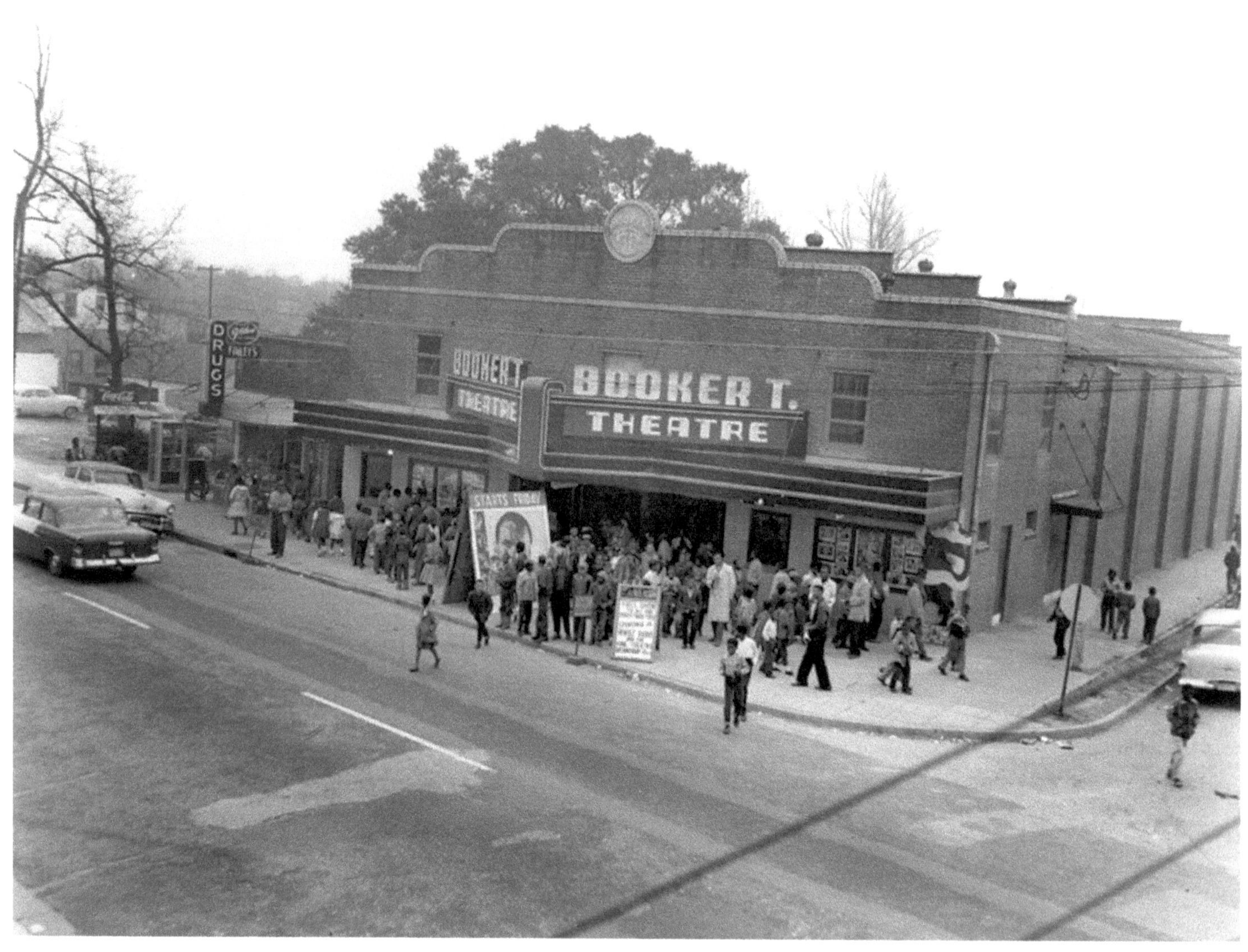

The Booker T. Washington Theatre in 1959. The sign in the center foreground of the photograph reads, "Free show to all kids. Christmas treat. Sponsored by WMOZ Radio and the King Theatres." On the far left is Finley's Pharmacy.

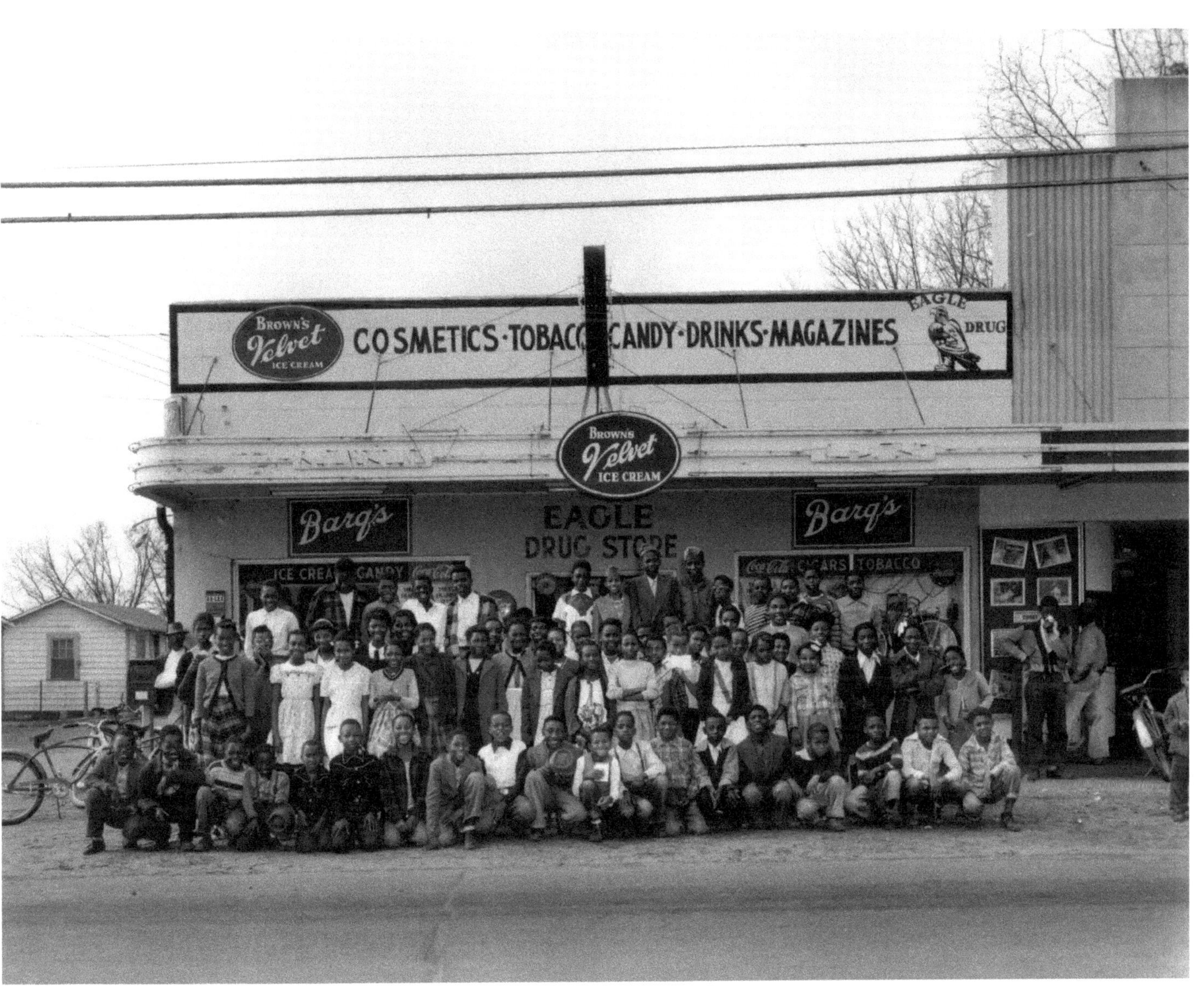

This group of children posed in front of the Eagle Drug Store on January 20, 1951. The reason for their congregation is lost to history, but, as the marker beneath the "Coca-Cola" sign reads, they may have been members of the Youth Training Club. Eagle Drug Store was located at 2801 St. Stephens Road in Toulminville.

A group of 1951 Azalea Trail maids pose in Bienville Square in the shadow of the Waterman and Merchants National Bank buildings. Begun in 1929 as a means of attracting tourists, the trail helped contribute to the growth of the area's nursery industry and to Mobile's being known as the Azalea City.

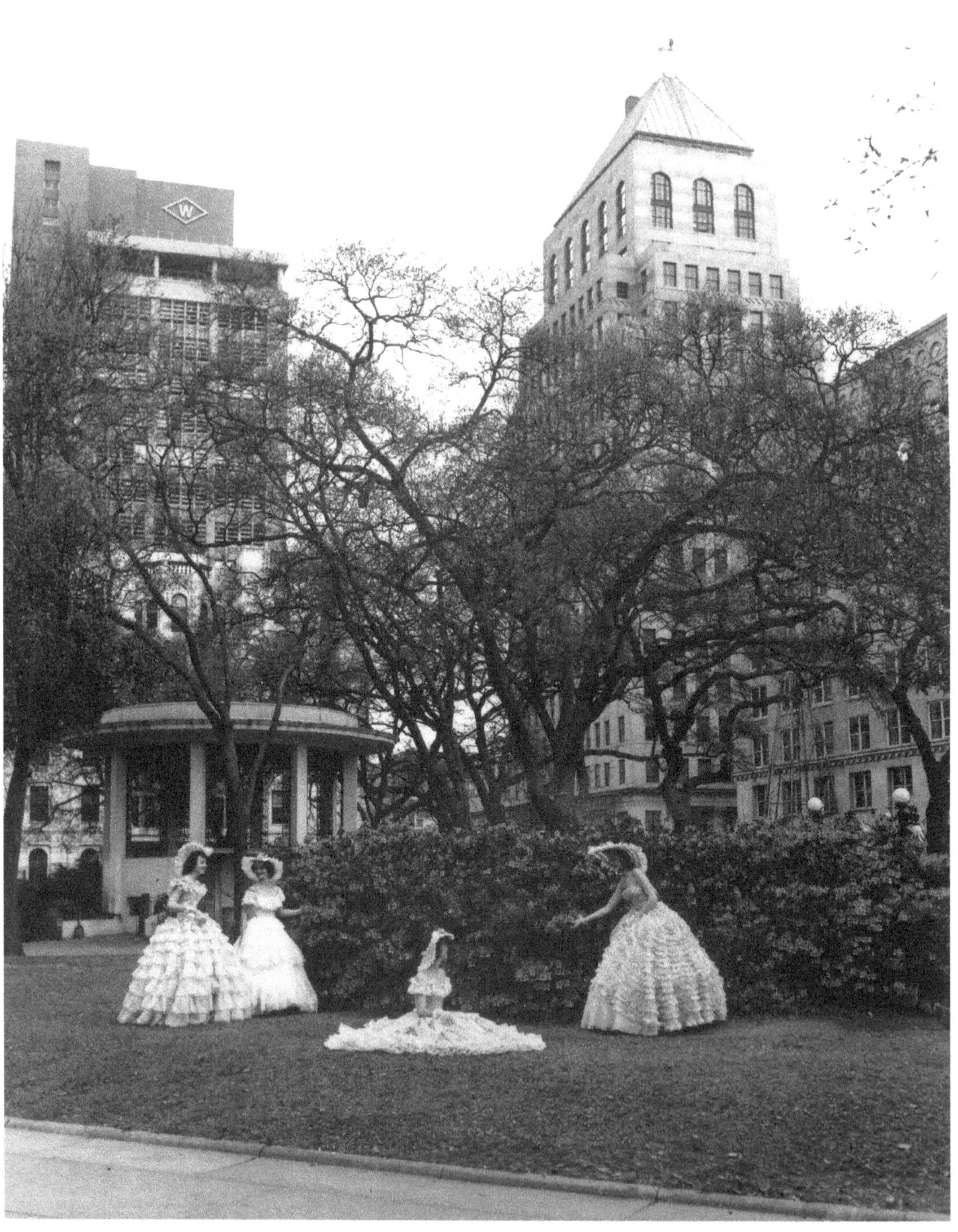

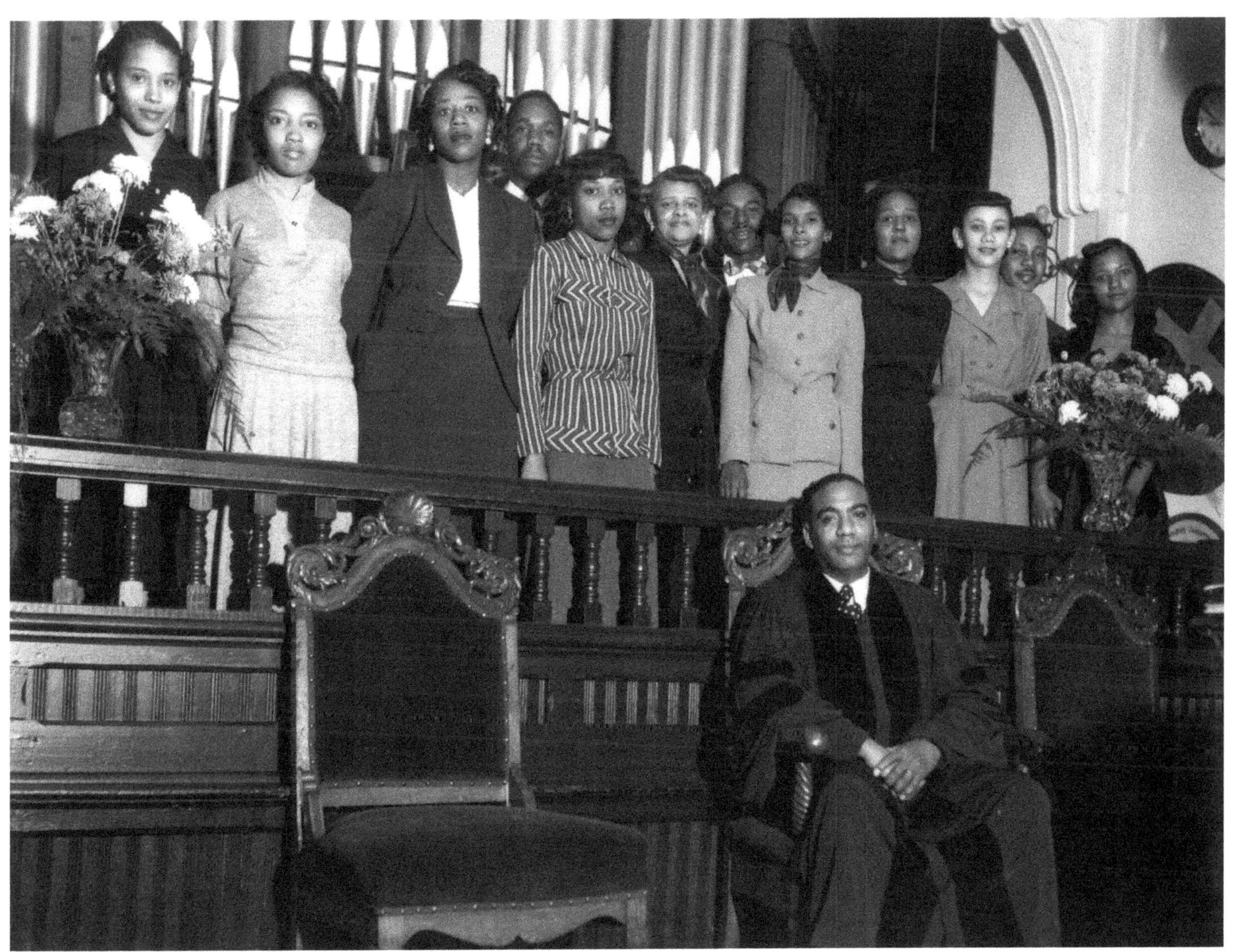

Members of the Big Zion AME choir, 1953. Bishop William Smith sits to the right.

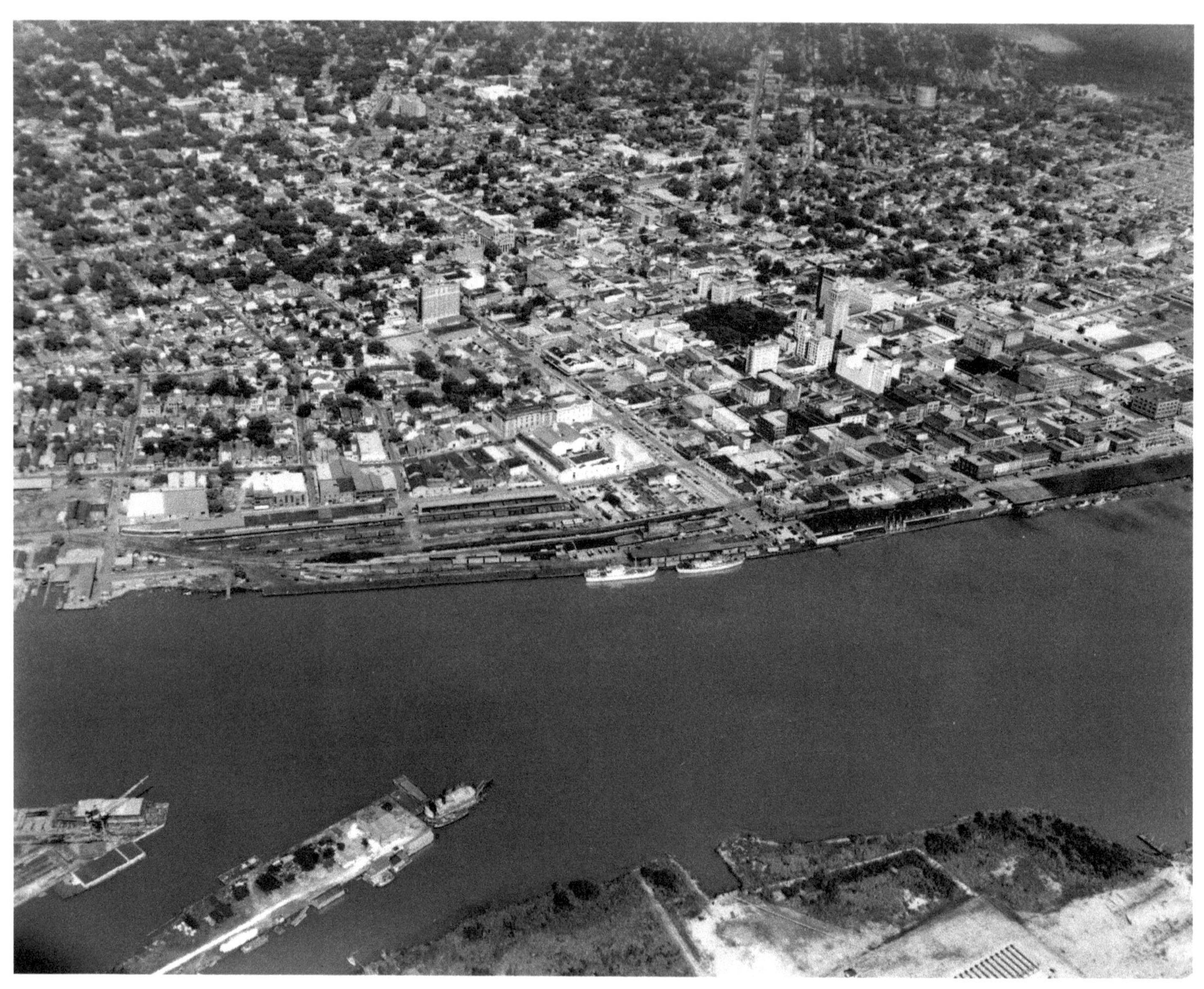

An aerial view of Mobile taken May 1952 and showing the Cathedral of the Immaculate Conception, the Merchants National Bank, the Admiral Semmes Hotel, and City Hall, among other things.

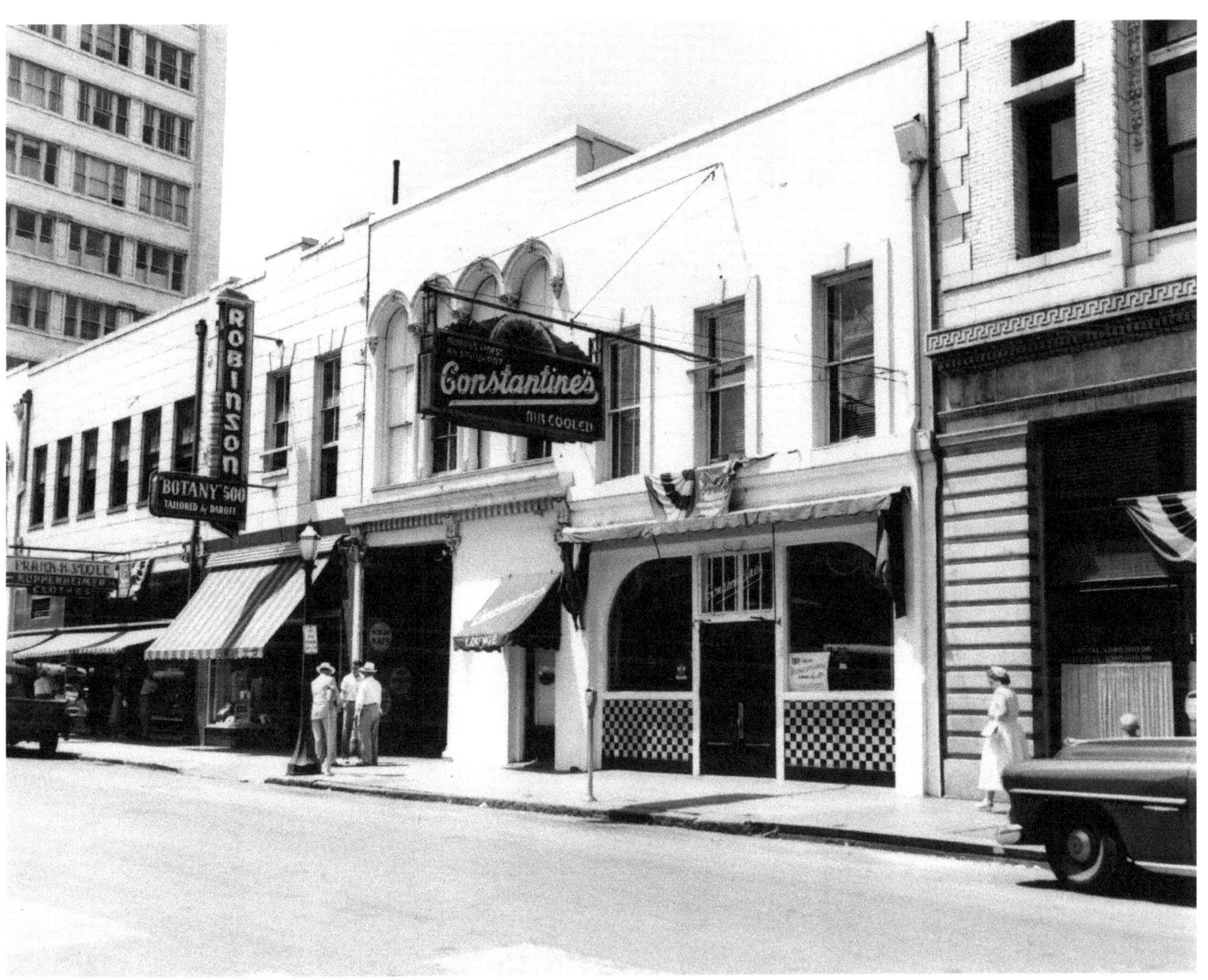

The exterior of Constantine's Restaurant, July 28, 1952. The restaurant's founder, Constantine Panayiotou, arrived in Mobile around 1932. He immediately opened a café at 80 St. Francis Street. By the time this image was taken, the business had moved to 9 Royal Street. The sign above the entrance displays the Stars and Bars and bids welcome to a Confederate group.

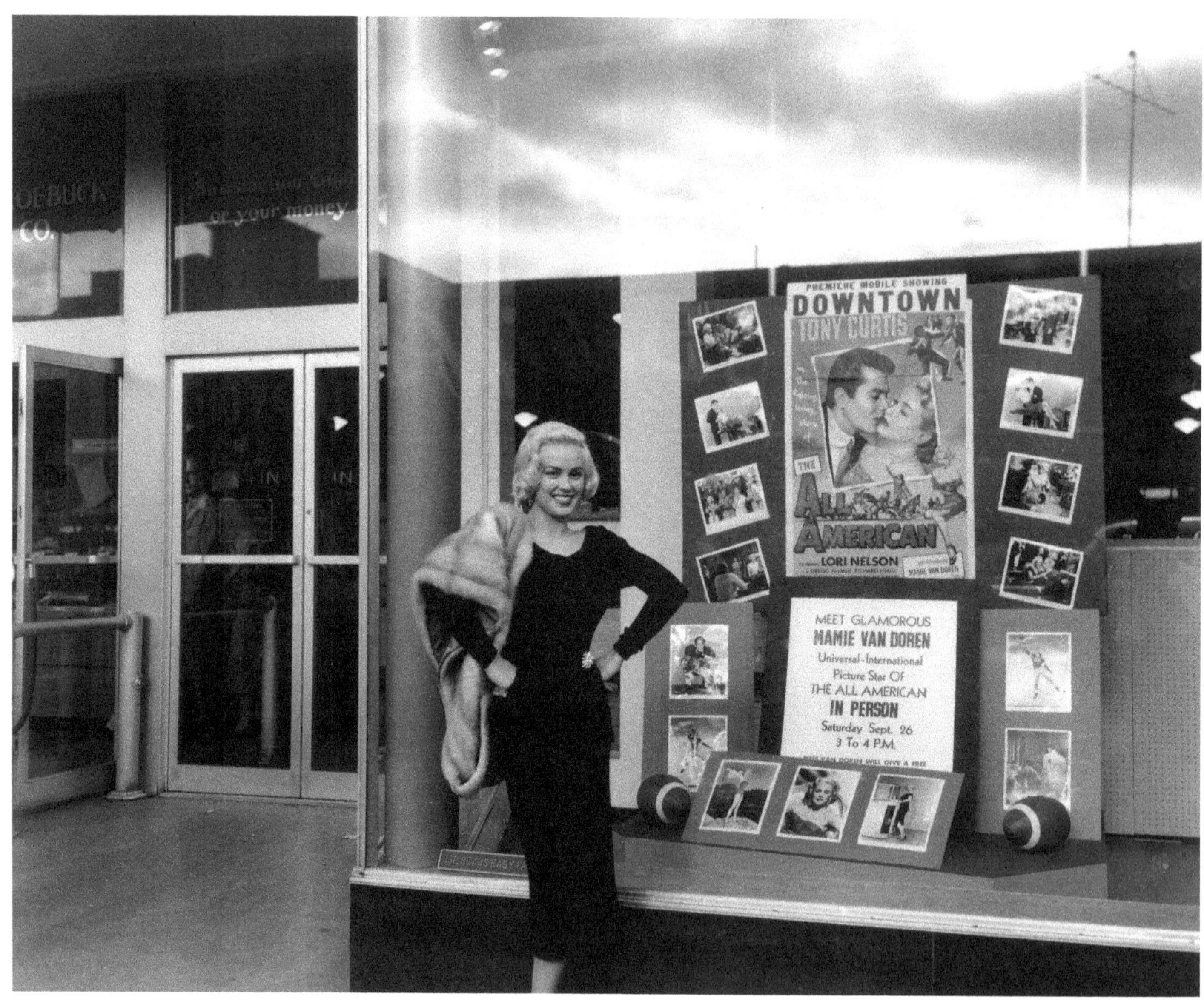

In town to promote her latest motion picture, actress Mamie Van Doren posed for this photograph on September 25, 1953.

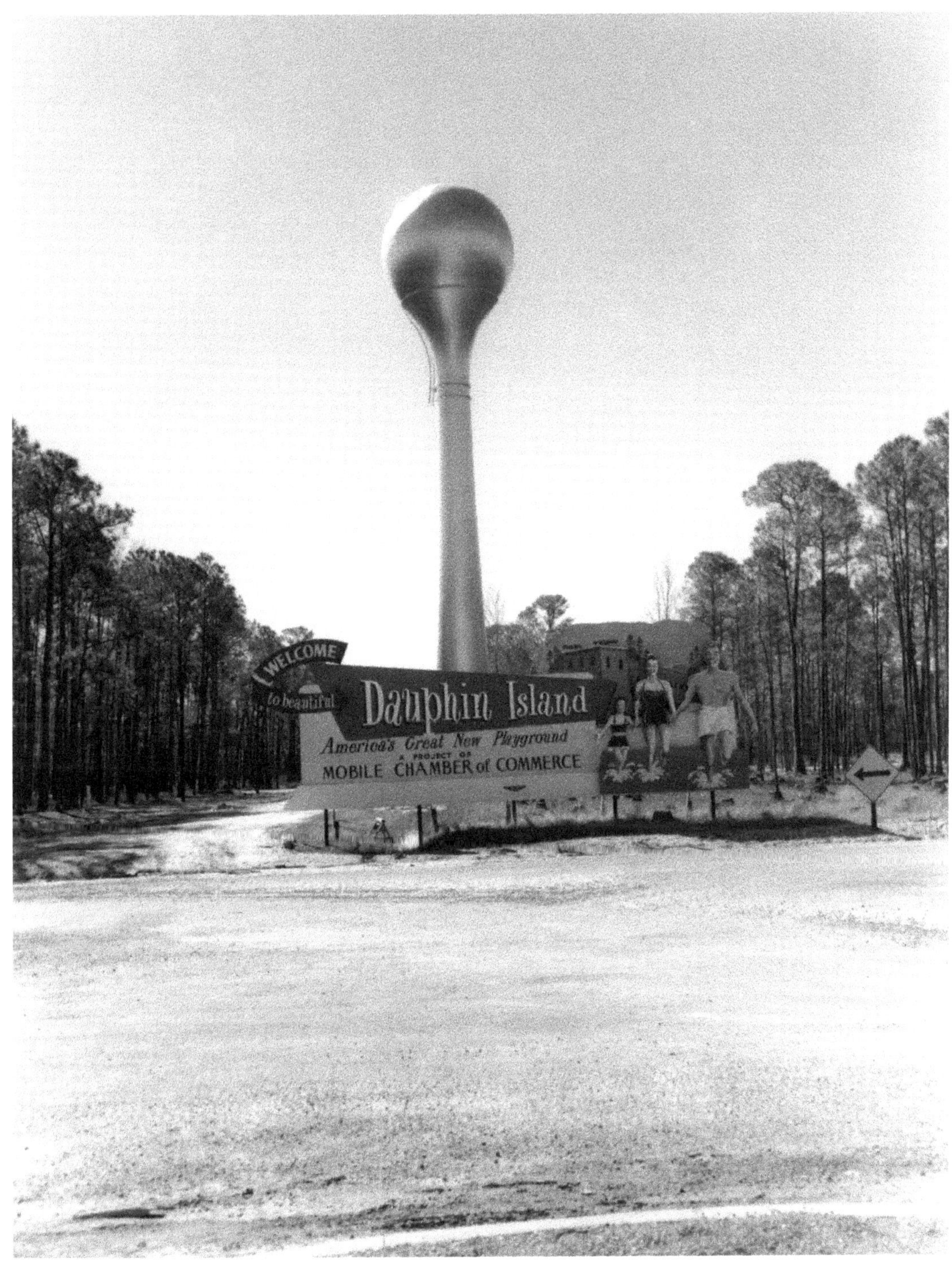

In the 1950s, this sign greeted visitors to Dauphin Island, Alabama, a barrier island in the Gulf of Mexico, long touted by the Mobile Chamber of Commerce as the Gulf Coast's "great new playground."

Laborers with the Mobile Typographical Union walk the picket line, February 13, 1958.

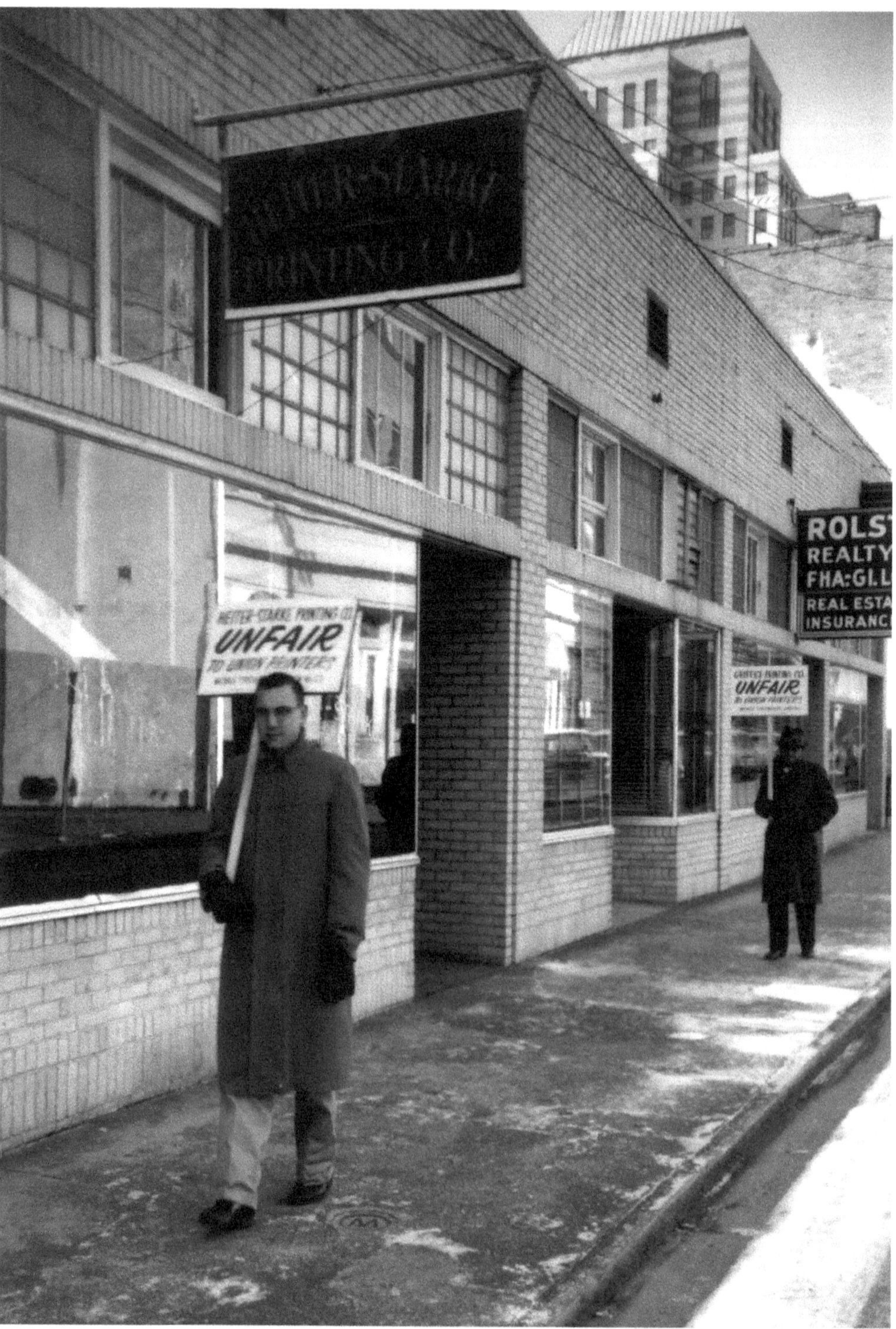

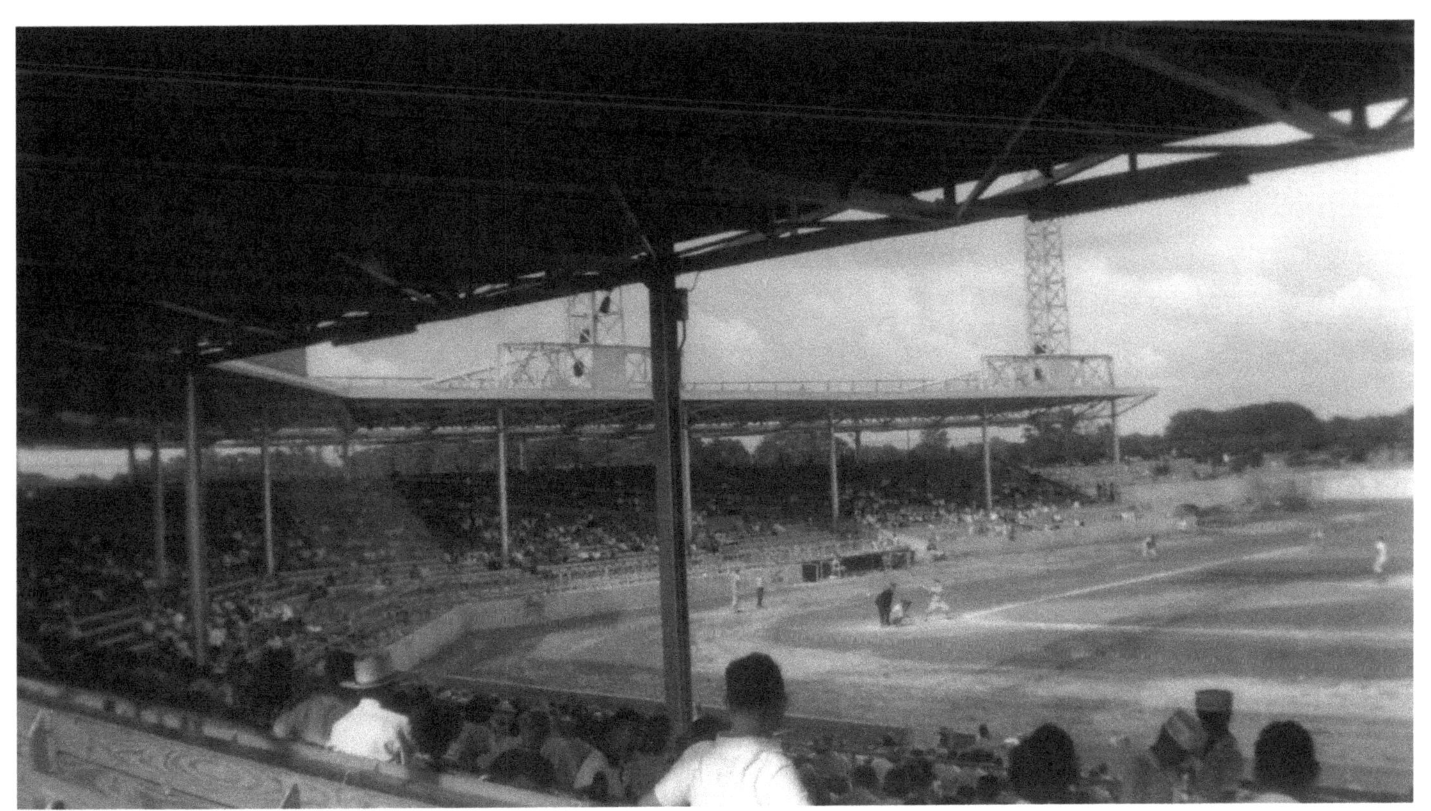

Baseball has been played in Mobile since at least the 1880s. This game—probably involving the Mobile Bears—was played at the old Hartwell Field in 1958.

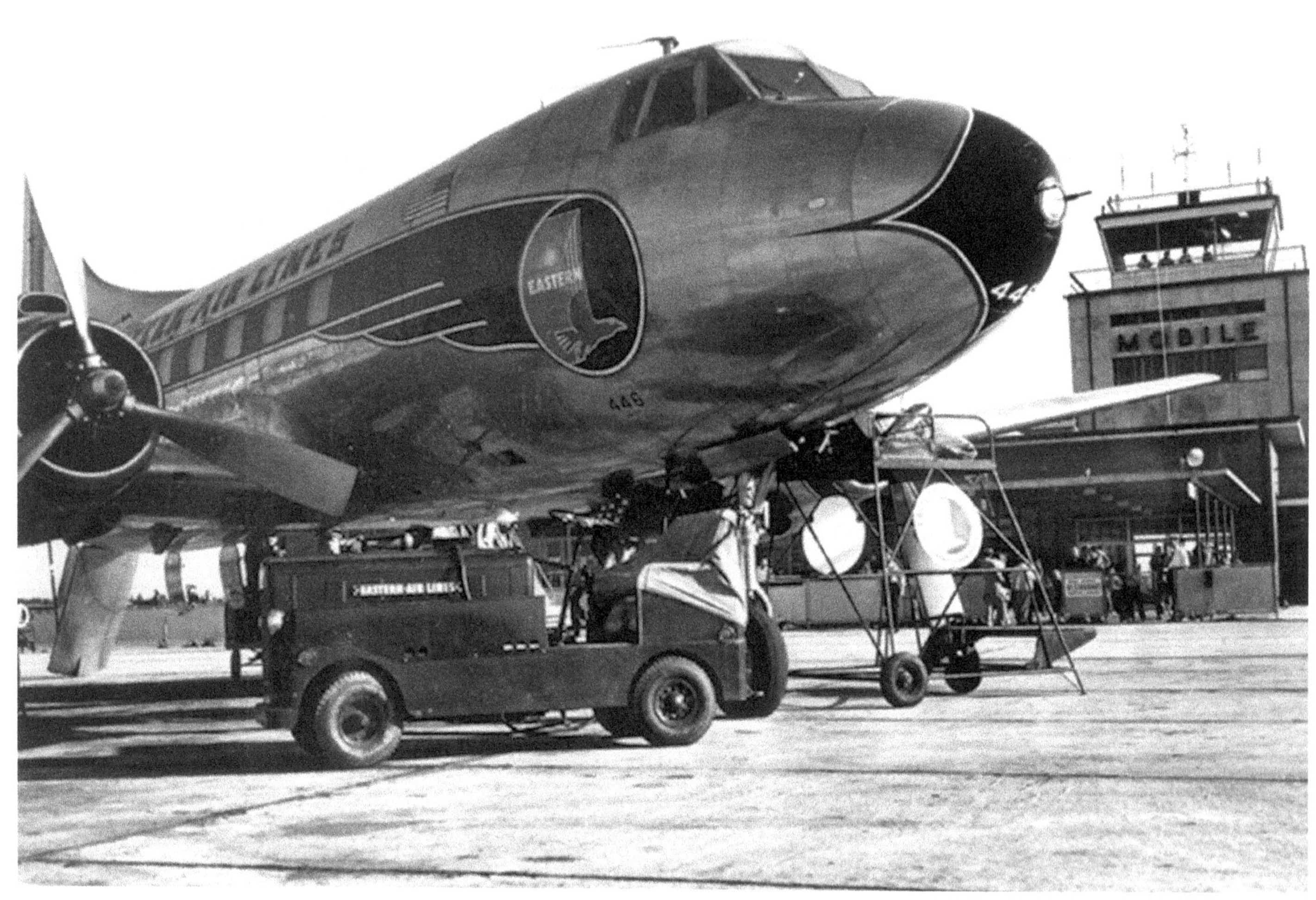

An Eastern Airlines plane on the tarmac at the Mobile airport around 1950.

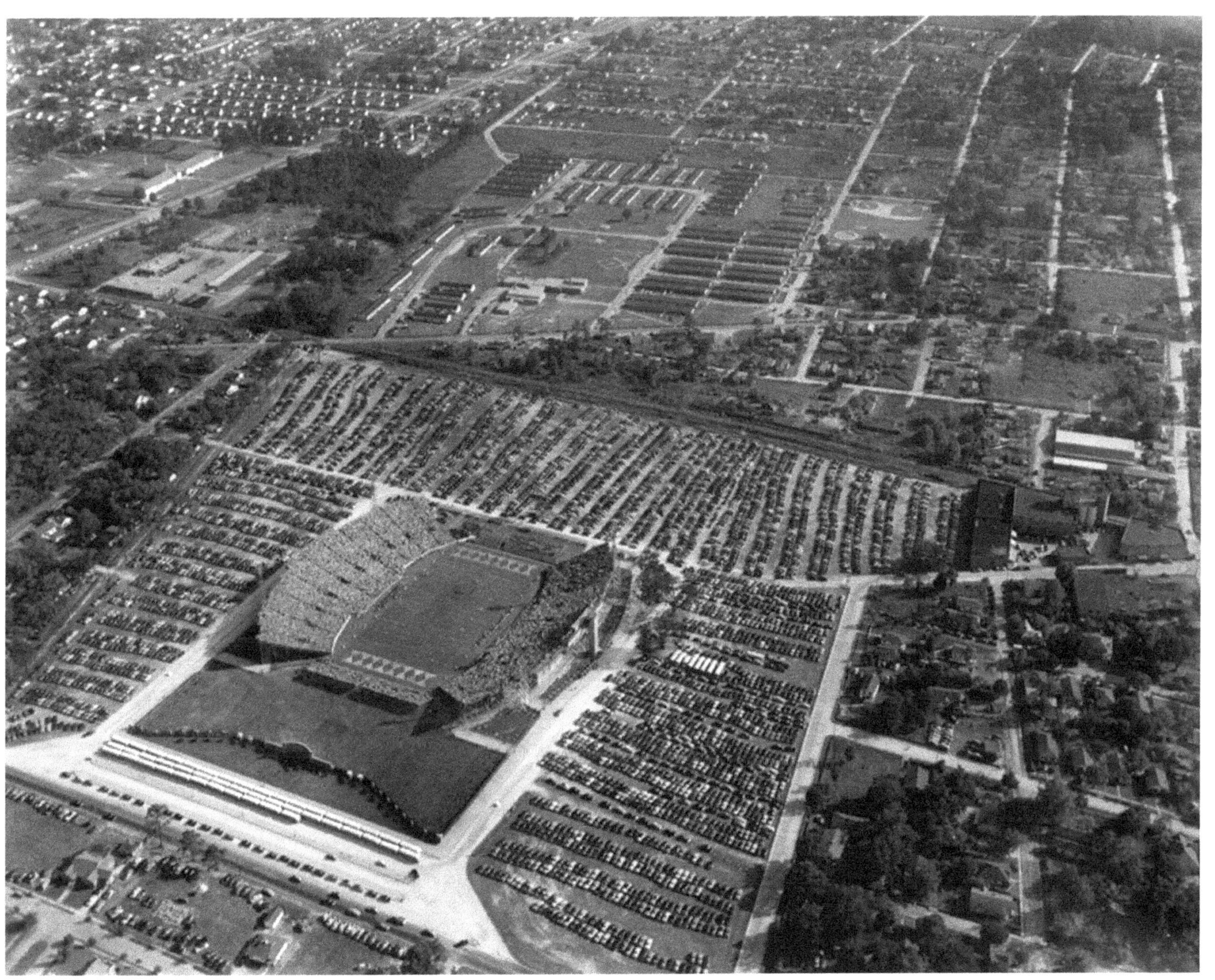

An aerial of Ladd Stadium, taken October 7, 1950. The occasion is probably a high school football game. Named in honor of Ernest F. Ladd, a former president of the Merchants National Bank, the stadium has been home to the Senior Bowl since 1951.

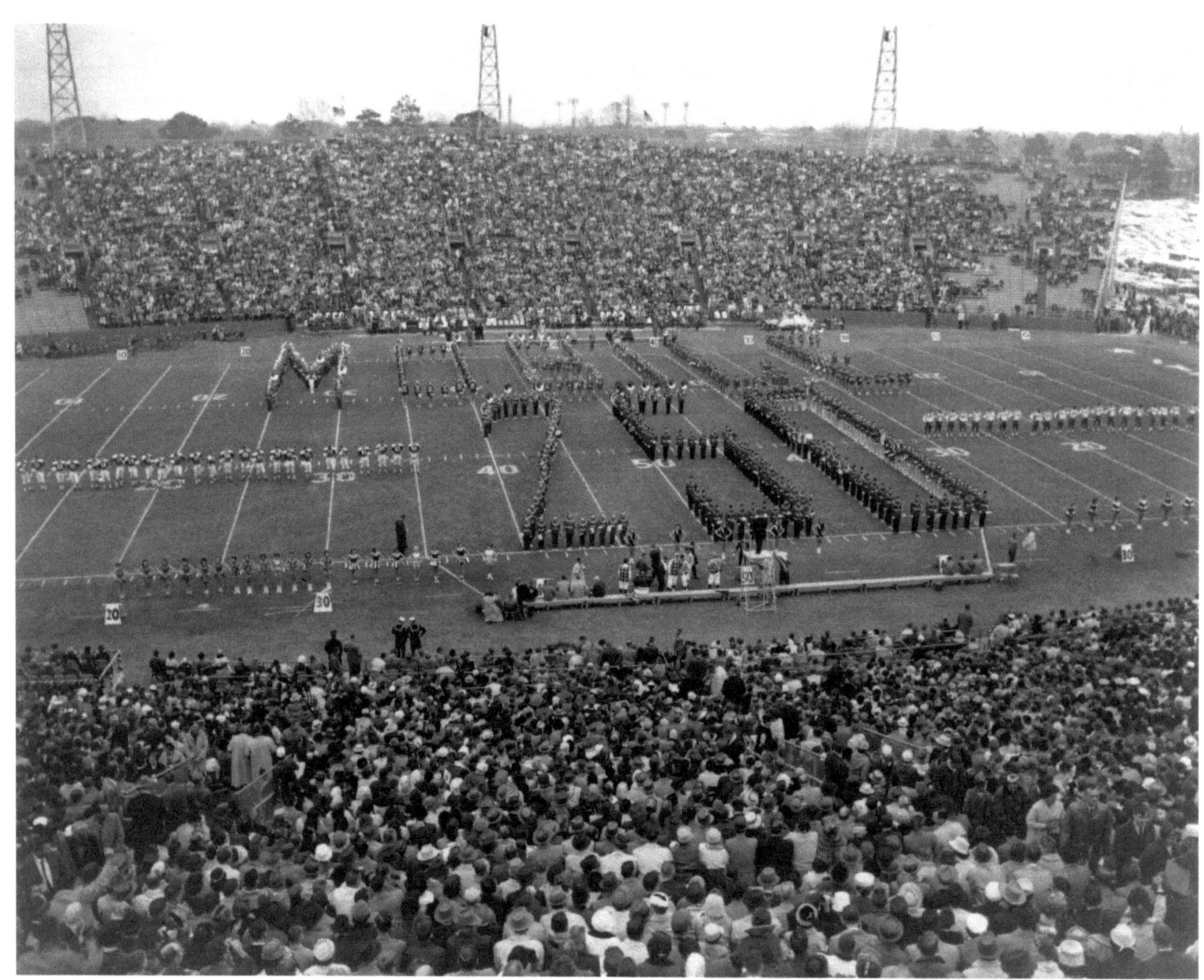

This image shows one of the events during Mobile's celebration of the 250th anniversary of its removal, in 1711, from Twenty-Seven Mile Bluff to its present location. Mayor Joseph Langan had decreed that all Mobile men grow beards and mustaches, uncommon in 1961, so that they would resemble the men who founded the city in 1702. This photograph was taken at Ladd Stadium.

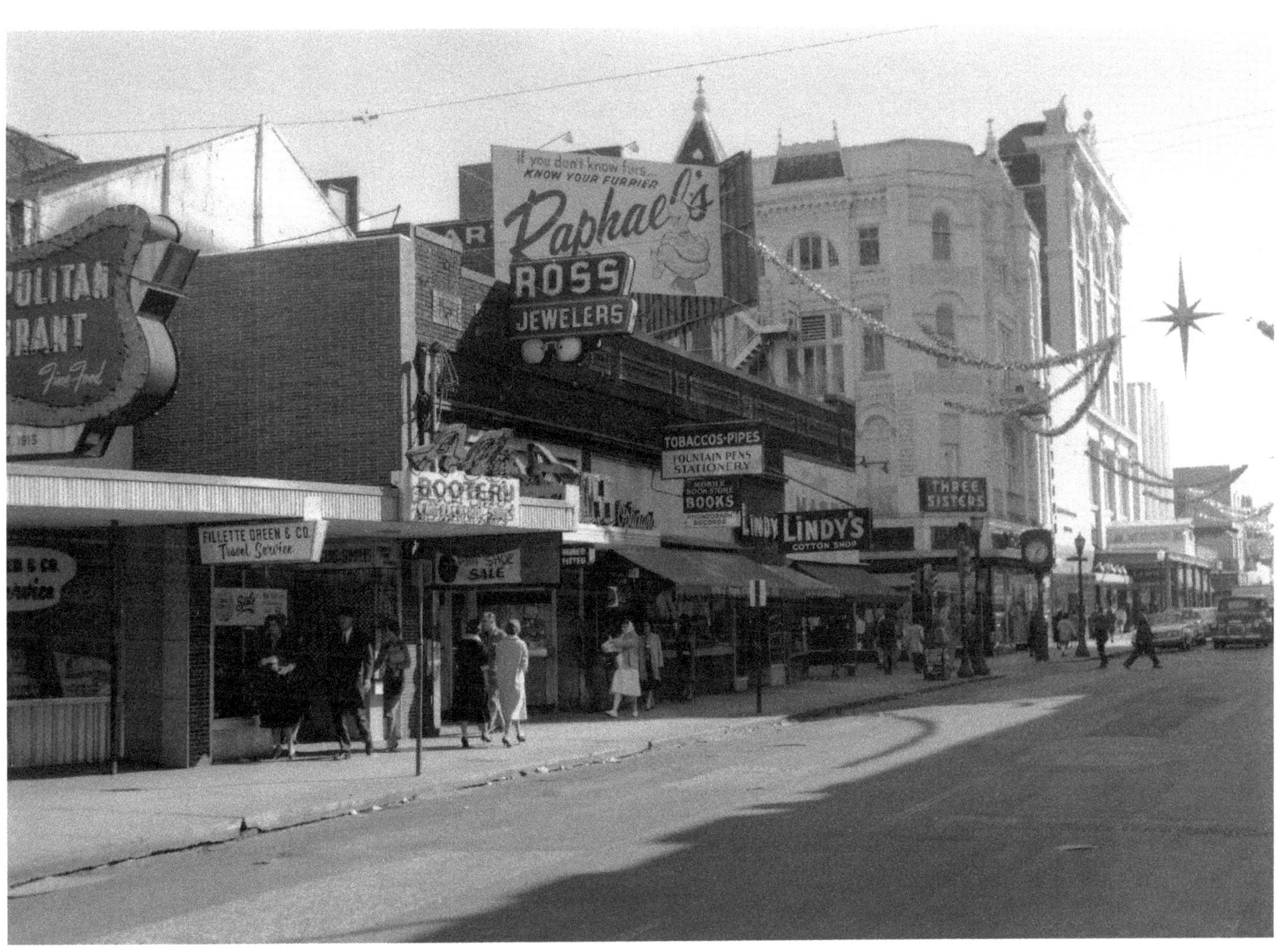

Royal Street, looking south toward Government around 1960. The Three Sisters is still in business and shares the preceding block with the Metropolitan Restaurant, Ross Jewelers, and Al's Bootery.

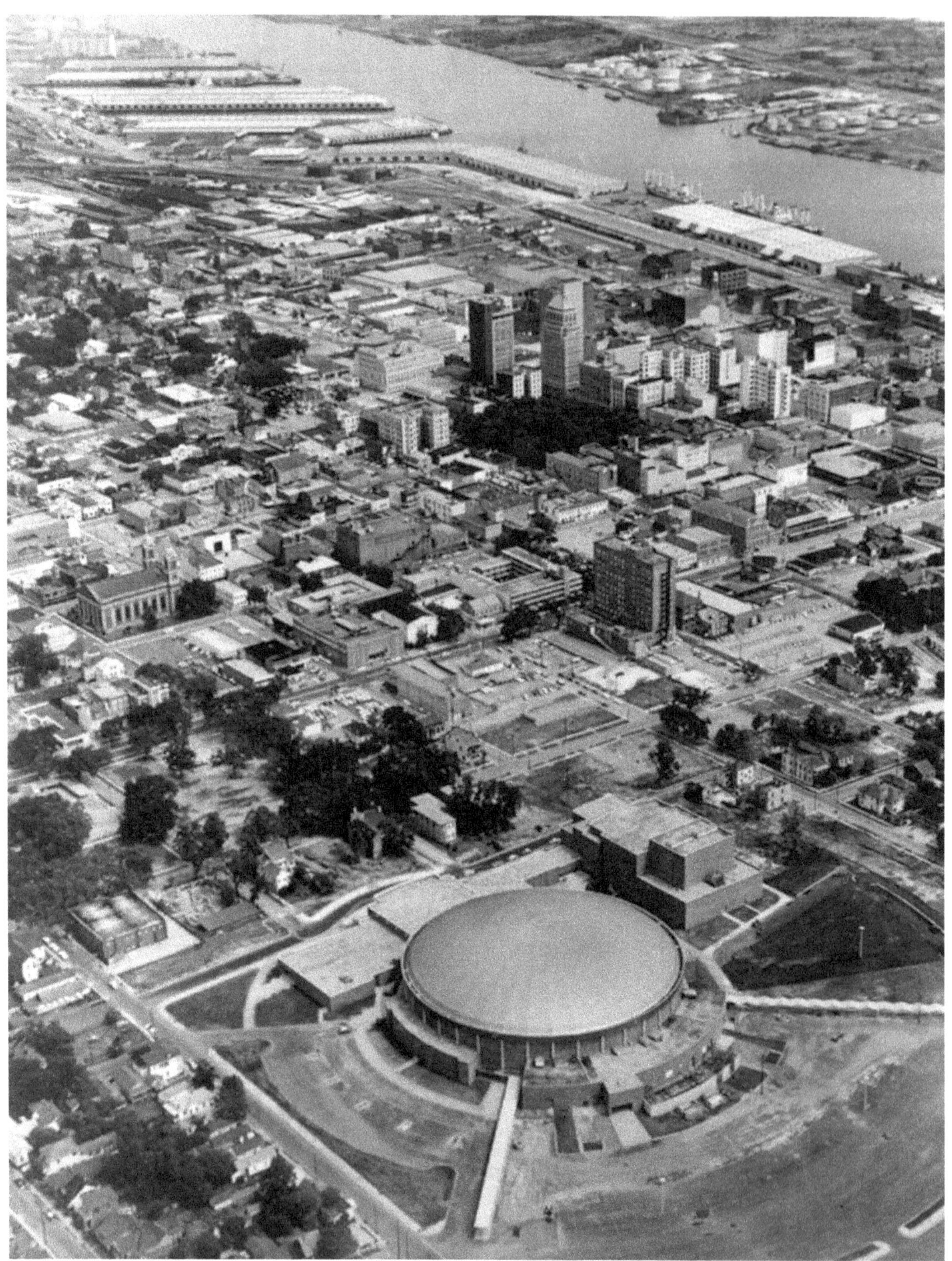

An aerial view of downtown Mobile, looking northeast from the Municipal Auditorium (ca. 1965).

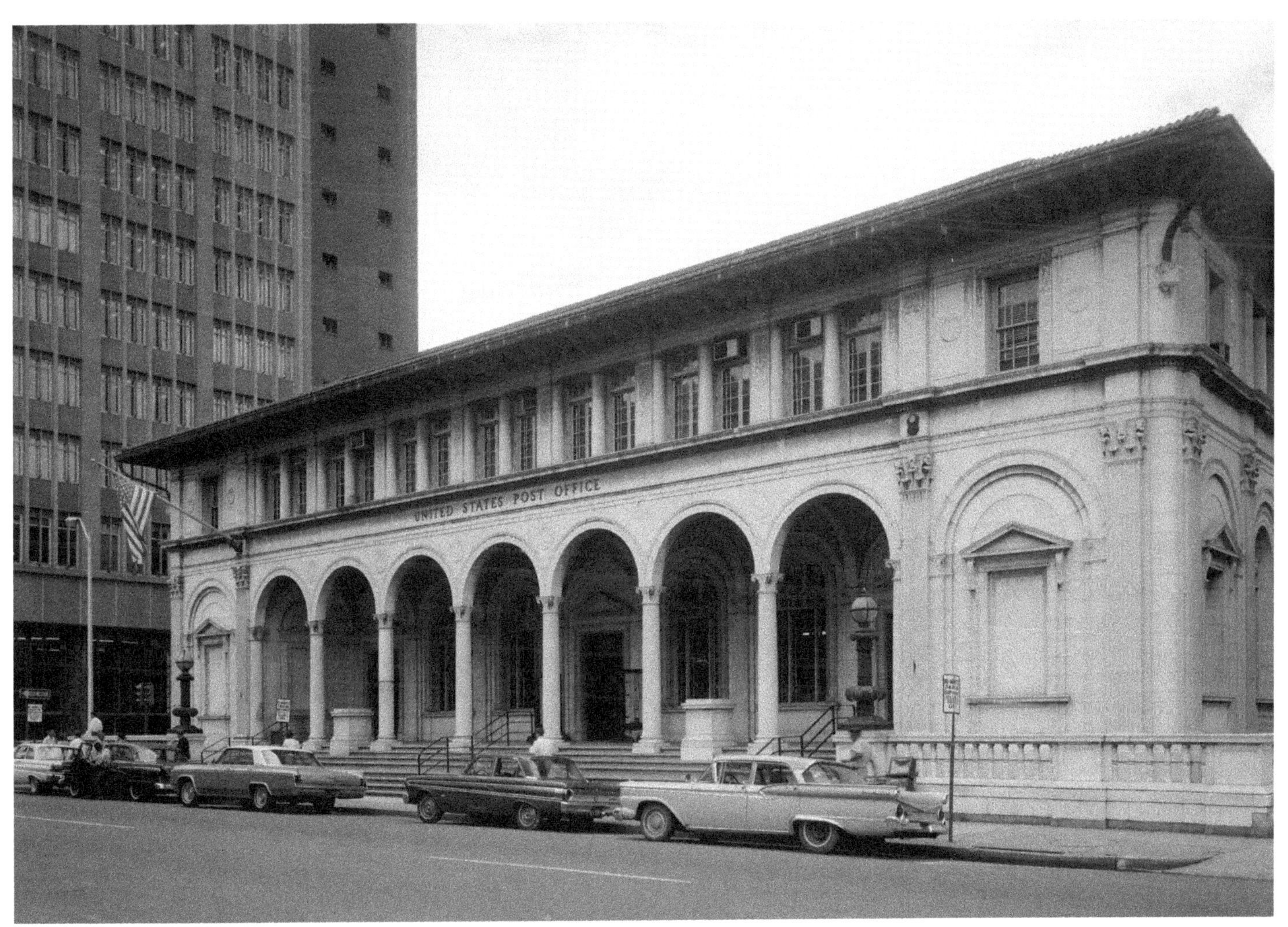

Reflecting the classical revival style, the old U.S. Post Office building was constructed in 1914. This image was taken in 1966, two years before the structure was demolished.

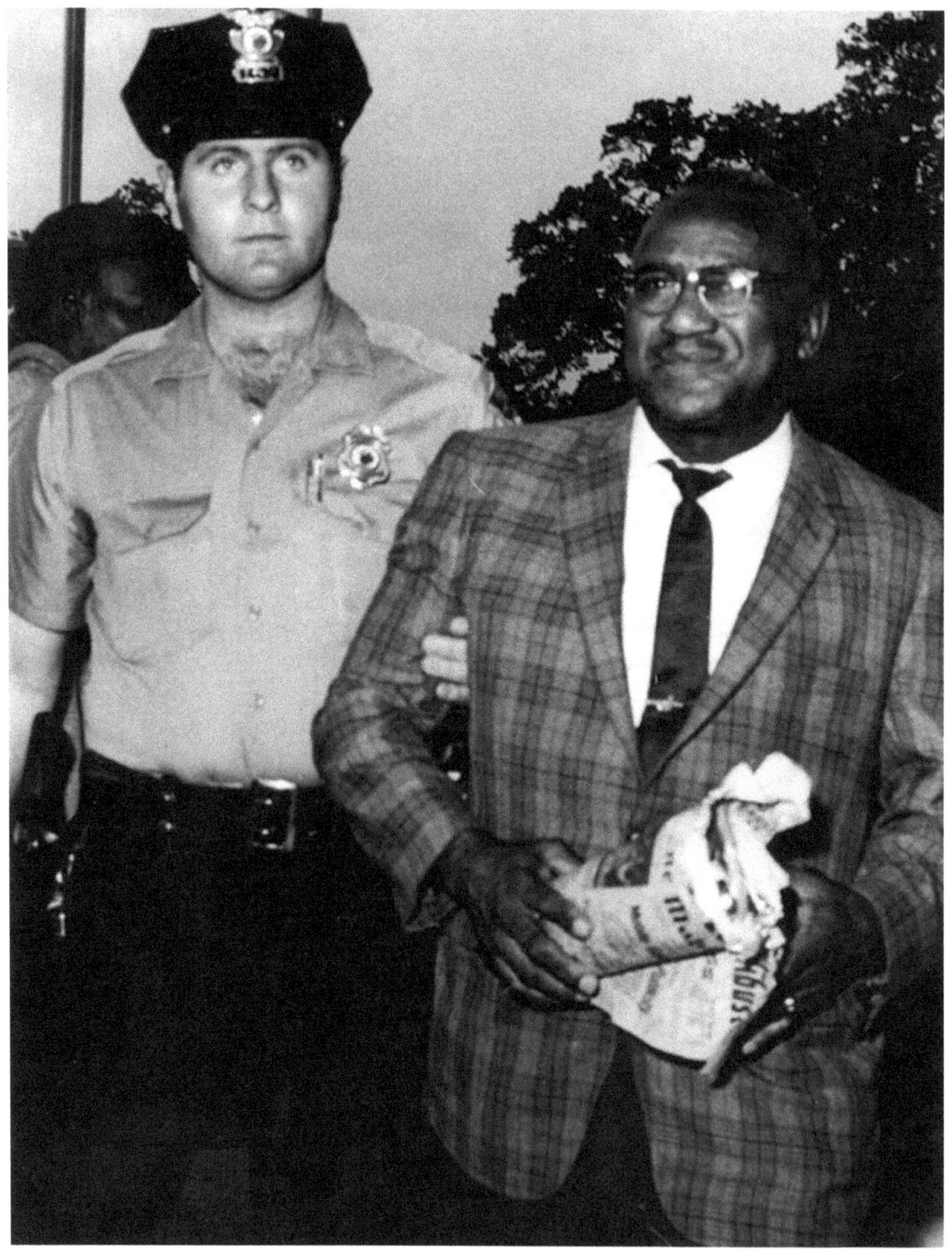

In 1969, John LeFlore was arrested outside the America's Junior Miss pageant. He and others were protesting the segregated venue in which the pageant was held.

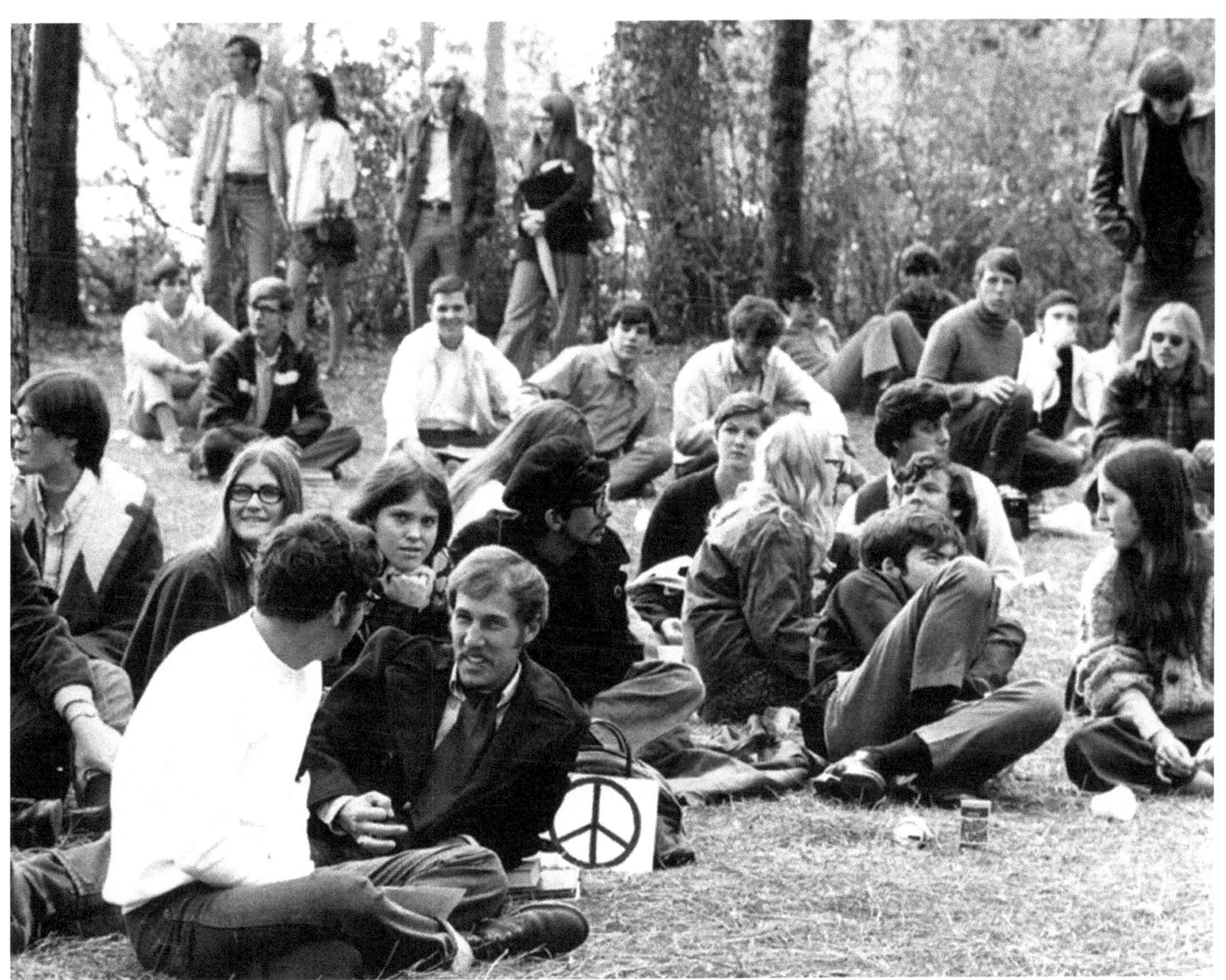

A group of University of South Alabama students "sit-down" in observance of the October 1969 Vietnam War Moratorium.

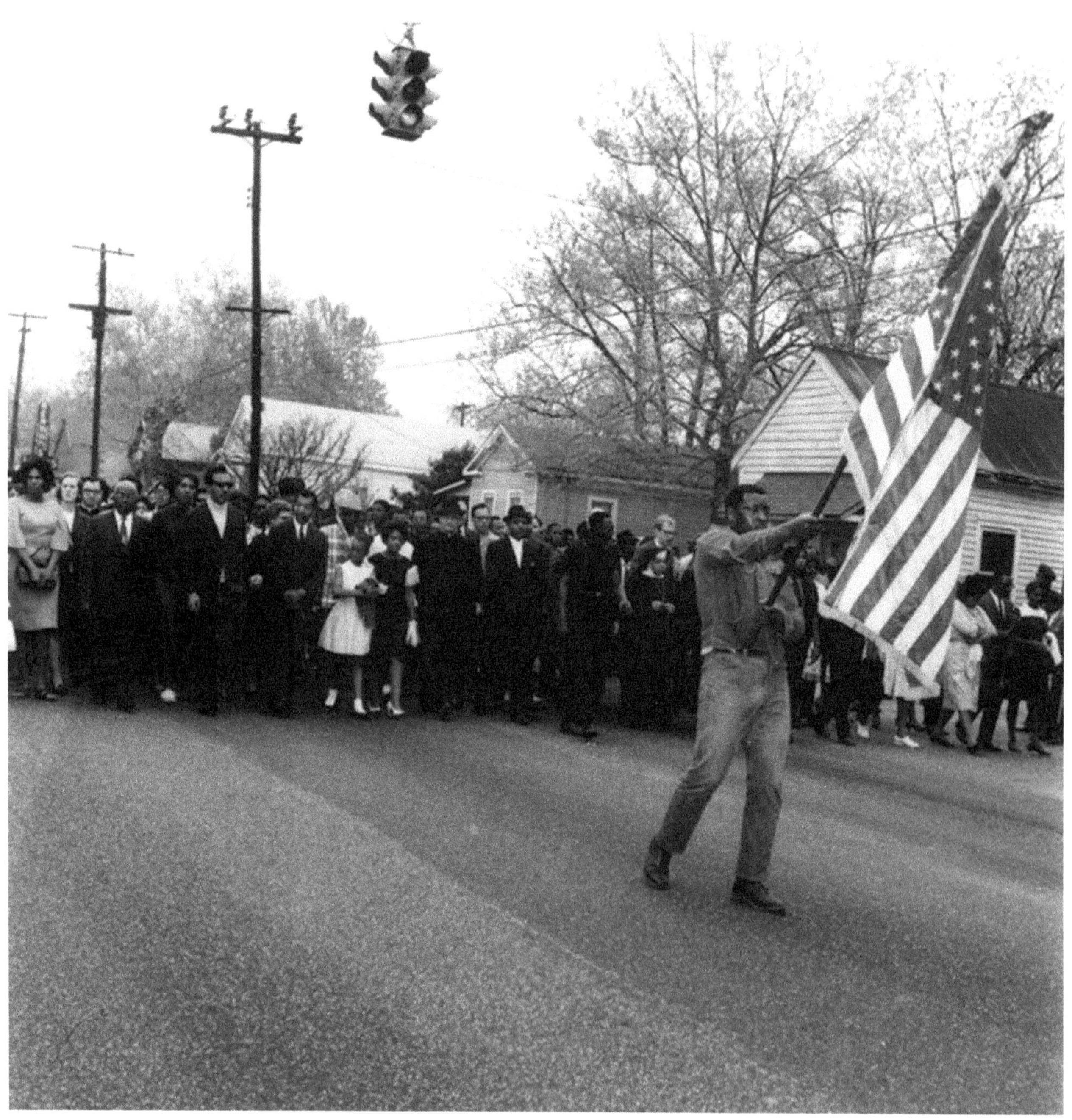

Members of the Mobile community march down Davis Avenue (now Martin Luther King Jr. Avenue) on April 7, 1968, in mourning after the assassination of the Reverend Dr. Martin Luther King, Jr. Jerry Pogue carries the flag.

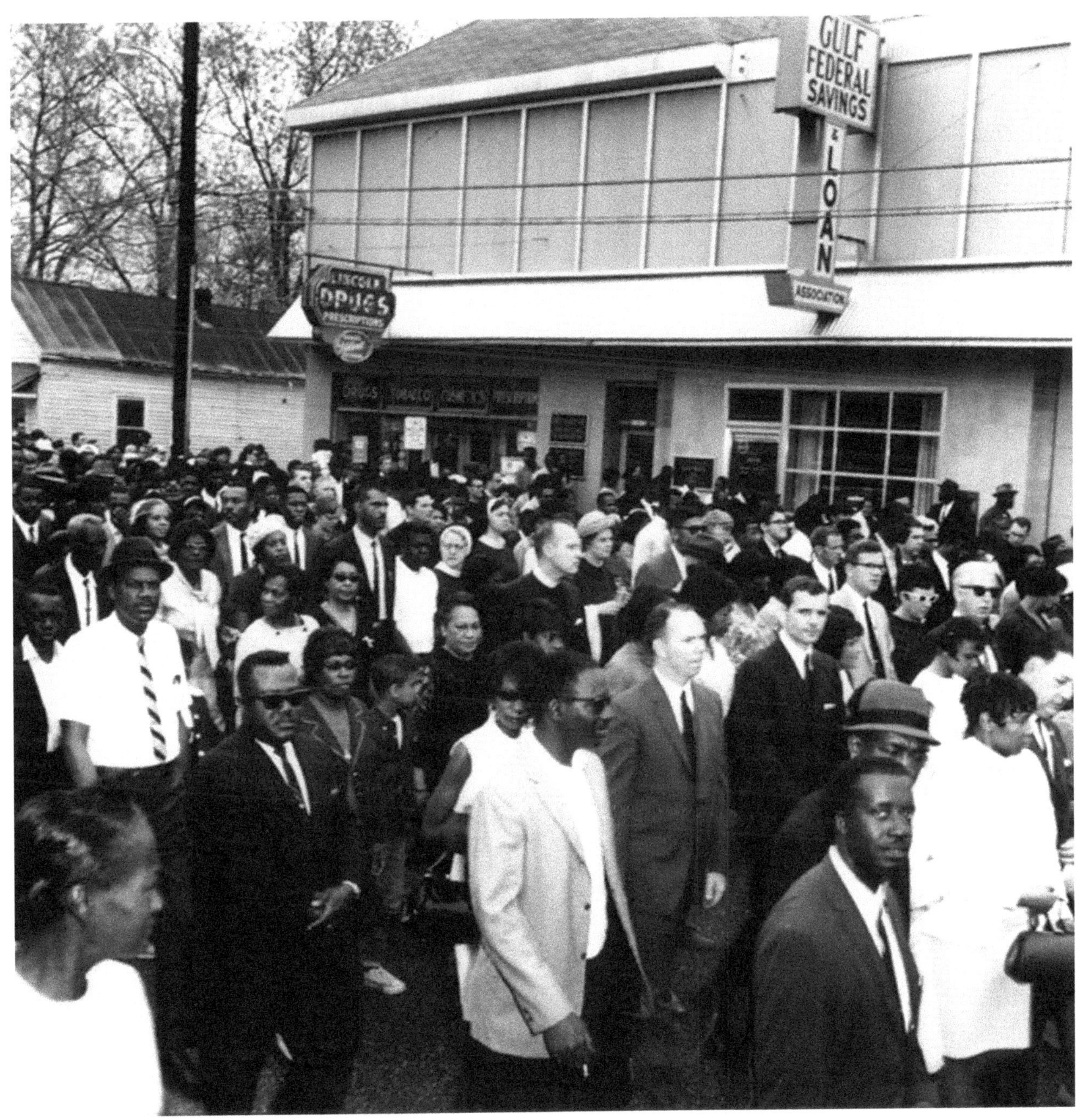

Following the assassination of the Reverend Dr. Martin Luther King, Jr., large crowds turned out to honor him with a march down Davis Avenue on April 7, 1968.

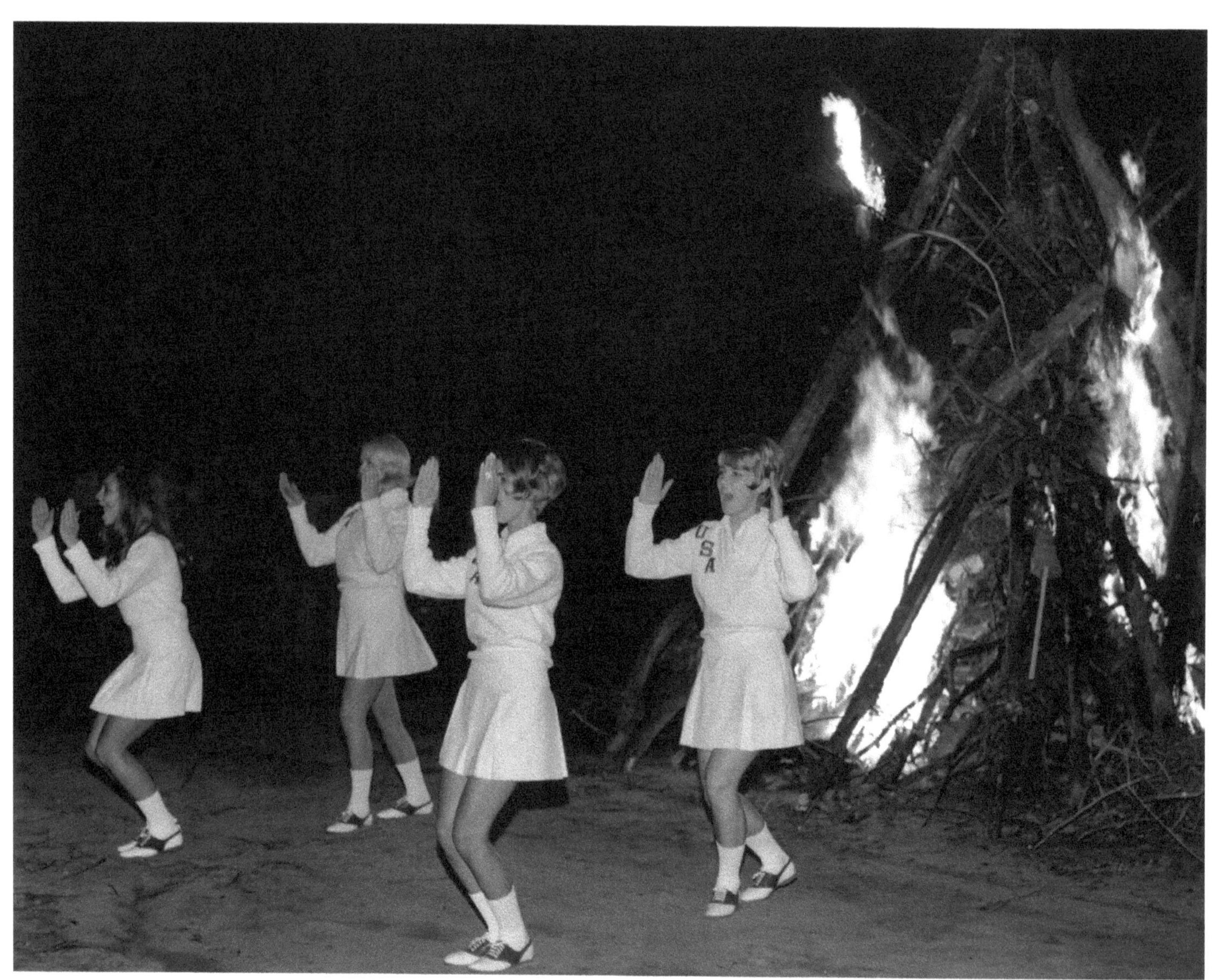

University of South Alabama cheerleaders around 1970.

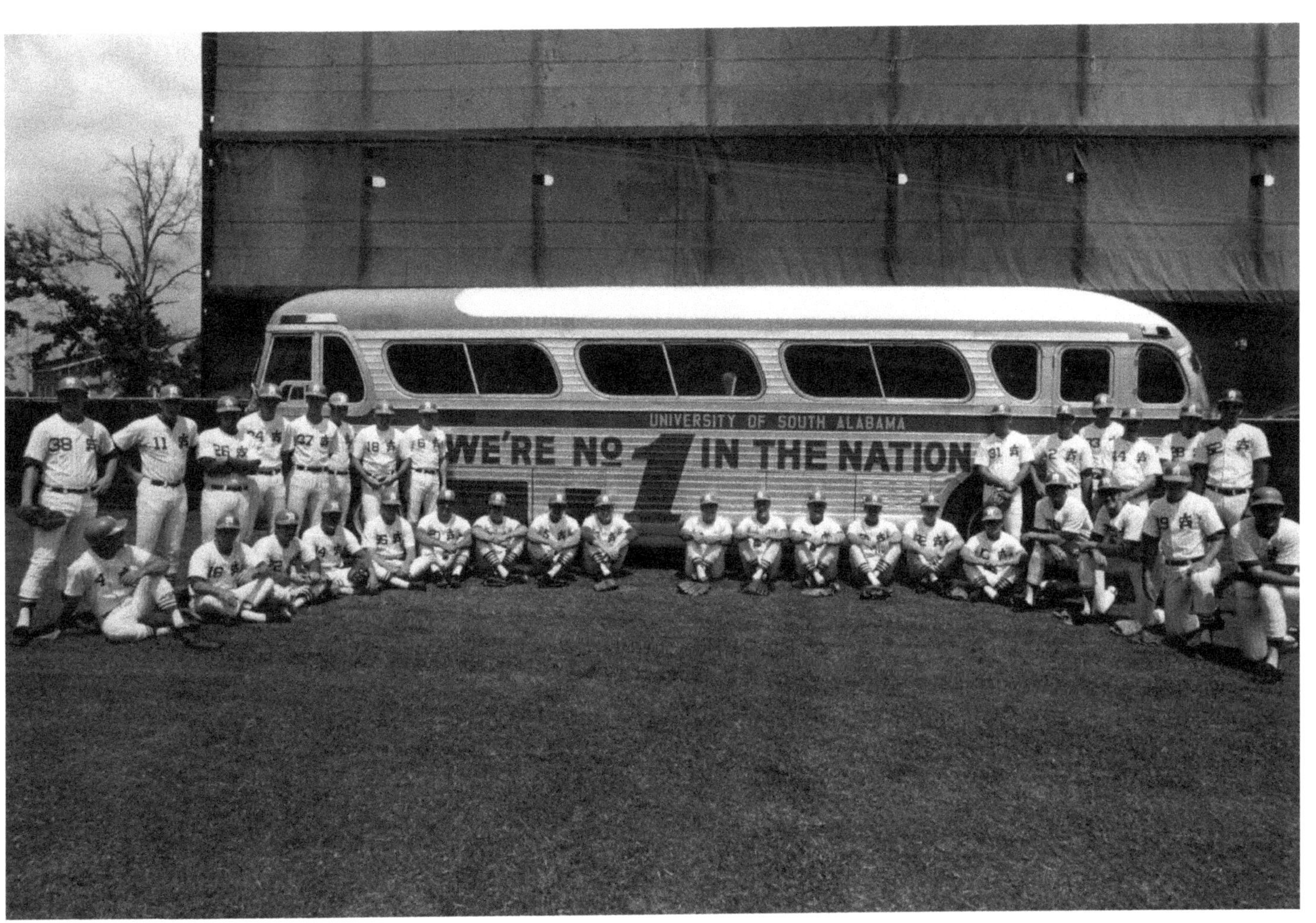

This photograph was taken in 1972, the year the University of South Alabama's baseball team, the Jaguars, were number one in the nation. They finished the season with a winning percentage of .818 and a record of 36–8.

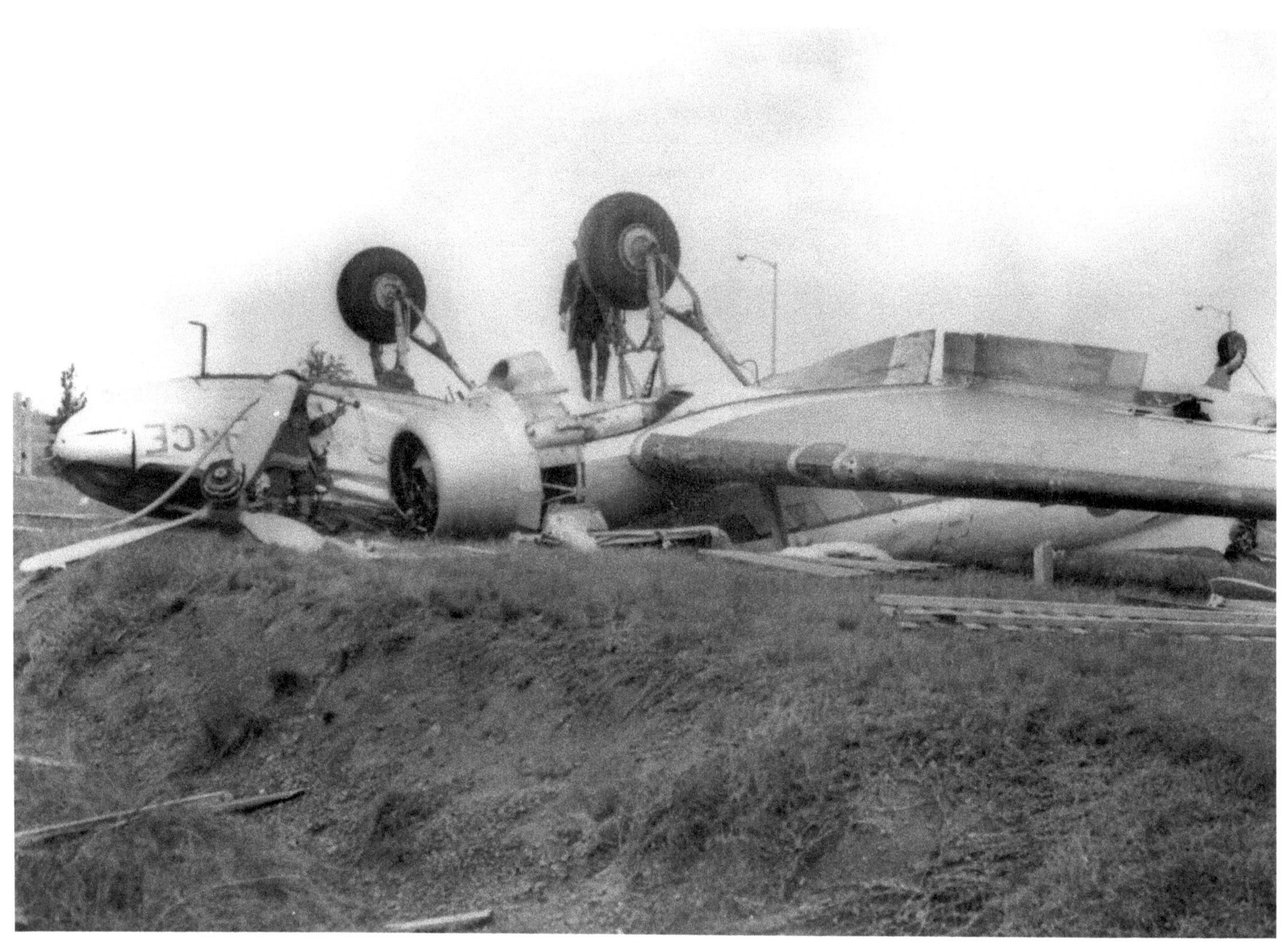

A U.S. Air Force plane lies on its back after the winds of Hurricane Frederick overturned it. Frederick hit the city on the night of September 12–13, 1979, causing extensive damage throughout the area.

NOTES ON THE PHOTOGRAPHS

These notes, listed by page number, attempt to include all aspects known of the photographs. Each of the photographs is identified by the page number, photograph's title or description, photographer and collection, archive, and call or box number when applicable. Although every attempt was made to collect all data, in some cases complete data was unavailable due to the age and condition of some of the photographs and records.

II **PANORAMIC FROM CAWTHON HOTEL**
University of South Alabama Archives
C9072G
Harris Photo, Conneaut, Oh.

VI **EMPIRE THEATER**
University of South Alabama Archives
N-1662

X **MOSES DISTRIBUTORS**
S. Marion Coffin Collection
University of South Alabama Archives
SMC-46

2 **CATHEDRAL OF THE IMMACULATE CONCEPTION**
Photo courtesy of F. V. White
University of South Alabama Archives
C-5031

3 **GOVERNMENT STREET, UNPAVED**
T. E. Armitstead Collection
University of South Alabama Archives
A-124

4 **GOVERNMENT STREET**
T. E. Armitstead Collection
University of South Alabama Archives
A-125

5 **RAILROAD**
T. E. Armitstead Collection
University of South Alabama Archives
A-22

6 **FOURTH MOBILE COUNTY COURTHOUSE**
T. E. Armitstead Collection
University of South Alabama Archives
A-122

7 **FIRE**
S. Blake McNeely Collection
University of South Alabama Archives
C-4254

8 **TIMBER AND RAILROADS**
T. E. Armitstead Collection
University of South Alabama Archives
A-317

9 **MOBILE'S MARDI GRAS**
Mobile Public Library Collection
University of South Alabama Archives
C-4017A

10 **AUCUSTA**
T. E. Armitstead Collection
University of South Alabama Archives
A-37

11 **DAY'S CATCH**
T. E. Armitstead Collection
University of South Alabama Archives
C-17,080

12 **SMITH'S BREAD**
Photo Courtesy of Jim Cool
University of South Alabama Archives
C-2109

13 **CLERKS**
Erik Overbey Collection
University of South Alabama Archives
S-3671A

14 **SALVATION ARMY**
Erik Overbey Collection
University of South Alabama Archives
G-297

15 **OYSTER BOATS**
Erik Overbey Collection
University of South Alabama Archives
G-2

16 **OYSTER DOCKS**
T. E. Armitstead Collection
University of South Alabama Archives
A-39

17 **BARTON ACADEMY**
T. E. Armitstead Collection
University of South Alabama Archives
A-56

18 **VAN ANTWERP AND SON**
Erik Overbey Collection
University of South Alabama Archives
N-2428

19 **DOCKWORKERS**
University of South Alabama Archives
Windsor-11-30

20 **COMMERCE**
University of South Alabama Archives
Misc-2

21 **WEST WARD SCHOOL**
T. E. Armitstead Collection
University of South Alabama Archives
A-57

22 **E. M. HUDSON'S ORCHARD**
T. E. Armitstead Collection
University of South Alabama Archives
A-159

23 **CITY AMBULANCE**
Gift of J. Eugene Bressingham,
University of South Alabama Archives
C-7003

24 **ST. FRANCIS STREET METHODIST CHURCH**
University of South Alabama Archives
C-5052

25 **DAUPHIN AND WATER**
Erik Overbey Collection
University of South Alabama Archives
G-340A

26 **AMERICAN LAUNDRY COMPANY**
Erik Overbey Collection
University of South Alabama Archives
C-34

27 Mobile & Ohio Docks
Mary Tucker Collection Clarke County Historical Society
Misc-104

28 John Fowler
Erik Overbey Collection
University of South Alabama Archives
N-3409B

30 Monument
Erik Overbey Collection
University of South Alabama Archives
G-494

31 People's Drugs
Erik Overbey Collection
University of South Alabama Archives
C-71

32 Mardi Gras Float
Erik Overbey Collection
University of South Alabama Archives
G-479

33 St. Joseph Street
Erik Overbey Collection
University of South Alabama Archives
G-344

34 Circus Performers
Courtesy of Bettie Champion, University of South Alabama Archives
05-02-348-N-6

35 Van Antwerp Building
Erik Overbey Collection
University of South Alabama Archives
G-230

36 Battle House Hotel
S. Blake McNeely Collection
University of South Alabama Archives
C81

37 Government Street
S. Marion Coffin Collection
University of South Alabama Archives
SMC-238N

38 Royal Family
Erik Overbey Collection
University of South Alabama Archives
G-474

39 Mobile City Hall
Library of Congress
LC-D4-19451

40 Magnolia House
Photo by Henry T. Hughes
Michael McEachern Collection, University of South Alabama Archives
C-374

41 Foster's Barbershop
Courtesy of V. Pratt Vereen
University of South Alabama Archives
C-259

42 Dauphin Street
Mobile: The Gateway to Panama (1900)
Courtesy of the Mobile Public Library
C-1161

43 Cargo Ships
Robert Brown Collection
University of South Alabama Archives
C-9067

44 Hurricane Damage
Courtesy of Larry Massey
University of South Alabama Archives
C-3257

45 Bienville Square
Image from the Harris Photo Company of Conneaut, Ohio
C-1107

46 King's Float
Erik Overbey Collection
University of South Alabama Archives
N-3661

47 St. Francis Street
Erik Overbey Collection
University of South Alabama Archives
G-343

48 Floral Decorations
Erik Overbey Collection
University of South Alabama Archives
C-4084

49 Fountain in Bienville Square
Library of Congress
LC-USZ62-113675

50 Washington Fire Engine Company
Photo by E. W. Russell
Historic American Buildings Survey
Library of Congress
HABS AL-2

51 Mobile Daily News
University of South Alabama Archives
C-102

52 Joseph Patt's Veterinary Hospital
Erik Overbey Collection
University of South Alabama Archives
G-207

53 Mobile Police Officers
Courtesy Mobile Public Library
C-7001

54 North Royal Street
Erik Overbey Collection
University of South Alabama Archives
C-1136

55 Barefoot Newsboy
Library of Congress
LOT 7480, v. 3, no. 3838

56 President Woodrow Wilson
Erik Overbey Collection
University of South Alabama Archives
C-15,010

57 Barker Mill
Library of Congress
LOT 7479, v. 6, no. 3798

58 Barker Cotton Mill Interior
Library of Congress
LOT 7479, v. 6, no. 3829

59 Uwanta Pressing Club
Courtesy of Flo Simmons
University of South Alabama Archives
C-278

60 Sunny South
Erik Overbey Collection
University of South Alabama Archives
C-3003

61 Toy Horse
Erik Overbey Collection
University of South Alabama Archives
G-419

62 Gayfer's Department Store "Cash Girl"
Library of Congress
LOT 7483, v. 2, no. 3802

63 Vessels
Philip Austin Collection
University of South Alabama Archives
C-3076

64 Carlisle Café
Courtesy of Tom Barkley
University of South Alabama Archives
C-7

65 Wrecked Automobile
Erik Overbey Collection
University of South Alabama Archives
N-5882

66 Admiral Raphael Semmes Monument
Erik Overbey Collection
University of South Alabama Archives
G-504

67 Hammel's Delivery Service
Hammel's Scrapbook University of South Alabama Archives
C-10, 064

68 Nurses
Erik Overbey Collection
University of South Alabama Archives
G-272

69 Operating Room
Erik Overbey Collection
University of South Alabama Archives
C-6007

70 Monroe Park
Photo by Erik Overbey; print courtesy of F. V. White
University of South Alabama Archives
C-16,047

71 General Store
University of South Alabama Archives
C-172

72 161-foot Apollo
Philip Austin Collection
University of South Alabama Archives
C-3072

73 July 4, 1916
Erik Overbey Collection
University of South Alabama Archives
G484

74 Hurricane Aftermath
Erik Overbey Collection
University of South Alabama Archives
N-3861

75 Mobile & Ohio Pier
Erik Overbey Collection
University of South Alabama Archives
N-3846

76 Spring Hill College
Library of Congress
PAN US GEOG-Alabama no. 22

77 Raphael Semmes Camp of the United Confederate Veterans
Erik Overbey Collection
University of South Alabama Archives
N-4238

78 Grocery Store
Courtesy of Wayne Meyer, University of South Alabama Archives
C-271

79 Gulf City Bicycle Shop
Sherwood C. McBroom Collection, University of South Alabama Archives
C-171

80 Government Street Rally
Erik Overbey Collection
University of South Alabama Archives
N-4258C

81 Celebration
Erik Overbey Collection
University of South Alabama Archives
N-4254

82 Fire Fighters
University of South Alabama Archives
C-7014

83 Fires
Courtesy of Benjamin Boutwell, University of South Alabama Archives
C-7120

84 Creole Fire Department 100th Anniversary
Erik Overbey Collection
University of South Alabama Archives
C-7004

86 Airplanes and Motor Vehicles
Erik Overbey Collection
University of South Alabama Archives
N-5614

87 South American Banana Trade
Erik Overbey Collection
University of South Alabama Archives
N-242

88 George Harness & Vehicle Company
Erik Overbey Collection
University of South Alabama Archives
N-1751

89 Bay Queen
Erik Overbey Collection
University of South Alabama Archives
C-3197

90 City of Mobile
Erik Overbey Collection
University of South Alabama Archives
N-804

91 Crown Theatre
Erik Overbey Collection
University of South Alabama Archives
N-1615

92 Monroe Park
Erik Overbey Collection
University of South Alabama Archives
N-4746

93 Bessie Morse Bellingrath
Courtesy of Harry Sackhoff, Bellingrath Gardens Collection, University of South Alabama Archives
Bellingrath 1920-126

94 Dauphine Theatre
Erik Overbey Collection
University of South Alabama Archives
N-1635

95 Dauphin Street
Erik Overbey Collection
University of South Alabama Archives
N-3128

96 Royal Street
Erik Overbey Collection
University of South Alabama Archives
C-1046

97 Biloxi Beach
Erik Overbey Collection
University of South Alabama Archives
N-4480

98 Curtis Feed Company
Courtesy Bay City Coin & Gun, Mader Studio Print, University of South Alabama Archives
C-74

100 Royal Street at Conti
Erik Overbey Collection
University of South Alabama Archives
N-3264

101 St. Emanuel Street
Erik Overbey Collection
University of South Alabama Archives
C-1158

102 Babe Ruth with a Group of Boys
Erik Overbey Collection
University of South Alabama Archives
C-15,001

103 Old Stove Round-up
Erik Overbey Collection
University of South Alabama Archives
C-1098

104 Dauphin at St. Joseph
Erik Overbey Collection
University of South Alabama Archives
N-3134

105 Cawthon Hotel
Erik Overbey Collection
University of South Alabama Archives
N-1543

106 Interior, Old Mobile Public Library
Erik Overbey Collection
University of South Alabama Archives
N-2219C

107 Between Joachim and Jackson
Erik Overbey Collection
University of South Alabama Archives
N-3176

108 Cochrane Bridge
Erik Overbey Collection
University of South Alabama Archives
N-4033

109 Swimming
Erik Overbey Collection
University of South Alabama Archives
N-2621

110 Reiss Mercantile Company Parade
Erik Overbey Collection
University of South Alabama Archives
N-4270C

111 St. Francis Street
Erik Overbey Collection
University of South Alabama Archives
N-4185

112 The Little Theatre
Erik Overbey Collection
University of South Alabama Archives
N-3601

114 Oyster Room
S. Blake McNeely Collection
University of South Alabama Archives
MN-661B

115 Murphy High School
Erik Overbey Collection
University of South Alabama Archives
N-2622

116 Naval Store Fire
S. Blake McNeely Collection
University of South Alabama Archives
MN-204B

117 Sam Impastato
Erik Overbey Collection
University of South Alabama Archives
N-2508

118 St. Emanuel Street
Erik Overbey Collection
University of South Alabama Archives
C-1146

119 Huxford Oil Company
Erik Overbey Collection
University of South Alabama Archives
N-1797

120 Albright and Wood
Erik Overbey Collection
University of South Alabama Archives
N-1451

121 Railroad Travel
Phillip Kotheimer Collection
University of South Alabama Archives
C-10,050

122 Football
Inge Family Album University of South Alabama Archives
C-4170

123 St. Joseph and St. Louis Streets
S. Blake McNeely Collection
University of South Alabama Archives
MN-313C

124 Kahn Manufacturing Company
Erik Overbey Collection
University of South Alabama Archives
N-1861

125 Gulf Coast Sign Company
McGill Studio Collection
University of South Alabama Archives
C-249

126 Malbis Bakery
Erik Overbey Collection
University of South Alabama Archives
S-960

127 Mardi Gras Floral Parade
Erik Overbey Collection
University of South Alabama Archives
N-3777

128 Trinity Episcopal Church
S. Blake McNeely Collection
University of South Alabama Archives
MN-114

129 View from Spanish Fort
Erik Overbey Collection
University of South Alabama Archives
N-4027

130 Civilian Conservation Corps
S. Blake McNeely Collection
University of South Alabama Archives
MN-162

131 Autogiro
S. Blake McNeely Collection
University of South Alabama Archives
MN-3

132 Cudjo Lewis
Erik Overbey Collection
University of South Alabama Archives
N-3446

133 McGill Institute
Photo by E. W. Russell
Library of Congress
HABS AL-77

134 Government Street
Photo by E. W. Russell
Historic American Buildings Survey
Library of Congress
HABS AL-62-G

135 National Range Month
Erik Overbey Collection
University of South Alabama Archives
C-322

136 Mobile Skyline
S. Blake McNeely Collection
University of South Alabama Archives
MN-278

137 Big Fish
Erik Overbey Collection
University of South Alabama Archives
C-16,198

138 Bankhead Tunnel
Erik Overbey Collection
University of South Alabama Archives
N-5426

139 Jim's Billiards
Courtesy of Mrs. Jim Dixie, University of South Alabama Archives
C-238

140 Interior of a Delchamp's Grocery Store
Erik Overbey Collection
University of South Alabama Archives
N-1651

141 Mobile Infirmary
Erik Overbey Collection
University of South Alabama Archives
N-2608

142 Old City Hospital
Photo by W. N. Manning
Historic American Buildings Survey
Library of Congress
HABS AL-13

143 Mule-drawn Carts
S. Blake McNeely Collection
University of South Alabama Archives
MN-213

144 Spring Hill College
Historic American Buildings Survey
Library of Congress
HABS-ALA, 49-SPRIHI,3B

146 Hammel's Department Store
Erik Overbey Collection
University of South Alabama Archives
C-24

147 Dauphin Street
Erik Overbey Collection
University of South Alabama Archives
C-1035

148 Crowd on Dauphin
McGill Studio Collection
University of South Alabama Archives
MG-74

149 Sha'arai Shomayim Synagogue
Erik Overbey Collection
University of South Alabama Archives
N-3068

150 Gone with the Wind
Erik Overbey Collection
University of South Alabama Archives
C-4045

151 Southern Bell Telephone Company
Erik Overbey Collection
University of South Alabama Archives
S-1181

152 Government Street
Erik Overbey Collection
University of South Alabama Archives
C-1010

153 Government Street
Erik Overbey Collection
University of South Alabama Archives
C-1186

154 Bemis Brothers Bag Company
Erik Overbey Collection
University of South Alabama Archives
S-701A

155 Alabama Dry Dock and Shipbuilding Company
Alabama Dry Dock and Shipbuilding Company Collection, University of South Alabama Archives
C-11,006

156 ADDSCO Women
Alabama Dry Dock and Shipbuilding Company Collection, University of South Alabama Archives
ADDSCO-071C

157 Merchants National Bank
Erik Overbey Collection, University of South Alabama Archives
C-88

158 Rally at ADDSCO
Alabama Dry Dock and Shipbuilding Company Collection, University of South Alabama Archives
ADDSCO-103A

159 Dauphin Way Baptist Church
Museum of Mobile Collection, University of South Alabama Archives
MOM-1498-3

160 Workers
S. Blake McNeely Collection
University of South Alabama Archives
MN-527A

161 Mobile's Shipbuilding Industry
Alabama Dry Dock and Shipbuilding Company Collection, University of South Alabama Archives
ADDSCO-015B

162 Brookley Field
Courtesy of Sherwood McBroom, University of South Alabama Archives
Brookley RG-14 SER8 #49

163 Bob Hope at White River Launch
Alabama Dry Dock and Shipbuilding Company Collection, University of South Alabama Archives
ADDSCO-383C

164 Three Sisters Clothing
Erik Overbey Collection
University of South Alabama Archives
S-1061

165 Dunbar High School
S. Blake McNeely Collection
University of South Alabama Archives
MN-461D

166 Coca-Cola Delivery
Erik Overbey Print from the Bellingrath Gardens Collection, University of South Alabama Archives
C-339

167 **Toulminville Drug Store**
Erik Overbey Collection
University of South Alabama Archives
S-4097

168 **Comic Books**
Alabama Dry Dock and Shipbuilding Company Collection, University of South Alabama Archives
ADDSCO-M34

170 **Dauphin Street at Conception**
Erik Overbey Collection
University of South Alabama Archives
C-1043

171 **Vernadean**
Museum of Mobile Collection, University of South Alabama Archives
MOM-1833

172 **Woolworth's Five and Dime**
Erik Overbey Collection
University of South Alabama Archives
S-4141

173 **Woolworth's Lunch Counter**
Erik Overbey Collection
University of South Alabama Archives
S-4141

174 **Dance**
Museum of Mobile Collection, University of South Alabama Archives
MOM-4455

175 **St. Joseph's Chapel**
Museum of Mobile Collection, University of South Alabama Archives
MOM-6895B-34

176 **City Furniture Company**
Museum of Mobile Collection, University of South Alabama Archives
MOM-4875

177 **The Gulf, Mobile, and Ohio Building**
Erik Overbey Collection
University of South Alabama Archives
S-1120

178 **Booker T. Washington Theatre**
Palmer Studio Collection
University of South Alabama Archives
Palmer-6234

179 **Eagle Drug Store**
Museum of Mobile Collection, University of South Alabama Archives
MOM-2606-1

180 **Azalea Trail Maids**
Museum of Mobile Collection, University of South Alabama Archives
MOM-2701-52

181 **Big Zion AME Choir**
Erik Overbey Collection
University of South Alabama Archives
S-3536

182 **Aerial View**
Museum of Mobile Collection, University of South Alabama Archives
MOM-4118-2

183 **Constantine's Restaurant**
Museum of Mobile Collection, University of South Alabama Archives
MOM-4288-12

184 **Mamie Van Doren**
Museum of Mobile Collection, University of South Alabama Archives
MOM-5765

185 **Dauphin Island**
Chamber of Commerce Collection, University of South Alabama Archives
COC-31

186 **Pickets**
Erik Overbey Collection
University of South Alabama Archives
S-4039

187 **Baseball**
Photo by Russell Brown
University of South Alabama Archives
00-03-356

188 **Eastern Airlines**
Photo by Erik Overbey Roy R. Froom Collection University of South Alabama Archives
C-10,085

189 **Ladd Stadium**
Museum of Mobile Collection, University of South Alabama Archives
MOM-2356

190 **Celebration**
William Lavendar Photo
University of South Alabama Archives
C-4153

191 **Royal Street**
Julius E. Marx Collection
University of South Alabama Archives
Marx-619-X

192 **Downtown Aerial**
Stephens G. Croom Collection, University of South Alabama Archives
C-9098

193 **U.S. Post Office**
Photo by Roy Thigpen
Historic American Buildings Survey
Library of Congress
HABS ALA, 49-MOBI,129-1

194 **John LeFlore**
John LeFlore Papers
University of South Alabama Archives
C-15,007

195 **University of South Alabama Students**
University of South Alabama Public Relations Collection
University of South Alabama Archives
USA-PR-3092

196 **March**
Palmer Studio Collection
University of South Alabama Archives
Palmer-7743

197 **Honoring Dr. Martin Luther King, Jr.**
Palmer Studio Collection
University of South Alabama Archives
Palmer-7743

198 **University of South Alabama Cheerleaders**
University of South Alabama Public Relations Collection
University of South Alabama Archives
USA-PR

199 **U. of South Alabama Baseball Team**
Mobile Press Register Collection, University of South Alabama Archives
PR-73772

200 **U.S. Air Force Plane**
Corps of Engineers Collection, University of South Alabama Archives
C-4196

HISTORIC PHOTOS OF MOBILE

Mobile's long history includes joyous Mardi Gras celebrations and tragic natural disasters. Civil War and segregation, shipping and manufacturing, dirt streets and booming wharves are part of its fascinating story. Cargo shipped to and from its busy docks gradually shifted from cotton to timber to bananas to manufactured goods. In World War II, its population grew exponentially as the city became an important shipbuilder for America's arsenal.

Historic Photos of Mobile transports readers to a time of hoop skirts and horse-drawn carriages, then shows them how the city changed during the first half of the twentieth century. Timeless, black-and-white images capture historic colleges, family-owned shops, the longest American flag ever displayed, hurricane damage, social change, tall ships, and scenes of daily life in generations long gone.

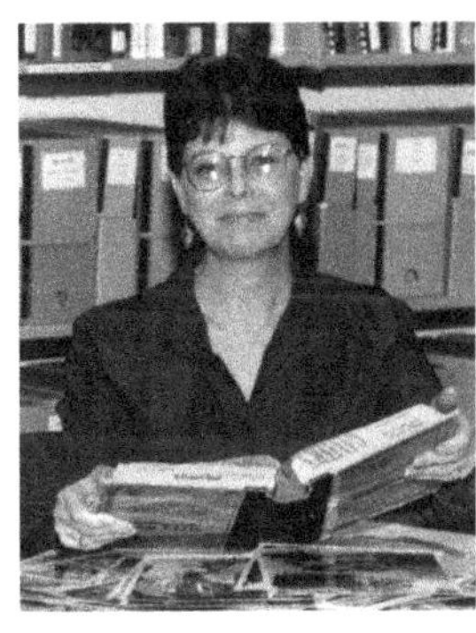

Carol Ellis was born in Frankfurt, Germany, to a career Army father. She moved with her family to Mobile in 1970. Carol currently serves as Archivist for the University of South Alabama, from which she earned both bachelor's and master's degrees in history. She serves on the executive boards of the Society of Alabama Archivists and the Gulf South Historical Association.

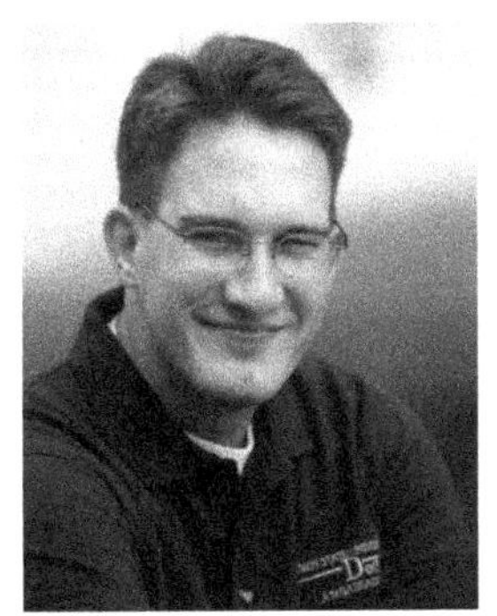

Scotty E. Kirkland is a graduate student in American history at the University of South Alabama and an assistant at the University Archives. His articles have appeared in *The Alabama Review* and *The Southern Historian.* He lives in Mobile with his wife, Jacqlyn.

WWW.TURNERPUBLISHING.COM

www.ingramcontent.com/pod-product-compliance
Lightning Source LLC
LaVergne TN
LVHW060612110826
845154LV00003B/71
9781684420100